Renward Brandstetter

An Introduction to Indonesian Linguistics

Salzwasser

Renward Brandstetter

An Introduction to Indonesian Linguistics

1. Auflage | ISBN: 978-3-84604-708-8

Erscheinungsort: Frankfurt, Deutschland

Erscheinungsjahr: 2020

Salzwasser Verlag GmbH

Reprint of the original, first published in 1916.

Asiatic Society Monographs

VOL. XV

AN INTRODUCTION TO
INDONESIAN
LINGUISTICS

BEING FOUR ESSAYS

BY

RENWARD BRANDSTETTER, Ph.D.

TRANSLATED BY

C. O. BLAGDEN, M.A., M.R.A.S.

LONDON
PUBLISHED BY THE ROYAL ASIATIC SOCIETY
22, ALBEMARLE STREET, W.

1916

PREFACE

THE Indonesian languages constitute the western division of the great Austronesian (or Malayo-Polynesian, or Oceanic) family of speech, which extends over a vast portion of the earth's surface, but has an almost entirely insular domain, reaching as it does from Madagascar, near the coast of Africa, to Easter Island, an outlying dependency of South America, and from Formosa and Hawaii in the North to New Zealand in the South. The whole family is of great interest and importance from the linguistic point of view and can fairly claim to rank with the great families of speech, such as the Indo-European, the Semitic, the Ural-Altaic, the Tibeto-Chinese, etc. Though but a small part of its area falls on the mainland of Asia, there is no reasonable doubt that it is of genuinely Asiatic origin, and of late years it has been linked up with another Asiatic family, which includes a number of the languages of India and Indo-China (e.g., Munda, Khasi, Mon. Khmer, Nicobarese, Sakai, etc.). The Indonesian division of the Austronesian family is the part that has best preserved the traces of its origin, and it forms therefore an essential clue to the study of the family as a whole. It has also been more thoroughly investigated than the other two divisions—viz., the Micronesian and Melanesian group and the Polynesian.

The Indonesian languages cover practically the whole area of Indonesia (otherwise called the Eastern, or Indian, or Malay, Archipelago, which includes the Philippines and extends from the north-western point of Sumatra to New Guinea), together with the whole of Madagascar, the greater part of the Malay Peninsula, the Mergui Archipelago off the coast of Tenasserim, some outlying tracts in Eastern Indo-China (which region there is much ground for regarding as the primitive home of the whole family), a considerable portion of Formosa, and a few island groups lying to the eastward of the Philippines. Its eastern boundary with the Micro-Melanesian division is still somewhat imperfectly ascertained, but appears to pass east of the Marian Islands and west of the Carolines to a point somewhere in (or near) the western extremity of New Guinea. The greater part of that large island lies outside the Indonesian division, much of its coast-line falling into the Melanesian section, while a very considerable portion is occupied by the entirely alien Papuan languages as is also in all probability the greater part of its imperfectly explored interior. Of the contents of the Indonesian area some details are given in Essay II, § 3, and need not be repeated here.

The scientific study of the Indonesian languages was initiated over half a century ago by two very eminent Dutch scholars, the late H. N. van der Tuuk and Professor Kern, to whom most of the good work that has been done in this field of research has been due, either directly or indirectly. Before their time many of the individual languages of the family had been studied, more or less systematically, but there had been no really scientific application of the comparative method, and consequently the conclusions arrived at by the earlier writers, such as Crawfurd and Logan, were founded on no solid basis. Many of them, in fact, have proved to be untenable and have been superseded by the sounder methods of the Dutch school. Unfortunately, however, most of the work of the modern school of Indonesian comparative philology has taken the form of articles in learned periodicals or notes in illustration of texts edited from time to time by one scholar or another; and by far the greater part of it is in Dutch. No comprehensive work dealing with the subject as a whole exists as yet in any language, and indeed it may be doubted whether the time has arrived for such a final synthesis to be made. There is still much pioneering work to be done in many outlying portions of the field.

Dr. Brandstetter, though thoroughly original in the handling of his materials, and by nationality a Swiss, is in the true line of succession of the Dutch school; and his monographis, of which four have been selected for translation into English, represent something like a new departure and are an important step towards the attainment of the ultimate aim. They deal in a comparative and synoptic manner with some of the leading branches of the subject, and are couched in a form which facilitates their use by students. The four Essays contained in this volume have been selected with an eye to the importance of the several matters discussed therein respectively, and that from the different points of view of three classes of students. I mean, in the first place, those who are interested in comparative philology in general (to whom the author's occasional comparisons of Indonesian with Indo-European phenomena will be of special interest and value); secondly, those whose desire it is to make a particular study of the comparative philology of the Indonesian languages, as an end in itself; and, thirdly, the considerable number of persons who are occupied primarily with some individual member of the family, but would like to see it in its proper perspective in relation to the cognate tongues, and are therefore impelled to give some attention to the family as a whole. By far the greater number of such special students are primarily interested in Malay, the best known and for practical purposes the most important of the Indonesian languages. But this very fact makes it the more desirable to present to them the results of the comparative work that has been done. For Malay is in many ways not a very typical member of the family: its grammar has been much worn down and simplified, and for various other reasons it is unfortunate that so many people are tempted to survey the whole Indonesian field, with its luxuriant diversity, through the rather distorting lens of a knowledge of Malay alone. There has been a very widespread tendency among Malay scholars to regard Malay as the standard or norm of the Indonesian family and to attempt to explain the differences which they noticed in the other languages as deviations from that standard; and that is very far from being the true view.

Further, even for those whose only object it is to master a

single language, there is some profit in devoting a part of their
energies to an acquaintance with the results of comparative
research. In every language there are words, phrases, and
idioms, which are obscure and cannot be adequately explained,
or indeed even thoroughly understood, by the mere light of
the language itself, whereas the comparative method often
helps to make them intelligible. And the moment a person
who has confined his attention to a single language attempts
to explain such things, he is liable to fall into all manner of
errors, unless he checks his theories by the results of linguistic
science. It is to be regretted that the excellent work done
by Dutch scholars (and some others) in the field of Indonesian
comparative philology has been neglected by most English
students of Malay, for the consequences have often been
decidedly unfortunate. Thus a comparatively recent English
work, of some importance in its own line, quotes extracts from
writings by Crawfurd printed in 1848 as if they represented the
latest light on the subject, though in fact hardly a single word
in them has stood the test of modern research and almost
every one of the theses they contain has been definitely and
completely disproved. Similarly, another book, somewhat
earlier in date, an admirable piece of scholarship in almost
every respect, is disfigured by an appendix on Malay etymology
that entirely ignores the work of the Dutch school and pro-
pounds various hypotheses which were plainly untenable
at the time they were published, having regard to the facts
then already made known to the world. And such instances
could easily be multiplied, if it were worth while. It is to be
hoped and expected, as a result of the publication of Dr.
Brandstetter's Essays in English, that in future such errors
will be avoided.

It is a great merit of Dr. Brandstetter that he incidentally
does much to teach his readers the scientific mode of procedure in linguistics. His grasp of the subject is equalled by
the soundness of his method and the perspicuity of his exposition. Though strictly scientific, his work is cast into a
form that renders it intelligible to the average reader as well
as to the specialist, and while the advanced student will find

much to learn from it, a beginner of ordinary intelligence and education can read it with profit and understanding.

In the translation the original has been closely followed, and such few modifications as have been made in the text have been carried out in consultation with the author himself and with his express approval. There are certain obvious disadvantages incidental to the fact that these Essays were originally written and issued as separate monographs: a considerable amount of repetition has been unavoidable, and it often happens that some point partially dealt with in an earlier Essay receives completer treatment in a subsequent one. An attempt has been made in this translation to remedy such inconveniences to some extent by giving references in footnotes; and these and other footnotes added by myself have been enclosed in square brackets. For the further convenience of students I have prefixed to each Essay a brief summary of its contents based mainly on the section headings of the original. For the sake of symmetry, the main divisions of Essay II have been numbered. In the Indonesian words and phrases quoted the author's spelling has been followed. On the other hand, in geographical names (including the names of the various languages discussed) and in the titles of works cited, etc., concessions have been made to ordinary usage and to the Hunterian system which is generally followed in English works where Malay words are spelt in the Roman character. Quotations appearing in German in the Essays have been translated; but when the ultimate source was in English the original words have been reproduced from that source.

My thanks are due to the Committee for Malay Studies of the Federated Malay States Government for having commissioned me to translate the work, to the author for his cordial consent and his assistance in clearing up doubtful points, and to the Council of the Royal Asiatic Society for having sanctioned the publication of the book by the Society.

The author also desires me to express his appreciation of the recognition thus accorded to his work.

C. O. B.

CONTENTS

ESSAY I

ESSAY I

ROOT AND WORD
IN THE INDONESIAN LANGUAGES

(The original was published in 1910.)

SUMMARY

THE THEME.

1.   When we open the dictionary of an Indonesian language we are at once struck by the fact that a very large proportion of the key-words in it are disyllabic.   Thus in the Mal.* vocabulary we find successively: *ikal*, " curl ", *ikan*, " fish ", *ikat*, " tie ".

But it is not only in the dictionary that we find such disyllabic formations, they also occur in actual speech, as witnessed by the following passage from the Old Jav.   Ādiparwa, edited by Juynboll, p. 49: *hana sira wiku* † *kapanguh in tĕgal, ri lĕpi nin āśrama* = " (It) happened (that) a hermit was met with in the field, at the edge of the hermitage " = " Then (the king) met in the field a hermit standing near his hermitage ".

Now these disyllabic words, *hana*, *tĕpi*, etc., may also live in the language in more extended forms, *hana* for example having a derivative *kahanan*, " existence "; but they do not, in the actual spoken language, exist in any shorter forms; therefore it is appropriate to call formations like *hana* " *word-bases* ".‡

2.   Now in the Old Jav. dictionary we find the following word-bases: *singul*, " to push ", *angul*, " to push away, to fend off ", *tangul*, " to defend against ", and finally *agul*, which is rendered by the Sanskrit *pragalbha* and accordingly signifies " determined, bold ".   Here we have a monosyllabic combination of sounds, viz., *gul*, which, to use Wundt's words,

<hr/>

* For the abbreviations see note on § 10, for the transcription § 11.

† *wiku*, being a loan-word, has no bearing on the present question.

‡ [The original has " Grundwörter," a term for which there is no thoroughly satisfactory English equivalent.   For explanations of the meaning of the term, and the author's reasons for selecting it, see § 110 and Essay II, §§ 143 *seqq.*)

can be pursued unchanged through a series of words with similar meanings. Now such a combination of sounds as this we style a *root*.

3. These roots and these word-bases are the *theme* of the present dissertation. Our first task will be to extract the root from the word-base; then we must describe the root; thirdly, we have to show how word-bases are formed from roots; our fourth and last duty will be to delineate the characteristics of the word-base.

4. IN linguistic formations are less compressed and more transparent than Indo-European ones; some living IN languages are archaic to a degree far surpassing that of any modern IE language, even the Lithuanian. The IN languages which are geographically furthest apart from each other, the IN dialects of Formosa and the Batan Islands on the one hand and the dialects of Madagascar on the other, stand in a much closer relation to one another than Hindustani and Irish. From all this it follows that we can recognize the root and its characteristics more clearly and certainly in IN than in IE research.

Here follows a short comparative table showing how closely Formosan and Batanese — according to Otto Scheerer's researches—are related in certain particulars to Mlg.

				Formosan.	Batanese.	Malagasy.
Fire	..	..	..	*apuy*	*apuy*	*afu*
Sinew, artery	..	..	*ugat*	*uyat*	*uzatra*
Child	..	..	..	*alak*	*anak*	*anaka*
Finger-nail	..	..	*kuku*	*kuku*	*huhu*
Five	..	..	..	*rima*	*dima*	*dimi*
Seven	..	..	..	*pito*	*pito*	*fitu*

5. An insight into the nature of roots and words is one of the more important factors in IN linguistic research. Bopp's attempt to prove a relationship between IN and IE was foredoomed to failure from the start because, for one thing, he made no effort whatever to acquire such an insight before

going on to his comparison. Thus on p. 5 he correlates the Sanskrit *priya* with the Common IN *pilih*. The first word means " beloved, worthy ", the second " to choose, to select out of a number of things ", in Mkb. also " to lift up from the ground ". Now Bopp says, quite arbitrarily, that *pilih* is based upon an older form *plih*, an *i* having been inserted to facilitate pronunciation: and this *plih* he then identifies with the Sanskrit root *prī*.—By the side of this IN *pilih*, however, are found Karo *kulih*, " to appropriate to oneself ", Mal. *olih*, " to acquire ", and Old Jav. *ulih*, " to get ". Now, surely, *pilih*, when compared with *ulih*, *olih*, and *kulih*, points to a nucleus *lih*, between which and the Sanskrit *prī* there can of course be no further possibility of comparison.

PRELIMINARY QUESTIONS OF METHOD.

6. The *first* indispensable requirement for the success of a work like the present is that it should be built up entirely on the basis of phonetic law. In former monographs the present writer, instead of appealing to phonetic laws, often had recourse to parallel instances, and that alternative may have sufficed for those cases. But here he will expressly formulate all the phonetic laws that may come into question.

This is perhaps a convenient place for stating summarily the two chief phonetic laws affecting IN vowels and consonants respectively. They are to be found in fuller form in the present writer's previous monographs, and the second one in particular detail in Brandes' "Bijdrage".

I. The pĕpĕt-law. Original IN *ĕ* remains *ĕ* in some languages, as in Old Jav. and Karo; in others it becomes *a*, as in Mak. and Mkb.; in others again *e*, as in Day.; in others *i*, as in Tag.; and finally in others *o*, as in Toba and Bis.*

II. The R-law. Original IN had two shades of the *r* sound. In several IN languages, for instance in Karo, these have been unified again into a single kind of *r*. In others the differentiation has developed further. Thereby the one kind of *r* has become *g* in certain languages, as in Bis.; in others it has become *h*, as in Day.; in others again this *h* has disappeared, as in Old Jav. The other kind of *r* sometimes persists as *r*, sometimes it appears as *l* or as *d*.†

7. The *second* indispensable condition consists in this, that the material should be surveyed in its entirety. That is the case here, for the present writer has in the course of years

---

* [See also Essay II, §§ 25-6, Essay III, §§ 28-9, and Essay IV, §§ 5, 121-8.]

† [See also Essay II, § 190, and Essay IV, §§ 99, 129-39.]

compiled for himself complete root dictionaries in MS, of the principal IN languages.

8. A *third* requirement for a work like the present is that the material should not be merely raked together out of dictionaries and grammars by the wooden processes of the amateur, but be vivified by the study of texts. This will be particularly necessary in Section IV, where we deal with the functions of the word-base.*

9. *Fourthly*, it will mean a decided saving of labour if we determine from the very start which of the numerous IN languages can render us the best services in our task. Speaking generally, the guiding principle here is that a language will be the more welcome to us the more archaic it is in its phonetic system, in the characteristic type of its words (particularly as regards final sounds), and in its word-store. Therefore we shall often cite Old Jav., but seldom Modern Jav., oftener Karo than Achinese, often the written forms of Toba and Mkb., but never the spoken forms of these two languages.† However, in certain cases we shall be able to get help even from languages that have suffered very serious changes in their character, as for instance Kissarese.

10. The following are the languages we shall make use of in general.

In the Philippines, Tagalog, Bisaya, and Iloko; in Sangir, Sangirese; in Northern Celebes, Tontemboan and Bulu; in Middle Celebes, Bareqe; in Southern Celebes, Bugis and Makassar; in Bali, Balinese; in Madura, Madurese; in Java, Javanese and Sundanese; in Borneo, Dayak;‡ in Sumatra, Minangkabau, Karo, Toba (these two being also commonly called Batak), Gayo, and Achinese; Mentaway in the island of that name; in the Malay Peninsula and neighbouring islands, Malay; in Madagascar, Malagasy, especially the Hova dialect,

---

* [*Cf.* Essay III, §§ 1-7.]

† Of course it frequently happens that in these two languages the written and spoken forms agree.—Similarly Old and Modern Jav. are often identical.

‡ [*I.e.*, Hardeland's Olo-Ngaju Dayak.]

the literary language. — In a few cases some other languages besides these will also be used.*

11. *Fifthly*, though not an absolute necessity, it will be a great convenience for our enquiry if we introduce the idea of the Original Indonesian mother-tongue as an auxiliary factor. Of this Original IN two features are of especial importance to our enquiry, viz., the phonetic system and the general type of words.

I.   The phonetic system of Original IN :†

$$i \quad e \quad a \quad o \quad u \quad \breve{e}$$

$$q‡$$
$$k \quad g \quad \dot{n}\,§$$
$$c\,§ \quad j \quad \tilde{n}\,§$$
$$t \quad d \quad n$$
$$p \quad b \quad m$$
$$y \quad r \quad l \quad w$$
$$s$$
$$h$$

The $\breve{e}$ is the rapidly pronounced, indeterminate vowel, styled after the Jav. manner " pĕpĕt "; q represents the hamzah, the glottal stop; many scholars, *e.g.* the two Adriani's, denote it by a symbol like the apostrophe, as also does Sievers (" Phonetik ", § 353). It has already been observed in § 6 that there were two shades of *r* in Original IN.

Some of the living languages have evolved sounds which were unknown to Original IN: thus Mlg. possesses the sonant sibilant *z* ; in Gayo there is an *ö*, which according to Hazeu sounds pretty much like the German *ö* in " hören "; in several Philippine languages, and also in Bimanese we find *f*, as appears from the dissertations of Conant and Jonker.¶

---

* The meaning of the various abbreviations used is self-evident, *e.g.*, IN = Indonesian; IE = Indo-European; Mal. = Malay; Mkb. = Minangkabau; Mlg. = Malagasy, etc.   [See also Essay II, § 15.]

† [See also Essay II, especially §§ 17-49, and Essay IV, especially §§ 39 *seqq.*]

‡ [In Romanized Malay commonly written *k* or *ḳ*.]

§ [In Romanized Malay commonly written *ng*, *ch*, and *ny*, respectively.]

‖ [See also Essay II, § 48, and Essay IV, §§ 40, 140 *seqq.*, 181 *seqq.*]

¶ [See also Essay II, § 48, and Essay IV, §§ 41-3.]

II. The word-type of Original IN: In Original IN any sound could be the initial of a word, but there could not be more than one consonant there. Any sound* could serve as a final, except the series *c j ñ* ; but here too only one consonant was allowed. In the interior of words, between the two vowels of disyllabic word-bases, there might be one consonant or two, the latter in very various combinations (see § 74).

A great part of the living IN languages has undergone changes in these respects. Some languages tolerate no consonants, or a very limited number of them, as finals; others admit very few combinations of consonants, for instance only nasal + cognate explosive, between the two vowels.

The reader will ask: How does the writer know this phonetic system and word-type of Original IN ? The writer answers: This knowledge is based on detailed comparative studies which will be submitted to the reader on some future occasion.† Besides, the whole of the present dissertation will show that these assertions are correct.

12. When in the modern IN languages a derivative is formed from a word-base, the formatives used for that purpose are usually put *before* the word-base, they are prefixes; thus Sang. possesses nearly a hundred prefixes but only six infixes and five suffixes, and Day. has only *one* suffix as against a great number of prefixes. Now it is to be presumed that in Original IN, at the time when the monosyllabic roots were used as nuclei for the formation of disyllabic or polysyllabic word-bases, the same principle prevailed. That may, *sixthly*, serve us as an indication as to which part of the word-base should receive our particular attention during our search for the root, viz. the last part.

This view, put forward here as a presumptive probability, will be shown by the whole course of our investigation to be the true one.

13. *Seventhly*, if our investigation were concerned with the IE languages, accent and quantity would be important

---

* [But *y* and *w* only in so far as they form part of diphthongs.]

† [See Essay II, especially §§ 54-74.]

factors in the enquiry.   But here in IN they are of secondary
significance.   That is because they exhibit so much uniformity:
e.g., the penultimate syllable is the accentuated one in an ex-
traordinarily large percentage of cases. — The influence of
accent will be referred to in § 32, II, that of quantity in § 32, I.*

14.   *Eighthly,* we will bear in mind what Delbrück (" Grund-
fragen ", pp. 115, 116) teaches us about the investigation
of roots, and accordingly we shall turn our attention not merely
to words of action but also to words denoting things and
mental states.

15.   *Finally,* let it be observed that only genuine IN words,
and never loan-words, can be used for the purposes of the
enquiry.   Of course when we quote Old Jav. sentences as
evidence, loan-words cannot be avoided, for the Old Jav.
literature is strongly impregnated with Sanskrit words; but
such sentences are used on account of their genuinely IN contents, not on account of the loan-words they may happen to
include.†

  * [See also Essay II, §§ 75 *seqq.*, and Essay IV, §§ 67 *seqq.*, 307 *seqq.*]
  † [See also Essay III, § 12, II.]

SECTION I : THE SEARCH FOR THE ROOT.

Seeking the Root in an Individual Language.

16. In addressing ourselves now to the task of detecting the root in IN word-bases, we will begin by undertaking this research in connexion with a single language and see what results we can obtain without comparing it with others. The language shall be Old Jav. Now we can draw up the following series of Old Jav. words showing in each case the root:

uṅkab, " to open ", *siṅkab,* " to uncover ": root *kab.*
pĕkul, " to clasp ", *raṅkul,* " to embrace ": root *kul.*
ikĕl, " curly ", *riṅkĕl,* " twisted ": root *kĕl.*
taṅkĕp, " to seize ", *sikĕp,* " to seize ": root *kĕp.*
saṅguh, " to consider as . . . . . ", *suṅguh,* " truly ": root *guh.*
iṅis, " to grin ", *taṅis,* " to weep ": root *ṅis.*
tutuk, " mouth ", *patuk,* " beak ": root *tuk.*
gantuṅ, " to hang ", *tĕluṅ,* " to hang down ": root *tuṅ.*
itĕk, " mud ", *latĕk,* " mud ": root *tĕk.*
atĕr, " to accompany ", *hantĕr,* " to follow ": root *tĕr.*
indĕl, " curdled ", *kandĕl,* " thick ": root *dĕl.*
unĕñ, " desire ", *sĕnĕñ,* " loved ": root *nĕñ.*
tapis, " small ", *pipis,* " to pound small ": root *pis.*
liput, " to cover ", *saput,* " to cover ": root *put.*
umbak, " wave ", *limbak,* " wave ": root *bak.*
bubuk, " insect that burrows in wood ", *hrĕbuk,* "dry rot ": root *buk.*
bayaṅ, " to rock to and fro ", *huyaṅ,* " restless ": root *yaṅ.*
rĕrĕp, " to fall asleep ", *sirĕp,* " to lull to sleep ": root *rĕp.*
pulaṅ, " dirt ", *wĕlaṅ,* " spotted ": root *laṅ.*
alih, " to return ", *pulih,* " to turn back ": root *lih.*
kĕlĕm, " to sink in ", *silĕm,* " to plunge in ": root *lĕm.*

17. Here then we have established a series of Old Jav. roots: *kab, kul, kĕl,* etc. With one single exception the elements by means of which the root is fashioned into a word-base stand, as we presumed in § 12, *before* the root. The exception is *tĕluñ,* in which we see an infix *-ĕl-.*

These roots are Old Jav.; whether they are also Original IN does not appear from our demonstration; in order to answer *that* question a comparative study would be necessary.

18. Kern's dissertations on the Old Jav. grammar are excellent, but Van der Tuuk's Old Jav. dictionary is in several respects an imperfect work. Therefore it is impossible to obtain such a complete survey of the Old Jav. root material as is necessary for our purpose, and accordingly we must look around for another source of information. — In fact the present writer, in preparing this dissertation, has used that dictionary very little; most of his material is derived from Juynboll's glossary to the Old Jav. Rāmāyaṇa or from his own reading.

Though it is to be regretted that we cannot make as much use of Old Jav. as we could have wished, yet we must not overlook the fact that it has suffered in a marked degree from the operation of two phonetic laws, which have impaired its archaic character: The *r* of the RGH series (§ 6) has disappeared; accordingly Original IN *tĕras,* "hard", which has been preserved in several languages, *e.g.* in Mal.. has become *tĕas* and finally *twas* in Old Jav.; and when in Original IN two vowels came together, they often suffered contraction in Old Jav.; thus Mal., Sund., etc., *daun,* "leaf", appears in Old Jav. as *roñ.*

19. So we see that we must look for a substitute for Old Jav. in cases where it is necessary to have a general survey. Now there are other IN languages which have preserved an archaic impress in phonetic system and word-type, though it is true we cannot seize them in their earlier historical phases. Amongst these Karo is in the first rank. It has undergone few such changes as would alienate it from the Original IN.

This appears clearly when we compare it with the better known and closely related Toba:

Original IN *ĕ* persists in Karo, in Toba it becomes *o**

  ,, ,, *k* ,, ,, ,, ,, ,, ,, ,, *h*†

  ,, ,, *h* ,, ,, ,, ,, ,, ,, ,, nil

All these laws are neatly illustrated by the following example : Original IN, and also Mal., Gayo, etc., *kĕsah*, " to breathe, to pant ", remains *kĕsah* in Karo, but appears in Toba as *hosa*.

20. There are two laws which affect Karo and estrange it from Original IN, but both these laws comprise only a few individual cases:

I. Original IN final diphthongs become simple vowels in Karo: *e.g.*, *uy* becomes *i*; thus Original IN, and Old Jav., Formosan, etc., *apuy* becomes Karo *api*. We need only mention this one case, the change of *uy* into *i*, for the rest do not happen to occur in our monograph.

II. Original IN final media becomes tenuis in Karo. Original IN *lawĕd*, " sea ", Bis. *lawod*,‡ is sounded *lawĕt* in Karo.

21. Now follow some series of Karo words, from which in each case the root can be deduced:

tiṅkah, " step ", *laṅkah*, " step ": root *kah*.

tĕguh, " firm ", *paṅguh*, " hard wood ": root *guh*.

liṅgĕm, " shadow ", *agĕm*, " cloudy sky ": root *gĕm*.

riṅut, " wrinkled ", *pĕrṅut*, " curled ": root *ṅut*.

antar, " to set up ", *batar*, " a stand ": root *tar*.

tutuṅ, " to burn ", *gĕstuṅ*, " to blaze up ": root *tuṅ*.

dodas, " unlucky in gambling ", *radas*, " ruined ": root *das*.

tulpak, " disappointed ", *lepak*, " to err ": root *pak*.

tembal, " crossed ", *gambal*, " scissors ": root *bal*.

lĕmbut, " soft ", *umbut*, " soft pith ": root *but*.

pusiṅ, " to turn round ", *gasiṅ*, " spinning top ": root *siṅ*.

---

* The first rule holds good both for written and spoken Toba; the second one for written Toba only, as the *h* may undergo a further change in actual pronunciation.

† Only in certain positions, not, for example, as a final.

‡ The *o* is in conformity with the law stated in § 25.

22.　Here the writer ends this list, for it occurs to him that the method therein followed might be objected to. A very severe critic might observe, that the several series of the preceding paragraph, and also those of § 16, consist of two terms only; that these coincidences might in some cases at any rate be determined by mere chance; and that a higher degree of certainty would be attained if the series comprised a greater number of terms. — Though the writer does not believe that these objections are well founded, he will nevertheless take them into account and will produce series of Karo words containing a larger number of terms:

igar, sĕgar, toṅgar, " to splinter ": root *gar.*
mĕgah, agah, juṅgah, " proud ": root *gah.*
anjuṅ, " to raise up ", *ujuṅ,* " summit ", *tanjuṅ,* " hill ":
root *juṅ.*
lintaṅ, " weal (on the body) ", *rintaṅ,* " row ", *listaṅ, tintaṅ,*
" rectilinear ": root *taṅ.*
idah, " to see ", *dedah,* " to look on at ", *cidah,* " to show ",
pĕdah, " to teach ": root *dah.*
ĕlah, " finished ", *alah,* " conquered ", *tĕlah,* " to end a strife
(by intervening) ": root *lah.*
sulit, salit, " to peel ", *kulit,* " skin ": root *lit.*

23.　The writer could extend this table further, but he desires that his monographs should not exceed a certain compass. As he is not aiming at the production of a vocabulary of roots, he cannot reasonably be required to enumerate every individual case; he need only produce as many examples as may be necessary on each occasion to give the reader a true insight into the matter in hand. Accordingly all the lists in this monograph will merely represent a selection of specially characteristic cases.

24.　The writer himself must, of course, take a general survey of the whole of the material, he must at this very point be in a position to answer the question whether it is possible to determine *all* the Karo roots by the process hitherto followed. The answer is: A great many, but by no means all, of the Karo roots can be detected in this way. For many of the Karo word-bases stand entirely isolated, *e.g.*, *lecek*, " to ask for ". There is no other Karo word of similar meaning and analogous sound; none at all, in fact, that ends in *cek*. After what has been said we may, no doubt, presume that *lecek* can be analyzed into the formative *le* and the root *cek*, but owing to the isolated position of the word we gain nothing thereby.

It is certainly interesting and quite legitimate to ascertain what results we can arrive at if we confine ourselves to the study of a single language; but for the solution of our further problems that method does not suffice, and we must proceed to the comparison of several languages.

Seeking the Root by means of the Comparison of Languages.

25. Turning now to the method of comparing several languages for the purpose of our theme, we will first make the experiment of comparing two only and will select Karo and Bis. to work with. The choice is thoroughly justified: The relationship between Karo and Bis. is one of intermediate degree, neither very close nor yet quite remote; moreover Karo in Sumatra, occupying a region which nowhere reaches the sea, and Bis. in the Philippines are absolutely separated from one another geographically, so that we need have no fear of any influence of the one language on the other which might disturb our conclusions.

Before proceeding to this comparison we must mention the phonetic laws affecting Bis. which come into question. — For the Karo laws see § 20. In Bis. the *r* of the RGH series (§ 6) appears as *g ;* the *r* of the RLD series appears under certain conditions as *dl ;* Original IN *ĕ* and *u* as *o ;** final *h* is not tolerated.

Now follow lists of roots common to Karo and Bis.

I. The roots are absolutely identical in both languages:

---

* On this point Bis. and other Philippine dictionaries are inconsistent: we find both *o* and *u*.

Karo *kilkil,* " to gnaw ", Bis. *baṅkil,* " to bite ": root *kil.*

Karo *deṅgal,* " unchaste ", Bis. *bogal,* " adulterous ": root *gal.*

Karo *bĕtat,* " slow ", Bis. *kotat,* " slothfulness ": root *tat.*

Karo *ĕrdan,* " stairs ", Bis. *hagdan,* " stairs ": root *dan.*

Karo *kanam,* " joyful ", Bis. *hinam,* " joyful ": root *nam.*

Karo *bebas,* " accustomed ", Bis. *basbas,* " to accustom ": root *bas.*

II.   The roots exhibit phonetic discrepancies, which however resolve themselves without difficulty in accordance with the above-mentioned phonetic laws of Karo and Bis.:

Karo *sĕlkut,* Bis. *dagkot,* " to kindle (a fire) ": root *kut: kot.*

Karo *api,* " fire ", Bis. *apuy,* " erysipelas ": root *pi: puy.*

Karo *gĕbuk,* " smoky ", Bis. *dabok,* " to burn straw ": root *buk : bok.*

Karo *lĕmĕs,* " to dissolve in water ", Bis. *damos,* " to wet ": root *mĕs : mos.*

Karo *ilar,* " to shine ", Bis. *dilag,* " bright ": root *lar : lag.*

Karo *bĕsur,* Bis. *bosog,* " satiated ": root *sur : sog.*

Karo *lawĕt,* Bis. *lawod*: see § 20.

26.   From these Karo-Bis. root-lists two conclusions follow:

I.   It was remarked in § 24 that from Karo alone, without the assistance of a comparison with other languages, only a part of the Karo roots could be detected. This portion is at once considerably augmented when Karo is compared even with only *one* other IN language, as here with Bis. Thus the word *bĕtat,* " slow ", stands quite alone in Karo, but Bis. provides a pendant, *kotat,* " slothfulness ", and from the comparison of these two word-bases we get the root *tat.*

II.   In § 25 it was shown that direct influence as between Karo and Bis. is inconceivable. How comes it then that they have roots in common? Surely, it can only come from the fact that those roots belonged to Original IN. The Karo-Bis. lists in § 25 are, therefore, also lists of Original IN roots.

27.   The severe critic of § 22 might raise against the final sentence of the last paragraph the same objection that he formerly expressed. Here too the writer will make a concession to him and will produce more comprehensive series of words.

At this point it will be convenient to mention two Mal. and two Mak. phonetic laws:

I. Original IN ĕ persists in Mal., save in the final syllable of a word, where it becomes *a*. Original IN, and also Old Jav., *tĕkĕn*, " staff ", becomes *tĕkan*.

Every final media of any other language is represented in Mal. by the corresponding tenuis. Bis. *olob*, " cavity ", appears in Mal. as *ulup*, " hawse-hole ".

II. Original IN pĕpĕt becomes *a* in Mak., and if this *a* is in the penultimate syllable the next following consonant is doubled.

When in Original IN a word ends in *l*, *r*, or *s*, then in Mak. the vowel preceding the liquid or *s* is repeated after it, and finally a hamzah is added.—Both these laws are illustrated by the example *sassalaq* from *sĕsĕl*.

28. Now follow as specimens five rather more comprehensive series; we shall meet with others later on.

Tag., Bis., Gayo *nipis*, " thin "; Tontb. *apis*, " small ", *tompis*, " sunken (of cheeks) "; Old Jav. *tapis*, " small ", Mak. *nipisiq*, " thin ": root *pis*.

Tag., Bis. *hasañ*; Bulu, Tontb. *asañ*; Gayo *isañ*; Mal. *insañ*, " gills ": root *sañ*.

Old Jav. *wĕñis*; Mal., Gayo *bĕñis*; written Mkb., Bis. *bañis*, " angry ": root *ñis*.

Old Jav. *sĕlañ*, " to take turns "; Mal. *sĕlañ*, " interval "; Gayo *kĕkĕlañ*, " between "; Karo *alañ*, " middling "; Bis. *alañ-alañ*, " undecided ": root *lañ*.

Bal. *sĕlsĕl*; Old Jav. *sĕsĕl*; Tonsea *manĕsĕl*; Bis. *basoi*, Mal. *sĕsal*; Mak. *sassalaq*, " repentance ": root *sĕl*.

As in each of these cases the same root appears in strict phonetic equivalence in so many different languages, we are entitled to assign these roots to Original IN.

29. In the course of our enquiry hitherto we have taken little notice of two important members of the IN family of speech, namely Bug. and Mlg. The reason was this: these

languages have been affected by the operation of so many
phonetic laws that the root can only be detected in them with
difficulty. The omission shall now be made good and a special
paragraph devoted to each of these two languages.

The Bug. phonetic laws chiefly affect the final of the word-
base; hence in the Bug. root it is particularly the third sound
that is modified, while the first and second are less liable to be
affected.

Bug. *giliṅ*, " to roll ": root *liṅ*. — Mal. *giliṅ*, Old Jav. *puliṅ*,
" to roll ". Here no phonetic law has been at work in Bug.

Bug. *pipiq*, " to pinch": root *pit*. — Mal. *apit*, Gayo *sĕpit*,
" to pinch ". — Law: Every IN final explosive appears in
Bug. as hamzah.

Bug. *pĕddĕṅ*, " to close the eyes ": root *dĕm*. — Old Jav.
idĕm, Karo *pĕdĕm*. — Laws: Every IN final nasal appears
in Bug as *ṅ*. — After the pĕpĕt in the penultimate, that is the
accentuated, syllable the consonant is doubled; see also
sĕssĕq below.

Bug. *wukaq*, " to open, to unfold " (intrans.): root *kar*. —
Old Jav. *wĕkar*, " to open ", Bal. *sĕkar*, " flower ". — Law:
IN final *r* appears in Bug. as hamzah, but remains unaltered
when a suffix is added, hence Bug. *pataqbukarĕṅ*,* " to open "
(trans.).†

Bug. *nipiq*, " thin ": root *pis*. — Tag. *nipis*, Tontb. *impis*,
" thin ". — Law: IN final *s* appears in Bug. as hamzah, but
remains unaltered when a suffix is added, hence Bug. *nipisi*,
" to make thin ".†

Bug. *sĕssĕq*, " repentance ": root *sĕl*. — Bis. *basol*, Mal.
sĕsal ‡. — Law: IN final *l* appears in Bug. as hamzah, but
before a suffix takes the form of *rr*, hence Bug. *pasĕssĕrrĕṅ*,
" reproof ".†

30. In Mlg. even more phonetic laws have been at work
than in Bug.; just as in Bug., they particularly affect the final,
but they also affect consonants in every position, the vowels
less; therefore the Mlg. root shows modification chiefly in the

---

* The *b* is due to the influence of the hamzah.
† [See also Essay IV, § 210.]
‡ As to the vowels *o* and *a*, see §§ 25 and 27.

first and third sound, less often in the middle one. — The Mlg.
phonetic laws have been determined by the present writer in
former works, and also more especially by Ferrand.

Mlg. *ambi*, "surplus": root *bih*. — Mal. *lĕbih*, "more",
Karo *ambih*, "to build an annexe". — Law: IN *h* disappears
in Mlg. in all positions without leaving a trace.*

Mlg. *haruna*, "basket": root *run*. — Old Jav. *kuruñ*, "to
enclose", Karo *baruñ*, "buffalo pen". — Law: Every IN
final nasal appears in Mlg. as *na*.†

Mlg. *idina*, "to pour out": root *liñ*. — Karo *iliñ*, "to pour
into", Bug. *paliñ*, "to pour into another vessel". — Law:
Before a primitive *i* (not an *i* derived from some other sound)
in Mlg., Original IN *l* appears as *d* ; this is a special case of the
great RLD-law.

Mlg. *ampatra*, "stretched out": root *pat*. — Karo *iapat*,
"stretched out", Mal. *pĕpat*, "smoothed out". — Law:
Every Original IN final *t* becomes *tra* in Mlg.

Mlg. *hindzaka*, "to stamp": root *jak*. — Old Jav. *tañjak*,
"to jump", Karo *anjak*, "to trot". — Law: Original IN *j*
after a nasal appears in Mlg. as *d + z*. Every Original IN
final *k* appears in Mlg. as *ka*.

Mlg. *lefa*, "away, done": root *pas*. — Mal. *lĕpas*, "loose,
free, finished", Tag. *lipas*, "past". — Laws: Original IN
p becomes *f* in Mlg., save after a nasal (see *ampatra*, above)
and save when final. Original IN final *s* disappears in Mlg.
but persists before a suffix, hence the imperative passive:
alefasu.‡

31. To conclude this Section we must now undertake
another investigation which, as shown amongst others by
Sütterlin ("Das Wesen der sprachlichen Gebilde", pp. 56
seqq.), is of great linguistic interest. If we know, for example,
that a word *iluh*, *aluh*, *luha*, etc., runs through nearly all the
IN languages with the meanings "to flow, to weep, tear",

---

* Where we find an *h* in Mlg. it has a different origin, it arises from
Original IN *k*—(save that as a final or after a nasal *k* persists unchanged).

† [See also Essay IV, § 206.]

‡ [See also Essay IV, § 210.]

and if we are compelled to deduce from it a monosyllabic
formation *luh*, is it not then conceivable that this *luh* might
exist in some language or other as a living word, by itself,
uncombined with other elements? In general terms: Do
the roots exist only as parts of word-bases or are they capable
of existing by themselves?

32. When we search for monosyllabic words in the IN languages and succeed in finding some, we must first enquire
whether their monosyllabism might not have arisen out of a
former disyllabism. For that has really happened in many
cases in IN.

I. In several IN languages consonants between the two
vowels of the word-base may disappear in conformity with
phonetic law, *e.g.*, in Old Jav. the *r* of the RGH series, in Bug.
h, in Mlg. *s*. Accordingly Old Jav. *wā*, " glowing fire ", Bug.
pōn, " trunk ", Mlg. *fu*, " heart ", are not roots that have
preserved their monosyllabic character; they are derived from
the forms *wara, pohon, pusu*, which have a wide distribution
in the IN languages and are to be regarded as Original IN.
The length of the vowel still serves as evidence of the contraction.

II. Achinese accentuates the final syllable, and hence it
has in many cases dropped the first, unaccented, syllable
of the originally disyllabic word-base, as Snouck Hurgronje
has shown. Thus in Achinese " leaf " is *un*, as compared with
the *daun* of many other IN languages. This *un*, however,
is not a primitive thing but the final product of a process of
evolution.

III. In Sund., disyllabic words when employed as the first
members of compound expressions are often reduced to monosyllables. " Tree " is *kai* (disyllabic), but the " Mĕraq tree "
is *ki mĕraq*.—

Other phenomena of this sort are to be found in the IN
languages; and the conclusion to be derived from these considerations is : Monosyllabic forms originating in such ways
as these must be avoided in our investigation.

33. We will now select from IN vocabularies some mono-syllabic words with regard to the original monosyllabism of which there is no doubt: Old Jav. *luh*, " tear ", *sih*, " pity ", *liṅ*, "to speak"; Karo *pĕt*, "to desire"; Gayo *tul*, "unable to get through (a narrow space)". — Other cases will follow later.

It will now be shown by the quotation of texts that such words exist not only in the dictionary but in actual speech. For this purpose we shall select extracts from a dead language, Old Jav., and a living one, Karo:

I.   Old Jav. examples.   Mahābhārata, edited by Juynboll, 9: *maṅkana liṅ saṅ Bhīma* = " Thus spake Bhima ". — Mahābhārata, *a*, 54: *deniṅ sih n ikaṅ śvāna* = " Out of pity for * this dog ". — Rāmāyaṇa, edited by Kern, VIII, 40, 4: *hunvili ta luh* = " Then (=*ta*) flowed tears ".

II.   Karo examples.   Si Laga Man, edited by Joustra, p. 7: *maka sĕkali lit sada bapa ; tubuh anak-na, tapi mate rusur; jadi anak-na sada igĕlari-na si Laga Man †, maka ‡ pĕt man, nina* = " There + was (= *lit*) once a father; (there) were + born children of + him, but (they) died one + after + another; (so it) came + to + pass + that of + (the) + children of + him one was + called by + him (= *na*) the greedy (in) eating that (it) might + desire to + eat, said + he " = " There was once a father who had children that all died one after another ; so he gave one the name of ' Glutton ', in order that, as he imagined, it might eat heartily ".

34. The number of roots used as actual words is nowhere large.§   Many languages have, apart from words of form,‖

---

* The construction is a genitive one, as in Latin, *n* being a genitive preposition.

† *man* is a doubtful case, it may be primitive or it may be a contrac-tion of *maan*, which is found, *e.g.*, in Gayo.

‡ *maka* has very various functions: it can introduce both principal and subordinate clauses, as in this extract.

§ [See § 71 and Essay II, §§ 51-2.]

‖ [In the original, " Formwörter ", the meaning of which term is illustrated by the examples given here and in § 72. See also Essay II, §§ 81, 84-114. " Words of form " must not be confounded with " for-matives" (which are not separate words, but mere affixes, though they were often originally independent " words of form "): see Essay II, § 80, and Essay III, §§ 34-5.]

not a single case; Karo has some five dozen. In the entire Prasthānikaparwa of the Old Jav. Mahābhārata there are, not counting words of form, four certain cases: *sih*, " pity ", *duk*, " moment of time ", *gön*, " big ", and *liñ*, " to speak ".

Roots used as words of form occur in every language, some having them in greater numbers than others, *e.g.*, Mal. only a few, Tontb. a fairly large number. A Tontb. sentence with such monosyllabic words of form: Story of Kĕrisĕn, edited by Schwarz, end: *taniqtuo si sisil an doroq i Cĕrisĕn* * = " Thus (runs) the story about Kĕrisĕn ".

35. It can be shown that the Original IN possessed a greater number of independently existing roots than any living IN language does. This is indicated by the fact that in Modern Jav. several words exist only in disyllabic form which in Old Jav. still lived in monosyllabic shape; accordingly as we go back in time the number of monosyllables increases. One of these cases is the Modern Jav. *duduh*, Old Jav. *duh*, " liquid ". But § 91 forbids us to assume that Original IN spoke entirely in monosyllabic words.

36. The existence of mere roots, not made up into word-bases, can serve us as a touchstone to test the correctness of the principles which we have developed above for the analysis of the word-bases. There is a widespread IN word-base *kasih*, " pity "; according to our principles we have to analyze it into *ka* + *sih* ; and the *sih* cited in § 33 confirms the correctness of the analysis.

It happens particularly frequently that a monosyllabic root survives in Toba while the closely related Karo only has a disyllabic word-base formed from it. Here, therefore, Toba offers us the desired guarantee. Examples:

Toba *gas*, " to break ", shows that Karo *tegas*, " to tear " = *te* + *gas*.

Toba *gañ*, " to stand on end ", shows that Karo *tĕgañ*, " erection " = *tĕ* + *gañ*.

---

* *c* for *k* in conformity with the law stated in § 74. [*i* is the article; as to the use of articles before proper names, see Essay II, §§ 85, 91 (and footnote).]

Toba *das*, " announced (of a message) ", shows that Karo *landas*, " evident " = *lan* + *das*.

Toba *ñal*, " too tight, short of breath ", shows that Karo *doñal*, " disheartened " = *do* + *ñal*.

37. It has been shown, particularly by the researches of W. Schmidt, that the Austroasiatic languages on the mainland of Asia are in some way related to the IN languages. And as the former possess many monosyllabic word-bases, the view has been expressed that light could be thrown from that quarter on the nature of the IN roots. That may be, but the IN material has become so extremely abundant, particularly through the classifying work of Dutch scholars, that IN research needs no such assistance. Further, the present writer knows that students of the Austroasiatic languages, such as Cabaton, Aymonier, Blagden, and Skeat, favour caution in proceeding along this line of comparative enquiry.

Such caution, however, will above all else imply that we must first study each of the two groups, the Austroasiatic and the IN, exhaustively by itself before we proceed to a comparison of the two. Further, Austroasiatic and Austronesian parted from one another in some remote prehistoric age. In each of these two fields of research we must, therefore, first endeavour with the help of phonetic laws to work back to the primitive forms and then compare these with each other.

Several scholars, particularly Kern, have also established some very interesting points of relationship between Indonesian and Polynesian. Nevertheless, as Wulff justly observed in his critique of the present writer's " Matahari ", we can and may pursue IN studies without introducing the Polynesian languages into our sphere of research.

SECTION II : THE CHARACTERISTICS OF THE ROOT.

Preliminary Observations.

38. The IN root has six characteristic points requiring to be discussed: (1) The fact that it consists of three sounds, (2) variation, (3) determination, (4) metathesis, (5) homophony, and (6) its meaning. It is not to be inferred that all these phenomena need necessarily occur in connexion with *every* root.

The Three Sounds of a Root.

39. The most striking characteristic of the root, obvious at once even on a cursory inspection, is the fact that it consists of three sounds, arranged thus: consonant + vowel + consonant. All the roots which we have thus far become acquainted with have three sounds.

40. We must, however, raise the question whether there are not in IN other roots of a type different from the norm set up in the preceding paragraph.

Let us first enquire after roots of two sounds. This investigation demands special care. For if in some language or other we happen to come across a root that apparently has two sounds, we must reckon with the possibility that it may have lost one of its component parts through the operation of phonetic laws. If we find in Tontb. a word *rĕqmba*, " to fall ", we must not at once set up a root with two sounds, viz. *ba* ; to be sure, Tontb. only drops one final consonant, namely *h*, but might not that just be the case here ? In actual fact it *is* the case, for other IN languages, which have no objection to final *h*, here have the form *bah*: Old Jav. and Mal. *rĕbah*,

" to fall ", Karo *tabah*, " to fell ". If therefore, in what follows, series of words are set out from which roots of two sounds are to be inferred in each case, the languages comprised in such series must include some that do not drop any sound whatsoever.

41. Here follow the series in question:

Old Jav. *ipi*, Bug. *nipi*, Mal. *mimpi*, Day. *nupi*, Tontb. *impi*, " to dream ": root *pi*.

Old Jav. *wĕli*, Bug. *ĕlli*, Mak. *balli* *, Mal. *bĕli*, Sund. *bŏli*, " to buy ": root *li*.

Old Jav. *tuju*, " to hit, to aim ", Mal. *tuju*, " to pursue a certain course ", Sund. *tuju*, " course ", Karo *tinju*, " to cuff ": root *ju*.

Old Jav., Mlg. *isi*, Mak. *assi* †, Sund. *ŏsi*, " contents ": root *si*.

42. Here then we have four roots of two sounds arranged in the order: consonant + vowel. All four roots run in perfect phonetic concordance through many languages, and can therefore be assigned to Original IN.

43. Roots formed otherwise than of three sounds or two, like those in the preceding paragraph, are quite exceptional and occur only in individual languages. Thus in the Philippine languages we meet with a sort of extension and subdivision of the vowel resulting in the production of roots of four sounds, with two interior vowels. The IN languages have a root *gĕm*, " to shut, to clench the fist, to seize "; in Jav. it exists as a monosyllabic word-base *gĕm*, Karo has *siṅgĕm*, " to fit closely ", but Bis. has *goom* ‡, " to shut the mouth ". — In Sund. and Gayo there are interjections beginning with a mute and a liquid, e.g. Sund. *drel*, an interjection used of the rattling of musketry fire. At a pinch one might regard the *-r-* as the infix discussed in § 86, in which case the root

---

* The doubling of the *l* in Bug. and Mak. is in conformity with the laws stated in §§ 27 and 29.

† The doubling of the *s* follows the same laws, as the *a* is not a primitive *a*.

‡ The *o* is in conformity with the law stated in § 25.

would only have three sounds, but the *r* seems to us so essential
to the symbolical representation of the sound of rattling that
we must decline on this occasion to take it for an infix.   Here
then we have another root of four sounds.   Interjections
of this type may conceivably have been Original IN, and in
that case the remark in § 11 about the Original IN initial
would require modification accordingly.

Variation.

44.   The concept of root-variation.   In Day. the word
tuli means " to land " and *talian* is " a landing place "; in
Karo the expression " to roll " can be rendered by *gulun*
and *gulan*.   Viewing the matter quite superficially, we find
in both languages the same process, an interchange between
a and *u*.   But if we look closer we notice great differences.
In Day. the change of *u* to *a* occurs frequently, it is bound up
with a certain condition — namely that a suffix containing
an *a* is annexed to the word — and it occurs with the strictest
regularity and necessity every time that condition is fulfilled.
Besides which it is to be observed that in Day. this phenomenon
affects the first vowel of the word-base, and the meaning
suffers no change. — In Karo we find this kind of vowel change
in some other cases besides that of *gulun* and *gulan*, to be
sure, but yet only in a limited number, forming no sort of
groups or series.   Nor can we detect any condition determining the occurrence of the vowel change.*   Moreover, the
phenomenon takes place in the second part of the word-base,
that is to say in the root, and is often accompanied by a
modification in meaning ; thus in this very case, *gulun* signifies " to roll up ", *gulan* " to roll down ".   — This phenomenon, which we observe in the two Karo words *gulun*,
gulan, we call root-variation.   It affects the consonants of the
root as well as the vowel and it occurs in all the IN languages
without exception.

* See however § 48.

45. Examples of root-variation in several IN languages:

I. In Karo:

 a. Variation of the vowel:

> *gĕgĕh,* " strength ", *tĕguh,* " firm ".
> *ripas,* " away ! ", *lĕpus,* " to escape ".

 β. Variation of a consonant:

> *ĕrlap,* " to shine ", *kilat,* " to shine ".
> *bańkir,* " to break ", *lukis,* " to carve (with a chisel) ".

 γ. Variation of both vowel and consonants:

> *pĕdĕh,* " to stand fast ".
> *tandĕk,* " to stand on ".
> *pajĕk,* " to ram (*e.g.,* posts into the ground) ".
> *pĕrjak,* " to set foot on ".

II. In other languages: Old Jav. *gantuń,* " to hang ", *tatiń,* " to hang down "; *indĕr, intĕr,* " to turn ". — Achinese *ulak, balik,* " to turn back ". — Tontb. *kompeń, kumpeq,* " low ".

Variation of both vowel and consonant:
Old Jav. *sasak, pasuk, susup,* " to enter, to penetrate ".

46. There are also cases of variation which affect more than one language and run through several. We cite two such cases, the one with change of vowel and the other with change of consonant:

	lań	*luń*
Old Jav.	*kalań,* " ring "	*guluń,* " to roll "
Sund.	*kalań,* " ring "	*guluń,* " roll "
Karo	*gulań,* " to roll "	*guluń,* " roll "
Achinese	*ilań,* " reel "	*guluń,* " to roll up "
Mlg.	*halana,* " to roll "	*huruna,* " to roll ".*

* The *r* is in conformity with the RLD-law; the final -*na* in accordance with the law stated in § 30.

	rit	*ris*
Old Jav.	*arit*	*hiris*
Toba	*arit*	*iris*
Tontb.	*gorit*	*riris*
Bis.	*kodlit* *	*kodlis.*

In this way it is possible to show the existence of a certain number of cases of variation which run through a number of languages and can therefore be attributed to Original IN.

47. Although variation does not occur in series or groups we do notice that certain kinds of it are of greater frequency than others. Thus we find:

I. Initially: frequent interchanges of tenuis and media; tenuis and cognate nasal; *s* and *n*.

II. In the interior vowel: *u* and *ĕ*.

III. In the final: tenuis and cognate nasal; *s* and *t*; *s* and *h*; *s* and *r*; *l* and *r*; *m, n,* and *ṅ*.

48. Now whence comes this phenomenon of variation? As it is probably based for the most part on Original IN processes, the question is a difficult one to answer. Nevertheless a good deal can be done to throw light upon it, and on this occasion the present writer will contribute the following:

I. When in the modern IN languages derivatives are formed by means of prefixes from word-bases, the initial surds *k, c, t, p, s*, very frequently, and often even the sonants *g, j, d, b*, change into the most closely related nasals. From the Old Jav. word-base *pupuh*, " to beat ", comes a passive *kapupuh*, but the active is *amupuh*; the active of the word-base *pet*, " to seek ", is *met*. Now in accordance with what has been said in § 47 we find in roots variations of the initial consonant exhibiting a similar change: *e.g.*, Karo has the variation *puk : muk*, in the word-bases *ripuk*, " to crumble ", and *mumuk*, " worm-eaten ". These variations of the initial of the root are therefore fossilized products of that same phonetic process, derived from a past epoch when IN em-

---

* The *dl* is in accordance with the law stated in § 25.—All these words mean " to cut ".

ployed a larger number of roots as word-bases than is the case
nowadays. — Other examples:

Karo: *kĕmkĕm*, " to shut in ", *jĕrñĕm*, " to clutch ".
Tontb.: *atĕp*, " to cover ", *ĕnĕp*, " to conceal ".
Mal.: *pusiñ*, " to turn round ", *pĕniñ*, " to feel giddy ".
Sund.: *babuk*, " to smite violently ", *amuk*, " to attack
furiously ".

II. In onomatopœic roots the variation of the interior
vowel may be symbolical: Mal. *ris* stands for a higher, *rus*
for a deeper, " rustling " sound. This phenomenon is extremely common.

III. Some IN languages have sentence-sandhi. Thus
in Mentaway a final nasal interchanges regularly with the
corresponding tenuis, according to the initial of the following
word, *e.g.*, *uran* with *urat*, " rain ". The same change is found
in Masaretese, but there it does duty in the formation of
words: *sefen*, " angry ", *epsefet*, " anger ".
Now according to § 47 there are variations in the final of
the root which exhibit the like change, so here again we have
fossilized relics of a former linguistic vitality. Examples:

Karo: *gĕbuk*, " cloud of dust ", *abuñ*, " ash ".
Old Jav.: *pĕpĕt*, " to cover ", *simpĕn*, " to conceal ".
Tontb.: *roñkap*, " to feel (an object) ", *roñkam*, " to touch
(an object) ".

49. Besides the ordinary style of speech several languages
also possess a higher one, specially appropriated to politeness,
sacred things, etc. In these gradations of style root-variation
is also employed. Thus in Modern Jav. *tĕpuñ* is the usual,
tĕpañ the polite, word for " to unite ". In the Day. dirge
Augh Olo Balian Hapa Tiwah, p. 215, we find: *hasambalut
tatekan* = " mixed with that which is cut off "; this *tatekan*
is explained by *tapekan*, so the variant *tek* denotes the religious,
pek the common, form of speech.
50. Root-variation is a complex subject in IN research and
will yet afford matter for many an academic thesis. But
at the same time there is no other field of study that holds out
such alluring temptations to the constructive fancy as this

one does, and the utmost caution is therefore to be observed in
approaching it. An identification has been suggested between
the roots of the Old Jav. words *kĕlĕm*, " to sink ", and *surup*,
" to become submerged ", so that *rup* and *lĕm* would be
variants of one another. The present writer formerly agreed
with this view, but has since had doubts on the subject. For
there is also a Karo word *kĕnĕn*, " to sink "; and why should
we not be allowed to identify this *nĕn* also with *lĕm*? That,
however, inevitably leads to the identification of *nĕn* and *rup*;
and then there would be an end to all serious research.

51. In raising the question of the universal validity of
phonetic law in IN, one must not use the phenomena of
root-variation as evidence against such validity. There is
a phonetic law of interchange of vowels as between Karo and
Toba (§ 19), whereby every Karo *ĕ* is represented in Toba by
o, and thus Karo *ĕnĕm*, " six ", is *onom* in Toba. Now the
pendant to the Karo *ikĕl*, " to laugh ", is not *eṅkol* in Toba
but *eṅkel*. But we have no right whatever to assert that this
is an exception to the law; on the contrary, the matter stands
thus: there was originally a root for " to laugh " with two
variants, *kĕl* and *kel*, whereof the first has been preserved in
Karo, the other in Toba.*

Determination.

52. In § 41 we were introduced to roots of two sounds,
such as *ju*, " to aim, to have a certain direction ", *li*, " to
buy ". Now alongside of these roots of two sounds there
always run roots of three, which have therefore another consonant after the vowel. Beside the above-mentioned root
li Karo has a root *lih*, " to appropriate to oneself "; beside
ju Sund. has *jul* in *tujul*, " to point, to direct a letter to someone "; beside *pi* in Old Jav. *ipi*, " to sleep ", there is *pit* in
ipit, " to talk in one's sleep ". Through many languages
there runs a root *kas* alongside of *ka*, " to open, to release ",
and the like:

* [See also Essay IV, § 348.]

ka		kas	
Tag.	*ouka*	Tag.	*bukas*
Bis.	*boka*	Bis.	*bokas*
Old Jav.	*buka*	Ponosakan	*wukas*
Sund.	*buka*	Tontb.	*ĕñkas*
Karo	*pulka*	Karo	*tĕlkas.*

53. Some of the phenomena that are usually regarded as variations could perhaps with equal justification be classed under the concept of determination. It is customary to say that *suk* in Old Jav. *asuk*, " to bring into ", and *sup* in *susup*, " to force one's way into ", stand in the relation of variation to one another. But it is also a tenable view that *suk* and *sup* are cases of the determination of a root of two sounds, *su*. But this would remain a mere figment of the imagination until it had been shown that such a root *su* had a real existence.

54. The explanation of the determining elements is more difficult in IN than in IE.* In the latter the formatives are affixed as suffixes, in the same place, that is, where the determinatives also appear, and thereby we are enabled to gain from the formatives some indications as to the nature of the determinatives (see Brugmann, " Kurze vergleichende Grammatik der indogermanischen Sprachen ", § 367). In IN the determinatives, it is true, are suffixed, but the formatives mostly appear as prefixes. There is only *one* universally distributed IN suffix, viz. *-an*, *-ĕn* or *-n*, which is used both in nominal and verbal derivation. By means of this suffix we are enabled, it is true, to explain one of the phenomena of determination. In § 41 we became acquainted with a root *si*, " contents "; in Tettum it has the form *sin*, occurring in *isin*, " contents ". In the determining *n* we may recognize the above-mentioned formative *-n*. This phenomenon is found chiefly in Masaretese and Tettum, which has twenty quite certain cases, but we also meet with it in other languages. Other examples:

* [See also Essay IV, § 348]

3

Common IN	*ina*	Tettum	*inan,*	" mother "
Day.	*ara*	Jav.	*aran,*	" name "
Day.	*olo*	Mlg.	*uluna,**	" man "
Jav.	*isi*	Masaretese	*isin,*	" contents ".†

Metathesis.

55.   Metathesis of the root occurs in IN in three forms:

I.   The two consonants of the root of three sounds change places.   Examples:

Tontb.	*kewoy*	and	*keyow,*	" to dirty "
Tontb.	*leqlew,*	" to peel "	*kawel,*	" to detach "
Sund.	*aduy*	and	*ayud,*	" soft "
Tonsea	*telew*	Bulu	*tewel,*	" to fly "
Old Jav.	*atus*	Iloko	*gasut,*	" hundred ".

This kind of metathesis is found in all the IN languages, in some more frequently than in others, but always in isolated cases, never in series or groups.

II.   The vowel and the final consonant of the root of three sounds change places.   This phenomenon occurs in Kissarese. But before we can examine it we must state the phonetic laws of Kissarese, as formulated by Rinnoy:

First Law : Original IN *k* is dropped.   Example: *iur,* " tail ", beside Mal., etc., *ekur.*

Second Law : Original IN *t* becomes *k*.   Example: *waku,* " stone ", beside Old Jav., etc., *watu.*

Third Law : Original IN *s* becomes *h*.   Example: *ahu,* " dog ", beside Old Jav., etc., *asu.*

Thus, in Kissarese, Original IN *kulit,* " skin ", first becomes *ulik* and finally by metathesis *ulki*; *walas,* " to repay ", *walah*

---

* Mlg. has no *o*; the final *-na* follows the law stated in § 30.

† [In " Der Artikel des Indonesischen verglichen mit des dem Indo-germanischen ", § 67, the author inclines to the view that in Tettum, at any rate, this final *n* may represent an affixed article.   The study of IN linguistics is still in progress, and very possibly new evidence may turn up some day which will assist in determining such doubtful points.]

and finally *walha*; *alas*, " forest ", *alah* and finally *alha*, etc.
The number of instances recognized by the present writer does
not suffice to decide whether these cases of metathesis in Kissarese are isolated phenomena, like those under I. above, or
whether they form a group subject to a phonetic law.

III. The two sounds in roots of two sounds change places.
This phenomenon occurs quite regularly in Kupangese, in a
consecutive context, apparently* when certain conditions
are fulfilled. Thus " to go " is, according to these circumstances, sometimes *lako* and sometimes *laok*; " to be able ",
bole and *boel*, etc. The etymological forms are *lako* and *bole*,
as is shown by Old Jav. *laku* and Mal. *boleh*. — This kind of
metathesis is found in quite isolated instances in various IN
languages, *e.g.* Tontb. *pair* as compared with Common IN
pari, " ray " (a species of fish).†

Homophony.

56. The concept of homophony:

In Old Jav. there is a word *atěr*, " to accompany ", and
another, *huntěr*, " to follow "; from these we infer a root *těr*.
Further, Old Jav. has a word *kětěr*, " to tremble ", and also
gěntěr, " to quake "; whence also follows a root *těr*. Both
roots have absolutely the same sound, but their meanings do
not admit of any identification whatever. This phenomenon
we style homophony of the root.

57. Examples from Karo:

First root *liñ*: *aliñ*, *saliñ*, " to hint at ".
Second root *liñ*: *tuñgaliñ*, " to fall ", *liñliñ*, " to have a
steep descent ".
Third root *liñ*: *baliñ*, "to turn ", *giliñ*, " to rub in a mortar".
Fourth root *liñ*: *kělaliñ*, " to float in the air ", *paliñ*, " to
blow away "
Fifth root *liñ*: *toliñ*, " to hold aslant ", *iliñ*, " to pour
out ".

* There is no Kupangese grammar, but Jonker has issued a Kupangese text in Bijdragen 1904, p. 252.
† [See also Essay IV, §§ 236-41.]

58. Such homophonies frequently extend through several languages. Example:

First root *liñ*, " to turn ": Old Jav. *puliñ*, " to roll ", Karo *baliñ*, " to turn ", Mal., Gayo *giliñ*, " to roll ", Bis. *galiñ*, " to spin ".

Second root *liñ*, " to look ": Old Jav. *dĕliñ*, " to look ", Bis. *hiliñ*, " to look carefully at ", Mal. *kĕrliñ*, " to give a side-long glance ".

Third root *liñ*, " word, sound ": Old Jav. *liñ*, *wĕliñ*, " to speak ", Gayo *liñ*, " word, sound ", Karo *aliliñ*, " echo ".

Homophonies that run through so many languages may be ascribed to Original IN.

59. An homophony deserving of particular notice is to be found among the words of form, to wit that one and the same word is at once a demonstrative pronoun (or, if weakened, an article) and a locative preposition.* Examples:

i: demonstrative or article in many languages.

i: preposition in many languages.

a: demonstrative or article in several languages.

a: preposition in Mlg.: *nusi*, " island ", *a-nusi*, " on the island ".

au: demonstrative in Bug. and as part of *itu* (in accordance with the phenomenon discussed in § 80) in several languages.

au: preposition in Toba.

ka: demonstrative, as part of *ika* (§ 80) in Old Jav.

ka: preposition in many languages.

Very probably, however, these are cases of something more than a merely superficial homophony.

60. This homophony of the root, a phenomenon of very frequent occurrence in all IN languages, has repeatedly been used as evidence to prove the inferiority of the Indonesian race as compared with the white one. It has been urged that it argues " a confused and clouded mental apparatus ". Such an assertion, however, merely proves the scientific inferiority and the inhumanity of its authors. This homophony by no

* [See also Essay II, §§ 84 *seqq.*, especially § 96.]

means leads to " confused and clouded " thinking: IN possesses sufficient linguistic means to avoid any such defect. It is true, for example, that the root *i* in Toba is both a preposition and also a demonstrative, but as a preposition it *precedes* the word with which it is in relation, and is proclitic with a weak stress, *e.g., na i danka* * = " those on the boughs ", while as a demonstrative it *follows* the word with which it is in relation, and has more stress than it, *e.g., pidon i* = " this bird ".

The Meaning of the Root.

61. In connexion with this theme we have to put two questions: What shades of meaning can a root have, and which is the primary one among such shades of meaning ? On this occasion we will deal with the matter by considering two instructive cases.

The root *lut* occurs in many IN languages. In Gayo we find as derivatives of it the words *balut*, " to wind, to twist ", *bĕlut*, " eel ", and *kalut*, " mental confusion ". One and the same root, therefore, yields a word-base denoting an action, another word-base denoting a concrete thing, and a third one denoting a psychical event. — Should anyone throw doubt on the relationship of these three words, we would draw his attention to the fact that precisely the same phenomenon is repeated in connexion with the Tontb. root *sey*: Tontb. *kĕsey* means " to wind " (intrans.), *kosey*, " eel ", and *pĕsey*, " doubt ".

62. Now which of the three shades of meaning of the root *lut* is the original one ?

This root has in many languages the meaning of " to twist, to entangle ", *e.g.* Karo *ulut*, " to twist ", Mal. *bulut*, " to wrap up hastily ", written Mkb. *bilut*, " irregularly shaped ", Bĕsĕmah *balot*, " to wrap round ", etc.; but only in quite a few languages does it mean " eel " or " mental confusion "; hence the first-named shade of meaning will probably be the original one.

---

* To be pronounced *dakka.*

To explain the *o* of Bĕsĕmah *balot* a phonetic law must be
mentioned, which affects the distribution of *u* and *o* in the
final syllable of the word-base: In the final syllable of Bĕsĕmah words *u* occurs as an absolute final and *o* before a final
consonant, no matter how these vowels may be distributed
in Original IN or in other languages; thus beside the Mal.
pasu, " pot ", there is also a Bĕsĕmah word *pasu*, but *pasuñ*,
" stocks ", is represented in Bĕsĕmah by *pasoñ*.

The second case referred to in § 61 is given in § 90.

SECTION III: THE FORMATION OF THE WORD-BASE FROM THE ROOT.

Preliminary Observations.

63. The word-base may be formed from the root in five different ways: first, the root itself may be a word-base; or, secondly, the reduplicated root; or, thirdly, two or more roots are combined; or, fourthly, formatives are added to the root; or, fifthly, a meaningless pĕpĕt is prefixed to the root.

The Root as Word-base.

64. Among the roots that can serve as word-bases we will proceed from the obscure formations of the emotional impulses to the clearer ones of the reason, thus mentioning *first* the *interjections* and ending with the words of form.*

65. The IN languages possess, to begin with, such interjections as are evoked by internal psychological processes, *e.g.*, *ah* used as an expression of mental anguish, etc., etc.

66. In the second place, there are the interjections that are elicited by some external event:

I. The interjection directly imitates by its sound the external event. Of such cases, which are numerous in most of the IN languages, let two be adduced as specimens:

    a. Toba: *sar*, " a rushing sound ".
        Mal.: *sar, sir, sur,* " a rushing sound ".
        Day.: *sar*, " rustling ", *sur*, " hissing ".
        Jav.: *sĕr*, " whirring ".
        Bĕsĕmah: *sar*, " hissing, as when water falls on fire ".
        Gayo: *sur*, exclamation when one sees a suddenly appearing ray of light.
        Sund.: *ser*, exclamation of sudden anger.

* [See also Essay II, §§ 81 *seqq.*]

The following examples illustrate the use of these interjections in the sentence:

Day.: *sindä mamaṅkih, sar basila* = "(When one) but once deals a cut (at it), '*sar*' (the wood) is split". Gayo: *sur itĕgudne luju e* = "'*Sur*', he pulled out his (= e) knife".

    β. Gayo: *kak,* "raven".
        Day.: *buroṅ kak,* "raven".
        Toba: *si-gak,* "the raven".
        Nabaloi: *uak,* "raven".

II.   The external event has the characteristic of being sudden or momentary, but it can scarcely be maintained that the form of the interjection is an imitation of the event. These cases are particularly numerous in Jav. and Sund. Examples from Sund.: *bĕs,* interjection used of diving; *bral,* at departing; *bray,* when it grows light; *jlog,* at a sudden arrival.

III.   The external event lacks the characteristic of suddenness. Sund. examples: *rĕd,* interjection when binding; *tret,* when writing.—

Obviously these groups are not sharply differentiated from one another. Gayo *sur* and Sund. *ser,* which owing to their sound have been included under I., might equally well have been put under II.

67.   Thirdly, the interjection expresses a complete judgment. Examples: Gayo *cup,* "that is against the rules!", but the same *cup* in Jav.: "Yes, that is so!"

68.   The *second* category is that of the words for *calling, frightening away,* and *urging on.* Examples: Mad. *yuh* incites dogs; Jav. *cik* calls dogs; Karo *ciṅ* calls cats, etc.

Through many languages there runs the call *kur,* which is used for calling fowls and summoning back the departing vital spirit of persons in a faint, etc. In Mal., Gayo, Jav., and written Mkb. it has the form *kur;* Bĕsĕmah, in accordance with the law stated in § 62, has *kor.*

69.   The *third* category is that of the "*suckling*" words of children's speech, or, as Paul in his "Prinzipien der Sprachgeschichte " calls it, " wet-nurse language ". These all contain the consonant *m*, for vowel they mostly have *a*; they signify: " to suck, breast, to drink, to eat, mother, father ". Some are used as imperatives and thus form a link with the preceding category. Examples: Mal. *mam*, " to suck "; Lampong *mah*, " breast "; Achinese *mom*, " breast "; Sund. *am* and *mam*, " eat ! "; Sund. *ma*, " mother "; Mentaway *mam* or *mai*, " father "; Mad. *maq*, " father ".

70. *Fourth* category: *forms of address.*

I. Single instances: Běsěmah *bě*, an expression used in addressing persons younger than the speaker; Běsěmah *cih*, used in addressing young girls; Sund. *nuñ*, " child ! "

II. Through several languages, though not with a phonetically concordant final, runs the root represented by Sund. *ka*, Mad. *kaq*, Jav. *kañ*, " elder brother ".

III. Often there is a disyllabic form alongside of the monosyllabic one: Sund. *bi* and *ěmbi*, " aunt ": Mad. *naq* and *anaq*, " child "; Mad. *ca* and *kanca*, " friend ". — In such cases the monosyllabic form is generally the one used for the vocative, while the disyllabic one performs the other functions. Some lexicographers are of opinion that the monosyllabic forms represent abbreviations of the disyllabic ones; that assumption is unnecessary, for the instances under I. show that such monosyllabic formations are capable of existing by themselves.*

71. *Fifth* category: *words of substance.* As stated in § 34, roots playing the part of words of substance are not numerous in any IN language.

I. Examples from a single language, viz. Karo: *buk*, " hair ", *dah*, " clay ", *kěm*, " impartial ", *rěh*, " to come ".

II. Examples running through two languages. — As in the following Gayo is often referred to, the principal phonetic law of that language must be stated here. It runs: Original IN *a* appears in Gayo as *a* or as *ö* in accordance with very complicated rules; thus Original IN, Old Jav., Mal., etc., *ikan*, " fish ", appears in Gayo as *ikön*; but Old Jav., Mal., etc., *kurañ*, " de-

* [But see Essay IV, § 276.]

ficiency ", remains *kuraṅ* in Gayo. The chief rule, which includes the majority of the individual cases, runs: *a* remains *a*
before final *ṅ*, as in the above-mentioned *kuraṅ*; exceptions:
böṅ, " a species of plantain ", and *röṅ*, " elderly ". Now follow
the examples:

    Karo and Gayo: *tul*, " unable to get through ".
    Karo and Gayo: *dah*, " clay ".
    Mal. and Bal.: *laṅ*, " kite ".
    Old Jav. and Daïri: *pu*, " master ".
    Old Jav. *bap*, " very ", Gayo *böp*, " brave ".
    Old Jav. *duk*, " to push ", Mentaway *duk*, " to stamp ".
    Old Jav. *pet*, " to seek ", Karo *pĕt*,* " to desire
        keenly ".

III.   Examples running through three languages:
Old Jav., Bal., Gayo: *luh*, " tear ".
Old Jav., Toba, Gayo: *liṅ*, " word, sound ".
Magindanao, Tontb., Mentaway: *kan*, " food ".†

72.   *Sixth* category: *words of form.*   There is a considerable
number of monosyllabic words of form in the **IN** languages.
Some of them run in unchanged shape through so many **IN**
languages that we must ascribe them to Original **IN**.   These
include:

n: genitive preposition.
i: locative preposition.
ka: the preposition " until, to, for ".
ku: possessive pronoun of the first person.
a: particle of uncertain judgment, hence in Bug. meaning
" or ", in Old Jav. " to be compared with ", in Bis. " what sort
of ? ".

The following examples exhibit the distribution of some of
these monosyllabic words of form, and at the same time
illustrate their application:

I.   The genitive preposition *n:*
Mlg.: *ra n usi*, " blood of a goat ".
Gayo: *gĕral n guru*, " name of the teacher ".

* With root-variation.
† [See also Essay II, §§ 51-2, 115.]

Mentaway: *uma n abak*, " house of boats " = " boat-house ".

Sangirese: *tinara su soa n Leiden*, " printed in (the) town of Leyden ".

Day.: *huma n papan*, " house for planks ".

II.   The locative preposition *i*:

Old Jav.: Arjuna-Wiwāha, edited by Kern, II, 19, *c*: *tan madoh i sor*, " not far at bottom " = " down there ".

Tag.: *i babaw*, " on the surface ".

Bug.: *i liwĕn*, " at the side ".

Gayo: *i umah*, " in the house ".

Mlg.: *i masu*, " before the eyes ".*

The Reduplicated Root as Word-base.

73.   The second method of fashioning word-bases from roots consists in the reduplication of the root. This reduplication may be of three kinds:

74.   *First* type: the root is set down twice, every sound of it.

a. Examples from Karo, which possesses a very large number of such formations:

Root *kap* : *kapkap*, " kite ". — Beside *tankap*, " to seize ".

Root *gĕr* : *gĕrgĕr*, " to cook ". — Beside *tangĕr*, " to cook ".

Root *kĕl* : *kĕlkĕl*, " to overcome all obstacles ". — Beside *donkĕl*, " obstacle ".

Root *bis* : *bisbis*, " pus ", etc.

β. Examples from Tontb., which also exhibits very many cases. — For the understanding of these examples it is necessary to mention three Tontb. laws, as formulated by the two Adriani's.

First law: Original IN final *h* is dropped; see the example *rĕqmba*, § 40.

Second law: *k* becomes *c* whenever an *i* precedes. From the root *koq*, " to push ", are formed both *sĕqkoq*, " impact (of collision) ", and *sicoq*, " knock, blow ".

* [See also Essay II, §§ 96 *seqq.*]

Third law: between the two vowels of the word-base only a few of the Original IN combinations of consonants are now tolerated, in most cases the first consonant has to become *q.* The following examples particularly illustrate this third law:

Root *kal : kaqkal,* " to stamp ". — Beside *taṅkal,* " to knock ".

Root *tas : taqtas,* " to cut through ". — Beside *wontas,* " notch ".

Root *las : laqlas,* " past ". — Beside *tĕlas,* " left over ".

Root *lĕt : lĕqlĕt,* " to penetrate ". — Beside *sĕlĕt,* " between ".

γ. Examples running through several languages:

Karo, Mad., Tag., Bis. *kaṅkaṅ,* " to sprawl ".
Old Jav., Karo, Iloko *laklak,* Tontb. *laqlak,* " to peel ".
Karo, Iloko *kupkup,* Tontb. *kuqkup,* Bis. *koqkop,* " to shut ".

This mode of forming the word-base by doubling the root, and likewise the actual cases cited under γ, may be ascribed to Original IN.

75. *Second* type: the root is doubled and between the two roots the root vowel is inserted. This type occurs very frequently in Iloko:

Root *bat : batabat,* " to check ". — Beside *albat,* " to hinder ".

Root *sim : simisim,* " to spy out ". — Beside *simsim,* " test ".

Root *pak : pakapak,* " foliage ". — Beside *palakpak,* " leaf ".

Root *muk* (§ 48): *mokomok,* " gold dust ".

In other languages this formation is rarer. Examples from Bis.: *bisibis* beside *bisbis,* " to pour out "; *hisihis,* " to trail along the ground ", beside Old Jav. *his,* " to stream ".

76. *Third* type: only the first two sounds of the root are reduplicated, as in Mal. *kikis,* " to scratch ".

a. In many languages, and precisely in Mal., it is difficult to recognize this formation. It is indeed by no means certain that Mal. *kikis* is really a case of partial reduplication; in fact, the word might be explained in three ways. First, it might be a partial reduplication. Secondly, it might be the final result of an originally complete doubling: Original IN *kiskis* would have to become *kikis* in Mal., for Mal. no longer admits the combination *s* + *k*. Thirdly, it is conceivable that *ki*- may not be a reduplication at all, but one of the formatives (like those given in § 87), as it is in Mal. *kipas*, " fan ", as compared with Toba *alpas*, " to wag ", and Karo *gurpas*, " to shake the wings ". — Precisely the same possibilities, for similar reasons, hold good in the case of the Day. *lalak*, " to strip bare of leaves ".

β. There are, however, means of determining whether it is a case of reduplication or of a formative. As an Original IN *laklak* has been established in § 74, it is surely simplest to regard Day. *lalak* as a product of this *laklak* ; and further, since a word *kiskis* occurs in many IN languages, we shall assert that this reduplication also accounts for the first syllable of Mal. *kikis*.

γ. Mad. possesses many striking cases of forms transitional between full and partial reduplication, as the following table shows:

Mad.	Mad. second form	Modern Jav.
sĕpsĕp	*sĕssĕp*	*sĕsĕp,* " to suck out ".
tĕptĕp	*tĕttĕp*	*tĕtĕp,* " firm ".
sĕksĕk	*sĕssĕk*	*sĕsĕk,* " narrow ".

δ. The writer has, however, no means at hand of deciding the question whether every case of partial reduplication of the root in IN languages has proceeded from an Original IN complete reduplication or whether partial reduplication existed in Original IN side by side with the complete form.*

77. The question now presents itself, whether reduplication of the root entails a definite modification of meaning. Now we actually do observe that an intensification of the idea of the root can be expressed by reduplication, as is shown by the following table of Karo words:

* [See also Essay II, §§ 57-9, and Essay IV, §§ 195-6, 198.]

kĕskĕs, " to bind tightly "	*biṅkĕs,* " to pack ".
parpar, " to fling down "	*ampar,* " to lie on the floor ".
gakgak, "to keep one's gaze fixed upwards "	*jurgak,* " to look upwards ".
kĕlkĕl, " to overcome all obstacles "	*doṅkĕl,* " obstacle ".
larlar, " very extended "	*wĕlar,** " broad, wide ".

We find similar phenomena in other languages as well. Thus, in Tontb., the precise meaning of *lĕqlĕt,* from *lĕtlĕt,* is " to force oneself into ", whereas *sĕlĕt* merely means " between ". Further *peqpet,* from *petpet,* means " to flatten ", while *kumpet* signifies " to cover ". There are similar cases in Mad. and elsewhere.

78.   The further question arises, whether this intensification of meaning is a regular concomitant of reduplication. Since the present writer, as stated in § 7, has taken a general survey of the whole store of simple and reduplicated roots in many languages, he is in a position to answer this question also.   And the answer is: no.   In the majority of the cases reduplication does not, after all, import any specific shade of meaning; that is shown by the following comparisons, here given as samples:

Karo

taptap, " to wash clothes "	*litap,* " wet clothes ".
datdat, " slow "	*kĕdat,* " lazy ".

Madurese

raṅraṅ, " seldom "	*jaraṅ,* " seldom ".
jhĕkjhĕk, " firm "	*ajhĕk,* " to stamp firm ".
terter or:	*eter,* " to sow in a row ".

79.   In the cases of complete reduplication hitherto mentioned the root was set down twice, sound for sound.   But we also find cases of reduplication with variation of the vowel. This phenomenon occurs in many languages, but the variation is nowhere found in manifold diversity, and the number of individual cases is nowhere great.

---

* Not Karo, but found in several other languages.

I. Toba has hardly any other type than the variation *u : a*, and the instances denote a noise or a discordance: *ñumñam*, " not harmonious", *suñsañ*, " inverted ", *lumlam*, " confused ", *juljal*, " to contradict oneself ".

II. Mad. shows no preference for any particular kind of variation; the meaning is again discordance: *cekcok*, " non-sensical ", *cokcak*, " strife ", *salsul*, " mistaken for something else ".

III. Day. does not employ complete reduplication at all, except in onomatopoeic words. The reduplication with the same vowel often denotes a mere repetition of the event, the one with a varying vowel a happening in many different places:

jakjak. " to hiss often "   *jikjak*, " to hiss everywhere".
geñgeñ, " to resound often "   *yoñgeñ*, " to resound every-where ".

The most frequently occurring variation is *i : a*, irrespective of whether the simple root has *i* or *a :*

lap, " to sip noisily "   reduplicated : *liplap*,
kis, " to sneeze "   ,,   *kiskas*.

We can observe such phenomena in several other languages besides, but, as Toba, Mad.. and Day. have sufficed to show, the various languages diverge to a very marked extent, so that there is no possibility here of drawing any conclusions as to Original IN conditions.

Combination of Roots to form the Word-base.

80. *First type* of combination of two or more roots to form the word-base: roots serving as words of form are combined. This is a very common phenomenon. Words of form, though very short, can nevertheless often be analysed, *e.g.* the three cases at the beginning of the Old Jav. inscription of the Śaka year 1272, edited by Kern in Bijdragen 1905: *irika diwaśa ni kamoktan Pāduka Bhaṭāra, sañ lumah ri Śiwabuddha* = " This (is the) time of the demise of His Majesty who rests in the Śivabuddha sanctuary ". Here *ni* is divisible into *n + i*.

saṅ into *sa* + *ṅ*, and *ri* into *r* + *i*, and all these roots of one sound exist by themselves in Old Jav. or in other languages. Old Jav., for instance, welds the two locative roots *i* and *r* into *ri*, and even then it can prefix another *i*, thus producing *iri*. Examples:

Mahābhārata, 42: *saṅ hyaṅ Indra umujar i sira* = "The god Indra spake to them".

Mahābhārata, 46: *majar ta saṅ Arjjuna ri wwaṅsānak nira kabeh* = "Then spake Arjjuna to his brothers all" (*nira* = "his").

Mahābhārata, *a*, 13: *wuwusan iri kita* = "Words to you".

Similarly Old Jav. *ika*, "this", consist of the two demonstrative elements *i* and *ka*. Mlg. *tsia*, "no", as compared with *tsi*, "not", contains an intensifying particle *a*, which in the form of *ah* also follows negatives in Day.: *dia*, "no", *dia ah*, "not at all!" The Bug. *kuwaetopa*, "just so", is composed of five parts, all of which also occur separately in Bug., viz. *ku* + *a* + *e* + *to* + *pa*.

We find in many languages the combination of the genitive preposition *n* (which we have repeatedly mentioned) with an *i*, which is a locative preposition, but may also perhaps be regarded as an article in certain cases. The resulting form *ni* is used as a genitive preposition. Examples:

Magindanao: *su walay ni Pedro*, "the house of Pedro".
Toba: *isi ni huta*, "inhabitants of the village".
Old Jav.: *anak ni ṅhulun*, "children of mine".

81. That a genitive and a locative preposition should coalesce is nothing remarkable. In IE also, as is well known, these two relations run into one another; Brugmann ("Kurze vergleichende Grammatik", § 539) cites the Vedic *sūrē duhitā*, "daughter of the sun", where of course *sūrē* is a locative. Moreover, there are IN languages which employ *i* directly as a genitive particle, *e.g.* Tontb. and Mlg. Tontb. example, Sisil 82, edited by Schwarz, p. 177: *siituoka sera mareṅomoṅe an tĕruṅ i apoq era* = "Then they (= *sera*) went back to the northward to the hut of their master" (lit. "to the hut of master their"). Mlg. example, from the text Ny

Vazimba in Julien's grammar: *ani andrefana misi fuku witsi-witsi, izay milaza, azi hu taranak' i ni* * *Wazimba* = " In the West there are several clans (= *fuku*) which say that they are descendants of the Wazimba ".

82. The combination of the genitive particle with the article in Old Jav. and Tag. deserves particular notice:

Old Jav. " the foe " *ṅ musuh.*
" of the foe " *niṅ musuh.*
Tag. " the man " *aṅ tawo.*
" of the man " *naṅ tawo.*

The formula for Old Jav., therefore, is $(n + i) + ṅ$, since *ni* consists of $n + i$; the Tag. formula is $n + (a + ṅ)$, since *aṅ* is composed of two articles, the *a* mentioned in § 59 and the *ṅ* which occurs in the Old Jav. The view that Tag. *naṅ* consists of *ni* + *aṅ* raises phonetic difficulties, nor is it necessary seeing that in § 72 we showed the existence of a preposition *n* without a vowel.

An illustration of Old Jav. *niṅ*, Kuñjarakarṇa, edited by Kern, p. 60, l. 2: *kumucak baṅu niṅ sāgara* = " The water of the sea moaned ".

83. *Second type :* combination of two roots of substance. Examples:

Sund. *bĕk*, " to beat " Sund. *bĕksĕk*, " to cut down ".
Sund. *sĕk*, " to fall down dead "
Old Jav. *ruk*, " to destroy "
Sund. *ruksak*, " to destroy ".
Old Jav. *sak*, " to devastate "
Mentaway *rok*, " in a straight line "
Mentaway *rokdaṅ*, " in a straight line ".
Karo *ledaṅ*, " in a straight line ".

84. *Third type :* combination of a root of substance with a root of form. The latter in these cases is the article *a*.
Old Jav. *luh*, " tear " Bagobo *luha*, " tear "
Old Jav. *buṅ*, " shoot " Common IN *buṅa*, "flower".
Toba *pus*, call to frighten away cats Day. *pusa*, " cat ".

* *ni* is an article in Mlg.

4

Coalescence of Formatives with the Root to form the Word-base.

85. The most important linguistic means whereby word-bases are fashioned from roots consists in the indissoluble union of a formative with the root, so that they solidify into a new entity. These formatives are put before, into, or after the root; they are prefixes, infixes, or suffixes.

86. As already observed, the number and importance of the infixes and suffixes are much less considerable than those of the prefixes. So far as infixes and suffixes are concerned the following remarks will suffice for our purposes:

I. Formatives serving as suffixes are: -*an*, otherwise -*ĕn* or -*n*, and -*i*. Examples: Old Jav. *gahan*, " renowned ", beside Gayo *gah*, " renown "; Karo *buni*, " to hide ", beside Karo *bunbun*, to cover ".

II. As infixes we find: -*ĕr*-, -*ĕl*-, -*um*-, -*in*-. Examples: Mal. *kĕriñ*, " dry ", beside Old Jav. *kiñ*, " dry "; Old Jav. *tĕluñ*, " to hang ", beside Old Jav. *gantuñ*, " to hang "; Day. *kuman*, " to eat ", beside Magindanao *kan*, " food "; Tontb. *tinĕp*, " to dive ", beside Tontb. *tĕqtĕp*, " to sink in ".

III. Examples of infixes that run through several languages: *kuman*, " to eat ", is not only Day. but also Sampit, Tonsea, and Bulu; Mal. *kĕras*, " hard " — beside Old Jav. *kas*, " hard " — is also Old Jav. and Gayo, and in conformity with the laws stated in § 19 the Toba *horas* is identical with it.

IV. All the six formatives mentioned under I. and II. have other functions as well. They occur, the one in one language, another in another, as means for forming out of word-bases actual living derivatives, mostly in great numbers, *e.g.*, -*um*- in Old Jav. serves to form the aorist. — Compare herewith the quite different conditions mentioned in § 95 in relation to the prefixes.

87. The use of prefixes in fashioning the word-base out of the root is far commoner than that of infixes and suffixes. The number of prefixes is very large and the investigation of them could supply material for many a dissertation. In conformity with § 23 we shall here confine our enquiry to the main features of the subject.

Our first duty will simply be to recognize the existence of such prefixes, beginning our enquiry with the examination of a single language. Now here Sund. can be of very good service to us. It possesses a considerable number of monosyllabic roots which actually live in the language, nearly all being interjections, and it *also* possesses many word-bases derived from those roots. Karo, which we have often cited on other occasions, would be less useful to us here; it also has a good many living monosyllabic roots, but in most cases no derivatives from them. We need only subtract the roots from the respective Sund. word-bases, and the formatives will appear. This is shown by the following list:

děk, interjection of touching	*aděk*, " to touch ": formative *a*.
bat, interjection of stretching	*ěmbat*, " facings ": formative *ěm*.
sěd, interjection of pushing	*isěd*, " to push to ": formative *i*.
rěd, interjection of binding	*urěd*, " to bind fast ": formative *u*.
bur, interjection of jerking away	*kabur*, " to flee ": formative *ka*.
gěn, interjection of setting down	*tagěn*, " to put upon something ": formative *ta*.
cok, interjection of picking	*pacok*, " to pick ": formative *pa*.
gěs, interjection of breaking	*rěgas*,* " brittle ": formative *rě*.
bar, interjection of spreading out	*sěbar*, " to sow ": formative *sě*.

Here then we have ascertained that the prefixes *a*-, *ěm*- or *ěn*- or *ěñ*-, *i*-, *u*-, *ka*-, *ta*-, *pa*-, *rě*-, and *sě*- are employed in Sund. for forming word-bases.

Now when we look through the various IN dictionaries, *e.g.* those of Old Jav., Karo, Mal., etc., we are at once struck by

* With variation of the root.

the number of words we meet with that begin with these nine syllables. Likewise we have also come across them very often in the analyses we have previously undertaken. Therefore these nine prefixes are amongst the most widely distributed and commonly employed formatives used for the formation of word-bases.

88. Up to now we have usually spoken of the IN word-base as being disyllabic, consisting of the root and *one* formative. That is really the case of most frequent occurrence, but a root may also be combined with more than one formative at a time. In Tontb. the root *pañ* forms *pom + pañ*, " hole in the ground ", but also *pa + im + pañ*, " hole in a tree ". The number of such combinations of formatives is exceedingly large. Some of them run through many languages, *e.g.*, *kĕ + rĕ*

Old Jav.	*kĕrĕkĕt,*	" to creak ".
Mal.	*kĕrĕpaq,*	" to crack ".
Sund.	*kĕrĕpuk,*	" to beat ".
Achinese	*kĕrĕluñ,*	" to scratch ".
Tonsea	*kĕrĕsot,*	" to squirt ".

This formation may be ascribed to Original IN.

89. We will now proceed to explain in greater detail a word-base containing two formatives which has been chosen at random as an example. In Tontb. there is a word-base *lincayoq*, " to swarm ". The root is *yoq*, which also occurs in *woyoq*, " to shake ". From this root there has been formed, to begin with, a word-base *kayoq*, which also exists and signifies " to stir about ". The formative *ka-* here used is also found, *e.g.* in *kaloy*, " to hang down loosely ", from the root *loy*, whence also is derived the synonymous word *loyloy*. In front of *kayoq* another formative, the prefix *lin-*, is then attached, and as this contains an *i* the *k* has to be changed to *c* in conformity with § 74, and hence the ultimate resultant is *lincayoq*. The formative *lin-* also occurs *e.g.* in *lintoy*, " to swing up and down ", from the root *toy*, whence also comes *kontoy*, " to settle down ".

90. We will now illustrate by a single case how a number of different formatives may combine with one and the same root in various IN languages. The root selected for the purpose is *suk*, which means " to enter, to bring into ".

Old Jav.: *pasuk*, " to enter "; *asuk*, " to bring into, to put on "; *raṅsuk*, " clothing "; *rasuk*, " fighting dress "; *susuk*, " to penetrate ", *isuk*, " morning ", *i.e.* " entry of day ".

Mal.: *masuq* (for *masuk*), " to enter, to be on a person's side ", *esuq* (for *esuk*), " morrow ".*

Karo: *pasuk*, " to knock in, to penetrate "; *sĕluk*, " to put on ".

Achinese: *rasuk*, " peg ".

Day.: *masuk*, " to enter, to become ".

Toba: *pasuk*, *susuk*, " to make into something, to found ".

Mlg.: *isuka*, " to become engaged ".†

Sund.: *tusuk*, " to stick into "; *tisuk*, " to stab ".

Tag.: *tosok*,‡ " to make a hole ".

Bis.: *dasok*, " to stuff into "; *osok*, " peg "; *bogsok*, " stake ".

Nabaloi: *usokan*, " entrance ".

Tiruray: *suku*, " sharp stake for stabbing ".§

91. A considerable number of word-bases recur in very many IN languages with absolute phonetic concordance, that is to say with the same root *and the same formative*. — At this juncture we must interpolate a phonetic law of Iloko: Original IN *ĕ* appears in Iloko as *e*, and when this *e* is in the penultimate syllable, the next following consonant is doubled. Accordingly Original IN, and also Karo, etc., *ĕnĕm*, " six ", appears in Iloko as *ennem*. — Now follow the examples:

Meaning: " to enclose, cage ". — Type: Old Jav., Mal., Karo, Gayo, Mak. *kuruṅ*; Tag. *koloṅ*, by the RLD-law. — Root *ruṅ*, whence also comes Karo *karuṅ*, " sack ".

Meaning: " past, away ". — Type: Old Jav., Mal., Sund. *lĕpas*; Toba *lopas*, by the law given in § 19; Mlg. *lefa*, in con-

---

* [Malay pronounces Original IN final *k* as *q* : see Essay IV, § 150, I.]
† *Cf.* Mal. " to be on a person's side."
‡ As to the *o* in Philippine languages, see the note to § 25.
§ [See also Essay II, § 116.]

formity with the laws of § 30; Iloko *leppas*, by the law stated
above. — Root *pas*, from which also is formed Karo *ripas*,
" away ! "

Meaning: " black ". — Type: Original IN *itĕm*; Tag. *itim*;
Bis. *itom*; Magindanao *item*; Mkb. *itam*; Mlg. dialect *itina*. —
Root *tĕm*, whence also Bis. *agtom*, " blacking ". — The vowels
correspond with the utmost accuracy to the requirements of
the pĕpĕt-law.

Meaning: " wave ". — Type: Old Jav., Mal., Achinese, Mkb.
alun; Bis. *alon*; Mlg. *aluna*, by the law given in § 30. — Root
lun, whence also Old Jav. *wĕlun*, " to whirl ".

Meaning: " skin ". — Type: Old Jav., Mal., Sund., Gayo,
written Mkb., Ponosakan, Sampit *kulit*; Mlg. *huditra*, by the
laws of § 30. — Root *lit*, whence also Karo *salit*, " to peel ".

Such word-bases as these we may ascribe in their disyllabic
form to Original IN.*

92. When a formative is prefixed to the root we often observe that the two syllables of the resulting word-base have
similar vowels. There is an IN root with the meaning " to
turn ", which occurs in three variants: *laṅ*, *liṅ*, *luṅ*, and we
find in many IN languages word-bases such as *galaṅ*, *giliṅ*,
guluṅ, that is to say, with vowel harmony; but alongside of
these there are also such forms as *gilaṅ*, *galuṅ*, etc., that is,
with dissonance of the vowels. So the harmony in the above
cases is merely fortuitous. Still, there are also certain
cases where we can clearly perceive a law. The following
phenomenon appears in Tontb.: when to any root there is prefixed the formative *i* + nasal and to this again some other
formative (no matter which) is prefixed, then the last-named
formative always has the same vowel as the root. This law
includes thirty-three individual cases, and is hardly subject to
a single exception. Examples: *wuimbuṅ*, " to knock all of a
heap ", from the root *buṅ*, which also appears, *e.g.*, in
Karo *ambuṅ*, " to throw "; *waimbaṅ*, " to throw away ",
from a variant of the root *buṅ*; *lĕindĕṅ*, " mist "; see also
§ 88.

* [See also Essay II, §§ 118-9.]

93. The question now suggests itself, what is the meaning, what the function, of each of these formatives that fashion word-bases out of roots ? This subject is enormously complex and will also furnish material for many a dissertation. As in some other cases, the present writer wishes merely to throw some light on this matter by the mention of a particular instance: in many IN dictionaries there is a not inconsiderable number of word-bases beginning with *dĕ-*. When we survey all the cases, the conclusion follows that this *dĕ-* forms verbal word-bases from interjections:

Mal.: *ciñ*, " jingle "	*dĕciñ*, " to jingle ".
Karo: *kuñ*, " cry of a quail "	*dĕkuñ*, " to cry like a quail ".
Gayo: *buk*, " bump ! "	*dĕbuk*, " to fall with a thud ".
Sund.: *ñek*, " shrill tone "	*dĕñek*, " to yell ".
Bulu: *	*dĕtup*, " to bang (like a shot) ".
Iloko: *	*dessoor*,* " to rustle ".

We may ascribe this formative *dĕ*, with the meaning assigned to it, to Original IN.

94. The further question arises, whether the formatives were not originally independent words. In actual fact this can, with considerable probability, be argued of many of them. Toba has word-bases like *tuliñ*, " to fall over, to be knocked over ", *tulak*, " to be turned back ", *tulus*, " to be realized, to come to pass "; these have passive or intransitive meanings. Now in Toba we also find that by means of the preposition *tu*, " to ", and word-bases, phrases are formed which are precisely equivalent to passive verbs: thus *gadis* is the word-base for " sale " and *tu gadis* means " to be sold ". Now it is quite credible that this preposition is also inherent in the above-named *tulak*, etc. In that case, however, we have here what are really combinations of two roots after the fashion mentioned in § 84.

---

* The Bulu and Iloko dictionaries do not give the corresponding interjections, but *tup* occurs in Gayo and Mal. has *sur*, which by the law of § 43 corresponds with an Iloko *soor*.—Iloko *e* has been dealt with in § 91.

95. Many of the formatives that serve to make word-bases may also perform other functions in the economy of language. Thus in several languages the above-named prefix *ka-* forms the passive.* Thereby it may happen that one and the same root carries two *ka-*'s, the one forming the word-base and the other the passive. So from the root *sut*, which occurs, *e.g.*, in Old Jav. *kusut*, "to move oneself to and fro", there is also formed an Old Jav. *kasut*, "to shake", and the passive thereto is *kakasut*. — But most of the formatives that serve to make word-bases are, in fact, confined to that function; thus the prefix *lis-*, wherever it occurs, only creates word-bases, and is nowhere employed in inflexion, etc. Examples:

Karo: *listaṅ*, "vertical", root *taṅ*, whence also Karo *rintaṅ*, "in a (straight) line".

Iloko: *lisdak*, "to liquefy", root *dak*, whence also Karo *mĕdak*, "liquid".

96. In the languages that possess a higher style (see § 49) the latter is often formed by adding to the root a different formative from the one used in the common style. "Paunchy" in Day. is *haknai* in ordinary speech, *baknai* in the language of religion; and in precisely the same way Sund. expresses the idea of "to rise out of the water" by *hanjat* in the common style and *banjat* in polite language.

Prefixing the Pĕpĕt.

97. In some languages which possess monosyllabic roots used as word-bases, these roots also often appear with a pĕpĕt prefixed. Thus "kite" in Mal. is *laṅ* or *ĕlaṅ*, "bend" is *luṅ* or *ĕluṅ*, etc. — Common IN *duri, ruri*, etc., "thorn", appears in Old Jav. as *rwi*, from an older *rui* from which the second *r* has disappeared in accordance with the law in § 18; Modern Jav. turns the word into *ri*, and alongside of that we find a form *ĕri*. — This pĕpĕt is also added to monosyllabic loan-words, thus the Dutch *paal*, "a certain measure of length", appears in Mal. either as *pal* or as *ĕpal*.

* [See Essay III, § 65.]

This pĕpĕt, as Poensen rightly asserts, is a meaningless initial syllable.   It owes its existence only to the impulse to achieve a disyllabic form in the word-base.

The addition of such a pĕpĕt must, however, in some cases have taken place at a fairly remote epoch, for in Toba it has followed the pĕpĕt-law.   Thus by the side of Mal. *lat, ĕlat*, " interval ", Toba has the word *olat*, " boundary ", and beside *guñ, ĕguñ*, " gong ", a form *oguñ*, etc.*

* [See also Essay IV, §§ 226 *seqq.*]

SECTION IV: THE CHARACTERISTICS OF THE WORD-BASE.

Preliminary Observations.

98. This Section deals in 'the first place with the structure of the word-base; but as that follows from the account already given above of the manner in which the word-base is formed from the root, there will be no scope here for more than a brief recapitulation. The second point is the homophony of the word-base; the third, the function in a continuous context of the simple word-base, uncompounded with any further formatives; the fourth subsection deals with the reduplication of the word-base; the fifth, with the extension of the word-base for the formation of derivative words and for inflexion.

Structure.

99. It has been shown in Section III that the IN word-base is either identical with the root; or with the reduplicated root; or that it consists of two or more roots welded together; or that in it the root is indissolubly combined with one or more formatives, which are mostly prefixed, more rarely infixed or suffixed; or, lastly, that a pĕpĕt is prefixed to the bare root. The commonest of these several modes of formation is the fourth, and within this mode the commonest case is that of the root combining with *one* prefix, so that the word-base appears as a disyllable.

Several IN languages have an objection to final consonants, and therefore either discard them or else add on a vowel to them. The latter occurs in Mlg. and Mak. Thus Original IN and Old Jav., etc., *anak*, Mal. *anaq*,* "child", appears in Mlg. as *anaka*. Accordingly, the dictionaries of such languages contain many trisyllabic word-bases.

* [See Essay IV, § 150, I.]

Homophony.

100. Homophony is as rare in the complete word-base as it is common in the root. That is due to the fact that the formatives which create word-bases from roots are very numerous.

Example of homophony in Old Jav.: *ulih* = (1) to get, (2) to deliberate, (3) to return.

Example of homophony running through many languages:

	I. *karan*:	II. *karan*:
Old. Jav.	crag, rock	to cut designs.
Mal.	reef	to make garlands, to compose.
Gayo	rock	to compose.
Day	gravel, crag	to compose.
Mak.	coral reef	to compose.

Function.

101. The word-base can be employed, just as it stands, in living speech. From the root *kit*,* " to rise ", which appears *e.g.* in Gayo *bankit*, " to rise ", there is also derived a widely distributed word-base *bukit*, " rising ground, hill, hill town ". Now the following sentences show that this word-base, without any further additions, is really capable of being used in speech:

Mal.: *bukit jadi paya*, " Hills become lowland swamps ". (A proverb.)

Day.: *äka-m hon bukit galeget*, " Thy (= -*m*) dwelling (is) in the distant highlands ".

Mlg.: *zana-buhitra*,† " suburb ".

The Old Jav. sentence given in § 1 contains four word-bases used in living speech.

102. Although it has been stated that word-bases can be used in speech just as they are, yet we must add that there are certain rules, or limitations, affecting their use.

* [A still more primitive form of this root was *kid* (see Essay II, § 65), but that point is not material in this connexion.]

† The -*ra* is not a formative suffix but merely the product of a phonetic process (see § 30).

103. In the case of *substantival word-bases* there are probably no limitations whatsoever.*

104. In regard to *adjectival word-bases* there is much divergence between the different IN languages. In many languages, *e.g.* Mal., Gayo, and Tettum, we find no sort of limitation in this matter either. In other languages, however, the adjectival word-base, in order to fit it for use in a sentence, has to undergo some extension, which mostly consists in the prefixing of the formative *ma-*, as Humboldt ("Kawisprache," II, 77 *seqq.*) rightly showed. In Mlg. a minority of the adjectives needs no such extension, but the majority requires *ma-*; in Toba *ma-* can be added or omitted, but in the latter case the accent is thrown on to the final syllable; "this tree is high" is accordingly expressed by *matimbo hau on* † or *timbó hau on.*—And similarly in other languages.

Examples of adjectival word-bases used in the sentence without any further formative: Mal., Hang Tuah, edited by Niemann, p. 49: *bĕndahara mantĕri yañ tuwa, barañ sĕmbah-ña harus-lah diturut* = "The Bĕndahara (= chief minister) is a councillor who (is) aged, every word of his (therefore) should be complied with".—Mlg., the text Ny Fambara in Julien's grammar, p. 158: *nisi kusa natauni-hue fambara sua* = "There were also good omens, so-called".‡—Mak., Jayalangkara, 1 : *barañ bajik aq aqbaine maraeñ* = "(It were) perhaps well (that) I marry another (one)".§

105. In many IN languages the *verbal word-base* is an imperative:

Old Jav.	*laku*	word-base for "going".
	lumaku	indicative.
	laku !	imperative.
Day.	*tiroh*	word-base for "sleeping".
	batiroh	indicative.
	tiroh !	imperative.

---

* [See also Essay II, § 162.]
† The order is: "High (is) tree this".
‡ The order is: "So-called omens good".
§ [See also Essay II, §§ 168 *seqq.*, 185.]

In the Old Jav. Wṛttasañcaya, Wasantatilaka, verse 3, there are several such imperative word-bases in succession: *prih! pet! rarah!* = " Exert yourself! seek! search out! " —Mal. example, Hang Tuah, p. 10: *kata-ña, hay anaq-ku, sĕgĕra-lah naiq kaatas kĕday ini* = "She said: 'O my (= *ku*) child, quickly mount on this (= *ini*) booth ! ' " *

106. At the same time, many IN languages possess a definite number of verbal word-bases, often denoting a mode of motion, which do duty as indicatives. Mal. has a good many such, Mlg. very few. Examples: Bug., Paupau Rika-dong, p. 7: *lao pole, naĕssoiwi riolo bola na puwanna* = " They went (and) returned (and) laid (the rice) in the sun before (= *riolo*) the house of their mistress ".—Mlg., the text Ny Vazimba in Julien's grammar: *karazan' uluna awi ani iwelani ni Huwa* = " A race of men come from abroad (are) the Hovas ".†—Mal., Ken Tambuhan, edited by Klinkert, p. 72, verse 31: *sañ nata pun duduq dĕkat anakanda* = " The monarch sat next to his princely son ".—Old Jav., Mahā-bhārata, 34: *hetu nira pĕjah tan-paśeṣa* = "(The) consequence thereof (was, that they) all died (= *pĕjah*).‡

107. The simple substantival word-base, neither extended by any formative nor qualified by any word of form, is in many languages plural. Examples: Old Jav., Mahābhārata, *a*, 36: *tikus mañigit kuku mwañ rambut* = " Mice nibbled (at their) nails and hair ".—Day., Augh Olo Balian, p. 286: *ñalaya tolañ rumpañ, ñaleleñ uhat leso* = " Give the weary bones a rest, brace up the slack sinews ".§—Mlg., the text Ny Fahafa-tesana, in Julien's grammar, p. 115: *ni* ‖ *fati dia* ¶ *mifunu anati lamba mena marumaru* ** = " The corpses are shrouded in several red cloths ".

* [See also Essay II, § 159, and Essay III, §§ 75 *seqq.*]

† *karazan'*, by elision for *karazana*. The meaning is : " The Hovas are a race, etc."

‡ [See also Essay III, especially §§ 17 *seqq.*]

§ [The order is: " Rest bones weary, brace-up sinews slack."]

‖ *ni* is the article for both singular and plural.

¶ *dia* is an untranslatable particle.

** The order is: " cloths red several ".

108. Word-bases which denote a quality, state or process, are very often substantives in the IN languages. Accordingly such substantival word-bases need no further formative; but the verbs and adjectives thereto belonging do. Thus in Day. *handaṅ* is "redness"; "red" is *bahandaṅ*; and "to make red" is *pahandaṅ*. In Mlg. *lemi* is "mildness", *malemi*, "mild". In Old Jav. *lara* is "sickness", *malara*, "sick"; Old Jav. example, Wṛttasañcaya, edited by Kern, strophe 45, 3 : *saṅ nitya mawch lara-unĕṅ* * = "Who always causes love-sickness".

As these word-bases are substantives, they of course require the substantival construction. As mentioned in § 72, *n* is a genitive preposition, and thus in Mlg. "mildness of temper" is *lemi n fanahi*, which by reason of the sandhi-laws has to be pronounced: *lemi m panahi*.

In this respect the IN conditions are mostly the opposite of the IE. Thus in the French *rouge : rougeur* it is the substantive that carries the formative, in Day. *handaṅ : bahandaṅ*, the adjective; and the same relation obtains between Mlg. *lemi : malemi* and the Latin *lenitudo : lenis*.

109. Word-bases in the IN languages often have more than one function:

I. A definite, but not large, number of Old Jav. word-bases, including *tĕka*, are used in threefold fashion: as substantives, *tĕka mu*, "thy coming", as indicatives, *tĕka ko*, "thou comest", and as imperatives, *tĕka*, "come !"

II. In Day. a definite, very large, number of word-bases, including *tiroh*, have a double function: as substantives, *maṅat tiroh ku*, "sound (was) my sleep", and as imperatives, *tiroh*, "sleep !"; the indicative is *batiroh*.

III. In Mlg. such words have only *one* function, viz. as substantives: *turi*, "sleep". The indicative is *maturi* and the imperative *maturia*.

110. The IN word-base resembles the IE stem. The structure of Karo *abat*, "obstacle", from the root *bat*, from

* In pronunciation *a* + *u* are contracted to *o*.

which also comes *rĕbat,* " barred, blocked ", is quite similar
to that of the Latin *fuga* from the root *fug;* the fact that in
the one case the formative *a* precedes while in the other it
follows, affects the matter but little.

There is, however, a difference between the IN word-base
and the IE stem. The IN word-base, as stated in § 101, is at
the same time a word, that is to say, it is a formation
ready for use in speech. But the IE stem is not, or at least
only exceptionally, *e.g.* in the vocative; " the IE word comprises *three* parts, root, suffix and termination ", as Meillet-
Printz (" Einführung ", p. 82) says. That is the reason why
the present writer adheres to the term " word-base " and does
not replace it by the expression " stem ".

It is true that there are also some cases in which a word-
base appears only in the vocabulary, and stands in need of a
formative in order to be employed in actual speech. Thus
the Mlg. word-base *itsu,* " green ", only exists in the dictionary; the actual language (in accordance with the principle
stated in § 104) can only say *maitsu.* In such cases one would,
no doubt, be justified in speaking of a " stem " instead of a
" word-base ".

Reduplication.*

111. As in the case of the root, so also in that of the word-
base we find the phenomenon of reduplication. Either the
whole word or merely some part of it may be repeated, and
thus several very different types of reduplication result:

I. Complete reduplication: Mal. *rumah,* " house ", *rumah-
rumah,* " various houses ".—This type may be modified by
variation, which gives rise to a great multiplicity of forms:
Mal. *boṅkar,* " to overthrow ", *boṅkar-baṅkir,* " to throw everything into confusion ".

II. The final consonant of the first word is omitted: Old
Jav., Mahābhārata, *a,* 41: *mawĕla-wĕlas ta manah nira* =
" His (= *nira*) heart then felt deep pity ", from *wĕlas,* " pity ".
—In Sanskrit loan-words often more than one sound is omitted:

* [See also Essay II, §§ 174 *seqq.*]

Mahābhārata, 2: *pratī-pratīta sira kabeh* = " They all rejoiced exceedingly ".

III. The first syllable of the first word is omitted: Mad. *soñay*, " river ", *ñay-soñayan*, " ditch ".

IV. Of the first word only the first two sounds are used: Tontb. *gorit*, " to saw ", *gogorit*, " saw ".

V. The word-base has only one consonant between the two vowels, and that consonant is then doubled: Iloko *ama*, " father ", *amma*, " fathers ".

The various significations expressed by reduplication of the word-base have been discussed with subtle insight by Misteli (" Charakteristik ", p. 235).

Extension.

112. I. Word-formation and inflexion take place in IN either by the reduplication of the word-base, discussed in the preceding paragraph, or by the addition of formatives, mostly prefixes, to the word-base, or else by means of independent words of form.

II. The formatives which combine indissolubly with the root to form the word-base and those which, together with the word-base, create living derivatives, are in part identical (see § 86).

III. Word-formation and inflexion are generally explained clearly and in detail in the several IN grammars; and Kern in particular has done a great deal for the comparative treatment of the subject. Nevertheless there still remains quite a wide field open for research here, especially as fresh IN languages are constantly being made available by the creation of dictionaries and grammars.—In this place the writer will merely touch the fringe of the subject by means of a few examples:

a. Word-formation, example from Mlg.:

> *hira*, word-base for " singing ".
> *mihira*, " to sing ".
> *mpihira*, " singer ".
> *fihirana*, " song ".

β. Declension, plurals with formatives containing an *r*:

Tiruray: *Antonio*, " Anthony ", *re-Antonio*, " Anthony and
his people ".

Sund.: *budak*, " child ", *barudak*, " children ".

Masaretese: *huma*, " house ", *humaro*, " houses ".

γ. Conjugation, formation of the past tense with *n*:

	Magindanao	Sangirese	Malagasy
Pres.	*mageda*	*mĕbĕbera*	*matahutra.* *
Past	*nageda*	*nĕbera*	*natahutra.*
Fut.	*mageda-bu*	*mĕbera*	*hatahutra.*†

* The three word-bases signify: " to go on board ", " to speak ", and
" to fear ", respectively.

† [See also Essay II, especially §§ 143-76, and Essay III, especially
§§ 26 *seqq.* and 93 *seqq.*]

ESSAY II

COMMON INDONESIAN AND
ORIGINAL INDONESIAN

*(The original was issued as an Appendix to the Annual Report
of the Cantonal School, Lucerne, 1911.)*

SUMMARY

INTRODUCTION.

1. In the Tagalog language of the Philippines the word for " sky " is *lañit*, and it has also the same form in the Tontemboan of Celebes, the Dayak of Borneo, the Javanese of Java, the Gayo of Sumatra, the Malay of the Malay Peninsula, the language of the Mentaway Islands (which lie to the south-west of Sumatra), and in many other Indonesian languages besides these. It is true that in the language of the Batan Islands, northward of the Philippines, we find *gañit*, in the Bimanese of Sumbawa, an island lying towards New Guinea, *lañi*, and in the Hova of Madagascar *lanitra*; but it can be proved by means of strict phonetic laws that these three tongues, in an earlier stage of their development, also used the form *lañit*.—We have, therefore, in many IN (= Indonesian) languages one and the same expression for " sky ", viz. *lañit*.

Note.—The accentuation of IN words, including therefore *lañit*, is dealt with in § 75.

2. Such IN linguistic material as recurs in many different languages either unchanged or modified only in accordance with strict phonetic laws, we style Common Indonesian. We say, therefore, that there is a Common IN name for the sky, viz. *lañit*.

3. The wider the distribution of an IN linguistic phenomenon, the more positively shall we be entitled to pronounce it to be Common IN. Our right to do so will be particularly strong when the phenomenon manifests itself at the most different points of the IN linguistic area: *i.e.*, to put the matter concretely, in the seven great insular regions and the three border districts.

Note I.—The seven great insular regions are: the Philippines, Celebes, Borneo, Java with Madura and Bali, Sumatra,

the Malay Peninsula with the adjacent islands, and lastly
Madagascar. — The three border districts are: in the North,
the Batan Islands and Formosa; in the East, the islands from
Lombok towards New Guinea, of whose languages the best
known to us are Bimanese, Kamberese, Sawunese, Rottinese,
Tettum, and Masaretese; in the South-West, the row of islands
behind Sumatra: Simalur, Nias and Mentaway. — Another
border district, viz. Halmahera * and the adjacent islands,
cannot be included in our survey because there is a doubt
whether it really belongs to the IN linguistic area: see Van
Hinloopen Labberton, " Handboek van Insulinde ", p. 88.

Note II.—It is of course not to be expected, and indeed it
will seldom happen, that we shall be able to demonstrate the
existence of one and the same linguistic phenomenon in all
these ten areas of distribution; the Malay Peninsula area in
particular, with its impoverished vernacular, will often fail
us.   Our normal standard will be nine, eight, or it may be
only seven areas: if the number is less than that, it will be
only with diffidence, if at all, that we shall pronounce a linguistic phenomenon to be Common IN.

4. When we confront together languages thus diversely
situated in geographical position, we are at the same time
comparing languages that are related in the most various
degrees of relationship.   It will happen, for instance, that we
shall compare the Malay of the Peninsula, the Minangkabau
of Sumatra, the Javanese, and the Masaretese of the eastern
border.   Now the Minangkabau is closely allied to the Malay,
the Javanese is more distantly connected, the Masaretese still
more distantly; and the same sort of thing will occur in all our
comparisons.   Now if we find one and the same linguistic
phenomenon occurring in several forms of speech which are
related to one another in the most various degrees, that is to
say, even in such as in other respects are most distant relatives,
then we can with perfect confidence regard such a phenomenon
as being Common IN.

* [This applies in particular to the northern part of Halmahera:
see Hueting's article in Bijdr. 1907-8, pp. 370 *seqq.*]

5. The word for "cloud" in the Pampanga of the Philippines is *biya*, in the Bugis of Celebes *ĕlluñ*, in the Malay of the Peninsula *awan*: in short, one might almost say that each IN language has its own special word for " cloud ". We therefore say: there is no Common IN expression for " cloud ".

6. Now the Common IN linguistic phenomena form the subject of *the first of the two principal parts* into which our monograph is divided.

7. Let us now take stock of the chief principles of method which must serve as our lodestars in this first part. Herein we must first of all realize that our delineation of the Common IN element must have two facets, a positive and a negative side. If we establish the fact that there are Common IN expressions for " sky ", " to weave ", and " ten ", we must also at once add that for the concepts " cloud ", " to spin ", and " eleven " there are no Common IN designations. If we gave the reader only the positive results, our sketch would be one-sided, partial, and too favourable.

8. Further, we must build up our demonstrations entirely upon the basis of phonetic laws. That is really self-evident, but it must nevertheless be particularly insisted on here, because this first part of the monograph has to yield us a thoroughly sound foundation for the second part, which is of a more hypothetical nature, and therefore less certain. We must not therefore content ourselves with maintaining, for example, that Bimanese *lañi* and Hova *lanitra* are derived from an original form *lañit*: we must formulate the laws in accordance with which *lañi* and *lanitra* have come into being. These laws are as follows: " In Bimanese and Sawunese all Common IN final consonants disappear ", therefore *lañi* < *lañit*.* — " Every Common IN *ñ* becomes *n* in Hova, except before a velar "; " every Common IN final *t* appears in Hova as *-tra* "; therefore *lanitra* < *lañit*. — As to Batanese *gañit*, see § 9.

* [The symbol < means " (is) derived from ", and similarly the symbol > signifies " (which) changes into ". In both cases the more archaic form is at the diverging end of the symbol, the more modern form at the converging end.]

9. Besides having recourse to phonetic laws we shall find references to parallel cases of great service. In Mentaway *lañit* no longer means " sky ", as it does in Common IN, but " the red tint of dawn and sunset ". This transition in meaning would hardly, I imagine, disconcert us: instead of the sky we have a phenomenon in the sky. But our confidence will be even greater when we observe that a parallel case occurs in a dialect of Formosa, where *arañit* < *lañit* means " cloud ": here, too, instead of the sky we have a phenomenon in the sky.

It is, however, not only in our researches into the varying significations of words, that this method of reference to parallel cases will assist us: we shall also occasionally apply it instead of the appeal to phonetic laws. As stated in § 1, Common IN *lañit*, " sky ", appears in Batanese under the form *gañit*. Now the hitherto published Batanese material includes barely a hundred words, and among these there are only three cases in which *ñ* represents Common IN *ñ*. Three cases are, however, too few to enable a phonetic law to be formulated with safety. Here, therefore, we take refuge in a parallel and say: In Batanese *gañit* < *lañit*, *ñ* represents Common IN *ñ*, as in *añin* < Common IN *añin*, " wind ".—Further, among those hundred words, the number of cases in which Batanese *g* represents Common IN *l* is somewhat larger, there are ten safe cases; but even that number seems to me too small to enable a phonetic law to be formulated on the strength of it; I therefore again apply the method of reference to a parallel and say: In Bat. *gañit* < *lañit*, *g* represents Common IN *l* as in *bugan* < Common IN *bulan*, " moon ".

10. We shall exhibit the Common IN linguistic phenomena from the following points of view: phonetic system, synthesis of sounds into words, word-accent, formal analysis of words, formation of derived words, reduplication of words, and synthesis of words into sentences (*i.e.* syntax).

11. The *second principal part* of the monograph will have for its subject the Original Indonesian language. We style Original IN the fundamental form of speech from which the individual IN languages are descended.

12. The basis upon which we shall reconstruct the Original IN is the Common IN as delineated in the first part.

13. Whereas in the first part we shall deal altogether with real facts, the second part will only yield results of hypothetical value.

14. The contents of this monograph are my own, both as regards substance and method. It is true that here and there in the writings of other scholars I have come across the remark that this or that linguistic phenomenon is to be regarded as being Common IN; but such observations are only to be found sparsely, in no great numbers, and often unsupported by the necessary evidence.

Note.—As it is my wish that my monographs should not exceed a moderate size, I shall not mention everything that I have recognized as being Common IN; but I shall include everything that seems to me specially important.

15. The following abbreviations will be used:

Bal.	=	Balinese.	Mad.	=	Madurese.
Bat.	=	Batanese.	Mak.	=	Makassar.
Bim.	=	Bimanese.	Mal.	=	Malay.
Bis.	=	Bisaya.	Mkb.	=	Minangkabau.
Bol.	=	Bolongan.	Mlg.	=	Malagasy.
Bont.	=	Bontok.	Pamp.	=	Pampanga.
Bug.	=	Bugis.	Sund.	=	Sundanese.
Day.	=	Dayak.*	Tag.	=	Tagalog.
Form.	=	Formosan.	Tar.	=	Tarakan.
Inv.	=	Inivatan.	Tontb.	=	Tontemboan.
Jav.	=	Javanese.			

Note I.—For languages which have short names, such as Bulu, Toba, Karo, and Hova, and also for such as are only rarely cited, as Bolaang-Mongondou, no abbreviations are used.

Note II.—The abbreviations of the titles of periodicals are those used in the Orientalische Bibliographie.

* [See Essay 1, § 10, footnote.]

16. The Formosan material is derived from the notices of Happart and Van der Vlis, and from O. Scheerer's " The Batan Dialect "; the Inivatan material, from a MS. vocabulary most kindly presented to me by O. Scheerer ; the Sumbawarese, from a text published by Jonker in Bijdr. 1904, pp. 273 *seqq.*

PART I

COMMON INDONESIAN

SECTION I : PHONETIC SYSTEM.

17. We have to recognize as belonging to Common IN the six *vowels : a, i, u, ě, e,* and *o.*

18. The vowel *a.* We meet with this vowel in the Common IN word *kayu,* " tree ". That *kayu* is a Common IN word is proved by the following table:

Tree. Philippines, Ibanag: *kayu* — Celebes, Tonsea: *kayu* — Borneo, Day.: *kayu* — Java, Jav.: *kayu* — Sumatra, Mkb.: *kayu* — Malay Peninsula, Mal.: *kayu* — Madagascar, Hova: *hazu* — Northern Border, Form. : *caiou* — South-Western Border, Simalurese: *ayu-ayu.*

Note I.—The spelling in Happart and Van der Vlis' Form. vocabularies is very awkward; we need have no hesitation in interpreting *caiou* as = *kayu.*

Note II.—Hova *hazu* < *kayu* in accordance with the two following phonetic laws: " Common IN *k* becomes *h* in Hova, except after the velar nasal or as a final ". — " Common IN *y* appears in Hova as *z* ".

Note III.—The disappearance of *k* in Simalurese *ayu-ayu* is supported by the parallel case of *iuq* as compared with the widespread Common IN *ikur,* " tail ".

Note IV.—The word *kayu* appears in a number of other IN languages besides the above, *e.g.* in Sumatra in Běsěmah, Lampong, Karo, and Gayo, as well as in Mkb., and everywhere unchanged in sound. But it will suffice if in each case we select one language out of each of the ten areas of distribution.

77

19. We have, therefore, demonstrated the existence of a Common IN word *kayu*, which contains the vowel *a*. We also became acquainted in § 1 with a Common IN *laṅit*, "sky", and later on we shall meet with the Common IN words *apuy*, "fire", *ama*, "father", *ina*, "mother", *ratus*, "hundred", and *a*, "the", as well as the Common IN formatives *ka-*, *ta-*, and *-an*. All these forms agree in containing the vowel *a*. The amount of this material is so large that we may without hesitation pronounce the vowel *a* to be Common IN.

20. The vowel *i*. This vowel is proved to be Common IN by the word *aṅin*, "wind", in accordance with the following table:

Wind. Philippines, Iloko: *aṅin* — Celebes, Bug.: *aṅiṅ* — Borneo, Sampit: *aṅin* — Java, Sund.: *aṅin* — Sumatra, Toba: *aṅin* — Malay Peninsula, Mal.: *aṅin* — Madagascar, Hova: *anina* — Eastern Border, Bim.: *aṅi* — South-Western Border, Simalurese: *aṅin*.

Note I.—Phonetic laws: "Bug. and Mak. unify all Common IN final nasals into *ṅ*", hence Bug. *aṅiṅ* < *aṅin*. — "Hova unifies all Common IN final nasals into *-na*", hence *anina* < *aṅin*.

Note II.—The law in accordance with which Common IN *ṅ* has become *n* in Hova, as in *anina* < *aṅin*, and the law in accordance with which final consonants disappear in Bim., as in *aṅi* < *aṅin*, have already been given. We assume that the reader will make a mental note of all such laws, and we therefore mention each of them only once.

21. We have become acquainted with a Common IN word *aṅin*, "wind", which contains the vowel *i*. In the course of our enquiry we shall meet with many other Common IN words containing the same vowel. But we will content ourselves with specifying this one instance, the word *aṅin*; the reader will, of course, notice the other cases; and in the sequel we shall pursue the same method. We therefore pronounce the vowel *i* to be Common IN.

22. The vowel *u*. This is proved to be Common IN by the word *kayu*, dealt with in § 18.

23. The vowel *ĕ*, an indeterminate, rapidly pronounced sound often called by its Jav. name *pĕpĕt*. This vowel establishes its claim to be styled Common IN by the evidence of the word *tĕñah*, " half, some ".

Half. Celebes, Bug.: *tĕñña* — Borneo, Bol.: *tĕñah* — Java, Sund.: *tĕñah* — Sumatra, Karo: *tĕñah* — Malay Peninsula, Mal.: *tĕñah* — Eastern Border, Sawunese: *tĕña* — South-Western Border, Simalurese: *tĕñah*.

Note.—The phonetic laws are: " Common IN final *h* disappears in Bug., Mak., and several other IN languages ".— " When in Common IN *ĕ*, of a non-final syllable, is followed by a *single* consonant, that consonant appears doubled in Bug." —Both these laws are exemplified by Bug. *tĕñña*.

24. The number of areas in which we have met with *ĕ* amounts only to seven; according to the principles enunciated in § 3 we ought therefore to have some hesitation in declaring it to be Common IN. Whereas *a*, *i*, and *u* are present everywhere, the pĕpĕt is wanting in some IN languages, which instead of it use another vowel: *e.g.* Day. does not say *tĕñah*, but *teñah*, Bis. says *toña*. But in several of these languages the pĕpĕt has left tangible traces of its former existence. In Mak. of Celebes the pĕpĕt appears as *a*; Mak. therefore possesses two etymologically distinct *a*'s, the one corresponding to the Common IN *a*, the other to the Common IN *ĕ*. But the second *a* causes certain consonants which follow it to be doubled, the first one does not affect them. So Common IN *anu*, " someone " (§ 135), appears in Mak. as *anu*, but Common IN *ĕnĕm*, " six ", as *annañ*, and Common IN *tĕkĕn*, " staff ", as *takkañ*. In this matter Bug. exhibits the intermediate stage, for it also doubles the consonant but it retains the pĕpĕt:

Common IN	*tĕkĕn*
Old and Modern Jav.	*tĕkĕn*
Bug.	*tĕkkĕn*
Mak.	*takkañ*

In precisely the same way Iloko in the Philippines, which has replaced *ĕ* by *e*, doubles the consonant and accordingly says *tekken.*—Further, in the Hova of Madagascar the pĕpĕt appears in an accentuated syllable as *e* but in an unaccented one as *i*; accordingly Common IN *ĕnĕm* appears in Hova as *enina*. Hova therefore has two etymologically distinct *i*'s, the one being Common IN and the other derived from the pĕpĕt. Now before the first of these *i*'s Common IN *l* becomes *d* in Hova, but before the second it remains unchanged. For Common IN *lima*, "five", Hova has *dimi*, but for *alĕm*, "night", *alina*.

Note.—In the final of Hova *dimi* we have a third *i*, originating from *a*, in accordance with the following law: " A Common IN final *a* is assimilated in Hova to an *i* of the preceding syllable ". Analogous cases of assimilation have been discussed by Conant in Anthropos 1911, pp. 143 *seqq.*

25. We have shown in the preceding paragraph that in Iloko and Hova the formerly existing pĕpĕt is still traceable to-day; we therefore add the Philippines and Madagascar to the number of the regions mentioned in § 23, and are thereby entitled to style the pĕpĕt a Common IN feature.*

26. The vowels *e* and *o*. In contrast to the pĕpĕt these vowels have, one might almost say, a universal distribution; though it is true that Hova has no *o* and Mentaway very few words that contain an *e*. But *e* and *o* have in many cases originated out of other sounds, *e.g.* in Mad. *pote*, which stands by the side of Common IN *putih*, "white". And secondly, words containing an original *e* or *o* can as a rule be traced only through a very limited number of languages. Perhaps the most widely distributed are the two words *bela*, " companion, avenger, to share the same fate ", and *sor*, " above " or " below ". The *e* and *o* in these words are original; at least I know of no indication whatever that they are derived from any other sounds.

To share the same fate. Celebes, Mak.: *bela* — Java, Jav.: *bela* — Sumatra, Gayo: *bela* — Malay Peninsula, Mal.: *bela* — Eastern Border, Bim.: *bela.*

* [See also Essay IV, § 5.]

Above, below.   Philippines, Tag.: *anor*, " to lift up, to carry "
— Celebes, Tontb.: *sosor*, " to go up " — Java, Old Jav.:
sor, " below " — Sumatra, Lampong: *ansor*, " to diminish "
— Northern Border, Form.: *masor*, " to exceed ".

Note I.—Tag. *anor* with *n* for *s* is formed in accordance with
the principles illustrated in § 149.

Note II.—The phenomenon that one and the same word
means both " above " and " below " finds a parallel in the
Rottinese *demak*, which signifies both " high " and " deep ".
For other cases see Kern, " Fidjitaal ", p. 211.

27.   In view of what has been said in the preceding paragraph, it is only with some hesitation that we can venture to
style *e* and *o* Common IN vowels.

28.   We must concede to Common IN the three *diphthongs*
uy, ay, au (which I prefer to write *aw*) .*   These appear only
as finals.   In the interior of words, as in Mal. *laut*, the two
vowels belong to different syllables.

29.   The diphthong *uy*.   This is shown to be Common IN
by means of the Common IN word *apuy*, " fire ".

Fire.   Philippines, Inv.: *apuy* — Celebes, West Mori: *apuy*
— Borneo, Tar.: *apuy* — Java, Old Jav.: *apuy* — Sumatra,
Achinese: *apuy* — Northern Border, Bat.: *apuy* — South-
Western Border, Simalurese: *ahoy*.

Note.—In Simalurese *ahoy* we find *oy* < *uy* in accordance
with the parallel *lanoy*, " to swim ", as compared with Old
Jav. *lanhuy*. — The *p* has disappeared as in the parallel *ulaw*,
" island ", beside the very widespread *pulaw*; the *h* is to be
regarded as the last remnant of the vanishing *p*.

30.   The diphthong *uy* becomes *u* in Hova, so we find *afu*
< *apuy*, *walu*, " to change, to turn back ", beside Old Jav.
waluy.   But when a suffix is appended to such word-bases
as these, the *y* is no longer a final and therefore need not dis-

* [In Romanized Malay these diphthongs are commonly written
ui, ai, and *au,* respectively.   For the reason why it is preferable (at
any rate in works like the present) to adopt the author's spelling, see
Essay IV, § 158.]

appear: it then becomes *z* in accordance with the law stated
in § 18.   Now in Old Jav. beside the indicative *waluy* there is
a conjunctive *waluya*, and with this there corresponds in
Hova, according to § 108, the imperative *mi-waluza*.   This
formation *mi-waluza* < *mi-waluya* therefore proves to us the
former existence of the diphthong *uy* in Madagascar.

31.   In view of the evidence set out in §§ 29 and 30 we may
pronounce the diphthong *uy* to be Common IN.

32.   The diphthongs *ay* and *aw*.   About as widely distributed as the Common IN *apuy* are also *patay*, " dead ", and
paraw, " hoarse ".   These two words therefore warrant us
in regarding the two diphthongs *ay* and *aw* as Common IN.

33.   The *semi-vowels* *y* and *w*.   The former is shown to be
Common IN by *kayu* (§ 18), the latter by means of the word
walu, " eight ".

Eight.   Philippines, Magindanao: *walu* — Celebes, Tondano:
walu — Borneo, Tar.: *walu* — Java, Old Jav.: *wwalu* — Sumatra, Gayo: *waluh* — Madagascar, Hova: *walu* — Northern
Border, Form. dialects: *walu* — Eastern Border, Tettum:
walu — South-Western Border, Mentaway: *balu*.

Note I.—The pronunciation of the *w* is not uniform everywhere; it appears to be chiefly bilabial, the Philippine textbooks often write it *u* or even *o*, thus *ualu*, *oalo*.

Note II.—Phonetic law: " Common IN *w* appears in Mentaway as *b* ", hence *balu* < *walu*.

Note III.—Old Jav. *wwalu* < *walu* in accordance with the
parallel *wwara*, " to exist ", as compared with *wara* elsewhere
(see § 188).

Note IV.—Gayo *waluh* has got its *h* through the influence
of neighbouring numerals which really possess a genuinely
primitive one, such as *tujuh*, " seven ".   Analogous changes
in numerals are mentioned in § 141.

34.   We must admit as Common IN the *velars* *k*, *g*, *ṅ*.*

---

* [See Essay I, § 11, I, footnotes.]

35. The velar *k* is evidenced by the word *kayu* (§ 18); the velar *ṅ* by *aṅin* (§ 20); the velar *g* by the word *dagaṅ*, " stranger, trader ".

Stranger. Philippines, Tag.: *dagaṅ* — Celebes, Bolaang-Mongondou: *dagaṅ* — Borneo, Day.: *dagaṅ* — Java, Sund.: *dagaṅ* — Sumatra, Toba: *dagaṅ* — Malay Peninsula, Mal.: *dagaṅ* — Eastern Border, Bim.: *daga*.

36. We must concede to Common IN the *palatals c,* j, ñ.* But the pronunciation of this series of sounds is not quite identical everywhere: in several languages they are palatalized dentals, in Bont. the two explosives are " frequently near *ds* and *ts* ", as Seidenadel says.

37. The tenuis *c*. This is shown to be Common IN by the word *racun*, " poison ".

Poison. Celebes, Bug.: *racuṅ* — Borneo, Sampit: *racun* — Java, Jav.: *racun* — Sumatra, Karo: *racun* — Malay Peninsula, Mal.: *racun* — Eastern Border, Bim.: *racu*.

38. The media *j*. This is proved to be Common IN by means of the word *jalan*, " path ".

Path. Philippines, Bont.: *jalan* — Celebes, Bareqe: *jaya* — Borneo, Sampit: *jalan* — Java, Sund.: *jalan* — Sumatra, Bĕsĕmah: *jalan* — Malay Peninsula, Mal.: *jalan* — Eastern Border, Sawunese: *jara*.

Note I.—Phonetic law: " Bareqe, like Bim. and Sawunese, tolerates no final consonants ", hence *jaya* < *jalan*.

Note II.—Parallels: Bareqe *jaya* with *y* < *l* as in *buyu*, " mountain ", beside Bug., etc., *buluq*. — Sawunese *jara* with *r* < *l* as in *mara*, " exhausted ", beside Mal., etc., *malas*.

39. The nasal *ñ*. This is shown to be Common IN by the word *añud*, " to drift ".

To drift. Philippines, Pamp.: *añud* — Celebes, Mak.: *añuq* — Borneo, Day.: *hañut* — Java, Old Jav.: *añud* — Sumatra, Bĕsĕmah: *añot* — Malay Peninsula, Mal.: *hañut*.

Note I.—Phonetic laws: " Day., Mal., Bĕsĕmah and other languages, particularly of Borneo and Sumatra, change

* [See Essay I, § 11, 1, footnotes.]

Common IN final media into tenuis ", hence Day., Mal. *hañut*. — " Bug. and Mak. change Common IN explosive final into *q* ", hence Mak. *añuq*.—" Bĕsĕmah renders Common IN ending *u* + consonant by *o* + consonant ", hence *añot*.

Note II.—The *h* in Day. and Mal. *hañut* is a petrified formative: Day., for instance, uses *ha-*, or *h-*, to form verbs from word-bases.

40. If we survey once more the area of distribution of the series *c, j, ñ*, we are compelled to admit that it is not extensive enough to justify us in declaring without hesitation that this series is Common IN. However, we find in Madagascar, in Old Mlg., a further piece of evidence, at any rate for *j*, in the spelling *dz*, which we meet with occasionally in Flacourt and may compare with Seidenadel's *ds* in § 36. Thus Flacourt mentions a word *idzin*, " dark ": see Ferrand's edition, p. 103. But this *idzin* coincides phonetically with Jav. *ijĕm*, in accordance with the phonetic law: " Common IN and also Old and Modern Jav. final -*ĕm* becomes -*ina* in Mlg.; but the older sources often represent it by -*in* ". See also *alina < alĕm*, § 24.—It is true that *idzin* means " dark " and *ijĕm* " green ", but we find in IN more than one parallel for the shift of meaning from " green " to " dark ". In Madagascar itself *maitsu* signifies " green " in some of the dialects and " black " in others; Mal. *hijau* means " green " and is also used to describe the glint of black hair.— In the Mlg. of to-day *z*, *i.e.* the sonant sibilant, is used for Flacourt's *dz*, that is, for Common IN *j*.

Note.—It is remarkable what a number of Day. words containing *j* occur also in Hova, including some that are peculiar to these two languages. Examples: Day. *jara*, " punishment " = Hova *zara*, " lot, luck " — *jera*, " to frighten away by beating " = *zera*, " to beat " — *jawoh*, " negligent " = *zawuzuru*, " to behave carelessly " — *joho*, " wantonness of spirit " = *zu* " fame ", etc.—I am of opinion that Hova, or Mlg., finds its nearest relative among the IN languages in this very Day. Besides the circumstance I have just mentioned there are a number of other observed facts that have led me to that opinion, such as their common possession of the passive in *buah*, their peculiar adverbial use of the numerals (§ 172). etc. —Porzezinski's contention with regard to the relationship of Mlg. to other languages (Porzezinski-Boehme, p. 77) is untenable.

41. We must attribute to Common IN the *dentals t, d, n.* The tenuis is evidenced by *lanit* (§ 1), the media by *dagan* (§ 35) and the nasal by *anin* (§ 20).

42. We must attribute to Common IN the labials *p, b, m.* The tenuis has been shown to be Common IN by the word *apuy* (§ 29).

43. The media *b.* This can be shown to be Common IN by means of the word *buna*, " flower ".

Flower. Philippines, Pamp.: *buna* — Celebes, Mak.: *buna* — Borneo, Bol.: *buna* — Near Java, Mad.: *buna* — Sumatra, Toba: *buna* — Malay Peninsula, Mal.: *buna* — Eastern Border, Bim.: *buna* — South-Western Border, Nias: *buna.*

Note.—Pamp. *buna* does not mean " flower " but " fruit ", and Mad. *buna* means " seed-bud ". Compare the parallel case that in Mentaway *bua*—which, by the way, has no etymological connexion with *buna*—means " flower " as well as " fruit ".

44. The nasal *m.* This is shown to be Common IN by means of the word *ama*, " father ".

Father. Philippines, Inv. : *ama* — Celebes, Bolaang-Mongondou: *ama* — Borneo, Bol.: *tama* — Java, Sund.: *ama* or *rama* — Sumatra, Gayo: *ama* — Madagascar, Mlg. dialects: *zama* — Northern Border, Form. dialects: *ama, rama, tama* — Eastern Border, Masaretese: *ama* — South-Western Border, Siberutese: *ama.*

Note I.—In *rama, tama* and *zama* the articles *ra, ta* and *i* have coalesced with the word *ama*: see §§ 93 and 187.—Mlg. *zama* has undergone the following development: *zama < yama*, in accordance with § 18, *< iama* = article *i* + *ama.* A parallel thereto is Mlg. *zahu*, beside *ahu*, " I ", *<* article *i* + *aku.* The intermediate form *yaku* is preserved in Day.: compare what has been said in § 40.

Note II.—Mlg. *zama* does not mean " father " but " uncle ". A parallel thereto is the Gayo *ama,* which signifies both " father " and " uncle ".

45. We must attribute to Common IN the *liquids r* and *l.* The sound *l* is evidenced by the Common IN *laṅit* (§ 1): the sound *r* by *karaṅ,* " rock, dry ground, reef, coral ". § 190 deals with the pronunciation of the *r.*

Rock. Philippines, Iloko: *kalaṅ* — Celebes, Mak.: *karaṅ* — Borneo, Day.: *karaṅ* — Java, Sund.: *karaṅ* — Sumatra, Gayo: *karaṅ* — Malay Peninsula, Mal.: *karaṅ* — Madagascar, Hova: *harana* — South-Western Border, Nias: *kara.*

Note.—Iloko *l* for *r* in accordance with the RLD-law (§ 190). — A phonetic law of Nias: " No final consonant is tolerated in Nias ".

46. We must attribute to Common IN the *sibilant s.* This is evidenced by the word *susu,* " breast, to suck ".

Breast. Philippines, Inv.: *susu* — Celebes, Tontb.: *susu* — Borneo, Bol.: *susu* — Java, Sund.: *susu* — Sumatra, Lampong: *susu* — Malay Peninsula, Mal.: *susu* — Northern Border, Bat.: *susu* — Eastern Border, Tettum: *susu* — South-Western Border, Nias: *susu.*

47. We must concede to Common IN the *aspirate h.* This is evidenced by the word *tahan,* " to hold fast, to retain ".

To retain. Philippines, Tag.: *tahan* — Celebes, Ponosakan: *mo-tahaṅ* — Borneo, Day.: *tahan* — Java, Sund.: *tahan* — Sumatra, Lampong: *tahan* — Malay Peninsula, Mal.: *tahan.*

Note.—It must be admitted that the distribution of *h* is of such a nature that we have some hesitation in pronouncing it to be Common IN.

48. We meet with other sounds besides these in the IN languages: thus in § 30 we became acquainted with an *f* in the Hova word *afu,* " fire ", and in § 44 with a *z* in the Hova *zahu,* " I "; and Bug. and Mak. have the glottal explosive *q.** etc.

* [See also Essay I, § 11, I, footnotes.]

But on the one hand these sounds are not very widely distributed, and on the other they are demonstrably of a secondary kind. Thus the Hova *f* originated in accordance with a phonetic law from the Common IN *p*, as is proved by the comparison of *afu* with Common IN *apuy*; and the law is: "Common IN *p* becomes *f* in Mlg., save after a labial or when final". On such sounds as these we cannot confer the title "Common IN."

49. Common IN, therefore, has the following phonetic system, though it must be admitted that some of the sounds have not been evidenced with absolute certainty: *

$$a \quad i \quad u \quad \breve{e} \quad e \quad o$$
$$k \quad g \quad \dot{n}\dagger$$
$$c\dagger \quad j \quad \tilde{n}\dagger$$
$$t \quad d \quad n$$
$$p \quad b \quad m$$
$$y \quad r \quad l \quad w$$
$$s$$
$$h$$

* [See also Essay IV, especially §§ 39 *seqq.*]
† [See Essay I, § 11, I, footnotes.]

SECTION II: SYNTHESIS OF SOUNDS INTO WORDS.

50. Apart from interjections and words of form, the words of the IN languages, as we meet them when we open the dictionaries (*i.e.* in the shape which is more accurately called the " word-base "), are mostly disyllabic. We may say, therefore, that as a general rule the primary synthesis of sounds is into a disyllabic structure. Thus in the Mal. version of the Rāmāyaṇa, where the story is told of how Hanuman was sent to Langkapura, there is the sentence: " Now Hanuman was sitting under a maja tree " = *Hanuman pun duduq-lah di bawah pohon maja*. Here we have four disyllabic word-bases in succession.

Note.—Mal. *lah* here serves to emphasize the predicate. — *di bawah* literally means " at (the) bottom (of) ".

51. Monosyllabic words of substance, *i.e.* verbs and nouns, are rare; some languages possess none at all; Old Jav. has the largest number. And we never find one and the same monosyllabic word of substance running through very many different languages. Probably the one that is most widely distributed is *kan*, " food ".

Food. Philippines, Magindanao: *kan* — Celebes, Tontb.: *kan* — Sumatra, Pabian dialect of Lampong: *kan* — Eastern Border, Masaretese: *ka* — South-Western Border, Mentaway: *kan*.

Note I.—It must not be imagined that this monosyllabic *kan* merely figures in the dictionary: it really exists in living speech. We find in the Mentaway story Ägä-mu-la-laibi the phrase: " There is no food " = *tata kan*, and that is a complete sentence. Again, in the Mentaway legend of the origin of the race we read: " There were plantains for food " = *aiat kan bago*; and that, too, is a complete sentence.

Note II.—In other languages *kan* is found as a radical constituent of disyllabic words of substance, as for instance in the Old Jav. *pañan*, " food ", where *k* has become *ñ* in conformity with the principles of § 149. Thus in Jonker's Book of Laws, Art. 15, there is the sentence: " If he is a minor lodging with another person, he is liable for his board " = " If is child under-age living with a man, owes food " = *yen hana rare alit, añheriñher iñ woñ, ahutañ pañan.*

52. If *kan*, which only appears in five areas of distribution, is the most widely spread monosyllabic word of substance, we must declare that we are unable to style any single monosyllabic word of substance " Common IN ".

53. There are also trisyllabic word-bases, but these, too, are not numerous, and we seldom find any one of them running through a number of languages. Perhaps the most widely distributed one is the word *banua*, " district, inhabited place ".

District. Philippines, Pamp.: *banua* — Celebes, Bareqe: *banuwa* — Java, Old Jav.: *wanwa* — Sumatra, Toba: *banua* — Malay Peninsula, Mal.: *běnuwa* — South-Western Border, Nias: *banua.*

Note I.—Old Jav. *w* for *b* as in the parallel *wuña*, " flower ", for Common IN *buña* (§ 43).

Note II.—Between the *u* and the *a* some of the languages have developed the transitional sound *w*, hence Bareqe *banuwa*; in Old Jav. the *u* before the *a* has become a consonant, hence *wanwa*. An exact parallel hereto is afforded by Common IN *buah*, " fruit ":

> Without transitional sound: Nias *banua, bua.*
> With transitional sound: Mal. *běnuwa, buwah.*
> *U* turned consonant: Old Jav. *wanwa, wwah.*

Note III.—In Mal. a full vowel preceding the accent is weakened into the pěpět. Parallel: the loan-word *sěrdadu* < *soldado*, " soldier ".

Note IV.—Pamp. *banua* means " sky ". We have a parallel to this transference of meaning in Bis., wherein *banoa* denotes both a region of the earth and a region of the sky. Likewise in Toba *banua ginjaṅ* = " upper *banua* " = " sky ", while *banua toṅa on* = " this middle *banua* " = " the earth ".

54. *The initial of words.* Every sound of the phonetic scheme set out in § 49 can serve as the initial of a Common IN word. Evidence in support of this is superfluous. But there cannot be more than *one* consonant at the beginning of a word. Initials of two consonants appear in quite isolated cases; thus Gayo has contracted Common IN *bĕli*, " to buy ", into *bli*.*

55. *The interior of words,* or more precisely, the consonantal element between the two vowels of disyllabic words. In this position every individual IN language admits one or two consonants, but not more.

56. The commonest case of the combination of two consonants is that of a nasal $+$ a cognate explosive, *e.g.*, $ṅ + k$ in Tonsea *duṅkud*, " to speak ironically ". This case occurs in every individual IN language, and can straightway be styled Common IN.†

57. Another common case of the combination of two consonants in the interior of a word arises from the reduplication of the root, which is one of the methods of forming words out of roots. Thus in Old Jav. from the root *kab*, " to move to and fro ", which does not occur in actual speech, we find the derivative formations *uṅkab* and, with reduplication, *kabkab*. Here we have the combination $b + k$.

58. Now some of the IN languages only tolerate the first of the two above-mentioned cases: nasal $+$ cognate explosive. Others also admit the second one, *e.g.* certain languages of the Philippines, Java, Sumatra, and the Northern and South-Western Borders. Thus Bis. in the Philippines says *kapkap* for " to touch ", but Day. in Borneo says *kakap*, and cannot say otherwise.

59. But we find certain indications which render it probable that the languages with the kakap type of combination

---

* [See Essay IV, §§ 187 *seqq.*]   † [See Essay IV, §§ 193 *seqq.*]

did in a previous stage of their development possess the kap-kap type instead of it.

The most important of these indications is based on such phenomena as are set out in the following table:

Mad.	taptap	Mad.	kapkap
Mad. dialect	tattap	Mad. dialect	kakkap
Sund.	tatap	Day.	kakap

Note.—*taptap* means " to strike with the flat of the hand ", and the like; *kapkap*, " to scratch, to touch ", and the like.

We have, therefore, in particular dialects of Mad. a transitional form, produced by assimilation, and accordingly think it credible that the languages which now only possess the kakap type have evolved it out of a pre-existing kapkap type.*

60. The result of the considerations in §§ 55–59 is:— Common IN tolerates one or two consonants in the interior of a word; in the latter case we find, on the one hand, the combination of nasal + cognate explosive, and on the other the kapkap type of combination.

61. *The final of words.* In Common IN any of the vowels may serve as a final; evidence in support of this is superfluous. Secondly, the diphthongs *uy*, *ay* and *aw*, as was shown in § 28 *seqq.* The investigation of the consonantal finals is a more complicated matter.†

62. From this investigation we must first exclude the palatals. The consonants of that series are incapable of doing duty as finals in any IN language, and accordingly it must be declared that Common IN does not tolerate final palatals. — Tontb. has a few words with final *c*, *e.g.*, *paliqpic*, " a certain part of the roof ". But this *c* is a secondary formation originating from *k* in accordance with the Tontb. law formulated by the two Adriani's: " In Tontb., *k* after *i* becomes *c* ". The original form with *k*, *palikpik*, occurs in Tonsea, a language closely related to Tontb.

* [See also Essay I, §§ 73 *seqq.*, and Essay IV, §§ 195-6 198.]
† [See Essay IV, §§ 200 *seqq.*]

Note.—The first *k* of *palikpik* appears in Tontb. as *q* in accordance with the following law, also formulated by the two Adriani's: " In the case of a Common IN combination of consonants, other than nasal + cognate explosive, the first of the two consonants becomes *q* in Tontb."

63. Setting the palatals aside, we find in the individual IN languages very various possibilities of consonantal endings, which the following three typical extracts from texts will at once serve to illustrate:

I. Sĕraway sentence, out of the Anday-Anday Riṅgan Sĕdayu: " The king had a son and a daughter " = King had son had daughter = *rajaw bĕranaq bujañ bĕranaq gadis.*

II. Nias sentence, out of the heroic song edited by Lagemann: " He is fallen into the broad sea " = Finished fallen he into sea broad = *no aeχu* ia ba nasi sebolo.*

III. Mak. sentence, out of the Jayalangkara, p. 101: " He did obeisance, bowing his head down to the ground " = He did obeisance, bowing head his down to earth the = *na aqñomba, sujuq ulu-nna nauñ ri butta ya.*

In the first sentence all the words end in consonants, even the loan-word *raja*, which elsewhere always terminates in a vowel, has acquired a final *w* in conformity with the phonetic law: " Final *a* of other languages appears in Sĕraway as *aw* ". † In the second sentence none of the words ends in a consonant. In the third sentence consonantal endings are in the minority.

Now among the various individual IN languages we notice three principal types of consonantal ending: Some languages tolerate no final consonants at all, or only very few, Bug. for instance, two, viz. *q* and *ñ*; other languages admit all the consonants, except the mediæ; others, again, allow all the consonants, including the mediæ, to serve as finals.

* According to Sundermann, the Nias sound *χ*, which he writes *ch*, is pronounced like the German *ch* in " wachen ".
[Much the same as the *ch* in Scotch " loch ", therefore.]

† [The Sĕraway vocabulary gives no indication as to the force of this final *w*, but it may be assumed that it forms a diphthong with the preceding vowel, wherein (it must be remembered) the second member is not a full vowel, but partakes of a consonantal nature.]

64. *The first group*, which tolerates no consonants, or very few of them, as final sounds — Bug., Bim., Nias, Hova, etc., languages which, by the way, are not closely related together — does not represent the Common IN condition. For it can frequently be proved that in these languages final consonants have become mute, *i.e.* they existed in a former stage of the evolution of the language; this can be shown by the evidence of derivative words built up from word-bases by means of suffixes. Common IN *nipis*, " thin ", appears in Hova as *nifi*, having lost its *s*. From *nifi* is formed a verb *manifi*, " to make thin ", and this forms its imperative with the suffix *-a*, as in § 30, but that imperative is not *ma-nifi-a*: it is *ma-nifis-a*, because here the *s*, having shifted into the interior of the word, is no longer liable to be affected by the laws that govern final consonants. Here, then, we have evidence that Hova also originally said *nifis < nipis*. And cases of this kind can be adduced in considerable numbers. But I have failed to discover in these languages any evidence of the former presence of final mediæ.

Note.—Progressive restriction in the choice of consonants serving as finals in the case of an Austroasiatic language has been illustrated by Blagden in JA, 1910, p. 498.

65. *The second group* includes languages which tolerate as finals all the consonants, with the exception of the mediæ. Where the languages of the third group exhibit mediæ, those of the second have tenues; thus Bis. *bokid*, " hill ", is represented by Mal. *bukit*, and *lawod*, " sea ", by *laut*. To this group belong in particular certain languages of Borneo, Sumatra, and the Malay Peninsula, languages, therefore, whose territories lie near to one another, and, furthermore, languages which are at any rate in part somewhat closely connected together. Nevertheless, in contrast with the languages of the first group, we are here in a position to show that these languages of the second group originally also possessed final mediæ. Only we cannot for this purpose use the evidence which served us in dealing with the first group, namely the extension of disyllabic word-bases by means of suffixes. Even when the above-mentioned word *laut*, " sea ", receives a suffix, *e.g.*, -*an*, the tenuis remains and no media appears, the result is *lautan*, " ocean ", and similarly in all the other cases. The evidence to which we must now have recourse is furnished by the formative process that has created disyllabic word-bases out of monosyllabic roots. We find in Old Jav. a root *rug*, which is used by itself without any further extension (*i.e.* after the fashion of *kan* in § 51) as a word, with the meaning of " devastated ". Mal. also possesses this root, though not as an independent word, but only as a constituent embodied in disyllabic word-bases. When it is combined with a prefixed element, the media *g* is a final, and must therefore change into the tenuis; but if the root is linked with a suffixed element, the media appears in the interior of the word and is preserved. Thus we get, on the one hand, Mal. *buruk* < *bu* + *rug*, " to fall to bits ", and on the other, *rugi* < *rug* + *i*, " to damage ". * — Other Mal. examples: *sigi*, " to dig with the fingers ", beside Old Jav. *sisig*, " to rub with the fingers ", *tubi*, " to persevere in a thing ", beside the Old Jav. *tub*, which has the same meaning. — These word-bases *rugi*, *sigi* and *tubi*, therefore, tell us that the Mal. of the Malay Peninsula in an earlier phase of its development tolerated the mediæ at the end of words.

Note.—The element -*i*, which occurs in *rugi*, is a very common phenomenon; it serves both to form word-bases out of roots, and also to give a further extension to word-bases (see § 156). The element *bu*- only serves to make word-bases out of roots, and it is of rarer occurrence; therefore we will add a parallel: From the root *way*, " to rock to and fro ", Old Jav. forms *a-way*, " to wave ", and Tag. has *bu-way*, " to see-saw ".

66. The same kind of evidence as has been given for Mal. can also be produced in the case of certain languages of Sumatra, *e.g.* Karo, Toba and Mkb. Old Jav., for instance, has a word-base *antĕg*, " to arrive at ", with a root *tĕg*; Toba has

* In Mal., *rugi* perhaps suggests rather a substantival sense, but in Gayo it is commonly used verbally, *e.g.*, *aku rugi*, " I have suffered loss ".

togi < *tog* + *i*, " to conduct to a place ", with *o* for *ĕ* in conformity with the law: " Common IN pĕpĕt appears in Toba as *o* ".—For Borneo, too, we have similar evidence: we merely add that *rugi* also exists in Day.

Note.—It will be seen in § 156 that the formative element -*i* serves to make transitive verbs, and it accords with this principle that the word *togi* is transitive, whereas *antĕy* is intransitive.

67. The conclusion to be drawn from the facts set out in §§ 65 and 66 is: The languages of Borneo, Sumatra and the Malay Peninsula in an earlier stage of their development also used the mediæ as finals.

68. *The third group* comprises the languages which tolerate all the consonants as finals, including the mediæ. To this group belong languages of the Philippines, Celebes, Java, and the Northern and South-Western Borders. But even in these the use of the mediæ as finals is not of very frequent occurrence, so we shall not rest content with asking the reader to glance at the dictionaries, but will give a few actual details of the matter.

69. We meet with final mediæ more frequently in Old Jav. and the Philippine languages than elsewhere. Examples:

" To manage, to take pains over ": Old Jav. *kĕpug*, Bis. *kopog*.
" Model, pattern ": Old Jav. *tulad*, Pamp. *tulad*.
" To conceal ": Old Jav. *kubkub*, Pamp. *kubkub*.

Note.—Phonetic law: " Common IN *ĕ* and Common IN *u* become *o* in Bis." , hence *kopog*.

70. Examples from the languages of Celebes:

Ponosakan *bowog* < *bobog*, beside Jav. *bog*, " to strike ".
Tonsea *tuud*, beside Old Jav. *tuwĕd*, " stump of a tree ".
Tonsawang *kokob*, beside Old Jav. *kubkub*, " to conceal ".

Note.—For the correspondence of *u* and *uĕ* in *tuud : tuwĕd* we have a parallel in Mal. *laut :* Karo *lawĕt*, " sea ". It must

be admitted, however, that the parallel is not very con-
clusive, inasmuch as it does not occur in the same two
languages.*

71. Examples from the Northern Border. The Form.
dialects are rich in cases of final mediæ, but there is often a
difficulty in finding parallels for them in other IN languages
and thus correlating them with IN. The cases for which no
such analogues can be discovered might, after all, be loan-
words from non-IN forms of speech. Therefore it has
seemed advisable to give a somewhat longer list in this connexion:

Form. *dobdob*	:	Tag. *dobdob*, " to poke the fire ".
Form. *laub*	:	Bis. *laob*, " to roast ".
Form. *soab*	:	Old Jav. *suwab*, " to yawn ".
Form. *abad*	:	Pamp. *babad*, " to become damp ".
Form. *utod*	:	Bis. *otod*, " crippled ".

72. Examples from the South-Western Border. The
Mentaway dictionary registers more than a dozen words with
final mediæ, *e.g.*, *jud-jud*, " high water ", which is etymologically related to the *añud* of § 39, and *bäb*, " to hit (the
goal) ", which is identical with the Achinese *bĕb*, " to fall
upon " (*cf.* Snouck Hurgronje, " Studien ", p. 62).

73. To sum up the results of this discussion on the final
mediæ (§§ 65-72), we have succeeded in showing that in the
Philippines, Celebes, Borneo, Java, Sumatra, the Malay Peninsula, and on the Northern and South-Western Borders, that
is in eight of our regions, there are languages which admit
all sounds as finals, including the mediæ, or else formerly
admitted them. Hence the conclusion: In Common IN any
sound can be a final, always excepting the palatal consonants.†

74. Let us now just recapitulate the propositions established in the present Section, " Synthesis of Sounds into
Words ": The Common IN word, apart from interjections

* [See Essay IV, § 126, 11.]
† [See also Essay IV, §§ 200 *seqq.*]

and words of form, is usually disyllabic. It may begin with any sound in the Common IN phonetic system. In the interior of it, between the two vowels, there may be one consonant, or two consonants, and in the latter case we find nasal + cognate explosive or else the manifold combinations of the kapkap type. At the end any sound can occur, excepting the palatals.

SECTION III : ACCENT.

75. The great majority of the IN languages accentuate their words, whether they be word-bases or extensions thereof, on the penultimate syllable. This must be regarded as the Common IN condition.*

76. Accentuation of the final syllable is found in three cases in the various individual IN languages:

77. *The first case :* The languages which still possess the pĕpĕt usually accentuate the final syllable when the penultimate contains a pĕpĕt, *e.g., lĕpás*, " free ".†

78. *The second case :* When a monosyllabic word-base is extended by means of a prefix, the accent in many IN languages remains on the final syllable, *i.e.* on the word-base.‡

Accentuation of the word-base. Celebes, Bug.: *maqnóq*, " to descend " < formative *maq* + word-base *noq* — Java, Jav.: *uwós*, " rice " < *u* + *wos*, see Poensen, Jav. Gr., p. 47 — Sumatra, Toba: *mandók*, "to speak", word-base *dok* — Madagascar, Hova: *wualá*, " denied ", word-base *la* — Eastern Border, Bim.: *kambé*, "to bleat", word-base *mbe*—South-Western Border, Mentaway: *patók*, " to draw ", word-base *tok*.

79. *The third case :* In many IN languages the vocative is accentuated on the final syllable.

Vocative accentuation. Sangir group, Sangirese: *amáṅ*, " o father ! " beside *amaṅ*, " father " — Celebes, Gorontalese: *naná*, " o mother ! " — Near Java, Mad.: *patéq*, " thou dog ! " — Sumatra, Toba: *amáṅ*, " o father ! " — Eastern Border, Bim.: *iná*, " o mother ! " — South-Western Border, Nias: *iná*, " o mother ! "

Note I.—Example of a sentence with vocative accentuation, from Breukink's Gorontalese dialogues: " Mother, come here ! " = *naná poolo*.

* [But see Essay IV, §§ 307 *seqq.*] † [See also Essay IV, § 311, I]
‡ [See also Essay IV, § 319.]

98

Note II.—It must be admitted that the second and third cases of the accentuation of the final syllable are not so widely distributed as to entitle us unhesitatingly to style them Common IN. On the other hand, it must be borne in mind that in many grammars this very question of accentuation has received the most inadequate treatment. Thus Hardeland says: " The accent remains on the final syllable of such few monosyllabic words as there are, even when they are extended into disyllables or polysyllables by means of prefixes ", and this would suffice to establish the case of the accentuation of the final for Borneo as well; but the instances he proceeds to give are dubious: *hāī*, whence *kahāī*, and the like must surely be disyllabic forms.—Again, Kruyt's Bareqe Grammar says nothing about the accentuation of the vocative, yet Adriani in Ts. Ind. t. l. vk.. 1910, p. 211, quotes vocatives of that kind, *e.g.*, *oñgá*, " friend ! " (addressed to a woman).

80. Words of form often lean proclitically or enclitically on the words which they accompany, and hence they are often written continuously with them in texts in the native alphabets. Thus we read in the Mak. epic Maqdi, towards the end: " And the burial service was read over his head " = *na nibaca mo talakkiñ a ri ulu-nna*. The words of form are: *na*, " and ", *mo*, emphatic particle, *a*, article, *ri*, " over ", *nna*, " his ". But in the original (Mak. Chrestomathy, p. 426) this sentence is written in three " complexes " or conglomerations, viz. $(n + n + i + b + c + m + o) - (t + l + k + i + ñ) - (r + i + u + l + a + n)$.* Hence, also, it is not uncommon for words of form to coalesce with the words they accompany, as illustrated by *rama, tama* and *zama* in § 44, and other cases which we shall meet with later on. And it is in this way that words of form have in some instances become formatives: the passive formative *ka-* is really the preposition *ka*, and Bug. *kacalla*, " to be accursed ", properly means " (to come) into a curse ".†

* [See also Essay IV, § 35, II.]
† [See also Essay III, §§ 35, I, 37, II.]

SECTION IV : FORMAL ANALYSIS OF WORDS.

Preliminary Observations.

81. Regarded from the point of view of their formal structure, the words of the IN languages fall into five classes:
interjections, words of form, words of substance, pronouns,
and numerals.

Interjections.

82. The interjections found in the several IN languages
are mostly monosyllabic formations, incapable of being analysed further. They can end either in a vowel or a consonant.
Example: the Tontb. Dirge for a Dead Mother begins: "Alas,
mother, o mother, o mother!" = *o inaq, e inaq, e inaq*. They
often appear in reduplicated form, *e.g.* Sund. *bobo* beside *bo*,
a word used in mild reproof; and the reduplication may be
accompanied by vowel change, particularly in cases where
the word is intended to imitate a sound (onomatopœia),
e.g. Day. *pikpak* beside *pak*, " smack ! pop ! "

83. We will take a closer view of one single interjection,
one that we are in a position to style Common IN. It is the
interjection of affirmation, and its form is *a*, or when reduplicated *aa*, or *ia*.

Yes. Philippines, Iloko : *a* — Borneo, Day.: *ia* — Near
Java, Bal.: *a* — Sumatra, Gayo: *a* — Malay Peninsula, Mal.:
iya — Madagascar, Tangkaranese: *ia* — Eastern Border,
Kamberese: *a* or *aa*.

Words of Form.

84. Like the interjections, the words of form are mostly
monosyllables incapable of further analysis. They often
consist of two sounds, and in that case usually end with the
vowel. This characteristic is illustrated, for example, by the
words of form contained in the following sentence from the

Old Jav. Śakuntalā: " He felt as if the mainstay of his heart were being cut off " = It was as if was being cut off now stalk of heart his = *kadi hiniris ta nāla ni hati nira.*

Note.—kadi, " it was as if ". — *hiniris,* passive of *hiris,* " to cut ". — The use of *nāla* in this sense may be compared with the Malay *tańkay* (*hati*).

In contrast with the interjections, the words of form are seldom reduplicated; one of the rare cases being the doubling of the negative *ta* to form *tata* in Mentaway. On the other hand they are capable of entering into the most manifold combinations with one another. Thus the two articles *i* and *tu* occur combined in Hova as *itu,* in Taimuruna as *tui,* and in Tontb. as *iitu.* These composite articles do duty as demonstrative pronouns. — Amongst the words of form we shall consider the articles, the prepositions, the *a* dubitativum, and the negative.

85. *The article i.* Philippines, Tiruray: *fantad,* " earth ", *i fantad,* " the earth " — Celebes, Bug.: *i Diyo,* " Madam Diyo " * — Borneo, Tar.: *i amaq,* " the father " — Java, Old Jav.: *i bapa,* " the father " — Sumatra, Toba: *pidoñ i,* " the bird " — Madagascar, Hova: *i Butu,* " the (young man) Butu " * — Eastern Border, Kamberese: *i ama,* " the father " — South-Western Border, Mentaway: *ka i tuan,* " to the master ".

Note I.—The position of the article in Toba, in *pidoñ i,* finds its parallel in another article, viz. the article *e,* which in Bug. is put after the noun, whereas in Nabaloi it precedes " The house " is *bola e* in Bug., but *e baley* in Nabaloi.

Note II.—The *i* in Toba is more accentuated, and is therefore a demonstrative, but when we look through a Toba text, such as the Mula ni debata idup in Meerwaldt, we see that it occurs extremely frequently, and does, after all, perform the functions of an article.

86. As already remarked in § 84, the article *i* also occurs as a component part of the demonstrative pronoun *itu,* and

* [As to the use of articles before proper names, see the footnote to § 91.]

this is also Mal.; it is likewise a constituent of the demonstrative *ai*, and this is Form. So we may now add the Malay Peninsula and Formosa (*i.e.* the Northern Border) to the eight areas of distribution set out in § 85. We therefore pronounce the article *i* to be Common IN.

Note.—Specimen sentence with the article *i*: Tarakan, from the Story of the Tailed Man: " He ordered his wife to go to Silimbatu " = It was ordered the wife his to go to Silimbatu = *sinusub i andu na makaw da Silimbatu.*

87. *The article a.* Philippines, Ibanag: *tolay a mapia,* " man a good " = " a good man " — Celebes, Mak.: *jaran a,* " the horse " — Sumatra, Gayo: *anak bujan a,* " boy big the " = " the youth " — Northern Border, Form.: *kairi a rima,* " left the hand " = " the left hand " — Eastern Border, Rottinese: *nau a,* " the grass ".

88. The article *a* is also a component of the Old Jav. article *an* < *a* + *n*, which is used pretty interchangeably with the simple *n*: *e.g., an anak* or *n anak,* " the child ". Similarly it is a component of the pronoun *anu,* " somebody " (§ 135), which occurs in nearly all the IN languages.

89. Like the article *i* (§ 44), the article *a* often becomes indissolubly attached to substantives. Thus beside the Old Jav. *bun,* " sprig ", there is the Common IN *buna,* " sprig, flower, fruit " (§ 43); beside Old Jav. *luh,* " tear ", the Bagobo *luha.* A particularly characteristic case is that of *pus,* " cat ", in Mad.. which in that language serves only as a vocative, whereas *pusa* in Day. does duty in all syntactical relations.

90. From what has been said in §§ 87-89 it follows that we must attribute the article *a* to Common IN.

91. *The article ra.* This occurs as a living element of speech in a few languages only: Java, Old Jav.: *ra hyan,* " the deity " — Madagascar, Hova: *ra Be,* " Mr. Big ". *

---

* [The original rendering here is: " der (Herr) Gross ", which illustrates better than the English translation the use of the article with a proper name (such as *Be* is in this context). Like German and Greek, but unlike English, Hova and some other IN languages admit the definite article before proper names of persons.]

92. The article *ra* (as was first shown by Kern, " Fidji-taal ", p. 163) has coalesced with the Common IN word *tu*, " master, lord ", to form *ratu*, and this word *ratu* occurs in very many IN languages.

93. Further, the article *ra* is found with particular frequency in inseparable combination with words of relationship, especially *ama* and *ina*, wherewith it forms *rama* and *rena*, which have been discussed in particular by Kern on several occasions. The word *rena* is found in Java, in Old Jav.; in Madagascar, in Hova, under the form *reni ;* and on the Northern Border, in Form.

Note.—Hova *ray*, " father ", is *ra + ayah*, *reni*, " mother ", is *ra + ina*, *raha*, " brother ", is *ra + aka*. *Ina* is Common IN, *ayah* is Simalurese, etc., and *aka*, " brother ", Sund., etc. — The phonetic characteristics of *reni* are explained in § 24 ad fin., those of *raha* follow from the law given in § 18, and those of *ray* from the following law: " Common IN *a + y + a*, or *a + y + a +* consonant, appear in Hova as *ay* ". Another instance is the Hova word *lay* < Common IN *layar*, " sail ". This law involves a limitation of the *y*-law of § 18.

94. From what has been said in §§ 91-93 it is plain that we may style the article *ra* a Common IN word.

95. The article *i* is in most languages a personal article, and as such it precedes personal names, words of relationship, and personal pronouns; the article *a* usually accompanies names of things; the article *ra* is an honorific particle. — These characteristics may be regarded as being Common IN.

96. *The prepositions.* Preliminary observation. Article and preposition are in a certain measure identical in IN. That which in one language is an article serves in another as a preposition; thus the two articles *i* and *a*, which we have just discussed, are prepositions in Hova, which language possesses the article *ni: e.g., a luha*, " in front ", *i masu*, " before (the) eyes ". Indeed, even in one and the same language it may happen that a word is both an article and a preposition: *e.g.* Bug. *i Diyo*, " Madam Diyo ", *i liwën*, " on

the other side ". — From §§ 86 and 97 it follows that we must
recognize in the double function of *i*, as both article and preposition, a Common IN feature; but in the case of *ra*, on the
other hand, only *one* function appears to be Common IN,
viz. its use as an article.

The articles can also serve as unemphatic pronouns of the
third person: *e.g.* Bug. *soroq i*, " he recedes "; Mak., from
the Zamenspraken (dialogues), p. 35 : *lino i*, " it is calm
(weather) ".

Note.—If the article in Mlg. is *ni*, why does it not appear
in the above-mentioned *a luha* and *i masu*? The answer is: In
phrases of the nature of formulas the article can be omitted.

97. *The preposition i.* Philippines, Tag.: *i baba*, " at the
bottom " — Celebes, Bug.: *i liwĕn*, " on the (other) side " —
Borneo, Day.: *i wa*, " at the bottom " — Java, Old Jav.:
i sira, " by him " — Sumatra, Gayo: *i Gayo*, " in the Gayo
country " — Madagascar, Hova: *i masu*, " before the eyes ".

Note.—In Tag. and Bug. the preposition *i* is no longer a
really living element of speech, it is only found in certain
formulas; but from the point of view of our monograph that
is immaterial.

98. Kamberese possesses a preposition *la*, " at, by ", with
a secondary form *lai*. This *lai* is the preposition *la* + the
preposition *i*. — Herewith we have a piece of evidence for
the existence of *i* on the Eastern Border also.

Note.—That we have rightly explained *lai* by *la* + *i*, is
proved by the following parallel: Old Jav. combines its two
prepositions *i* and *ri* into *iri*, and all three forms have pretty
much the same meaning, viz. " at, to ". See also Hazeu,
Gayo Vocabulary, p. 532.

99. The preposition *i* also does duty as a word-base for
verbal forms. The one we meet with most frequently is *ma-i*,
" to go (to) ", with the formative *ma-*, for which see § 148.
This verb is found in many languages, from Form. on the
Northern Border to Simalurese on the South-Western one. So
now we have evidence for *i* in two more areas of distribution.

Note.—That our explanation of the verb *mai* is the right one is proved by the parallel *matu* $<$ *ma* + preposition *tu*, " to ". This verb signifies " to set about (doing a thing) "; in Bug. it indicates the future.

100. The facts set out in §§ 97-99 justify us in pronouncing the preposition *i* to be Common IN.

101. Specimen sentence with the preposition *i*: Old Jav., Sang hyang Kamahāyānikan, *a* 49: " The space between the lower and the upper row of teeth " $=$ Space of the teeth, in the lower part, in the upper part $=$ *sĕla ni ṅ huntu i sor i ruhur*.

102. *The preposition n.* Philippines, Tag.: *aṅ tawo*, " the man ", *n aṅ tawo*, " of the man " — Near Celebes, Talautese, the Cursing of the Fowl, third sentence from the end: *laia n awaqa*, " heat of the body " — Borneo, Day.: *bau n andaw*, " face of the sky ", *i.e.* " cloud " — Java, Old Jav.: *tanaya n tani*, " people of the district " — Sumatra, Gayo: *gĕral n guru*, " name of the teacher " — Madagascar, Hova: *ra n usi*, " blood of goats " — Northern Border, Bat.: *chinamañanak* * *n i santa Maria*, " born of the blessed Mary " — South-Western Border, Mentaway: *uma n abak*, " house for boats ".

On the strength of this evidence we may pronounce the preposition *n* to be Common IN.

103. *The preposition ka.* Philippines, Bagobo: *ka kuda*, " to the horse " — Borneo, Day.: *ka Sampit*, " to (the place called) Sampit " — Java, Sund.: *ka Banduṅ*, " to (the place called) Bandung " — Sumatra, Toba: *ha duru*, " on to the side " — Malay Peninsula, Mal.: *ka darat*, " to the mainland " — Madagascar, Hova: *ha tratra*, " up to the breast " — South-Western Border, Mentaway: *ka lagay*, " into the village ".

Note.—Phonetic law: " Toba changes Common IN *k* into *h*, save after a nasal or when final, in which cases *k* persists ", hence *ha* $<$ Common IN *ka*.

* The writer has no information as to the force of the *ch* in this word, or in Batanese in general.

[Perhaps, like *ch* in Nabaloi, it is the sound rendered by *c* in these Essays: see Essay III, § 162, footnote.]

104. The preposition *ka* is also used as a conjunction, meaning "in order to, until"; Mkb. example: "Rice to be eaten" = *nasi ka dimakan*. In some other languages a verb *maka* has been formed from it, after the fashion of *mai* in § 99, with the meaning "to have an object, or a task". Mak. example: "Has he the task of reading it ?" = Has task he, to read it ? = *maka iya lambaca i*. Thereby *ka* is shown to exist in Celebes also; and see § 80 for additional evidence.

105. From the facts set out in §§ 103 and 104 we acquire the right to pronounce *ka* to be a Common IN preposition.

106. As is shown by the examples in §§ 97-104, the preposition *i* as a rule indicates the place where, the preposition *n* the place whence, the genitive, and the preposition *ka* the place whither. This usage may be regarded as Common IN.

107. The *a* dubitativum, a word of form used conjunctively, dubitatively, interrogatively, to weaken the force of a proposition, comparatively, and disjunctively.

The a dubitativum. Philippines, Bis.: "What manner of snake is this ?" = Which snake what this ? = *onsañ halas a kana* — Celebes, Bug.: "Is this a slave or a freedman ?" = Slave + interrogative particle *g* for *ga* + this or freedman = *ata-g-iro a maradeka* — Java, Old Jav.: "Like a tongue" = Tongue as = *ilat a* — Sumatra, Mkb.: "Whatever it may be" = Something, whatever = *barañ a* — Eastern Border, Kamberese: "Only a little" = *hakudu a*.

108. Besides the dubitative there is also an imperative *a*: Northern Border, Form.: *madis-a*, "Hasten!", from the word-base *madis*, "quick" — Madagascar, Hova: *mi-waluza*, discussed in § 30. We may assume that the imperative use has grown out of the dubitative one delineated in the preceding paragraph. We are justified in doing so when we note the fact that whereas in Old Jav. *a*, besides indicating comparison, also forms the conjunctive, in Modern Jav. it forms the conjunctive *and* the imperative, and in Hova the imperative alone. — If we now add the imperative *a* of the Northern

Border and Madagascar to the dubitative *a* of the preceding paragraph, we may pronounce this particle to be Common IN.

109. Specimen sentence with an *a* dubitativum, used conjunctively: Old Jav., Mahābhārata, Āśramawasanaparwa, 13: "It is not seemly that thou shouldst come with us" = Not seemly, thou shouldst-come-with with us = *tan yogya kita milwa ri kami*. — The indicative is *milu*, the conjunctive *milwa* < *milu* + *a*. — An *a* dubitativum, used to limit the force of the verb: Kamberese, from the Story of the Civetcat: "Come here, we wish to deliberate a little!" = Come thou, we deliberate a little only! = *mai kaw, ta batan hakudu a*.

110. *The negative.* Among the negatives of the several IN languages, *di*, either standing by itself or used as the nucleus of a word, has the widest distribution; we therefore style *di* Common IN.

The negative di, "not". Philippines, Tag.: *di* — Celebes, Bolaang-Mongondou: *diya* — Borneo, Day.: *dia* — Near Java, Mad.: *ĕnjaq* — Sumatra, Sĕraway: *ĕndiaq* — Malay Peninsula, Mal.: *janan*—Madagascar, Hova: *dia-hue*, "not so".

111. Here we have a Common IN nucleus *di*, which is mostly accompanied by a formative *a*, hence Day. *dia*, Bont. *adi*. For this attendant *a* we have many parallels in IN. In several languages there is also a negative *ti* (which, by the way, does *not* result by phonetic law from *di*), as well as another negative *ta*; and beside these short forms we find in Bulu a form *tiya* < *ti* + *a*, and in Mentaway a form *ata* < *a* + *ta*.

This attendant *a* is the article *a*; that appears from the following parallel: The Bug. negative is *deq*, but the Wajorese dialect of Bug. says *deq-sa*, and *sa* is a weak demonstrative in Bug.

112. In Mal. *janan* < *di* + *anan* and in Mad. *ĕnjaq* < *ĕn* + *di* + *aq*, as the Sĕraway still says, the *i* before the vowel *a* was first weakened into the consonantal *y* as in Day. *yaku* < *i* + *aku* (§ 44), and then *d* + *y* became *j*. — How the *q* in Sĕraway *ĕndiaq* and Mad. *ĕnjaq*, beside Day. *dia*, is to be

interpreted. I cannot say: I can only point to the parallel fact
that Bug. *ajaq*, "lest", also has a *q*, while Old Jav. *aja* has not.*

113. Specimen sentence with a negative: Bont., Kolling,
near the end: "Come thou down, that we may eat! Then
came he not" = Down, thou, that eat we; then not = *banad
ka ta mañan tako ; isaed adi.*

114. Among the *conjunctions* we can hardly discover a
case that we may venture to call Common IN. Though the
conjunction *pa* is very widely distributed, it has such very
different meanings in the several languages that the matter
becomes quite uncertain.

Words of Substance.

115. Words of substance — verbs, substantives and adjectives — are mostly disyllabic. They contain a monosyllabic
material nucleus, which we call the root, and a formative element; or else they are formed by the reduplication of the root,
or by the union of two different roots. It seldom happens
that the monosyllabic root by itself does duty as a word of
substance, like *kan* in § 51.

116. We will now, in the first place, take an individual
root and show that it is Common IN, choosing for that purpose
the root *suk*, "to enter, to force oneself into, to strike into",
and the like.

Root suk. Philippines, Pamp.: *tusuk*, "to pierce through"
— Celebes, Mak.: *usuq* < *usuk*, "to pierce with a needle"
— Borneo, Day.: *masok*, "to enter, to become". — Java,
Old Jav.: *asuk*, "to bring into" — Sumatra, Karo: *pasuk*,
"to knock in" — Malay Peninsula, Mal.: *masuq*, "to
enter, to take sides with a party, to be on a person's side" —
Madagascar, various dialects: *isuka*, "to become engaged".†

117. In accordance with the method delineated in the
Introduction, we may pronounce the following roots, amongst
others, to be Common IN: *kan*, root for word-bases signifying

* [See also Essay IV, § 144.]
† [See also Essay I, § 90 (and footnote).]

" food, to eat, to give food to " — *kit*, " pain, to pain, to punish " — *kis*, " to file " — *ñis*, " to howl " — *tuk*, " to knock " — *tuñ*, " to hang " — *tut*, " flatulence " — *num*. " to drink " — *pas*, " free, loose " — *buk*, " dry rot, worm that burrows in wood " — *bah*, " to revere, to pray to " — *raw*, " sun, day " — *ruñ*, " beak, nose, handle " — *lañ*, " to wind, to twist " — *lik*, " to turn back " — *lit*, " skin, to peel " — *lĕm*, " to dive, evening " — *sih*, " pity, love, to love ". — For the concept " to live " there is no Common IN root.

118. It may happen that only the root itself runs through a number of different languages, while the elements that accompany it vary, as in the case of the root *suk* in § 116. Or both parts, the root *and* the formative element, may extend through a number of languages. From the root *lit* mentioned in § 117, there is formed the verb *salit*, " to peel ", which only occurs in a few languages; but, on the other hand, the same root also goes to form *kulit*, " skin " (and also " to peel "). which we must class as Common IN.*

Skin. Philippines, Iloko: *kulit* — Celebes, Tontb.: *kulit* — Borneo, Sampit: *kulit* — Java, Sund.: *kulit* — Sumatra. Lampong: *kulik* — Malay Peninsula, Mal.: *kulit* — Madagascar, Hova: *huditra* — Eastern Border, Tettum: *kulit* — South-Western Border, Mentaway: *kulit*.

Note.—Lampong *kulik* beside Common IN *kulit* in conformity with the parallel: *lañik* beside Common IN *lañit*.

119. In accordance with our method, the following words of substance, amongst others, can be shown to be Common IN. in their complete disyllabic form, sound for sound: *lañit*, " sky ", *bulan*, " moon "; but not " sun " — *apuy*, " fire ". *tunu*, " to burn ", *añin*, " wind "; but not " warm " or " cold " — *buluh*, " bamboo "; but not " plant " — *lintah*, " leech "; but not " animal " — *ulu*, " head ", *mata*, " eye ", *kulit*. " skin "; but not " foot " — *ina*, " mother ", *ama*, " father ", *anak*, " child "; but not " step- " (mother, etc.) — *takut*. " fear "; but not " joy " — *pilih*, " to choose "; but not " to wish " — *tĕnun*, " to weave "; but not " to spin " — *tĕkĕn*

* [See also Essay 1, § 91.]

" staff ", *tali*, " cord ", *suliň*, " fife "; but not " hammer " — *putih*, " white "; but not " red " — *těňah*, " half "; but not " whole ".

120. The following Karo sentence from Si Laga Man: " Then they saw the half of the stone dug out, and now they applied the lifting pole to it " = *ěňgo me si těňah batu idah ikuruk, e maka ioňkil na*: contains five words of substance, of which two, *těňah*, " half ", and *batu*, " stone ", are Common IN, and precisely in that identical form; but the other three, *idah*, " to see ", *kuruk*, " to dig ", *oňkil*, " to apply a lifting pole ", are not.

Pronouns.*

121. The pronouns are very often disyllabic; they are mostly combinations of a specifically pronominal nucleus with formatives, which are mostly articles. Thus, as Seidenadel has shown, the Bont. pronoun *sika*, " thou ", consists of the article *si* and the nucleus *ka*.

122. The monosyllabic nuclei also have an independent existence, in one language or another, but as a rule they are not very widely distributed. The disyllabic *anu* (§ 135) is Common IN, while the monosyllabic *nu* is found in a few languages only, *e.g.* in Sund. The monosyllabic forms of the personal pronouns have recently been discussed in exemplary fashion by Jonker.

123. Specimen sentences with long and short forms. Bug. letter Nomoroq 13, in Matthes: " I have nothing of the kind at home " = But not anything thus I have = *nae deqsa anu maqkuwa u taro.* — Sund., Nyai Sumur Bandung, p. 66: " We will tell now of her who dwells in Bitung Wulung " = It is told, who dwells in place Bitung Wulung = *kacarios nu calik di nagara Bituň Wuluň.*

124. *The personal pronouns.* The following forms can be shown to be Common IN: *aku*, " I ", *kaw*, " thou ", *ia*, " he ", *kami*, " we ", *kamu*, " you "; in the pronoun of the third

* [As to the use of the personal pronouns, see Essay III, §§ 118 *seqq.*]

person plural only the nucleus *ra* is Common IN, the attendant articles vary, they are chiefly *i* or *si*, thus forming *ira* or *sira*.

125. *The pronoun " I "*. Philippines, Bis.: *ako* — Celebes, Tontb.: *aku* — Borneo, Day.: *aku* — Java, Old Jav.: *aku* — Sumatra, Gayo: *aku* — Malay Peninsula, Mal.: *aku* — Madagascar, Hova: *ahu* and *zahu* $<$ *i* + *aku* (§ 44) — Northern Border, Bat.: *ako* — Eastern Border, Masaretese: *yako* $<$ *i* + *ako* — South-Western Border, Mentaway: *aku*.

126. *The pronoun " thou "*. Philippines, Bis.: *ikao* $<$ *i* + *kaw* — Celebes, Mak.: *kaw* — Borneo, Day.: *ikaw* — Java, Old Jav.: *ko* — Sumatra, Mkb.: *kaw* — Malay Peninsula, Mal.: *kaw* and *ĕṅkaw* — Eastern Border, Sumbawarese: *kaw*.

Note.—Old Jav. *ko* for *kaw* in accordance with the parallel: *lod* $<$ *lawd* $<$ *laud*.

127. *The pronoun " he "*. Philippines, Ibanag: *ya* — Celebes, Mak.: *iya* — Borneo, Sampit: *iyac* — Near Java, Bal.: *iya* — Sumatra, Angkola: *ia* — Malay Peninsula, Mal.: *iya* — Madagascar, Hova: *izi* $<$ *iya* (§§ 18 and 24) — Eastern Border, Sumbawarese: *ia* — South-Western Border, Nias: *ia*.

128. *The pronoun " we "*. Philippines, Inv.: *kami* — Celebes, Tontb.: *kami* — Borneo, Bol.: *kami* — Java, Old Jav.: *kami* — Sumatra, Gayo: *kami* — Malay Peninsula, Mal.: *kami* — Eastern Border, Masaretese: *kami*.

129. *The pronoun " you "*. Philippines, Ibanag: *kamu* — Celebes, Tontb.: *kamu* — Java, Old Jav.: *kamu* —Sumatra, Karo, in certain districts: *kamu* — Malay Peninsula, Mal.: *kamu*.

Note.—Of all the above-mentioned personal pronouns *kamu* has the most restricted distribution, and accordingly we have some hesitation in pronouncing it to be Common IN.

130. *The pronoun " they "*. Philippines, Ibanag: *ira* — Celebes, Bareqe: *sira* — Borneo, Bol.: *sida* — Java, Old Jav.: *sira* — Sumatra, Toba: *nasida* — Eastern Border, Masaretese: *sira* — South-Western Border, Nias: *ira*.

Note I.—In *sida, d* stands for *r* in accordance with the RLD-law (see § 190).

Note II.—Nias *ira* and *ia* (§ 127) only occur in certain syntactical combinations.

Note III.—Old Jav. *sira* is also singular.

131. The plural pronoun *ra* and the honorific particle *ra* (§§ 91 *seqq.*) are identical. We have a parallel in the Karo pronoun *kena.* This is the pronoun of the second person plural, " you ", without any nuance of politeness, but it can also be used in addressing a single person, and then it is polite.

132. *The demonstrative pronoun.* Amongst the numerous demonstrative pronouns of the several individual IN languages we may pronounce *itu,* " this "*, to be Common **IN.** It is a combination of the two articles *i* and *tu.*

The pronoun " this ". Philippines, Bis.: *ito* — Celebes, Tontb.: *itu* — Borneo, Bol.: *itu* — Java, Sund.: *itu* — Sumatra, Běsěmah: *itu* — Malay Peninsula, Mal.: *itu* — Madagascar, Hova: *itu* — Northern Border, Form.: *iχo.*

Note.—Form. *iχo* with *χ.*† as in the parallel: *maχa,* "eye", spelt *magcha,* beside Common IN *mata;* for other examples see § 151 ad fin.

133. *The interrogative pronoun.* The Common IN form is *apa.* " what ", which consists of the article *a* and the nucleus *pa.*

The pronoun " what ". Philippines, Pamp.: *apa* — Celebes, Mak.: *apa* — Java, Old Jav.: *apa* — Sumatra, Karo: *apa,* " anything ", *apai,* " which " — Malay Peninsula, Mal.: *apa* — Eastern Border, Laoranese: *apa* — South-Western Border, Mentaway: *apa.*

Note.—Pamp. *apa* serves only as a word-base for forming verbal derivatives, which mean " to go and see how (or what) a thing is ", *e.g., mañapa.* Hereto we have the parallel case

---

* Or " that ": the force varies in the different languages, *e.g.* in Bol. and Hova it means " this ", in Mal. " that ".

† The Formosan sound written *ch* is most probably the velar spirant resembling the *ch* in the German " wachen," commonly rendered by *χ.*

that Bis. *onsa*, " what ", forms derivatives which are translated by " buscar, querer " (" to seek ") and the like.

134. The pronoun " who " has a number of equivalents in
the IN languages, but none of them can be held to be Common
IN.

135. *The indefinite pronoun.* The Common IN form of
this is *anu*.

The pronoun " somebody, something ". Philippines, Bis.:
ano — Celebes, Tontb.: *anu* — Borneo, Sampit: *yanu* —
Java, Sund.: *anu* — Sumatra, Gayo: *anu* — Malay Peninsula, Mal.: *anu* — Madagascar, Hova: *anuna* — South-Western
Border, Mentaway: *anu*.

Note.—In Old Jav. *anu* has to be accompanied by the article
ñ in certain syntactical combinations, and to this *anu* + *ñ*
the Hova *anuna* corresponds. Thus in the Hova *anuna* an
article has got inseparably attached at the end of the word,
while in the Sampit *yanu* < *i* + *anu* another article has attached itself to the beginning.

Numerals.

136. The *numerals* are almost exclusively disyllabic formations; their analysis and the positive explanation of their
component parts present great difficulties.

137. The numerals " one, ten, hundred, thousand " are
Common IN in the forms *sa*, *puluh*, *ratus*, and *ribu*.

138. *The numeral " one "*. Philippines, Tag.: *isa* —
Celebes, Tontb.: *sa*, *ěsa* — Borneo, Tar.: *isa* — Java, Sund.:
sa — Sumatra, Gayo: *sa*, *sara* — Malay Peninsula, Mal.: *sa* —
Madagascar, Hova: *isa* — Northern Border, Form., Puyuma
dialect: *sa* — Eastern Border, Sumbawarese: *sa* — South-
Western Border, Nias: *sa*, *sara*.

139. *The numeral " ten "*. Philippines, Bis.: *polo* —
Celebes, Tontb.: *puluq* — Borneo, Tar.: *puloh* — Java, Old
Jav.: *puluh* — Sumatra, written Mkb.: *puluh* — Malay Penin-
sula, Mal.: *puluh* — Madagascar, Hova: *fulu* — Northern

Border, Form., various dialects: *pulo* — Eastern Border, Sumbanese: *kĕmbuluh* — South-Western Border, Mentaway: *pulu*.

Note.—Several IN languages, particularly in the Philippines, tolerate no *h* as a final. — Hova *fulu* follows the law: " Common IN *p* appears in Hova as *f*, save after labials or when final ". — I do not know how to explain the final *q* in Tontb. *puluq.**

140. *The numeral " hundred ".* Philippines, Bis.: *gatos* — Celebes, Bug.: *ratuq* — Borneo, Tar.: *ratus* — Java, Sund.: *ratus*, Old Jav. *atus* — Sumatra, Gayo: *ratus* — Malay Peninsula, Mal.: *ratus* — Madagascar, Hova: *zatu* — Eastern Border, Bim.: *ratu*.

Note.—The initial of *gatos* and that of *zatu* follow the RGH-law, for which see Conant, JAOS, XXXI, I, pp. 70 *seqq.* The final of *ratuq* follows the law: " Common IN final consonants, except nasals, become *q* in Bug.".

141. *The numeral " thousand ".* Philippines, Iloko: *ribu* — Celebes, Tonsawang: *mo-ribu* — Borneo, Tar.: *ribu* — Java, Old Jav.: *iwu* — Sumatra, Gayo: *ribu* — Malay Peninsula, Mal.: *ribu* — Madagascar, Hova: *a-riwu* — Eastern Border, Bim.: *riwu*.

Note.—In Old Jav. *iwu* the *r* ought not to have disappeared, for it was originally an *r* of a different shade from the one in *ratus*, where the *r* has rightly disappeared in strict accordance with the R-laws in Old Jav. (see § 190). The *r* in *iwu* < *ribu* ought, according to phonetic law, to have persisted, as the following table shows:

Mal.	Bis.	Old Jav.
ratus	*gatos*	*atus*
rimbit	*limbit*	*rimbit*, " to take pains "
ribu	*libo*	**riwu*

Parallels like *rimbit* show that where Mal. has an *r* and Bis. an *l* Old Jav. also exhibits an *r*. But the word for "hundred"

* [See Essay IV, § 116, and also §§ 144 *seqq.*, 185 *seqq.*]

has influenced the word for " thousand ", and so both *r*'s, that of *ratus* and that of *ribu*, have been dropped. — For analogous modifications of numerals through the influence of other numerals, see §§ 33 and 183, where *nomu* has acquired its *u* from *pitu*.

142. There is no Common IN type for the formation of the numerals 11-19.

SECTION V: EXTENSION OF THE WORD-BASE.

Preliminary Observations.

143. In the preceding Section, §§ 81-142, we have been discussing word-bases. The term "word-base"* is thoroughly appropriate and legitimate. For, in the first place, the word-bases are the shortest, and so the most fundamental, forms that have a real living existence in actual speech: and, secondly, they serve as a basis or foundation for the further formation of derivatives.

144. Word-bases may either do duty in a sentence just as they are, without any addition, or else they may require certain extensions to enable them to perform that task. In the Kupangese text communicated by Jonker we find the sentence: "I shall go to-morrow" = To-morrow then I go = *cla kam auk lako*. Here the Kupangese word-base *lako* is used as a predicate without any change whatsoever. In Juanmarti's Magindanao dialogues we read: "I too am well" = *mikapia aku den*. Here the word-base *pia*, "good", has had to undergo an extension in order to fit it for serving as a predicate.

145. In works on the IN languages one often meets with the technical term "stem" (German "Stamm"): see Misteli, "Charakteristik", pp. 229 *seqq.*, and Finck, "Haupttypen", pp. 84 *seqq.* But I notice that some scholars when they speak of the "stem" refer to the word-base, while others thereby denote the forms produced by extension of the word-base. And, after all, either usage can be justified, for (as has already been remarked in § 65) the elements that are used for forming the word-base from the root and those that are used in extending the latter, are in a great measure identically the same. I

* [In the original, "Grundwort": see Essay I, § 1, footnote.]

therefore avoid the term " stem " and speak of the word-base on the one hand and its extensions on the other.

146. As was observed in § 80, a considerable number of the formatives used in these extensions are identical with words of form. And it often happens that one and the same formative serves in the formation of both verb and substantive, and so on. Here are two problems which we cannot pursue further in the present monograph.*

The Verb.†

147. Among the verbal formatives that we find in the various individual IN languages, we can show the following to be Common IN: four active formatives: *ma-*, *maṅ-*, *ba-*, *-um-*; three passive formatives: *ka-*, *ta-*, *-in-*; one transitive formative: *-i*; and one causative formative: *pa-*.

148. *The active formative ma-.* Philippines, Magindanao: *maulug,* " to fall ", word-base *ulug* — Celebes, Tontb.: *masowat,* " to answer " — Borneo, Day.: *marabit,* " to tear " — Java, Old Jav.: *matukar,* " to contend, to fight " — Sumatra, Toba: *madabu,* " to fall " — Malay Peninsula, Mal.: *makan,* " to eat ", word-base *kan,* " food " — Madagascar, Hova: *mahita,* " to see " — Northern Border, Form.: *makairi,* " to work left-handed " — Eastern Border, Bin.: *malampa,* " to go " — South-Western Border, Nias: *midiwa,* " to move (oneself) ".

149. *The active formative maṅ-.* In most of the IN languages the final *ṅ* of the formative is assimilated to the initial of the word-base, so that *ṅ* persists only before velars and before vowels; and when the initial consonant of the word-base is a surd, that initial disappears. Accordingly in Old Jav. *maṅgĕtĕm,* " to pinch ", < *maṅ* + *gĕtĕm,* the final of the prefix and the initial of the word-base have remained unaffected; whereas in Tag. *mamokot,* " to fish ", < *maṅ* + *pokot,* an *m* has

---

* [See Essay III, §§ 35, 138.]

† [On this subject see Essay III, particularly §§ 43-117.]

appeared in place of *ň* + *p*. — These processes also occur in the case of other prefixes, see *e.g.*, *pañan* from the word-base *kan* (§ 51).

The active formative mañ-. Philippines, Tag.: *mamokot*, word-base *pokot* — Celebes, Tontb.: *mamoñkor*, " to fish ", word-base *poñkor* — Borneo, Day.: *mañaput*, " to darken ", word-base *kaput* — Java, Old Jav.: *manurun*, " to descend ", word-base *turun* — Sumatra, Toba: *manurat*, " to write ", word-base *surat* — Madagascar, Hova: *manasa*, " to wash ", word-base *sasa* — South-Western Border, Simalurese: *manasai*, " to wash ", word-base *sasa* ; as to the -*i* see § 156.

150. *The active formative ba-*. Philippines, Bis.: *baigad*, " to stroke ", the word-base thereto being found in Iloko, viz. *igad*, " to stroke " — Celebes, Bug.: *baluka*, " to be loose, to be free " — Borneo, Day.: *badaha*, " to bleed " — Java, Sund.: *baganti*, " to interchange " — Sumatra, Lampong: *baguna*, " to be useful " — Madagascar, Hova: *wawenti*, " to be bulky, to be massive " — Eastern Border, Sumbawarese: *basiñin*, " to bear a name, to be called " — South-Western Border, Mentaway: *baliyu*, " to fill ", word-base in Mak., viz. *liyu*, " filled ".

Note I.—Hova *wa* < *ba* follows the law: " Common IN *b* appears in Hova as *w* except after *m* ".

Note II.—In Lampong *baguna* the word-base *guna* is, of course, a loan-word from the Sanskrit; but the example is cited on account of the *ba-* and not on account of the *guna*.

Note III.—In Bis. and in Mentaway, formations with *ba-* are not numerous, so that *ba-* is no longer felt to be a formative, but is rather regarded as part of the word-base; that fact, however, is immaterial here, having regard to the purpose of our monograph. The disyllabic word-bases corresponding to Bis. *baigad* and Mentaway *baliyu* are no longer to be found in these two languages. We have therefore had to seek them in other languages, and analogous cases occur *infra*.

151. *The active formative -um-*. Philippines, Inv.: *kuman*, " to eat ", word-base *kan* (see § 51) — Celebes, Tontb.: *kuman*

— Borneo, Day.: *kuman* — Java, Old Jav.: *lumaṅlaṅ*, "to
roam about", word-base *laṅlaṅ* — Sumatra, Toba: *sumurut*,
"to recede", word-base *surut* — Malay Peninsula, Mal.:
gumilaṅ, "to glitter", word-base *gilaṅ* — Madagascar, Hova:
humana < *kuman* — Northern Border, Form.: *χumme*, "to
evacuate excrement", word-base *χe*, "dung" — South-
Western Border, Simalurese: *lumaṅoy*, "to swim", word-
base *laṅoy*.

Note I.—We remarked in § 18 that the spelling of Form.
words in Vlis and Happart was defective, but the striking
doubling of the *m* in -*umm*-, *e.g.* in *χumme*, is consistently
carried out by them.

Note II.—Form. *χe*, "dung", stands in the same relation
to Common IN *tai* as in the parallel case of *χo*, "man", beside the widely distributed *tau*.

152. *The passive formative ka-.* Philippines, Bont.: *ka-
laṅo*, "dried up", word-base *laṅo* — Celebes, Bug.: *kacalla*,
"accursed" — Borneo, Tar.: *kasukab*, "opened" — Java,
Old Jav.: *katon*, "seen", word-base *ton* — Sumatra, Lampong: *kadĕṅi*, "heard" — Madagascar, Hova: *hadinu*, "forgotten", word-base in Pamp., viz. *liṅao*, "forgetful" —
Eastern Border, Kamberese: *kahira*, "torn".

Note.—Hova *hadinu* has been affected by the operation
of *four* different phonetic laws, three of which have already
been quoted; the fourth is: "Common IN final *aw* — for which
Pamp. has *ao* — appears in Hova as *u*".

153. *The passive formative ta-.* Philippines, Bis.: *takiliṅ*,
"to incline", word-base *kiliṅ* — Celebes, Tontb.: *talicur*, "to
turn the back towards" — Borneo, Day.: *tabiṅkis*, "to be
banished" — Java, Sund.: *talaṅke*, "hesitating", word-base
in Old Jav., viz. *lĕṅke*, "slow" — Sumatra, Toba: *talentes*,
"to stand open" — Madagascar, Hova: *taburuaka*, "bored
through", word-base *buruaka*, "hole" — Eastern Border,
Kamberese: *tabuṅgahu*, "opened", word-base *buṅgahu*, "to
open" — South-Western Border, Mentaway: *taico*, "to become visible".

154. *The passive formative -in-.* Philippines, Tag.: *tina-wag*, "called", word-base *tawag* — Celebes, Bulu: *winunu*, "killed", word-base *wunu* — Borneo, Day.: *kinan*, "eaten", word-base *kan* — Java, Old Jav.: *ginĕgö*, "held fast", word-base *gĕgö* — Sumatra, Toba: *tinogu*, "led", word-base *togu* — Madagascar, Hova: *tinapaka*, "broken", word-base *tapaka* — Northern Border, Bat.: *binobun*, "buried"; a cognate, though not etymologically identical, word-base hereto is Day. *bumbon*, "to conceal under something" — South-Western Border, Mentaway: *tinibo*, "exposed to the action of smoke".

155. *The signification of the active and passive formatives.* We have translated the above-mentioned active and passive forms in a convenient but rough and inadequate way by infinitives and participles. In reality these formatives indicate a number of finer shades of meaning, some in one language, others, it may be, in another. And the number of these is so large that we cannot pronounce any one of them to be Common IN. The most widely spread case is the force of the formative *-um-* in forming the aorist.

156. *The verbal formative -i.* This is added to word-bases or to extensions of word-bases and makes them transitive.

The transitive formative -i. Philippines, Tag.: *gaway*, "to bewitch" < word-base *gawa* + *i* — Celebes, Bug.: *joppai*, "to tread on", word-base *joppa*, "to tread" — Borneo, Tidung: *taṅkubi*, "to cover" — Java, Jav.: *nulis*, "to write", *nulisi*, "to write upon, to cover (*e.g.* a sheet of paper) with writing" — Sumatra, Mkb.: *manañih*, "to weep", *manañihi*, "to bewail" — Malay Peninsula, Mal.: *mĕnañis*, "to weep", *mĕnañisi*, "to bewail" — Madagascar, Old Mlg.: *ame*, "to give presents to" (see Note) — South-Western Border, Mentaway: *gagabai*, "to seek", word-base *gaba* or *gagaba*.

Note I.—Tag. *gaway* < *gawa* + *i* signifies "to bewitch", the word-base *gawa* means "to make". For this we have a parallel in Jav., where *gawe* < *gawa* + *i* means "to make", but *ma-gawe* "to produce an effect by witchcraft".

Note II.—Old Jav. has a verb *amah*, "to hand over, to give, to give rise to an emotion". Now the above Old Mlg. *ame* (which is given by Houtman) is for *amah + i*, with *e* for *a + (h) + i* like *reni < ra + ina* (§§ 24 and 93), to which is superadded the operation of the Mlg. phonetic law: "An *h* of other languages is not represented in Mlg.". Beside Old Mlg. *ame* Modern Mlg. (Hova) exhibits an *ume*, "to give, to give rise to an emotion", which we have to explain as *umah + i*. It is true that neither in Old Jav. nor elsewhere, so far as I know, is there any such word as *umah*, but such a form is *possible*, as is shown by the parallel that in Old Jav. *ajar*, "to impart to", is accompanied by a synonymous *ujar.* — As a consequence of its contraction *ume* is accentuated on the final syllable.

Note III.—Houtman's editors in the "Collection des ouvrages anciens concernant Madagascar" are of opinion that Old Mlg. *ame* is merely misspelt, the "orthographie vraie" being *ume*. But we have shown that the form *ame* is a possible one, and the word occurs in Houtman eight times in all, and each time spelt with an *a*. It would really be strange if that author had made precisely the same mistake in spelling eight times over, and in doing so had managed to hit on something sensible as well.

157. *The causative formative pa-.* Philippines, Nabaloi: *pabunu*, "to cause to be killed", word-base *bunu* — Celebes, Bug.: *padara*, "to allow to bleed" — Borneo, Tar.: *pakalap*, "to make possible" — Java, Sund.: *pasih*, "to give", word-base *sih*, "favour" — Sumatra, Angkola: *pauli*, "to beautify" — Northern Border, Form.: *pakiol*, "to sharpen" — Eastern Border, Laoranese: *padeta*, "to elevate" — South-Western Border, Mentaway: *pakom*, "to give food to", word-base *kom*, "to eat".

158. The case also occurs of one and the same word-base *joined to* the same formative running through many languages, so that one can declare the *whole* formation to be Common IN: Such a case is *minum*, from the word-base *inum*, "to drink".

"*To drink*", *verb with formative.*   Philippines, **Tag.**: *minum* — Celebes, Bug.: *minuǹ* — Java, Old Jav.: *minum* — Sumatra, Toba: *minum* — Malay Peninsula, Mal.: *minum* — Madagascar, Hova: *minuma* — South-Western Border, Nias: *minu.*

159.   In many IN languages the verbal word-base unaccompanied by any formative is imperative, and this usage must be regarded as Common IN.*

Word-base as imperative.   Philippines, Magindanao: *sulat,* " write ! " — Celebes, Mak.: *lampa,* " go ! " — Borneo, Day.: *tiroh,* " sleep ! " — Java, Old Jav.: *laku,* " go ! "—Sumatra, Toba: *buwat,* " take ! " — Malay Peninsula, Mal.: *paṅgil,* " call ! " — Madagascar, Hova: *fuha,* " wake up ! " — Eastern Border, Kamberese: *laku,* " go ! " — South-Western Border, Mentaway: *ala,* " take ! "

Note.—Hova has -*a* as a regular imperative formative (see § 30), but Richardson expressly states that *fuha* is also used as an imperative: the regular imperative alongside of it is *fuha-z-a.*

160.   Specimen sentence with a word-base as an imperative: Kamberese, from the Story of the Civetcat: " Wait till we kill you ! " = Wait, (we) kill you ! = *napa, mapameti kau.*

161.   The languages of the Philippines, North Celebes, Madagascar, and some other islands also have formatives for the formation of tenses, but the distribution of these formatives is not wide enough to entitle us to call them Common IN. The most widely spread case is that of *n*-, as a sign of the past tense.†

The Substantive.

162.   Substantives occur much more frequently without extension than verbs do.   In the Banggaya sentence from the text communicated by Riedel: " We were going to the village of Seasea " = *ikami ambakon do i lipu Seasea*: the verb *ambakon* has a formative, but the substantive *lipu*, " village ", has not.

163. Among the substantival formatives the prefix *ka-*, the infix *-an-* and the suffix *-an* can be shown to be Common IN. The formative *ka-* forms abstract nouns, *-an-* mostly indicates concrete things, *-an* denotes place.

164. *The substantival formative ka-.* Philippines, Magindanao: *kaputi*, "whiteness", word-base *puti* — Celebes, Tontb.: *kawĕlar*, "breadth" — Borneo, Day.: *kagogop*, "care, sorrow", word-base *gogop*, "worried, troubled" — Java, Sund.: *kañaho*, "knowledge" — Sumatra, Toba: *halinu*, "image produced by reflection in a mirror or in water", word-base in Old Bug., viz. *lino*, "to mirror oneself" — Madagascar, Hova: *hatsara*, "goodness".

165. *The substantival formative -an-.* Philippines, Bis.: *tanoptop*, "sound from afar", from the widely distributed root *tup*, which denotes various kinds of noises — Celebes, Bug.: *kanuku*, "talon", beside Common IN *kuku* — Near Java, Mad.: *sanolap*, "jugglery", word-base in Jav., viz. *sulap*, "to juggle" — Sumatra, Toba: *hanapa*, "involucre", word-base in Kawi Jav., viz. *kapa*, "covering" — Northern Border, Form.: *kalonkon*, "talon", word-base in Iloko, viz. *konkon*, "to scratch" — Eastern Border, Kamberese: *tanai*, "intestines", beside Common IN *tai*, "dung" — South-Western Border, Mentaway: *tanai*, "dung".

Note.—Form. *l* for *n* in *kalonkon* in accordance with the parallel *alak*, "child", beside Common IN *anak*.

166. *The substantival formative -an.* Philippines, Magindanao: *niugan*, "coconut grove", word-base *niug*, "coconut palm" — Celebes, Bug.: *labuwan*, "anchorage" — Borneo, Day.: *kayuan*, "forest" — Java, Sund.: *tanjakan*, "rising ground" — Sumatra, Toba: *hundulan*, "place to sit on" — Malay Peninsula, Mal.: *labuhan*, "anchorage" — Madagascar, Hova: *sampanana*, "bifurcation", word-base *sampana*, "to bifurcate" — South-Western Border, Simalurese: *kubanan*, "pool where buffaloes wallow", word-base in Mal., viz. *kuban*, "to wallow in the mire".

167. In several languages we find a formative *pa-* used for indicating the agent, but it competes with *mpa-*, *par-*, *pañ-*, etc., which are of course related to it, but are not identical with it; hence we cannot infer any Common IN factor here.

The Adjective.*

168. The Common IN formative for the formation of adjectives is *ma-*. In the Tag. riddle about the five fingers, in Starr, "Filipino Riddles": "Five coconut trees, one is high (= higher than the others)" = *limañ puno nañ niog, isa i malayog*: *malayog* is an adjective, formed by means of *ma-* from the word-base *layog*.

169. *The adjectival formative ma-.* Philippines, Inv.: *mapia*, "good", word-base *pia*, "goodness" — Celebes, Ponosakan: *mapiha*, "good" — Borneo, Day.: *manis*, "sweet" < *ma* + *anis*, "sweetness" — Java, Old Jav.: *maputih*, "white" — Sumatra, Toba: *matimbo*, "high" — Madagascar, Hova: *malutu*, "dirty" — Northern Border, Form.: *matakot*, "timid" — Eastern Border, Kamberese: *maliñu*, "useful" — South-Western Border, Mentaway: *mabatu*, "stony".

170. Several IN languages possess a *formative for the comparative*, usually -*an* or -*ĕn*, but it is not distributed widely enough to enable us to call it Common IN.

The Adverb.

171. In the IN languages the adverb is mostly identical with the adjective, or it is a prepositional construction, or a substantive may be used adverbially without a preposition, and the like. Example: In Ranawaluna's Book of Laws, Article II, we find: "Theft of rice, by mowing it by night in the field" = The mowing rice (by) night there in the field = *ni midzindza wari alina ani an tsaha*. In this Hova sentence the substantive *alina*, "night", is used without change or addition as an adverb.

* [See also § 185.]

172. But there are also formatives for the forming of adverbs, and among them *ka-*, which makes adverbs of time, is to be regarded as Common IN.

The adverbial formative ka-. Philippines, Tag.: *kagabi*, "yesterday", word-base *gabi*, "night" — Sangir Group, Sangirese: *kahĕbi*, "yesterday" — Celebes, Tontb.: *kaawiqi*, "yesterday" — Borneo, Day.: *katelo*, "for (*i.e.* during, lasting for) three days", word-base *telo*, "three" — Sumatra, Mkb.: *kapataṅ*, "yesterday", word-base *pataṅ*, "evening"; *kini*, "now" < *ka* + *ini*, word-base *ini*, "this" — Madagascar, Hova: *halina*, "last night" < *ka* + *alina* — Eastern Border, Bim.: *ka-sa-nai*, "on one day".

Note.—The Day. formula *katelo*, "for three days", has its pendant in the Mlg. *harua*, "for two days", word-base *rua*, "two".

The Numeral.

173. For the *ordinals* there is a Common IN formative, namely *ka-*. The *multiplicatives* and *distributives* also have their special formatives in the various individual IN languages, but none of them can be shown to be Common IN.

The formation of the ordinals. Philippines, Bagobo: *ka-tlo*, "the third" — Celebes, Tontb.: *ka-tĕlu* — Borneo, Tar.: *katalu* — Java, Sund.: *katilu* — Sumatra, Lampong: *katĕlu* — Malay Peninsula, Mal.: *ka-tiga*, "the third" — Eastern Border, Laoranese: *kalima*, "the fifth".

SECTION VI : REDUPLICATION OF THE WORD-BASE.

174. There are, to begin with, two methods of doubling words. According to the first one the whole word is set down twice over. Thus in the Mak. children's song Daeng Camum-muq there is the sentence: " Slowly, slowly swallow (the food) down your (= -nu) throat ! " = *palemeq-lemeq namaq-nauṅ ri kallon-nu.* Here the whole word-base *lemeq* is reduplicated. The second case is: First the word is set down as far as the second vowel, inclusively, and then it is set down in its entirety. Thus the Day. dirge Augh Olo Balian Hapa Tiwah begins with the words: " Flee, soul of (the) dead ! " = *lila-lilan liau matäy.* Here *lilan* is reduplicated according to the second method. The omission of the final consonant is not the result of any sandhi-laws of the several languages; that phenomenon is an ancient heritage. A third kind of reduplication merely repeats the first two sounds of the word-base, *e.g.* Bont. *nonoan,* " toy buffalo ", beside *noan* " real buffalo ."

The first two kinds of reduplication convey an intensification of the fundamental meaning, or, occasionally, the opposite, a weakening of it. The third kind indicates a thing, mostly a tool.

175. *Reduplication to the second vowel.* Philippines, Ibanag: *sinnu-sinnun,* " garments ", word-base *sinnun,* " garment " — Celebes, Tontb.: *londe-londey,* " all sorts of ships " — Borneo, Day.: *humo-humon,* " somewhat stupid " — Java, Old Jav.: *sulu-sulun,* " to swarm pell-mell " — Madagascar, Hova: *tiṅgi-tiṅgina,* " to sit at the edge of " — Northern Border, Form.: *darra-darrab,* " to line clothes thickly " — South-Western Border, Mentaway: *boli-bolit,* " to twist one-self ".

176. *Reduplication of the first two sounds.* Philippines, Bont.: *nonoañ*, " toy buffalo " — Celebes, Bulu: *tutura*, " pole for pushing ", word-base *tura*, " to push " — Borneo, Day.: *gagada*, " vane ", beside the synonymous Mal. *gada-gada* — Java, Jav.: *wĕwĕdi*, " scarecrow ", word-base *wĕdi*, " timid " — Northern Border, Form.: *wawarigbig*, " borer ", word-base *warigbig*, " to bore " — Eastern Border, Rottinese: *sisilo*, " gun ", word-base *silo*, " to shoot " — South-Western Border, Mentaway: *tutura*, " pole for pushing ".

Note.—The first kind of reduplication, the doubling of the entire word-base, is so very widely distributed that examples are superfluous.

Synthesis of Words into Sentences.

177. As already announced elsewhere, I shall publish a special monograph on this subject.*

* [The monograph here referred to appeared in 1914 under the title " Indonesisch und Indogermanisch im Satzbau ".]

PART II

ORIGINAL INDONESIAN

178. We saw in § 1 that the word *lańit*, either unchanged or modified only in conformity with strict phonetic law, runs through a number of IN languages. How do we account for that fact ? By the assumption that there was once a uniform original IN language, which possessed the word *lańit*, and from which its offshoots, when they parted away from it, took the word with them.

179. Having in § 2 styled the word *lańit* " Common IN ", we now call it " Original Indonesian ", and we also apply this epithet to all the linguistic phenomena which in Part I have been pronounced to be Common IN.

180. It is self-evident that this Original Indonesian also went through a process of evolution: when we speak of the Original IN mother-tongue in this monograph we are referring to its last phase, immediately before its subdivision.

181. Indo-European research also speaks of an original mother-tongue, though with more reserve nowadays than formerly: see Meillet-Printz, p. 17, and compare therewith Porzezinski-Boehme, p. 198.

182. In the field of IN research the conditions are more favourable to the hypothesis of a common original mother-tongue. That, surely, has been proved by the whole of our dissertation on Common IN. But we will single out a few particularly striking points.

183. The several IN languages, although they extend over such an enormous area, are more closely related together than the Indo-European ones. We may illustrate that fact, for example, by the case of the numerals. We give here the numerals 1-10 of the four most outlying regions.

Northern Border	Eastern Border	South-Western Border	Western Border
Puyuma	Sumbanese	Mentaway	Hova
sa	sa	ša, šara	isa
rua	dua	rua	rua
tero	tilu	tälu	telu
spat	patu	äpat	efatra
rima	lima	lima	dimi, dima
unum	nomu	änäm	enina, enem
pitu	pitu	pitu	fitu
waro	'walu	balu	walu
iwa	siwa	šiba	siwi
purru	kĕmbuluh	pulu	fulu

Note I.—The sibilant in Mentaway *ša, šara, šiba* and **Hova** *siwi* somewhat resembles our " sh ".

Note II.—**Hova** *dima* and *enem* occur before suffixes or in composition.

Note III.—The resemblance of *dua* to the corresponding Indo-European numeral is merely fortuitous; *dua* also occurs in languages which have no Sanskrit loan-words at all.

184. The conservative character of the IN languages is further illustrated by the way in which onomatopœic formations run unchanged through the several individual languages. Thus flatulence is imitated by the phonetic series $t + u + t$, and though $p + u + t$ or $p + u + p$ would be equally appropriate, the nucleus *tut* always recurs.

Flatulence, to break wind. Philippines, Pamp.: *atut* — Celebes, Tontb.: *ĕntut* — Borneo, Day.: *ketut* — Java, Sund.: *hitut* — Sumatra, written Mkb.: *kantut* — Malay Peninsula, Mal.: *kĕntut* — Madagascar, Hova: *etutra* — Northern Border, Form.: *matut* — South-Western Border, Mentaway: *ätut*.

185. Finally we will illustrate the closeness of the relationship between the IN languages by reference to an entire section of their linguistic life, viz. the adjective, comparing for that purpose the Kamberese adjective on the Eastern Border and the Hova adjective on the Western Border.

I. In both languages some word-bases, without the addition of any formative, may serve as adjectives: Kamb. *bokul*, " big "; Hova *keli*, " small ".

II. In both languages *ma-* is the chief adjectival formative: Kamb. *maliñu*, " useful "; Hova *malutu*, " dirty ".

III. Both languages also use the formatives *ka-*, *pa-*, *ta-*, before vowels *k-*, *p-*, *t-*, in order to form a limited number of adjectives: Kamb. *kapatañ*, " dark ", word-base in Mal., viz. *pĕtañ*, " evening "; Hova *hetri* < *ka* + *etri*, " growing slowly ", word-base *etri*, " to diminish " — Kamb. *tabaña*, " full "; Hova *taburi*, " round " — Kamb. *paita*, " visible "; Hova *fulaka* < *pa* + *ulaka*, " folded, bent ", word-base *ulaka*, " bend ".

IV. Neither language possesses any adjectives denoting the material of which a thing consists. The substantival name of the material is simply put after the word that is to be qualified. A " stone house " is " house + stone ": Kamb. *uma watu*; Hova *tranu watu*.

V. Both languages can turn the adjective into a substantive by means of the article: Kamb. *na mahamu*, " the good (thing) "; Hova *ni marina*, " the right (thing) ".

VI. After adjectives which express a state of mind the word for " mind " is added without any connecting word of form: Kamb. *mahamu eti* = " good + heart " = " good-hearted "; Hova *afa-pu*, by sandhi from *afaka fu* = " free + heart " = " contented ".

186. There is one IN language, and one only, that has a history, viz. Jav. The oldest phase of it is what we call Old Jav. Now it is a reasonable assumption that this Old Jav. would be particularly closely related to the Original IN. And that is really the case. By far the greater number of the phenomena which we have shown to be Common IN, and now call Original IN, are to be found in Old Jav.* It is true that in the section dealing with Common IN we did not always

* This disposes of the hasty and premature observation in my " Prodromus ", § 8, *ad fin.*

adduce the Old Jav. as evidence, but that was merely because
we wished to let the other languages of the Javanese region,
which includes Bali and Madura as well, have their say too.
Let us just make special mention of one item in the general
agreement between Old Jav. and Common IN, or Original IN,
viz. the phonetic type of the word. Old Jav. possesses the
five common vowels and in addition to them the pĕpĕt; in
the interior of a word it tolerates the kapkap type of consonantal combination; at the end of a word it admits any
consonant save the palatals, thus tolerating the mediæ: and
these are also the chief characteristics of the Original IN type
of word.* — Modern Jav. has departed much further from
Original IN. For example, it has turned part of its pĕpĕts
into another sound, it has given up the sulu-suluñ type of
reduplication, its passive with the formative -in- is in the act
of dying out, etc.

187. Of the earlier phases of Mlg. and Bug. there are also
documentary records available, though they are far less important than the Old Jav. ones. Here too we observe that
the earlier phases approach more closely to the Original IN
than do the modern forms of these languages. Thus in § 44
we worked back from the modern Mlg. zama to iama, and the
latter form really occurs in Houtman, p. 360. And in the
Old Bug. epic La-Galigo there is an expression, no longer in
use nowadays, viz. amesorĕñ, "a place where one can lie
down". In § 26 we had occasion to regret that the word sor
runs through only a few languages; in Old Bug. amesorĕñ <
a + me + sor + ĕñ we have a fresh piece of evidence in support
of it.

188. The sum total of the linguistic facts which we have
shown to be Common IN and now call Original IN is quite a
considerable quantity. It is true that beside these there are
a good many linguistic phenomena which we could only style
Common IN with hesitation, or not at all. But that is not to
say that they *cannot* be Original IN. Bim. on the Eastern
Border has a word wara, "to be, to be found somewhere",

* [See also Essay IV, §§ 3, 6, 8.]

which recurs in Nabaloi in the Philippines as *guara*, in Old
Jav. in Java as *wwara*, and in Mentaway, on the South-Western
Border, as *bara*. The original form is *wara*, with a *w* ; the other
initials follow in strict accordance with phonetic law from
that *w*. Now this word only appears in four areas of distribution, the Philippines, Java, the Eastern Border, and the
South-Western Border; on our principles we cannot possibly
pronounce it to be Common IN. Yet how shall we explain
the fact that it occurs at these four widely separated points ?
Has each of these languages created it by itself ? That would
indeed be a remarkable coincidence, particularly in view of
the perfect phonetic agreement. Has the word migrated ?
Words with that kind of meaning are not much in the habit
of migrating from one language to another; and how could it
have skipped so many intervening territories ? There will
be no alternative left but to pronounce *wara* to be an Original
IN word like so many others.

Note.—Nabaloi *guara* < *wara* in conformity with the phonetic law: " Initial *w* appears in Nabaloi as *gu* ", hence also
gualo, " eight " < *walu*. The phonetic laws which have produced Old Jav. *wwara* and Mentaway *bara* have already been
mentioned.

189. The Original IN did not differ *essentially* from the
modern living IN languages. One important point of difference may be said to consist in the fact that it used more
monosyllabic words of substance than the modern languages
do. Modern Jav. has a considerable number of disyllabic
words of substance which in Old Jav. were still monosyllabic:
thus Old Jav. said *duh*, " gravy ", but Modern Jav. says
duduh. Accordingly, as we go back from Modern Jav. to
Old Jav. the number of monosyllabic words of substance
increases; and when we go back from Old Jav. to Original IN
it is to be expected that there would be a further increase.

190. The Original IN *phonetic system* had two distinct *r*'s;
in several of the modern languages the two *r*'s have become
fused into one; in others, again, the one *r* has turned into *g*
or *h*, and the other *r* into *l* or *d*. These vicissitudes of the *r*

sound, particularly the RGH series, have been studied in considerable detail by Dutch scholars, *e.g.* quite recently by Talens and Adriani for the dialects of the Talaut Archipelago; and also by Conant for the Philippine languages.*

191. In *morphology* some of the IN languages, *e.g.* Sangirese, exhibit great luxuriance, others, *e.g.* Bim., a slighter development, while Old Jav. occupies an intermediate position in this respect. And some such intermediate position, it may be inferred from the data set out in §§ 143-173, was also occupied by the Original IN.

* [See also Essay IV, §§ 40, 11. 99, 129 *seqq.*]

ESSAY III

THE INDONESIAN VERB:
A DELINEATION BASED UPON AN
ANALYSIS OF THE BEST TEXTS IN
TWENTY-FOUR LANGUAGES

(The original was published in 1912.)

SUMMARY

137

139-62. Section IX : The Verb in the Sentence. 139. The
Connecting Links of the Sentence. 140. Prepositions.
141. The Copula. 142. The Status Constructus.
143. Emphasizing the Predicate. 144. Sentences
without a Subject. 145. Sentences without a Verbal
Predicate. 146-62. Connexion of the Predicate with
other Parts of the Sentence.

SECTION I : METHOD AND SOURCES.

1. I have observed that comparative philologists, whether they happen to operate in the Indo-European, Indonesian, or any other branch of the subject, seem, for the most part, to diverge along two different lines. The one school delves deeply into the texts of the several literatures that bear upon the subject, the other is inclined to depend more on manuals and vocabularies. The second method, though it may not give perfect satisfaction, certainly has the advantage of greater facility and rapidity; but as the special character of the present IN (= Indonesian) monograph compels me to follow in the footsteps of the first school, I will endeavour to justify my procedure in the eyes of those who pursue other methods.

2. There are, to be sure, a large number of IN grammars and vocabularies, and amongst them we meet with not a few that deserve to be styled "exemplary". Still, numerous as these are, there are quite as many languages that are represented only by inadequate manuals, or none at all. — Moreover, the point of view of the grammarian dealing with a single language is not the same as that of the comparative philologist. The grammarian will fail to observe some things which are of interest to the comparative philologist, or even if he does observe them, he may perhaps omit to include them in his delineation. For example: we shall have to deal later on with a causative formative *paka-* which occurs *e.g.* in Bugis (in Southern Celebes), in which language we find *e.g.* the form *pakatanre*, "to heighten", derived from the WB (= word-base) *tanre*, "high". In the language of Nias (an island at the back of Sumatra), in conformity with its phonetic laws, as to which more will be said hereafter, this *paka-* has to become *faqa-*. Now the formative *faqa-* is not mentioned in the Nias grammar, but we find it in the texts.

Illustration: in the story of " Samagowaulu in the South "
is the sentence: " Do let me go, Father ! " = Let-go me only
yet, father = *faqamoi do mano sa, ama*. Here we have the
causative *faqamoi*, " to let go ", derived from the WB *moi*,
" to go ".

3.   The literatures of the IN nations are rich, particularly
in popular productions which are most welcome material, not
only for the folklorist, but also for the student of comparative
philology.   And fortunately such texts have been published
in plenty, thanks to the zeal of Dutch scholars especially,
who, in this department, headed by Kern, have done admirable work.   In a good many cases we have got texts of languages for which there are at present no manuals, and that
happens just to apply to some languages which are particularly important to the comparative student, as for instance
Kupangese. — It is only in the special department of Philippine studies that the texts published up to now are deficient
in number.   It would, therefore, be a fruitful task for such
scholars as Scheerer, Conant and Seidenadel to remedy this
defect.

4.   There is *one* scientific operation that is practicable only
on the basis of a study of texts, viz. enumeration.   I do not
by any means regard enumeration as a species of child's play:
it is, amongst other things, a matter of scientific importance
to know *how often* a linguistic phenomenon occurs. — Specimen enumeration: as Section IX shows, IN, like other languages, have reflexive verbs; Malay has an expression parallel
to the German " sich begeben " (" to betake oneself "),
Bugis a parallel to the French " se repentir ".   Now an
analysis of the Malay popular historical romance Hang Tuah
yields a dozen reflexive verbs in 112 printed pages.   A German
or French text of the like compass would exhibit more of them.
The result of the enumeration, therefore, is: Malay has reflexive verbs as German and French have, but they are less
numerous in Malay than in these two languages.   Moreover,
we shall find on more than one occasion that an enumeration
actually decides a doubtful question.

5. Even those scholars who merely wish to study comparative phonology, must not think that this limitation of their aims dispenses them from the study of texts. I will emphasize that point by means of an example: one phenomenon of very frequent occurrence in IN is metathesis. Thus the Common IN* word *pari*, " ray " (a species of fish), appears in Tontemboan, of Northern Celebes, under the form *pair*. Such metatheses are inexplicable without the aid of a study of Kupangese texts. In Kupangese, a language spoken in Timor (an island lying near New Guinea), metathesis appears quite regularly in certain contexts. Common IN *laku*, " to go ", and *kali*, " to dig ", are *lako* and *kali* in Kupangese; but the sentence " Then I went and dug a hole ", in the Story of the Fool (literally " then I went (to) dig hole ") is *mo auk laok kail bolo*. — Or, to give another example of the importance of texts even for the phonologist: in Minangkabau (in Sumatra) pronunciation and spelling diverge to a marked degree, and as a rule the spelling represents an older phase of pronunciation; hence the written language is of importance for comparative phonology. Now the grammar, with its practical tendency, only gives the spoken forms of words, not the written; and even the very carefully compiled vocabulary occasionally gives merely the spoken form. In such a case we can find the form which for us is the more important one only in texts printed in the native character. The word for " generation ", for instance, appears in the vocabulary only under the form *sunduiq*; but in the texts I find *sundut*, and that this find may be relied on, *i.e.* that this spelling really embodies the older pronunciation of the word, is proved by the fact that Karo, another Sumatran language, actually says *sundut*. Here then we have a phonetic phenomenon which only a text could reveal, both grammar and vocabulary having failed us.

Illustration: in the Minangkabau popular story entitled Manjau Ari, in the third line from the beginning, we find the words " from generation to generation ", which in the spoken language are *sunduiq basunduiq*, written $s + u + n + d + u + t$ $b + r + s + u + n + d + u + t$.

* Common IN = occurring in all or at any rate most IN languages [See Essay II, especially §§ 2-4.]

6. Lastly, I have not infrequently met with discrepancies as between texts and manuals, and in such cases it was always the text that was in the right. The Makassar grammar says that the auxiliary word of form *la* is " generally " employed in order to indicate future time. So I said to myself: If that is the case, I shall meet with the particle indicating the future particularly frequently in the two prophecies contained in the romance Jayalangkara, for there the predicates refer to future events. But in the first prophecy, among a dozen predicates, the sign of the future only figures three times, and in the second one not at all. And the same proportion is exhibited, apart from the prophecies, by the whole text of the romance. So the grammar ought to have formulated the rule thus: " Makassar possesses the capacity of expressing the future; but usually, when future time is intended, it simply uses the general form of the verb, which does not imply any time in particular."

7. The present monograph treats of the IN verb. It is based upon a detailed analysis of IN texts. I do not say that I owe nothing at all to grammars, but I do say that for me the analysis of texts has everywhere been the primary factor, and has formed the groundwork of my edifice. And in all cases, where I have consulted a grammar, I have verified its assertions by the help of texts. All the illustrations occurring in this monograph have been collected by myself out of the texts mentioned in § 11 (or the other texts referred to in § 14); should any of the illustrations also figure in some manual, it would be a coincidence that has escaped my notice.

8. A monograph should have something of an artistic form. Now there is no art in raking things together into a heap. Art involves selection and limitation, lucidity of structure, and intelligible exposition. Particularly selection and limitation; I shall therefore by no means submit to the reader every one of the observations I have made, but only such as appear to me to be especially characteristic and interesting. By " characteristic " I mean in relation to the IN structure, and when I say " interesting ", I have in mind, above all, the interests of Indo-European and general linguistic study. I will explain that by an example. The IN languages of the Philippines have a copula, which links the subject with the predicate, and has the form *ay*, or *i*, or *ya*. So the passage near the beginning of the Tagalog version of " Wilhelm Tell ": " The boy fell asleep ": reads *an bata i naidlip*. There are, however, certain cases in which the copula is omitted, *e.g.* where Tell says to Johannes Parricida: " Stand up ! " = Stand + up you = *tumindig kayo*. Now the appearance of the copula is a linguistic phenomenon which is characteristic from the point of view of IN and interesting for the Indo-European student, and therefore I shall speak of it in Section IX; but the limitations of its use are of much less importance, and accordingly I shall say nothing about them.

If it should appear that any part of this monograph has been expressed too concisely, the defect can easily be remedied: I shall simply expand such portion into an additional monograph.

9. Amongst the numerous IN languages I have chosen the following for the basis of my delineation:

Philippines: 1. Bontok. — 2. Tagalog.

Northern Celebes: 3. Tontemboan.

Central Celebes: 4. Bareqe.

Southern Celebes: 5. Makassar. — 6. Bugis.

Borneo: 7. Dayak.* — 8. Basa Sangiang.

Java: 9. Old Javanese. — 10. Modern Javanese.

Islands towards New Guinea: 11. Kamberese. — 12. Kupangese. — 13. Rottinese. — 14. Masaretese.

Sumatra: 15. Minangkabau. — 16. Toba. — 17. Karo. — 18. Gayo. — 19. Achinese.

Islands at the back of Sumatra: 20. Mentaway. — 21. Nias.

Malay Peninsula: 22. Malay.

Madagascar: 23. Hova. — 24. Old Malagasy, *i.e.* the more archaic dialect of Ferrand's texts, which is indeed related to Hova but nevertheless independent of it.

10. Justification of the choice of these twenty-four languages. — The reason why I selected just these languages

* [See Essay I, § 10, footnote.]

consists merely in this, that they appeared to me to be the most fruitful for my theme. It is only the inclusion of the Basa Sangiang that demands a more detailed explanation. The name Basa Sangiang means " language of the spirits ", the genitive " of the spirits " being indicated merely by position, without any special formative. It is the liturgical language of the Dayaks. It differs from the Dayak proper in vocabulary and morphology. Thus in the last of the Songs of the Dead we find the sentence: " She has for cradle a spider's web " = Has + cradle spider's + web " = *batuyan lawa*. Here by means of the formative *ba-* is derived from the WB *tuyan*, " cradle ", the verb *batuyan*, " to have a cradle "; ordinary Dayak says *hatuyan*. However the Basa Sangiang may have originated, its formatives are strictly IN. Thus one of the formatives which it specially affects, viz. *na-*, or *nam-*, occurs in another language of Borneo, namely in Tidung:

Tidung: *nalikut*, " to bind ", from WB *likut*.
　　　　 nampuki, " to abuse ", from WB *puki*.
Basa Sangiang: *nalayan*, " to rest ", from WB *layan*.
　　　　　　　 nampelek, " to interrupt ", from WB *pelek*.

In a similar way all the special features of the verb in the Basa Sangiang can be shown to be genuine IN; therefore I am justified in including it among the twenty-four languages.

11. Now follows a list of the texts of the twenty-four languages selected as a basis for my investigations and delineations:

1. Bontok: mythical stories, accounts of battles, headhunters' ceremonies, working songs.

2. Tagalog: Guillermo Tell ni Schiller.

3. Tontemboan: mythical stories, descriptions of sacrifices, prayers at sacrifices, legends, ghost stories, tales.

4. Bareqe: stories about animals, funny stories, popular songs, riddles.

5. Makassar: the war epic Maqdi, the romance Jayalangkara, elegies, children's songs.

6.   Bugis: the edifying tale of King Injilai with the three moral tales of the executioners interwoven therewith, love songs, epigrams against cowardice, letters.

7.   Dayak: popular stories.

8.   Basa Sangiang: the songs at the festival of the dead.

9.   Old Javanese: the published portions of the Mahābhārata, the philosophical legend Kuñjarakarṇa, the philosophical work Kamahāyānikan, Jonker's Book of Laws, Mpu Tanakung's Prosody (= Wṛttasañcaya) with a sentimental tale interwoven therewith.

10.   Modern Javanese : the history of the kingdom of Kĕḍiri, the historical drama Prabu Dewa Sukma.

11.   Kamberese: stories about animals, dancing songs, harvest songs, songs at house-building.

12.   Kupangese: the Story of the Fool.

13.   Rottinese: the play "Cock and Ape", wherein the characters are animals.

14.   Masaretese: stories about animals, historical legends, forms of oaths.

15.   Minangkabau: the popular tale Manjau Ari.

16.   Toba: the Contest of Sangmaima for the spear that was an heirloom.

17.   Karo: the Story of the Glutton.

18.   Gayo: the Legend of the Blue Princess. Small vignettes illustrating social life.

19.   Achinese: the Story of the Pelican.

20.   Mentaway: love dialogues, polite dialogues, conversations about the priesthood, medicine, custom, and law.

21.   Nias: popular tales, wedding songs, proverbs, the great heroic hymn of Lagemann.

22.   Malay: the familiar epic Bidasari, the historical romance Hang Tuah, Abdullah's Journey to Kĕlantan, etc.

23.   Hova: the ethical Testament of Umbiasa, the old funeral oration of Imerina, Rahidy's fables.

24.   Old Malagasy: Muhammadan sermons and prayers.

12.   Justification of the choice of these texts. — By far the greater number of the selected texts are of an original and popular kind; they are therefore precisely such as a student of language desires. The exceptions are the Tag., Old Jav. and Old Mlg.* texts, whose inclusion must accordingly be justified.

I. The Tag. translation of Tell is by Rizal. To everyone who knows the name of Rizal the idea will at once suggest itself that this translation must contain the purest and most genuine Tag.

II. The Old Jav. literature, or so much of it as has been published up to the present time, is in the highest sense a product of conscious art, dependent in a great measure on the ancient Indian literature. This relation of dependence is reflected by the word-store of Old Jav., which displays a large percentage of ancient Indian loan-words. The Rāmā-yaṇa begins with a characterization of considerable length, wherein the " epitheta ornantia " are for the most part Sanskrit words, the native ones being pretty well confined to *rěñön*, " renowned ", *dumilah*, " brilliant ", and *māsih*, " kind-hearted ". — But this alien element has only affected the vocabulary: morphology and syntax, and therefore also the character of the verb, have hardly been modified in the slightest. The same is true of the foreign element in other IN languages, as the researches on that subject, *e.g.* those of Van Ronkel, have shown. — Accordingly we shall not only use the Old Javanese texts without scruples, but shall also find them to be the most fruitful of all texts for our purpose.

III. The Old Mlg. texts display much the same character as the Old Jav.; they contain a fairly considerable quantity of Arabic loan-words, but for the rest their inclusion may be justified by the same arguments as have been used concerning the Old Jav. texts.

13. Some IN dictionaries give such lengthy illustrative quotations in support of the words they explain, that they may be said to amount to complete, though short, texts. This may be seen, for example, in Aymonier and Cabaton's

* [As to the abbreviations, see Essay II, § 15.]

Cham dictionary or in Hazeu's dictionary of Gayo.   The
" small vignettes illustrating social life ", mentioned in my
list of sources, consist of such lengthy quotations in Hazeu's
dictionary.

14. The texts enumerated in § 11 vary in compass and
contents, but in almost every instance these sufficed for the
requirements of the present monograph.   Where that was not
the case, I have drawn upon additional texts.   An example:
in Hova we meet with an interesting imperative *fuha*, " wake
up ! ", a form which constitutes an exception to the regular
modes of formation.   But this *fuha* occurs neither in Umbiasa's Testament, nor in the funeral oration, nor in the fables;
but it does figure in the oracular formulas of Amurunkay and
Vunizungu; in treating of the imperative I shall therefore
have to quote from these formulas. — Just as I shall occasionally make use of other texts besides those mentioned in § 11,
so too it will occasionally happen that other languages besides
those enumerated in § 9 will be called upon to give evidence.

15. The majority of the texts mentioned in § 11 are accompanied by translations.   The comparative philologist prefers
such translations as, without being woodenly literal, do not
depart widely from the wording of the original.   I consider as
a model in this respect the style and manner in which Kern,
the two Adriani's, and Blagden do translations.   Of the two
versions of the Sangmaima, the more elegant one by Pleyte
is more convenient for the student of literature, the more
literal one by Schreiber more suitable for the student of language.   Van der Toorn's translation of the Manjau Ari is in
places too free for the requirements of the linguistic student.
For instance, in the description of the character of the Banda-
haro, there is a sentence: " He used to slay and pay no wer-
gild, he wounded and paid no fine " = Killed, not paid + wer-
gild, wounded, not paid + fine = *mambunuah inday mam-
bahun, mancancan inday mamampeh*.   This he renders by " He
disposed freely over the life and death of his subjects ". —
In my translations, which constituted the beginning of my
IN studies and a preparation for my work in comparative

philology, I have taken several different lines. My Hang
Tuah and Paupau Rikadong may serve both for the student of
literature and the comparative philologist; the Jayalangkara is
a decided abridgment of a somewhat diffuse original, so the
student of language would do well not to tackle it; on the other
hand, the translation of the Injilai has been specially designed to
meet the requirements of the linguistic student, and even the
beginner. Parts that were more than usually troublesome
to read have been transliterated in the footnotes and every
passage that offers any sort of difficulty is literally translated
and explained. I did this because in my opinion an accurate
knowledge of Bug. is indispensable to IN comparative philologists. — The requirements of students are met even more
fully by Snouck Hurgronje's translation of the Blue Princess
or Jonker's Kupangese translation : the former translates
word for word, the latter gives a double version, an interlinear
one and a free one.

16. My monograph has been preceded by five works, all
of great value, dealing with some parts of its theme. Kern
has written several essays on the Old Jav. verb; Jonker
has described the ways in which the IN verb indicates person;
Brandes has dealt with the infix -in-; Van Ophuijsen has discussed certain phenomena of the Mal. verb; Adriani has
scattered in his manuals many acute observations. — It has
been my endeavour to find something new to say even on
these subjects.

SECTION II : THE VERBAL WORD-BASE.

17. In relation to the objects of our monograph we can divide IN words into two classes: word-bases and words derived from word-bases by means of formatives. The latter may be called "derived" words, for short. The WB, which is mostly a disyllable, occasionally a monosyllable or a trisyllable, is the shortest formation actually existing in living speech; the fact that it is possible to analyse the WB further theoretically does not concern us in this monograph. In the Nias verse from the heroic hymn of Lagemann: "He went and clasped the shaft of the spear" = W. cl. sh. sp. = *moi muraqu dotou hulayo*, the word *moi*, "to go", is a WB, *muraqu*, "to clasp", is a derived word, formed from the WB *raqu*. So here there are both kinds, a WB and a derived word, used in living speech, in the sentence.

18. WB's that denote action, or it may be suffering. or a state, we style verbal WB's. In the fourth canto of the Malay epic Bidasari there is a verse: "Day by day he sat there sorrowing" = Every every d. sat sor. = *tiyap tiyap hari duduq bĕrcinta*. Here *duduq* is a verbal WB. it means "to sit"; and everywhere, wherever it occurs, it means "to sit", not "seat", for that is *kadudukan*.

19. There are not a few verbal WB's which, either quite unchanged or modified only in strict conformity with phonetic law, run through so many IN languages that we have to call them Common IN. Such a word is *takut*, otherwise *takot*, etc.. "to fear, to be afraid". — Illustrations: In the Tagalog Tell where Friesshardt says: "And we are not afraid of the waters of the Alps" = And not are + afraid of the w. of the A. = *at di natatakot sa maña ilog nan Alpes*. In the Bugis History of the Founding of Luwuq we find: "His servants were afraid"

149

= Feared s. his = *metauqna ata na*. In the Malay work
Hang Tuah, Hang Jĕbat says: " I am not afraid to die " =
Not I fear to die = *tiyada aku takut akan mati*. In the Hova
Fable of the Donkey we find: " There was no one who did not
fear him " = Not was, not feared him = *tsi nisi tsi nata-
hutra azi.*

Note.—In support of the assertion that *takut* is Common **IN**
I have only given illustrations from four areas of distribution,
viz. the Philippines. Celebes, the Malay Peninsula, and Madagascar. Strictly speaking, I ought to give illustrations from
all the twenty-four languages, or at any rate from a majority
of them, in order to convince the reader that *takut* really is
Common IN. But that procedure would involve such an
accumulation of ballast as to deprive my monograph of the
character which, as stated in § 8, I wish it to have. Accordingly both here and in the following I confine myself to mentioning merely three or four of the illustrations I have collected; but in doing so I always strictly observe the precau-
tion of quoting from languages which in each case are most
remote from one another both from the point of view of
relationship and also geographically, as in the present instance
of Tag., Bug., Mal. and Hova.

20. We have seen above that both simple WB verbs and
derived verbs can do duty as the predicate of a sentence. In
most IN languages the derived verbs bulk much more largely
than the others, and yet we always find alongside of them a
minority of simple WB verbs. This state of things must be
regarded as Common IN. Only in the languages spoken near
New Guinea. *e.g.* in Masaretese. do I observe the reverse,
viz. that the simple verbs predominate in the texts. — This
statement shall be emphasized by an enumeration. In the
part of the Tag. Tell. where Baumgarten relates Wolfen-
schiess' suggestions, all the verbs are derivative; in the passage " The castellan lies in my house " the idea of lying is replaced by that of being (*i.e.* being present in) and is not expressed verbally, for reasons which will be dealt with hereafter. In the Tontemboan Story of the Defeat of the Antel-

ope by the Water Snail there are hardly any but derived verbs
in 23 lines of print. On the other hand, in the Masaretese
Story of the Ghost with Seven Cords we find in 39 lines of
print only 5 derived verbs: *eptea* $<$ formative *ep* + WB *tea*,
" to set ", *ephatak*, " to sacrifice ", *danewen* $<$ *da* + *newen*,
" to live ", *damata*, " to die ", and *epmata*, " to kill ".

21. Having learnt that verbal WB's, without any formatives, are capable of being used in the sentence, if we now proceed to enquire whether any particular categories of verbs are
used in that way, we get the following result from an analysis
of the texts: the WB's most commonly thus used as predicates are those which have a passive or neutral sense; more
rarely the dative ones, *i.e.* such as link themselves with the
object by means of a preposition; and very seldom accusative *
ones, which take an object without a preposition. — Illustrations: Day., from the Story of Sangumang: " He wishes
to be addressed " = *blaku tiñak*. Kamberese, from the Riddle
about Maize: " He stands up " = *na hadañ*. Old Jav.,
from the Ādiparwa: " To be versed in the spiritual life "
= *wěruh ri ambĕk*. Mal., from the Hang Tuah: " To have
breeding " = Know speech = *tahu bahasa*. — Here then we
have the passive WB *tiñak*, " to be spoken to ", the neutral
hadañ, " to stand ", the dative *wěruh*, " to be versed in ", and
the accusative *tahu*, " to know ", used in sentences.

That the passive WB's are really passive in their nature, is
proved by the circumstance that they can be accompanied by
an agent linked with them by means of the same preposition
as in the case of a derived passive, *e.g.* in Mal. by means of
oleh, " by ". — Illustration from the Sějarah Mělayu: " This
king was defeated by King Alexander " = Was + defeated k.
this by K. A. = (*maka*) *alah* (*lah*) *raja itu oleh raja Iskan-
der.*

Note.—The IN languages are rich in particles. Such particles often merely serve the purpose of beginning the sentence,
like the above *maka*, or laying stress on some part of it, like

* [*I.e.* what are commonly called transitive verbs, the others (so
far as they are active) being intransitive.]

the above *lah*, or marking an antithesis, and then they are untranslatable. For the greater convenience of the reader I put them between parentheses: let the reader simply pass them by.

22. In practically all the IN languages the verb " to be " — not our copula " to be " but " to be " in the sense of " to exist, to occur somewhere " — is devoid of a formative; this phenomenon must be styled Common IN. — Illustrations: Magindanao, from the collection of dialogues in Juanmarti's work: " There is someone there " = Is someone = *aden saka-tau*. Mad., from the story Paman Manceng: " There was once a man " = Was one man male = *bada setton oren lakeq*. Sĕraway, from the story Ringan Sĕdayu: " There was once a king " = Formerly w. a k. = *bĕmulaw adaw suqatu rajaw*.

23. Enumerations bearing on §§ 21 and 22.

I. In the Old Jav. story of the evil serpent Takshaka in the Ādiparwa of the Mahābhārata we find many neutral, some passive, some dative, and one accusative verbal WB, viz. *tungan*, " to sit on ". — Illustration: " It sat on the hill " = *tungan parwata*.

II. In the part of the Mal. Hang Tuah which relates the early history of the hero we meet with the same state of things as in Old Jav. Amidst many neutral WB's there are a few passive and dative ones, and a single accusative one, *tahu*, " to know ". — Illustration: " To have breeding " = *tahu bahasa*.

III. In the Day. story Asang Baratih the proportion is again similar, only there we come across more accusative WB's, namely such as denote motion, which will be dealt with hereafter.

IV. In the collection of Hova fables by Rahidy the neutral and passive WB's are in the majority, the dative ones are represented by a single case: " to say to (a person) " = *hui;* accusative ones are wanting. But in contrast with the Old

Jav. (see I. above) the relation between the neutral and passive WB's is that the latter, *e.g.*, *hita*, " to be seen ", balance the former.

24. Now when it is desired to use derived verbs and not simply verbal WB's, the language is able to fashion them out of the most diverse materials, from any part of speech and even from " complexes " or agglomerations of words.

I. Derived verb formed from a WB which in itself is already of a verbal nature. In Old Jav., at the beginning of the episode of the death of Abhimanyu in the Bhārata-Yuddha: " The son of Dharma was dismayed " = *san dharm-masuta atĕgĕg*, we have a derived verb *atĕgĕg*, formed from the WB *tĕgĕg*, " to be dismayed ", which in itself is also verbal.

II. Derivatives from substantival WB's. Example: Old Bug. *pajuṅ*, " royal parasol ", *maqpajuṅ*, " to wield the royal parasol ". — Illustration from the History of the Founding of Luwuq: " They went to him who wielded the royal parasol " = Went to r. + p. + wielding the = *menreq ri maqpajuṅ e*.

III. Derivatives from other parts of speech. From the interrogative pronoun *apa* Old Jav. forms the verb *aṅapa*, " to do what, to desire what ? "; from the word *en*, " yes ", in Tontemboan comes *men* < *ma* + *en*, " to say ' yes ' ", the past tense of which is *nimen*; from the interjection of clearing the throat, *chem*, Day. forms the verb *ñaṅehem*, " to clear the throat, to say ' h'm ' ". — Illustrations: Old Jav., from the Mausalaparwa: " What ailed the Brahmans that they cursed ? " = W. + a. the B. c.? = *aṅapa (ta) sira brāhmana sumāpa*. Tontb., from the Story of the Python: " The youngest, she said ' yes ' " = *si caakaran isia (ka) nimen*. Day., from the Story about saying H'm: " He cleared his throat ' h'm ' " = *iä ñaṅehem cheehem*.

IV. Derivatives from conglomerates or " complexes ". In Mak., " to ask " is *palaq* and " help " is *tuluṅ*, but " to ask for help " is *papalaqtuluṅ*. In this case a verb has been formed by means of the two formatives *pa-* and *-i* out of the

conglomerate *palaq tuluñ*. — Illustration, from the Jayalangkara: " None other can we ask to help save only the serpent "
= Not other can we ask + for + help except serpent the only
= *taena maraeñ maka kiq papalaqtuluñi pasañalinna naga
ya ji.*

25. Concluding observation of Section II: Delimitation
of the verb as against the substantive and the adjective.

I. Verb and substantive. There are verbal WB's and
there are substantival ones. The Mal. WB *duduq* means " to
sit ", and not " seat ", the Bug. WB *api* signifies " fire ",
and not " to burn "; in Mal. " seat " is expressed by *kadudukan*, in Bug. " to burn " by *tunu*. It is true that the vocabularies speak of certain WB's as being both verbs and substantives; but in very many cases the texts tell us that that
is merely apparently the case. In all Mal. dictionaries we
find the statement that *tidor* means " sleep " and " to sleep ";
but *tidor*, " sleep ". when used in a context, requires different
pronouns from *tidor*, " to sleep ". " He sleeps " is *tidor iya*,
" his sleep " on the other hand is *tidor ña*. So verb and substantive are at least distinguished by the construction. Again
another case: Toba *pintu* means both " door " and " shut ";
but *pintu*, " door ". has the accent in the usual Common **IN**
fashion on the *i*, while *pintu*, " shut ", has it on the *u*. — It
often happens that the same formatives are used to form
both verbs and substantives; Bug. *-eñ* serves both purposes.
But here too the language knows how to guard itself from
confusion. Bug. WB's often have two or three forms, differing from one another in the final, a subject discussed by me
in a former monograph.* Thus *gauq*, the WB for the idea
" to make ". also occurs in the variants *gauk* and *gaur*. And
the variant *gauk* is used by the language to form the substantive: *gaukeñ*. " thing ", while from the variant *gaur* it
creates the verb: *gaureñ*. " to make ".

II. Verb and adjective. In the department of the adjective we also find the phenomenon that formatives are used

* [" Sprachvergleichendes Charakterbild eines indonesischen
Idiomes", especially §§ 46 *seqq.*]

which do duty for the verb as well. Thus in Hova *ma-* forms both verbs and adjectives, but still it hardly ever happens that this *ma-* is employed with *one and the same* WB to form a verb and an adjective. From the WB *tewina*, "thick", the language does, it is true, make the adjective *matewina*, but for the verb it employs another mode of formation: *manatewina*, "to make thick".

SECTION III: THE FORMATIVES OF THE VERB.

26. We have already learnt that the verbal WB may do duty as a predicate either with or without the addition of other linguistic elements. In the Nias proverb: "You need not close your hand when you have no tobacco in it" = Not shut h. when not t. = *boi goχoi daña, na lo bago*, the word *goχoi* is an unmodified WB and acts as a predicate. In the passage from the Masaretese oath formula: "He will die in eight days' time" = In days eight die he = *la beto etruwa damata di*, the WB *mata* has taken on another linguistic element, the formative *da-*, in order to play the part of a predicate.

27. Now of such linguistic elements there are two kinds. Either they are syllables which unite with the WB to make a new formation, which is a unit and is governed by a *single* accent. Or they are independent words, which, though they attach themselves to the WB, do not coalesce with it. The first are called formatives, the latter auxiliary words of form. In the phrase from a Bug. love-song : "Indifference changes into passion" = I. the becomes p. = *lĕbba e mañcaji señĕrrĕñ*, the syllable *mañ-* in *mañcaji* is a formative. But in another Bug. love-song: "He has deceived" = Has he d. = *pura na bĕlle*, the word *pura*, which really means "done" but here indicates the past, is an auxiliary word of form. — In the course of the present Section we shall only concern ourselves with the formatives; the auxiliary words of form will be discussed hereafter.

28. As phonetic law constitutes the basis of comparative philology, we must now, after the introductory observations of the two preceding paragraphs, concern ourselves with the phonetic conditions of the IN verbal formatives. But not

156

all the twenty-four languages call for special notice under this head.

I. Bontok. Common IN pĕpĕt, that is to say the rapidly pronounced, indifferent vowel ĕ, becomes e in Bont.; hence the Common IN formative -ĕn appears in Bont. as -en.

II. Tagalog. Common IN ĕ becomes i in Tag., hence the same formative becomes -in < -ĕn. — Some of the Common IN r's appear in Tag. as g, by the RGH-law; hence the Tag. formative mag- < mar-. Thus beside Toba mar-somba there is a Tag. mag-simba, " to worship ".

III. Bugis. A Common IN consonant, other than a nasal, immediately preceding another consonant becomes q in Bug.; thus beside Toba martaru there is a Bug. form maqtaro < mar + taro, " to put ". By analogy this maq- can also be put before a vowel, as in maqeñeq, " to shine ", from the WB eñeq. — All Common IN final nasals are unified into ñ in Bug., which therefore has -ĕñ and -añ for Common IN -ĕn and -an.

IV. Makassar. Mak. shares the laws which under III. above have been ascribed to its near relative Bugis, and adds to them the following: Common IN ĕ is represented in Makassar by a, hence Bug. -ĕñ and -añ both appear as -añ in Mak.

V. Toba. Common IN ĕ appears in Toba as o, hence the Toba -on < -ĕn. That is the reason why in I. above we found Toba marsomba corresponding with Tag. magsimba, both being from an original marsĕnbah.

VI. Hova. Common IN initial b becomes w in Hova, hence the formative wa- < ba-. — Unaccentuated Common IN ĕ is represented in Hova by i; a Common IN final nasal of every kind by -na; hence the repeatedly mentioned formative -ĕn appears in Hova as -ina. — Common IN k becomes a spirant in Hova, hence it has hu-, as compared with the Karo ku-.

29. The phonetic laws of the above-named languages have all been dealt with by me in previous monographs, so I need only state them here, without giving any evidence in support of them. It is otherwise with Nias. No one has as yet said anything about the phonetic laws of Nias, and therefore I must be more discursive on that matter.

I. Common **IN** ĕ becomes *o* in Nias.* Hence:

Common **IN** *ĕnĕm*, " six "	:	Nias *ono*
Common **IN** *tĕlĕn*, " to swallow "	:	Nias *tolo*
Common **IN** *kĕna*, " hit "	:	Nias *gona*.

II. Common **IN** final consonant disappears in Nias.† Hence:

Common **IN** *ĕnĕm*, " six "	:	Nias *ono*
Common **IN** *tĕlĕn*, " to swallow "	:	Nias *tolo*
Common **IN** *takut*, " to fear "	:	Nias *taqu*.

III. Common **IN** initial *k* appears in Nias as *g*.‡ Hence:

Common **IN** *kaka*, "elder brother"	:	Nias *gaqa*
Common **IN** *kima*, " shell-fish "	:	Nias *gima*
Common **IN** *kĕna*, " hit "	:	Nias *gona*.

IV. Common **IN** *k* in the interior of a word turns into *q*.§ Hence:

Common **IN** *takut*, " to fear "	:	Nias *taqu*
Common **IN** *buku*, " knot, joint "	:	Nias *buqu*
Common **IN** *kaka*, " elder brother "	:	Nias *gaqa*.

V. Common **IN** initial *p* becomes a spirant.| Hence:

Common **IN** *pitu*, " seven "	:	Nias *fitu*
Common **IN** *puri*, " behind "	:	Nias *furi*
Common **IN** *panah*, " shooting weapon "	:	Nias *fana*.

VI. In conformity with these phonetic laws the formatives show the following changes:

Common **IN** -*ĕn*	:	Nias -*o*
Common **IN** *ka*-	:	Nias *ga*-
Common **IN** *paka*-	:	Nias *faqa*-.

---

* [See also Essay IV, § 5, IV.]   † [See Essay IV, § 205.]
‡ [But see Essay IV, § 349, II.]   § [See also Essay IV, § 143.]
[See also Essay IV, § 112, II.]

30. Particular attention should be paid to the phonetic processes which take place in the various IN languages in connexion with the prefixing of the formative *ṅ :*

I. There is a Common IN formative *ṅ-*, about which we shall have a good deal more to say. Thus from the WB *atta* Bugis forms the verb *ṅatta*, " to be ready ", from the WB *golek* Modern Javanese makes the verb *ṅgolek*, " to seek ".

II. Now IN very rarely tolerates two consonants together at the beginning of a word. Consequently the addition of the formative *ṅ-* to WB's beginning with a consonant has led to a variety of compromises. The most important are the following, which may be styled Common IN:

$$ṅ + k > ṅ$$
$$ṅ + t > n$$
$$ṅ + p > m.$$

Examples from Modern Javanese:

$$ṅ + \text{WB } kirim > ṅirim, \text{ " to send "}$$
$$ṅ + \text{WB } tumbas > numbas, \text{ " to buy "}$$
$$ṅ + \text{WB } pakah > makah, \text{ " to ramify "}.$$

III. Now it often happens, as we shall explain in detail later on, that several verbal formatives together become attached to the verbal WB. Thus it is a Common IN phenomenon for the formative *ṅ* to combine with the formative *ma-*, as *ma + ṅ*; somewhat rarer are the combinations *a- + ṅ*, *ar- + ṅ*, and *mar- + ṅ*. The agglutination of these additional formatives entails no change in the function or meaning of the *ṅ-*. Alongside of the above-mentioned *ṅgolek* Modern Jav. also says *aṅgolek*, and both mean the same thing.— Here, in subsection III, the *ṅ* occurs under other conditions than in II.; it is in the interior of the word. Accordingly the phonetic phenomena that manifest themselves here are of a different nature, they are mostly simple assimilations; thus in Dayak *ma + ṅ + tarik > mantarik*, " to throw ".

IV. So we find, quite naturally, a different treatment of the case when the formative occurs in the middle of a word from that which it receives when the formative is initial.

Nevertheless a number of compromises have been made, consisting substantially in this, that the phenomena applicable to the case of the formative as initial have imposed themselves on the cases where it is medial. Thus in Day., *ñ + taluson*, " torch " > *naluson*, " to make torches "; *ma + ñ + taluson*, should. in conformity with III., become *mantaluson*, but in fact it is *manaluson*. — Compromises of this kind are to be found in so many IN languages that we are compelled to style them Common IN.

V. As these compromises occur even in the interior of words, we can understand how it happens that there are sometimes alternative forms. an indication that the compromise is not yet a perfect one. Thus from the WB *baläh*, " to requite ", Day. forms both *mambaläh* and *mamaläh*.

31. In the last few paragraphs we have been discussing such phonetic phenomena affecting the formatives as we can grasp and comprehend from the point of view of phonetic law. But we also meet with a minority of phonetic phenomena which do not admit of that possibility at present. Beside the Common IN formative *ta-*, which forms a passive, the Sund. displays a *ti-*. Now a Common IN *a* is represented in Sund., without exception. by *a*; so the Sund. *ti-* is not a regular phonetic equivalent of the Common IN *ta-*. How then shall we explain the relation of *ti-* to *ta-* ? Shall we simply declare that they have nothing to do with each other ? That will hardly do, for after all the consonant is the same, and the meaning is identical. So we cherish the hope that the progress of research will throw light on this point, and we call phenomena like this *ta : ti* by the provisional name of " variation ".

32. There are, however, cases of variation that can be tackled more effectually; we will mention a few of them here.

I. Day. has a formative *me-*, which fashions verbs from onomatopœic words. Thus from the interjections *kap!*, *bus!*, *rok!*, are formed the verbs *mekap*, *mebus*, *merok*; but *riñ*, " tinkle ! ", produces *miriñ*, " to tinkle "; so here appar-

ently, we have a variation *me : mi*. If however we look
into the matter more closely, it becomes plain to us that the
interjections with the vowel *i* take the formative *mi-*, as we
also find *mi-tip, mi-sir*. Here, therefore, the variation is a
product of assimilation.

II. Alongside of the Common IN, or at any rate widely
distributed, formatives *ma-, man- < ma + n. ber-. tar-*, Mal.
has *mĕ-, mĕn-, bĕr-, tĕr-*. Now Mal. has the tendency to weaken
into *ĕ* the vowel (whatever it may be in Common IN) that
precedes the accentuated syllable; examples: Common IN
banuwa, "country" > Mal. *bĕnuwa*, Common IN *kɔlilin̄*,
"around" > *kĕlilin̄*; and the two loan-words *pĕriksa*, "enquiry", and *sĕrdadu*, "soldier", also illustrate the same process.
Now the above-mentioned formatives also invariably *precede*
the accentuated syllable, and therefore they too have undergone this weakening, and so *mĕ-*, etc., are secondary forms of
the more original *ma-*, etc.

An exception to this principle is the formative *lĕ-* which
fashions verbs out of onomatopœic interjections. *e.g.*, *lĕtak*,
"to tap" *< lĕ + tak*. Here the equivalent of the *ĕ* in other
languages is not *a*, but *e.g.* in Day. *e*, as in *leyop < le + gop*,
"to tap", and in Toba *o*, as in *lon̄in̄ < lo + n̄in̄*, "to make
a shrill sound". But where the vowels correspond to one
another in that way, the *ĕ*, as Mal. has it, represents the
original condition, in conformity with the pĕpĕt-law.

33. To conclude our considerations on the phonetic characteristics of the formatives, we will make some remarks on
infixes. One of the Common IN verbal infixes is *-um-*, *e.g.*
in Old Jav. *lumaku*, "to go", from the WB *laku*. In
place of this infix *-um-* we find in some other languages, *e.g.*
Mentaway and Nias, a prefix *mu-*. Thus from the WB *hede*
Nias forms the verb *muhede*, "to speak". But the texts
show that the *mu + he* in *muhede* can be replaced by *hu + me*,
according to individual taste and fancy. In the Wedding
Song we find the sentence: "Thus spake the old chieftain"
= *hulo muhede lafauluo*; but in the Story of the Captain:
"Why don't you speak?" = Why not s. you? = *hanawa lo*

humede o. Here then a perfectly arbitrary metathesis is permitted; and as it seems to us more natural to assume that prefixes are the more primitive type of formative, we infer from this instance that infixes originated from prefixes through metathesis.

34. We have now dealt with the phonetic aspects of the formatives and turn to the further consideration of these verb-forming syllables. At the beginning of this Section we drew a distinction between formatives and auxiliary words of form. We will now supplement what we said on that subject by adding that the limits of the two concepts are often somewhat vague, inasmuch as the word of form can turn into a formative. By means of the word *buah*, "hit", Day. fashions a passive formula, which is used when it is necessary to speak of pain, disadvantage, and the like; example: *buah rugi*, "to be damaged", really "to be hit (by) damage". Here *buah* is still felt to be an independent word, and therefore it is not joined to the substantive, in this instance *rugi*. But in Hova, where in conformity with phonetic law *buah* appears as *wua*, its use is no longer confined to words that denote damage, disadvantage, or the like; one can also say, for example, *wuasuratra*, "written"; so the root-meaning has faded, and *wua* is now felt to be a formative, and is written together with the WB, in this instance *suratra*. — Illustration from the Testament of Umbiasa: "Written in this book here" = W. in this b. this = *wuasuratra amin iti taratasi iti.*

35. From what has been said in the preceding paragraph it also follows that it is sometimes possible to *explain the origin* of the IN verbal formatives. I will give several such cases here:

I. Many formatives were originally prepositions. Thus a whole series of prepositions meaning "to, towards", in Latin "ad, versus", are used to form the future. In Mkb. *ka*, in Mal. *akan* (an extension of *ka*), in Hova *hu* < *ku* (a variant of *ka*), in Mak. *la*, in Bont. *ad*. In the Bont. sentence from the Story of the Stars: "Then their mother flies up to the sky" = Then flies the m. their to sky =

keceñ tumayaw nan ina ca ad caya, the word *ad* is a preposition; in the sentence from the Battle of Kaloqokan:
" They will appear " = Will a. they = *ad-umali ca*, it is the
sign of the future. In Mak. *la* is no longer a preposition,
but only the sign of the future, while in the languages of the
islands that lie over against New Guinea it is still a preposition. That is shown by the following Kamberese sentence
from the Dirge of the Crocodile for his Dead Friend: " Let us
go to the deep water " = We go to w. d. = *ta laku la wai
mamanjoluñ*. In Sawunese we meet with a use of this *la*
which represents a striking transition from the preposition
to the sign of the future: *la* is only used when the idea of
direction " thither " is combined with the idea of futurity.
Thus in the text Bale ri ane there is a sentence: " It was an
order that one should buy rice " = Order. that " *la* " buy
rice = *li ta la wĕli lailudu*. That means: " The order was
given to *go* and buy rice ". Had the meaning been " The
order was given to come *here* and buy rice ", *la* would not
have been used.

II. Other formatives were originally articles. Thus the
Nias active participle consists of the indicative verb and the
agglutinated article *si*. In the Story of Buruti: " Didn't
you see any man passing just now ? " = Not was + seen by
+ you just + now man passing ? = *lo niila u mege niha
sanoro*, the form *sanoro* consists of the verb *anoro* and the
article *s* < *si*.

Similarly the formative *ñ*, discussed above, was originally
none other than the widely distributed article *ñ*. Originally,
therefore, the Modern Jav. *ula ñuntal*, " the snake swallows ", was *ula ñ untal*, " the snake (is) the swallowing (creature) ". It is true that the fundamental meaning has generally faded away, but there are plenty of cases in which it can
still be perceived. The sentence out of the Bol. dialogues
in Beech: " He abused me " = *saq ñampuki da-aku*, can also,
without doing violence to the meaning, be taken as " He (is
the one) that abused me " = *saq ñ ampuki da-aku*. — This
phenomenon, of the formative *ñ* being really an article, has
another IN parallel, which will occupy us in Section VII.

Just as they say "The snake is *the* swallowing creature", so
they also say, as we shall there see: "The snake, *it* is sleeping".
Here, too, the fundamental meaning has generally faded away,
and the whole thing means no more than: "The snake is
sleeping".

III. We have already met with a *verbal* WB, *buah*, which
has become a formative. Later on we shall come across an
adjective or adverb, *pura*, that has had the same fate. The
causative formative *pa-* is identical with the causal *conjunc-*
tion pa. And so on.

36. The IN verb possesses formatives to express, above
all, the three genera, active, causative and passive; and that
condition of things must be styled Common IN. In the
Bis. Riddle about the Ship, in Starr's Collection of Riddles:
"It runs with its back" = Runs goes + on + its + back =
nagalakat nagahayan, naga- is an active formative. In the
Tarakan Story of the Tailed Man: "You made me go" = You
made + go me = *dudu palakaw daka, pa-* is a causative formative. In the Talautese Cursing of the Fowl: "It shall be
borne in mind" = *papaghiana, -ana* is a passive formative.

37. It happens not infrequently that verbal formatives
have different meanings in different languages. We will
mention some of these cases:

I. The prefix *ma-* sometimes forms causative, sometimes
accusative,* sometimes neutral, and sometimes passive, verbs.
Examples:

> Day.: *ma-haban*, "to make sick"
> Day.: *ma-haga*, "to guard"
> Day.: *ma-lelak*, "to bloom"
> Bont.: *ma-oto*, "to be cooked".

The WB's are *haban*, "sick", *lelak*, "flower", etc. — We
can comprehend these shiftings of meaning, if we assume
that the neutral signification, as in *malelak*, "to bloom",
was the original one. One can very well understand a transition from the neutral meaning to the active and causative

* [*I.e.* transitive.]

on the one hand, and to the passive on the other.   And there
are languages in which *ma-* is exclusively neutral.   Similarly
we often find uses that fluctuate between the one type and the
other, as in the sentence from the Mentaway Fishermen's
Stories: " The fat fish is now hemmed in " = Fat + fish is
+ hemmed + in = *mokmok maipit.*

II.   The formative *ka*, originally, as shown above, a preposition, does duty in some languages as the sign of the future
active, in others as the sign of the passive without any implication of tense.   Thus the Minangkabau *katiṅa*, " to be about
to stay ", is future; the Bug. *kaҫalla*, " to be accursed ", is
passive.   Here, too, we can give a rational account of the
double evolution of the meaning.   We shall see later on that
in the IN sentence verbs of motion can often be omitted altogether, so that one may simply say: " I into the forest ", " I
out of the town ".   Now if we think of sentences like " I
(am going) to (= *ka*) dinner ", we can well understand that a
future in *ka-* might be evolved out of them;* but it is equally
comprehensible that a passive in *ka-* might grow out of sentences like " I (get) into (= *ka*) the curse ". — Illustrations:
Minangkabau, from the Manjau Ari: " You will stay, I shall
go " = *aṅku ka-tiṅa, den ka-pai.*   Sundanese, from the
Story of Nyai Sumur Bandung: " The story is told, how
Rangga Wayang reached the centre of the town " = It is
told. R. W. reaching to c. t. = *ka-curios Raṅa Wayaṅ sumpiṅ
ka hulu dayöh.*

III.   Common IN has a formative *-ĕn* for forming the imperative passive.   Alongside of this there is a formative *-ĕn*
that has an accusative or causative force; in accordance with
the phonetic laws set forth above it appears in Bug. as *-ĕṅ.*
in Nias as *-o, e.g.* in Nias *balio*, " to transform ", beside *bali*.
" to turn back, to return." — Now here, in the case of these
two *-ĕn*'s, the imperative passive and the causative active
one, I can think of no connecting link, nor have I found any-

* [The analogy of the English " I am going to dine " is so close that
the author would doubtless have mentioned it if he had been writing
in English or for English readers.]

where anything that looked like an intermediate stage between them.

38. The IN verbal formatives have as a rule three functions: a single IN verbal form represents, first, the infinitive, secondly, the participle, and, thirdly, the finite verb, of Indo-European languages. This state of things is to be styled Common IN, although we have, as above in Nias, found exceptions to it, and shall meet with others hereafter. Thus the Old Jav. *atukar* $<$ *a* + WB *tukar*, according to the context, must sometimes be rendered by " to brawl ", sometimes by " brawling ", or by " (I) brawl, (you) brawl ", etc. The same thing applies to the Hova *milefa*, " to flee ", the Bug. *maqrola*, " to prosecute ", etc., etc. — Illustrations:

I. Old Jav., Jonker's Book of Laws, from the sections about brawling: " Struck by the kĕris of the brawlers " = S. through the k. of the brawling (persons) = *kasuduk deni ñ kĕris i ñ atukar.* " If he begins to brawl " = *yen ambakalana atukar.*

II. Hova, Book of the Laws of Ranawaluna, from the sections about fugitive slaves: " A fleeing slave, if he steals " = A sl. f., if st. = *ni andewu milefa, raha mañgalatra.* " The slave of a soldier, if he flees " = *ni andewu n ni miaramila, raha milefa.*

III. Bug., Book of Laws of Amanna Gappa, from the sections about judicial procedure: " The prosecutor speaks first " = Person prosecuting the first speaks = *to maqrola e riyolo maqtuqtu.*

39. The addition of formatives to a WB not infrequently entails modifications, either slight or more pronounced, in the meaning of the word. In some languages, *e.g.* Day., this is less marked than in others, *e.g.* Bug. or Mak. Example:

I. Dayak.

WB *sala*	" wrong "
basala	" to be in the wrong, to do wrong "
mañala	" to accuse, to act wrongly ".

II. Makassar.

WB *salu*	" wrong, fault "
maqsala	" to be different "
maqñala	" to be guilty "
pisala	" to miss (in shooting) "
pisalai	" to frustrate (a plan) "
pasalu	" to pay a penalty (in money) "
pasalañi	" to impose a fine "
pañalañi	" to infringe (a regulation) "
kasalai	" to be undutiful (towards one's parents) ".

40. The number of formatives that can be attached to the WB *at one time* varies in the different IN languages, but hardly ever exceeds four. From the point of view of its capacity to form these combinations, the most interesting language is perhaps the Bug. In the Tiruray sentence from the collection of dialogues of an anonymous author: " I am hungry " $=$ *melayaf u*, the verb has only the one formative, *me-*. In the Bug. sentence from the Injilai: " She was recognized everywhere " $= $ W. $+$ r. $+$ e. s. $=$ *riasiisĕñi (n) i*, we have, to begin with, the WB *isĕñ*, " to know ", and then four formatives: *a*, which simply turns the WB into a verb; *i*, which makes it transitive; *si*, which expresses the " everywhere " ; and *ri*, the passive formative.

41. The number of formatives possessed by the several IN languages varies greatly. The richest in this respect are the languages of the North, of Formosa, the Philippines, the intervening islands, and Northern Celebes; Sangirese, for instance, has about a hundred. The poorest in formatives are the languages of the East, Bim., for example, having only two, viz. *ma-* and *ka-*. The remaining regions occupy an intermediate position in this respect.

42. Lastly, the formative methods of fashioning verbs also include the method of reduplication, which is a particularly common IN feature in other parts of speech besides the verb, occurs in the most various shapes, and mostly indicates plurality, intensification, and the like. The following are selected cases of specifically verbal reduplication; none of them can be called Common IN.

I. Mentaway has a *threefold* or *fourfold* repetition, wherein the final consonant is omitted except at the very end, when the WB appears for the last time. Illustration from the Fishermen's Stories: "He goes, wanders continually, comes to his mother" = Goes he, w. c., c. to m. his = *konat ña. toro-toro-toro-torot, śägä ka ina iña.*

Note.—Initial *ś* in Mentaway, as in *śägä,* sounds pretty much like *sch* in the German " schön ".*

II. Bug. has a *threefold* repetition, with the formative *ka-* or *si-* interpolated in between. — Illustrations, from the Injilai: "He went hither and thither" = *na lao na ka-lao-lao.* "He wept continually" = *těrri si-těrri-těrri na.*

Note.—The first *na,* the one before *lao,* means " he "; the other two are particles of emphasis.

III. Mak. has a *twofold* repetition, with interpolation of the word of form *sañga* or *sañge.* — Illustration, from the Epic Maqdi: "Then were urgently summoned the four pillars of the state " = *nikiyoq-m-i-sañga-kiyoq toqdoq appak a.*

Note A.—The *m* < *mo* is the particle of emphasis, and *i* means " they ". *appak,* " four ", *a,* " the ".

Note B.—This Mak. type of reduplication is not common. An analysis of the whole of the Maqdi only yields one case, viz. the one quoted above. In the whole of the Epic Datu Museng there are two cases: *kiyoq-sañge-kiyoq* and *kape-sañge-kape,* " to beckon repeatedly ".

IV. In several of the Philippine languages, which have a real system of moods and tenses, reduplication plays a great part, whereof we shall have to speak hereafter.

* [In English " sh ", as in " shine ".]

SECTION IV: THE THREE GENERA, THE PRINCIPAL CHARACTERISTIC OF THE INDONESIAN VERB.

43. The great majority of IN languages possess the capacity of forming the three genera of the verb: the active, the causative, and the passive. This phenomenon, therefore, is Common IN. It is the chief characteristic of the IN verb.

44. We have learnt that the languages of the East are very poor morphologically. So it is striking that even there we still find languages that possess the three genera, as, for example, Kamberese. Illustrations:

I. Active, formative *ma-*. From the Song at House-building: " Marapu, who created men " = *na Marapu na mawulu tau.*

II. Causative, formative *pa-*. From the Harvest Song: " Let this arrive at the top ! " = L. ÷ a. this to top = *patoama ña la pinu.*

III. Passive, formative *ka-*. From the Song against the Son-in-law: " She runs around, as though maddened " = *na laku biñu katoaba.*

45. We have seen above that there are WB's that can do duty in the sentence as active or passive verbs, without the help of any formative. But the usual rule is that the language requires formatives. I have never come across causatives without a formative.

46. *The Active.* The Common IN formatives for forming the active are:

> *ma-*
> *ñ-*, or in place thereof *mañ-* < *ma* ÷ *ñ*
> *um-*, or *-um-*.

The formative *um* is a prefix with words having an initial vowel, an infix where they have an initial consonant.

47. The active formative *ma-*. Proof that it is Common IN:

Formosa, Form. dialect: *matagga*, " to bleed ".
Philippines, Bont.:   *masuyep*, " to sleep ".
Celebes, Bungku: *mahaki*, " to be sick ".
Borneo, Basa Sangiang: *mahampan*, " to have a border ".
Near Java. Bal.:   *mahumah*, " to dwell ".
Islands near New Guinea,
   Kamberese: *malala*. " to cook ".
Sumatra, Lampong: *mabursog*, " to speak through the nose ".
Islands at the back of
   Sumatra, Mentaway: *maloto*, " to be afraid ".
Madagascar. Sakalava: *mataotra*, " to fear ".

48. The active formative *ñ-*, or its substitute *mañ-*. Proof that it is Common IN:

Philippines, Bont.:   *managñi*, " to dance ".
Celebes, Bug.:   *ñanro*, " to ask ".
Togian Islands. Bajo: *ñinum*. " to drink ".
Borneo, Basa Sangiang: *ñujan*, " to rain ".
Java, Modern Jav.:   *ñutus*, " to send ".
Islands near New Guinea.
   Sumbawarese: *ñaji*, " to teach ".
Sumatra, Karo: *ñapit*, " to pinch ".
Islands at the back of
   Sumatra, Mentaway: *mañaray*, " to climb ".
Madagascar. Old Mlg.:   *nilu*, " to shine ".

Note A.—The WB's of these verbs are: *sagñi, kanro, inum, ujan, utus, aji. apit. karay.* and *ilu.* The phonetic processes here displayed, *e.g.* by *ñanro*, have been discussed above. Old Mlg. *nilu* is for *ñilu*, in strict conformity with phonetic law.

Note B.—Hova and the Mlg. of Ferrand's texts usually have the longer form of the prefix: *man- < mañ-*. *nilu* is one of the few examples known to me of the shorter form; it occurs at the beginning of the sermon Tonih Zañahary.

49. The active formative *um-* or *-um-*. Proof that it is Common IN:

Formosa, Form. dialect: *comma*, " to speak ".
Philippines, Bont.:   *uminum*, " to drink ".
Celebes, Tontb.:   *kuman*, " to eat ".
Borneo, Day.:   *kuman*, " to eat ".
Java, Old Jav.:   *kuměmit*, " to watch ".
Sumatra, Toba: *sumuruṅ*, " to improve ".
Islands at the back of
  Sumatra, Simalurese: *lumañoy*, " to swim ".
Malay Peninsula, Mal.:   *gumilaṅ*, " to shine ".
Madagascar, Hova: *humana*, " to eat ".

Note A.—The WB's are *ka, inum, kan, kěmit*, etc.

Note B.—The number of cases in which this formation occurs in Day. and Hova is small.

Note C.—The Form. *comma* has been left unaltered in its clumsy spelling; it corresponds with the Tontb. *kuma*, WB *ka*.

50. Illustrations of the three active formatives. Old Jav., from the Kuñjarakarṇa: " Others ran away " = *waneh malayū*; from the Śakuntalā: " He then saw a woman " = S. t. he w. = *anon ta sira strī*; from the Kamahāyānikan: " To penetrate into the holy mystery " = *tumama ri saṅ hyaṅ paramarahasya*. Modern Jav., from Meijer Ranneft's Collection of Riddles: " A snake swallows a mountain " = *ula ṅuntal gunuṅ*.

Note.—*anon* is *a* + *ṅ* + WB *ton*.

51. Specific signification of the three active formatives. In several languages *ma-* is intransitive, *ṅ-* or *maṅ-* transitive; but in other languages the active formatives apparently only serve to form the active, without any other shade of meaning. The formative *-um-* usually plays the part of an aorist, inchoative, or future, and that state of things may perhaps be styled Common IN. — Illustrations of this force of the formative *-um-*. Bont., from the Head-hunters' Ceremonies: " They start for the settlement " = Start they to t. s. = *sumaa ca is nan fobfüy*. Tontemboan, from the Story of the Demon

that haunts women at childbirth: " She came quickly, in order
to clutch them " = *sia mĕlaqu-laqus (omai) tumaṅkaq isera*.
Old Jav. from Mpu Tanakung's Prosody: " Startled by the
birds bathing (they—the gaudily-coloured fish—) flashed
upwards " = S. by the birds b., flashed-up = *kagyat dem ṅ
paksi madyus kumĕlab*.

52. Alongside of the three principal active formatives,
ma-, *-ṅ*, *-um-*, there are secondary formatives. I call them so
because they are less widely distributed. I would mention
the following as being the most interesting of them:

I. The formative *r-*, which can also unite with the formative *a-* to form *ar-*, and with *ma-* to form *mar-*. Here, too, as
between *r-* and *mar-* we have the same relation as in the case of
ṅ- and *maṅ-*. This *r-*, just like *ṅ-*, was originally an article, in
Old Jav. it is an unemphatic pronoun of the third person.
The shorter form *r-* is rare, it is found in Karo, *e.g.*, *rĕlbuh*, " to
call " < *r* + WB *ĕlbuh*. The longer form is spread over
Sumatra, Java, Celebes, Borneo, and the Philippines. In
Bug. and Mak. the formative is *maq-* or *aq-*, in Tag. *mag-*, in
conformity with the phonetic laws already explained. — Illustrations of the active formatives *r-* and *mar-*. Karo, from
the Story of the Glutton: " There is somebody calling from
down below " = Calls from below hither = *rĕlbuh i tĕruh nari*.
Bug., from a letter of Lasiri's to Matthes, wherein he complains
that the police arrest him when he is going about by night to
make enquiries for Matthes about rare Bug. words: " If it is
possible, (give me a letter of attestation) " = If possible + is
it = *bara maqkulle i*. Mak., from the anonymous collection
of Mak. Dialogues: " Do not shoot so hastily ! " = Not you
hastily shoot = *teya ko karo-karo aqmaqdiliq*.

II. The formative *ba-*, which can also combine with the
formative *r-* into *bar-*, without change of meaning. This
formative is widely distributed. But as a *living* formative it
only exists in a few languages, for example in Day., which
has both *ba-* and *bar-*, and in that Sumbawarese dialect which
is known to us only by the Story of the Dog's Dung. This
text only contains 27 lines, and yet there are to be found in it

5 distinct cases of verbs in *ba-*, such as *ba-lañan*, " to go ",
ba-rari, " to run away "; but when we find in 27 lines 5 cases
of verbs formed with *ba-*, we are entitled to regard that formative as a living one. The Day. *ba-* forms intransitive verbs,
and such too are the 5 Sumbawarese ones. — Apart from this
there are *isolated cases* in many IN languages of verbs formed
with *ba*.

Philippines, Bis.:	*baigad*, " to scrape ".
Celebes, Mak.:	*baloliq*, " to roll up ".
Java, Sund.:	*bagĕnah*, " to be happy ".
Islands at the back of Sumatra,	
Mentaway:	*baliyu*, " to fill ".
Madagascar, Hova:	*wawenti*, " to be massive ".

Note.—The WB of Bis. *baigad*, viz. *igad*, does not exist in
Bis. itself, but is found in Iloko; similarly, the WB of Mentaway *baliyu* occurs in Mak.

53. Besides these active formatives there are very many
others that occur occasionally in one language or another,
e.g. Old Jav. *a-*, which alternates with *ma-*; Bug. *keq-*, which
denotes possession; Day. *me-* or *mi-*, which has been discussed
above, etc., etc.

54. Now of all these active formatives one language will
possess a larger stock, another a smaller one. By way of
example, let us enumerate all the living active formatives that
are found in Toba:

Formative	*ma-*	*maribak*, " to be torn ".
	mañ-	*mañanto*, " to pay attention ".
	mar-	*marhosa*, " to breathe ".
	masi-	*masihoda*, " to buy horses ".
	marsi-	*marsibuni*, " to hide oneself ".
	marha-	*marhapili*, " to be biassed ".
	marhu-	*marhuraja*, " to beseech ".
	mañin-	*mañintubu*, " to beget ".
	mañun-	*mañunsande*, " to lean against ".
	patu-	*patuñosños*, " to clench the teeth (with
	-um-	*humordit*, " to shiver ". pain) ".
	-ar- or *-al-*	*dumarede*, " to trickle ".

55. Now there are also cases in which the same WB and the same active formative run *together* through so many languages, that one is compelled to style the whole formation a Common IN one. Such a case is *manali*, " to bind " < *man* +*tali*, " cord ".

Philippines, Tag.:	*manali*
Borneo, Day.:	*manali*
Java, Old Jav.:	*manali*
Sumatra, Toba:	*manali*
Islands at the back of Sumatra, Nias:	*manali*
Madagascar, Hova:	*manadi* < *manali*.

56. *The Causative.* There is *one* Common IN causative formative, namely *pa-*. Proof that it is Common IN:

Formosa, Form. dialect:	*paita*, " to let see ".
Philippines, Nabaloi:	*pabunu*, " to cause to kill ".
Celebes, Bug.:	*papole*, " to cause to come ".
Borneo, Tar.:	*paakan*, " to let eat ".
Java, Sund.:	*pasak*, " to make well done (*i.e.* completely cooked) ".
Islands near New Guinea, Kamberese:	*palaku*, " to let go ".
Sumatra, Angkola:	*pauli*, " to make beautiful ".
Islands behind Sumatra, Mentaway:	*pakom*, " to let eat ".
Madagascar, Hova:	*mam-paturi*, " to let sleep ".

57. Illustrations of the causative: Bont., from the Story of the Stars: " The mother made the brother fly " = Made + f. m. b. = *inpatayaw ina kawwaan*. Bug., from the Injilai: " He made them go aboard his vessel " = He made + mount them in ship his = *na panoq i ri lopi na*. Mentaway, from the Dialogues about the Priesthood: " They make them healthy " = Make + healthy = *paaru*.

Note.—In *inpatayaw* the *in-* is the sign of the past tense. The WB of *panoq* is *noq*, " to mount up into ".

58. In several languages the causative formative *pa-* takes one or other of the active formatives in front of it, without any modification of meaning; thus in Day. we find by the side of *pa-* a form *mampa-*, and it is a point not to be overlooked that Hova also has *mampa-*, whence the above *mampaturi*, " to let sleep ".

59. Alongside of *pa-*, the chief formative of the causative, there is the less widely distributed secondary form *paka-*. We find it in the Philippines, Celebes, Java, and the islands at the back of Sumatra, *e.g.* in Nias under the form *faqa-*. — Illustration of this causative formative: Bareqe, from the Story of the Deer and the Water-Snail: " Pay particular attention ! " = You let + be + alive ears yours = *ni pakanaa taliña mi*. The WB is *naa*.

60. Besides the above-named formatives there are a considerable number of others forming the causative that occur more occasionally, in one language or another, *e.g.*, *pe-*, *pu-*, and in Bug. *-ĕñ*, with which (as we already know) Nias *-o* is identical, etc.

61. As in the case of the active, so here too in that of the causative we will enumerate all the formatives that occur in a particular language. In this instance we select Bug., the examples are all from the Injilai:

Formative *pa-*   *panoq*, " to let mount ".
           maqpa-   *maqpatĕlloñ*, " to erect ".
           po-   *powata*, " to make a slave of ".
           paka-   *pakĕda* < *paka* + *ĕda*, " to let speak ".
           -ĕñ   *lĕppĕssĕñ*, " to set free ".

62. As in the case of the active, we will give an instance here of the same WB and the same causative formative running *together* through a number of languages. The WB is *iram*, which also appears under the forms *idam*, *injam*, etc.. according to the phonetic peculiarities of the several languages. The WB means " loan ", the causative, therefore, " to effect a loan ", which expression is used sometimes for " borrowing " and sometimes for " lending ".

Philippines. Tag.:	*magpahiram*
Celebes, Mak.:	*painran*
Borneo, Bol.:	*painjam*
Near Java, Mad.:	*apaenjham*
Madagascar, Hova:	*mampindrana.*

63. *The passive.* There are two passive formatives that we can call Common IN: *ta-* and *in.* The latter, like the active formative *um,* is a prefix before words that begin with a vowel and almost always an infix in those that begin with a consonant. Proof that the passive formative *ta-* is Common IN:

Philippines, Bis.:	*takilid,* " to be inclined ".
Celebes, Bungku:	*tapeha,* " to be broken ".
Borneo, Tar.:	*tadagu.* " to be spoken ".
Java, Old Jav.:	*tawurag,* " to be scattered ".
Islands near New Guinea,	
Sawunese:	*tabolo.* " to be submerged ".
Sumatra, Toba:	*talentes,* " to be opened ".
Islands at the back of Sum-	
atra, Mentaway:	*taico,* " to be seen ".
Madagascar, Hova:	*taburnaka,* " to be pierced ".

64. The second passive formative is *in.* Proof that it is Common IN:

Philippines, Tag.:	*tinawag,* " to be called ".
Celebes, Bulu:	*winunu.* " to be killed ".
Borneo, Bol.:	*jinawal,* " to be lost ".
Java, Old Jav.:	*inambah,* " to be trodden on ".
Islands near New Guinea,	
Kupangese:	*inka,* " to be eaten ".
Sumatra, Lampong:	*tinabor,* " to be strewn ".
Islands at the back of Sum-	
atra, Mentaway:	*tinibo,* " to be dried ".
Madagascar, Hova:	*tinapaka,* " to be broken ".

65. Other important passive formatives that are fairly widely distributed are, above all, *ka-,* next *tar-,* for which Bug. and Mak. have *taq-,* further *-an,* etc.

66. Illustrations of the passive formatives. Mak., from the Jayalangkara: " (Jayalangkara saw the snake), then he was frightened " = Was + frightened J. = *taq-baṅka* (*mi*) *Jayalaṅkara*. Old Malagasy, from the sermon Tonih Zaña-hary: " Noah was saved alive " = The N. was + saved + alive = *ra Nuhu winelun*. Basa Sangiang, from the 14th Dirge: " Supported by the sheath of a sword " = S. sword-sheath = *kañokah kumpan̄*. Modern Jav., from the drama Prabu Dewa Sukma, 8th Act: " It is not known whether the corpse has been hacked to pieces or burnt " = Not + know, hacked + to + pieces, burnt = *tambuh cinacah kabĕsmi*.

67. Shades of meaning conveyed by the passive formatives. Of the two chief passive formatives, *in* and *ta-*, or *tar-*, the first generally forms a pure passive, the other often involves a sug-gestion of unintentional action, chance happening, or possi-bility. — Illustrations. Mak., from the third Elegy: " (I would keep her) in a casket that could not be opened " = In c. not to + be + opened that = *ri patti ta taqsuṅke ya*. Mkb., from the Manjau Ari: " Innumerable is the number of the prawns " = Not to + be + counted number prawns = *tiduq tabado bañaq udan̄*.

68. As in the cases of the active and causative, we will here enumerate all the passive formatives that are to be found in a particular language; in this instance we select Day.:

Formative	*ba-*	*bakunci*, " to be locked ".
	i-	*iagah*, " to be led ".
	ta-	*talenten̄*, " to be lopped ".
	tar-	*tarajar*, " to be teachable ".
	tapa-	*tapaisä*, " to be counted ".

Note.—The Day. formative *tapa-* also appears, as *tafa-*, in Hova, a point not to be overlooked.

69. As in the cases of the active and causative so here too in connexion with the passive we will give an instance of the same WB and the same formative running *together* through a

number of languages.   The WB is *bunu*, "to kill", also " to
fight ", or in other forms *wunu, bono*, etc.

Philippines, Tag.:	*binono*
Celebes, Bulu:	*winunu*
Java, Old Jav.:	*winunuh*
Sumatra, Toba:	*binunu*
Madagascar, Hova:	*wununu.*

Note.—In the Hova form the *i* of the infix has become assim -
ilated to the *u* of the WB.   In Section III we met with an
analogous assimilation in Day., a point that is not to be overlooked.

70.   Correlation of the passive with the active.

I.   It very often happens that certain passive formations are
closely connected with certain active ones.   Old Jav. -*um*-
forms actives with an aorist sense, and the like shade of meaning is indicated by the passive *ka*-; hence the active in -*um*-
and the passive in *ka*- are correlated together.

II.   But just as often no such close connexion exists between active and passive forms respectively.   Old Jav. has
an active formative *ma*-, which mostly forms intransitive
verbs, but also transitive ones: thus in the Śakuntalā there is
the sentence: " No one did evil " = Not was man did evil =
tātan hana wwan magawe hala.   This active in *ma*- in Old Jav.
has no specific passive correlative.

III.   In Bug. there is a passive derived from the WB *gauq*,
" blue ", viz. *rigauq*, " to be coloured blue ", but there is no
corresponding active. — Alongside of the Hova *manduka*, " to
throw a spear ", from the WB *luka*, there are two passives:
aluka, " to be thrown ", said of the spear, and *lukana*, " to be
hit ", said of the person.

IV.   In certain IN languages it has become a regular
custom for the transitive active to be accompanied by two
passives.   The Mlg. grammar calls one of them simply " the
passive ", the other " the relative ".

71.   Use of the passive.   The passive is used much more
frequently in IN than it is in the better-known Indo-European

languages. And this phenomenon is so widespread that we must style it Common IN. Proof:

I. By the evidence of translations. The expression in the Sanskrit original of the Prasthānikaparwa: *phalam prāpnoti* is in the Old Jav. recension rendered by: *phala pinaṅgih*.* The *prāpnoti* of the original is active, *pinaṅgih* on the other hand is a passive, formed with the infix -*in*-. — The passage in Tell, where Stüssi says: " He is now gone to fetch the bride at Imisee ", is rendered by Rizal by the passive construction: " The bride at Imisee is now being fetched (= *susunduin*) by him ".

II. By the evidence of enumerations. In the Day. story of the Chopper and the Buffaloes there are upwards of 24 passives in something under 100 lines. — The short episode beginning " *sĕrta ditikamña* " in the battle of the five friends with the pirates in the Hang Tuah contains 9 actives and 6 passives. — In the detailed account of the battle in the Old Jav. Mausalaparwa the number of actives and passives is approximately equal; *e.g.* the following passage occurs: " Reeds were pulled up, they were used as weapons, for they turned into clubs wherewith blows were dealt on the adversaries ".

72. The frequency of the passive is to be explained as follows: In all the IN languages it is a matter of great moment to emphasize by linguistic means that element of the sentence which is considered the most important one. These means include: intonation, unusual syntactical order, particles of emphasis, and also the choice between the active and the passive construction. If the subject is to be put into the foreground, the active is chosen; if it be desired to lay stress on the object, recourse is had to the passive construction, *i.e.* the object is made the subject. In the Toba Sangmaima, therefore, the construction is not as might have been expected: " The mother went to cook and killed a fowl for the dinner ", but: " and a fowl was killed by her "; for the point of importance is not that *she* killed, but rather *what it was* that she killed.

* *I.e.,* " to get one's due ".

73. The verbal systems.

I. We have learnt that the IN languages often have several
formatives that perform precisely the same function. If, for
example, we analyse the Hova descriptive piece " Fiana-
kaviana " in Julien, we see that the two formatives *mi* and
man < *ma* + *n̄* occur in it particularly frequently. It contains
6 verbs in *man-* and 7 in *mi-*. In all the 13 cases the formative
simply creates an active transitive verb, without any special
shade of meaning; *manasa lamba* means " to wash clothes ",
but *mitutu wari* " to pound rice ". — In Old Jav. the two
active formatives *a-* and *ma-* can be used for one another at
pleasure, and the same applies to the Bug. *aq-* and *maq-*.
If we analyse the Prasthānikaparwa from that point of view,
we see that *e.g.* "he made" is represented on some occasions by
sira agawe and on others by *sira magawe*. The meaning is
absolutely the same, and so is the situation: in both cases the
word that precedes the verb ends in *-a*.

II. On the basis of the condition sketched in I. above,
several of the IN languages have elaborated a series of verbal
systems running parallel and side by side with one another,
much like the Latin conjugations in *a* and *e*. As a specimen
I here exhibit the two systems of Mentaway:

THE *a*- SYSTEM.

Active	Causative	Passive
ma-loto, " to be afraid "	*pa-äru*, " to make healthy "	*ta-ico*, " to be seen "

THE *u*- SYSTEM.

Active	Causative	Passive
mu-kom, " to eat "	*pu-jinin̄*, " to cause to sound "	*tu-bätäk*, " to be bent (as a bow)"

The fullest development of this principle is the elaboration
of the Bug. verbal systems in *a* and *e*, which I have dealt with
in a former monograph.*

* [" Sprachvergleichendes Charakterbild eines indonesischen Idiomes ", §§ 84-99.]

SECTION V : THE MOODS.

74. Among the moods the imperative is the one that is most elaborated in **IN**; it displays the greatest number of formatives. The conjunctive is much more scantily equipped. The modal shades of meaning represented by " can, may, must, shall, and will " are mostly expressed with the aid of auxiliary words of form, though the conjunctive can also perform those functions. The same applies to the irrealis. And it often happens that the sentence contains no linguistic element at all, apart from intonation. whereby we can recognize the mood.

75. *The imperative.* Nearly all the IN languages possess imperative WB's, *i.e.* WB's that exist only as imperatives. Examples: Nias *aine*, " come ! ", Karo *ota*, " let us go ! ", Day. *hua*, " attention ! " — Illustration, Karo, from the Story of the Glutton: " Let us go home ! " = *ota ku rumah.*

It is deserving of particular notice that practically all the IN languages have an imperative word for the idea " lo ! ", " behold ! ", though each language has a different one: Bont. *nay,* Nias *hiza*, Hova *indru*, etc. — Illustrations. Nias, from the Consecration Song on the gold ornament: " Finished is the jewel, behold ! perfected is the glittering of the gold " = *noaway ganaqa, hiza ! nomaulu zaquso.* Hova, from the Testament of Umbiasa: " Behold, (my) son, the counsels" = *indru anaka ni anatra.*

76. Apart from these imperative WB's, the *active imperative* is formed, in the *first* place, by omitting the formatives, or to express it more accurately, by uttering the WB in a tone of command, request, entreaty, and the like, so as to express this mood. Thus in the Day. Story about saying " H'm " we find the sentence: " Fetch the sirih-vessel and bring it here ! " = F. v. s., b. h. = *duan sarahan sipa, imbit katoh.* The indicatives of these imperatives are *manduan* $<$ *maṅ + duan* and *mimbit* $<$ *ma + imbit*. This kind of imperative formation is found in all the IN languages, and is accordingly Common IN; even languages that generally employ some other method always exhibit a few cases of the one just described. In Hova I know only the one instance: *fuha*, " wake up ! ", the indicative of which is *mifuha*.— Illustrations. Old Jav., from the Kuñjarakarṇa: " Go, then, into the underworld ! " = *laku ta mareṅ Yamaloka*. Modern Jav., from the drama Prabu Dewa Sukma. Act I.: " And, elder brother, hasten ! " = *lan, kakaṅ, gupuḥ*. Bug., from the Epigrams against Cowardice: " Retire, you cowards ! " = R. y. c. the = *esaq ko kelow e*. Hova, from the Oracular Formulas of Amurunkay: " Awake, oracle !" = *fuha sikidi*. Achinese, from the Story of the Wise Judge: " Speak the truth ! " = S. with truth = *kĕhĕn bak tĕpat*.

77. *Secondly,* a very widespread mode of forming the imperative is to use the indicative as imperative without any change save in intonation. Of all the Mentaway texts the second Story of the Great Bear contains the greatest number of imperatives: therein we find formations like: " You, fish !" = *äkäw manuba*. This *manuba* $<$ *maṅ + tuba* is also indicative. Alongside of it there are formations like *pana*, " shoot !" This *pana* is also indicative, so here there is nothing omitted in the imperative, as there was in the Day. *duan* above. — In Matthijsen's Tettum dialogues there is a passage: " Where shall I lay them ? Lay them here !" = Shall lay where ? Lay here ! = *atu tau basa? tau banee*. Here the same word *tau* is both indicative and imperative. it is a simple, underived verb. — In the Tontb. Sacrificial Prayer there is a sentence " Drink there. you gods !" = *mĕlĕp aṅe, e kasuruan ;* and in the Dirge for the Dead Mother we find: " It is not yet time to drink " = Not + yet time drink = *raqipeq toro mĕlĕp*. Here the same form *mĕlĕp* is both indicative and imperative, and it is a derived verb, formed from the WB *ĕlĕp*.

78. A *third* mode of forming the imperative consists in the use of specific imperative formatives differing from those of the indicative and conjunctive.

I. A fairly widely distributed formative is *pa-*, which in this case has, of course, no causative meaning. It is found in the Philippines, in Magindanao; in Java, in Old Javanese; in Sumatra, in Toba; in the islands at the back of Sumatra, in Nias. — Illustrations. Old Jav., from the Kuñjarakarṇa: "Clasp his feet!" = C. f. h. = *paměkuli jön ira*. Magindanao, from Juanmarti's Collection of Dialogues: "Wake up! I am awake already" = Awake! Am + awake I already = *pagedam! nakagedam aku den*.

II. Nias has the formatives *a-* and *o-*, *i.e.* the *m* of the indicative form beginning with *ma-* or *mo-* is omitted. Thus from a WB *gule*, "vegetables", are formed an indicative *mogule*, "to cook vegetables", and an imperative *ogule*. Illustration, from the Story of the Strange Cook: "Well, cook vegetables!" = *lau, ogule*.

We have noticed on several occasions that Hova has special relations with Day. But it also shares all sorts of peculiarities with the languages of Sumatra and the islands at the back of Sumatra. Thus the Nias mode of forming the imperative is also found in Hova: from *leha*, "step", are formed the indicative *mandeha*, "to go", and the imperative *andeha*. Illustration, from Rahidy's Fable of the Crocodile: "Let us (= *isika*) go (and) swear blood-brotherhood!" = *andeha isika hifamatidra*.

79. A *fourth* kind of imperative is constituted by using the conjunctive as an imperative.

I. In Old Jav. *-a* forms the conjunctive, in Modern Jav. the formations in *-a* are used as conjunctives *and* as imperatives, in the dialects of Madagascar only as imperatives. Still, even in Old Jav. we already find passages where *-a* has an imperative function. — Illustrations. Old Javanese, from the Āśramawasanaparwa: "Conclude an agreement!" = *gumawayakěna ñ sandhi*. Old Mlg., from the sermon Harireunau: "Assent!" = *meteza hanaw* (= 2nd person singular pronoun).

II. We have learnt that the formative *-um-* produces aorists, futures, and conjunctives. Hence in some languages it is also used to form imperatives as well, *e.g.* in Tontb. Illustration, from the Dirge for the Dead Mother: " Step down here !" = *tumuli mai*. — In Tag. *-um-* is the regular formative of the imperative, the indicative having a different one. — Illustration, from Tell: " Quick, old man, set to work !" = *dali, matanda, gumawa*.

80.   We know that the IN languages have no word corresponding to the Indo-European copula " to be ". Therefore sentences in which, in our languages, the copula forms, or introduces, the predicate, have no verb in IN. In such cases the imperative is expressed merely by intonation. Illustration, Mentaway, from the Fishermen's Stories : " Be my bride !" = Bride my you = *madi ku äkäw*.

81.   The imperative of the *causative* is analogous to that of the active. In Hova *maturi* is " to sleep ", *mampaturi*, " to cause to sleep "; the corresponding imperatives are: *maturia* and *mampaturia*. In Bug. the causative *patĕttoñ* is both indicative and imperative. — Illustration, from the first executioner's story in the Injilai: " Erect it (= the house) at midday !" = At midday of day the you erect it = *ri tĕñĕsso na ĕssow e mu patĕttoñ i*.

82.   The imperative of the *passive* has the formative *-ĕn*, in Tag. *-in*, in Toba *-on*, in conformity with the phonetic laws already stated. This formative has a considerable distribution, being found in the languages of the Philippines, Northern Celebes, Java, and Sumatra. — Illustrations. Tag., from Tell: " Forget it now (and live only for joy) !" = Must + be + forgotten by + you = *limutin mo*. Tontb., from the first Vampire Story: " Let us only look for crabs !" = Must + be + sought by + us only c. = *umuñĕn ta reqe komañ*. Toba, from the Sangmaima: " What then must be done by me ?" = *beha ma bahenon ku*.

83.   The imperative is often accompanied by particles, which make it stronger, or milder, or more polite, and so on. This usage may be called Common IN. In Old Jav. and Bont. *ta* is used in that way, in Day. *has*, etc., etc. Illustrations.

Old Jav., from Mpu Tanakung's Prosody: " Do hurry !" =
D. h. you = *ta iṅgal kita*. Bont., from the Story of the
Brothers and the Rat: " Do let us go into my house !" = Do
go we i. h. m. = *ta umü̈y tako is afoṅ ko*. Day., from the Story
of the Inner Bark of the Tree: " Well," said Hatalla, " be it
so !" = *has, koan Hatalla, jadi*.

84. Later on we shall meet with a widespread particle *ma*,
mo, *mĕ*, *ma-ma*, *ma-lah*, etc., which serves to emphasize the
predicate. It is also used extremely often with the imperative.
Illustrations. Toba, from the Sangmaima: " Prepare provisions !" = *bahen ma bohal*. Mkb., from the Manjau Ari:
" Do smoke tobacco !" = *isoq malah santo*. Mak., from the
Epic Maqdi: " Only say it (and we will act according to your
words) " = Say only = *maqkana mama*.

85. The IN languages have two kinds of negatives, one for
the indicative and another for the imperative. This phenomenon is so widespread that we must call it Common IN.
Thus Masaretese has the two negatives *mohe* and *bara*. — Illustrations. Masaretese, from the Garuda Story: " His children
did not grow big " = His children the not big = *rinenake anat
ro mohe haat*; " Do not be malicious !" =Not you m. = *bara
kimi walekuk*.

But in many IN languages the prohibitive negative takes
the indicative, not the imperative. In Hova " to rule " is, in
the indicative, *mandzáka*, the imperative is *mandzaká* <
mandzaka + *a*. Now in the Testament of Umbiasa we find:
" Do not rule with the flesh, rule with the spirit !" = *aza
mandzáka ami ni nufu, mandzaká ami ni fanahi*.

86. *The Conjunctive*. Only a few IN languages have a
formative for this mood; it is, therefore, not a Common IN
phenomenon. Frequently it is not expressed at all; or else
only by means of auxiliary words of form, such as the Mal.
baraṅ, " possibly ". Special conjunctive formatives exist in
particular in Old Jav. and Bont., the former using *-a*, the
latter *-ed*, or after a vowel *-d*. As already mentioned, the
formative *-um-* may also be used to form the conjunctive;
that occurs in Tontb.

I. The conjunctive in Bont. Illustration, from the Battle of Kaloqokan: " We ought to go to Bontok " = G. w. should to B. = *umüy kami-d ad Funtok*.

II. The conjunctive in Tontemboan. Illustration, from the Story of the Burning of the Vampire: " Do go and tell them ! " = Go do tell to them = *mañe oka kumua an isera*. Here the conjunctive *kumua*, from the WB *kua*, is dependent on the imperative *mañe*.

In Bont. and Tontb. the conjunctive is not often used; in the Battle of Kaloqokan — 192 lines of print — there are only 2 cases. But it occurs quite regularly in Old Jav.

87. The conjunctive in Old Javanese. Its use, whether as a dependent verb or independently, coincides almost completely with the Latin usage.* Thus an analysis of the whole of the Kamahāyānikan — 63 printed pages — has yielded the following results:

I. The conjunctive of reserved utterance : " (You have now been instructed, and so your defects) have probably disappeared " = *hilaña*, corresponding to the indicative *hilaṅ*.

II. The conjunctive of request : " Let (rice, drink, etc.) be offered " = *wehakĕna*.

III. The conjunctive of condition : " If (freedom from desire) be attained (then Buddhahood is also won) " = *an kapaṅguha*.

IV. The concessive conjunctive : " Even though (no beauty) is seen (in your teacher, nevertheless be amiable towards him) " = *yadyapi katona*.

V. The conjunctive in sentences denoting intention : " (Strive after Advaya), in order that (your defects) may disappear " = *yatānyan hilaña*.

VI. The conjunctive after verbs of command : " (The order shall be given) that (these men) be slain " = *pĕjahana*.

* [The reader will notice that English idiom does not always make it convenient to render these IX conjunctives by our corresponding mood.]

VII. The conjunctive after verbs of permission: " (It is not permitted) to indulge in (love in the temple) " = *gumawa-yakĕna.*

VIII. The conjunctive after verbs of doubt and hesitation: " (Do not hesitate) to practise (the holy Samaya) " = *gumawa-yakĕna.*

88. The *Optative* is either an imperative, or else it makes use of special auxiliary verbs, or, most frequently, the above-mentioned particles of emphasis, *ma, mama, lah, malah,* etc. — Illustration, Mkb., from the Manjau Ari: " May he quickly grow big ! " = Quickly " *lah* " big = *dareh lah gadaṅ.*

89. The *Potential* has the formative *maka-,* which has a considerable distribution, being found in the Philippines, Celebes, and Madagascar. — Illustration, Bont., from the Story of the Stars: " But he cannot fly " = But not can fly = *ya adi makatayaw.* — Or else auxiliary verbs meaning " can " are used, *e.g.* in Karo *banci.* — Illustration, from the Story of the Glutton: " What then can (one) do ? " = *kuga kin banci bahan.*

90. The modal shade of meaning represented by " *I will* " is often expressed by the future, which in Nias for example has the formative *da-;* or by the conjunctive; or by means of auxiliary verbs meaning " will ", *e.g.* in Gayo *male.* Illustrations. Nias, from the Story of the Old Cat: " Where is the old thing, I want to kick it to death " = Where old + one, " *da* " + I + kick + dead = *hezo nina, da-u-hundrago.* Gayo, from the small vignettes: " I will turn back " = *aku male ulak.*

91. The modal shades of meaning represented by " *must, shall, may* " are rendered by paraphrases like " it is necessary, it is good, it is seemly ", etc.; and this type of phrase is so widely distributed that we must style it Common IX. Illustration, Toba, from the Sangmaima: " The spear Siringis must not get lost " = Not good, lost + go s. S. = *naso tupa mago hujur Siriñis.*

92. *The Irrealis.* On account of the interesting character of this mood from the point of view of general comparative philology, we must consider it in some detail. It has several different modes of formation, but none of them are Common IN.

I. Formation of the irrealis by reduplication of the first syllable of the verbal WB. This is found in Mentaway; but an analysis of all the Mentaway texts — 80 pages of print — has only yielded three instances of it. Illustration, from the Love Dialogues: " Then there would be naught good in me " = Not would + be good in + me = *ta babara uktuk ku.*

II. The irrealis is expressed with the same means as the conjunctive, future, or passive imperative. — Illustrations. Mkb., from the Manjau Ari: " Who should have taught me ?" = W. s. + h. + t. me = *siya ka-maajari den.* Karo, from the Story of the Glutton: " One would have thought he was dead " = *mate ninĕn.* — *ka-* is the sign of the future, *-ĕn* the sign of the passive imperative.

III. Nias has a special auxiliary word of form for the irrealis, viz., *enao*, which is put after the verb. Illustration, from the Story of Kawofo: " Fain would Kawofo have eaten " = F. K. eat " *enao*" = *omasi Gawofo ia enao.*

Note.—The initial of Gawofo follows from the laws of the " status constructus ", which will be dealt with in Section IX.

SECTION VI: THE TENSES.

93. The IN languages have three means of forming tenses: formatives, auxiliary words of form, and reduplication.

94. *The Present Active.* We have given, in Section IV, the formation of the three genera. The verbal forms of the active, which we there ascertained, are in some languages presents, in others they have no implication of any particular time, and so can be used for the present. — To that rule there are, however, exceptions. We have already learnt that the formative *-um-* is used in certain languages as a future, in others as an imperative.

95. *The Past Active.* The past tense is formed either by means of formatives or with the help of auxiliary words of form. The first type of past has formatives which are characterized by the possession of the sound *n*. This mode of formation is found in the Philippines; the intermediate islands south of the Philippines; in Northern Celebes; in Nias, at the back of Sumatra; and in Madagascar. So its distribution is quite a wide one; but, on the other hand, it is to be noted that this type is wanting in Old Jav.; and, moreover, the formative is not the same in all the above languages, though it everywhere contains an *n*.

96. Now the *first* way of forming the past tense is to add to the active form, as delineated in Section IV, the formative *ni-* or *no-* or *in-* or *-in-*.

Formosa, Form. dialect:	*linummis*, Pres. *lummis*, " to glow ".
Philippines, Bont.:	*inumjanak*, Pres. *umjanak*, " to arrive ".
Intermediate islands, Talautese:	*inumire*, Fut. *umire*, " to nod ".

189

Northern Celebes, Tontb.:	*nimaali*, Pres. *maali*, " to bring ".
Islands at the back of Sumatra, Nias:	*nomofano*, Pres. *mofano*, " to start ".
Madagascar, Hova:	*nutunena*, Pres. *tunena*, " to be calmed ".

Note I.—The Form. vocabulary only gives the forms, without telling us what tenses they represent; thus we simply find: *lummis, linummis*. But as the better known Magindanao conjugates precisely like this particular Form. dialect, we may conclude from it that *linummis* is a past tense:

Word-base	Present	Past
	Magindanao	
lutad, " to lower "	*lumutad*	*linumutad*
	Formosan dialect	
lis, " to glow "	*lummis*	*linummis*

Note II.—Hova *nu-* and Nias *no-* are identical; in accordance with phonetic law Hova represents the *o* of other languages by *u*.

Note III.—In Talautese the form with an *m* is not a present but a future.

Note IV.—The past formative *nu-* is also found in Toba (in Sumatra) in the extended form *nuñ* or *nuña*. This consists of *nu* and the emphatic particle *ña* or *ñě*, which recurs in several IN languages; in Karo, which is closely related to Toba, *ñě* after vowels also appears as *ñ*, e.g. in the Story of the Glutton, l. 28.

97. Illustrations of the past formations of the preceding paragraph. Tontb., from the Story of the Founding of the Village of Kapoya: " But Asaq set forth from Sondĕr " = *sapaka si Asaq (ya) nicumĕsot (ai) an Sondĕr*. Nias, from the Story of Buruti: " My mother has gone away " = G. + a. mother my = *nomofano nina gu*. Toba, from the Sangmaima: " The spear is lost, (dragged away by wild pigs) " = " *nuña* " lose spear = *nuña mago hujur*.

98. *Secondly*, the past tense is formed by replacing by *n* the *m* of the present formatives *ma-*, *mar-*, *mi-*, etc., which we became acquainted with in Section IV.

Philippines, Bont.:	*nalufug*, Pres. *malufug*.	" to perish ".
Intermediate islands, Talautese:	*namali*, Fut. *mamali*,	" to buy ".
Madagascar, Hova:	*natahutra*, Pres. *matahutra*,	" to fear ".

99. Illustrations of the past formation of the preceding paragraph. Bont., from the Lumawig: " Then all the people had perished " = *kecen nalufug amin nan taku*. Hova, from the Fable of the Crocodile: " Then replied the hedgehog " = *dia namali ni sukina*.

100. *Thirdly*, the past tense is indicated by auxiliary words of form. Nearly all these words mean " finished, completed ". This linguistic phenomenon may therefore be characterized as Common IN. But the same identical word of form seldom runs through several languages: thus Bug. uses *pura*, while the closely related Mak. has *leqbaq*, Old Jav. *huwus*, Kupangese *hidi*, etc. — Illustrations of this type of past tense. Old Jav., from the Kuñjarakarṇa: " Your words have entered into my bones " = " *huwus* " the w. your penetrate come into the b. = *huwus ika pawarah ta anusup těka i ñ tahulan*. Kupangese, from the Story of the Fool: " We have now made the hole " = We make " *hidi* " hole now = *kit sukun hidi bolo son*.

101. Words of form such as have been given in the preceding paragraph are not, as a general rule, used to indicate merely that the action took place in the past; there is nearly always an idea of completion or of the pluperfect bound up with them. When it is merely a matter of past time, these words of form are hardly ever used, the present, or rather the verbal form implying no particular time, then does duty as a past tense. — Illustrations, from Bug. letters: " I have drunk the whole of the medicine (and now my motions are really not so painful as they were) " = Completely " *pura* " I drink m.

= *aṅkana pura uw inuṅ pabura*. — " I have bought a house (and now I have not got enough money to pay for it) " = House I buy = *bola uw ĕlli*. — In the first case the idea of completion is emphasized. hence the use of *pura*; in the second case that notion is not present, so the word is not used. — In the sentence from the second executioner's story in the Injilai: " Scarcely had it taken (the poison, when it died) " = " *pura* " it takes = *pura na ĕmmĕ*, the word *pura* indicates the pluperfect.

102. In the languages which form the past by means of genuine formatives, the formative may either simply indicate past time. or completion, or the pluperfect, as well. Should it, however. be desired to throw special emphasis on the fact of completion or the pluperfect, then these languages, *besides* using the formative, also add words of form meaning " finished, complete ", like those mentioned above. Thus Hova uses *efa*. which is identical with the Nias *efa* in *aefa*, " finished ". — Illustration from the Testament of Umbiasa: " When knowledge has entered into our mind (it cannot be taken away from us again) " = The k., when " *efa* " entered into m. = *ni fahendrena, raha efa tafiditra an tsaina*.

103. Those languages which possess genuine formatives for expressing the past employ them in a very consistent manner. So in the Hova sentence from the Fable of the Cuckoo: " They would not receive him ". both verbs, " would " and " receive ", are in the past tense: Not would have + received him = *tsi neti nandray azi*. — In this respect Nias is an exception; it does not use its past formative *no-* very frequently. In the Story of Buruti — 46 lines of print — *no-* only occurs about half a dozen times. That, however, is without counting the phrase *no-mege*, " above mentioned ", as its meaning has faded and it almost does duty as an article.

104. The languages which express the past by means of words of form employ them, as already stated, almost exclusively in cases where it is desired to express completion or the idea of the pluperfect; but even in such cases the words of form are often omitted. In the second executioner's story in the Injilai, we find in 147 lines of print less than half a dozen *pura*'s.

105. *The Future Active.* This tense has four modes of formation in IN: first, it is expressed by genuine formatives; secondly, by enclitic, mostly monosyllabic, words of form, which are on the way to become formatives; thirdly, by di-syllabic, somewhat more independent, words of form; and, fourthly, by syllabic reduplication.

106. *First:* the future made by means of formatives. None of these formatives has a wide distribution, none therefore can be styled Common IN.

I. Hova replaces the *m* of formatives beginning with *m* by *h*. Example: " to kiss " = *miuruka*, " to have kissed " = *miuruka*, " to be about to kiss " = *hiuruka*. This *h*-formation has originated by analogy with the *hu*-formation, which will be discussed hereafter.

II. Sund. forms the future by means of the prefix *pi-* and suffix *-ön, e.g., pidatañön,* " to be about to come ".

III. In some languages the aorist formative *um* is used to form the future, *e.g.,* in Tontb. and Bont., thus Bont. *umoto,* " to be going to cook ".

IV. Some languages employ for the future the formatives beginning with *m-*, which are elsewhere present or have no implication of time; so Talautese *mamali,* " to be going to buy ".

V. Old Jav. uses its conjunctive formative *-a* as a future, *e.g., matya < mati + a,* " to be going to die ".

107. Illustrations to the foregoing paragraph. Old Jav., Mausalaparwa, from the prophecy of the angry Brahman: " Baladewa will not die at the same time " = *Baladewa tan ilu matya.* Hova, from the Testament of Umbiasa: " I shall be gathered to the forefathers " (*i.e.,* shall die) = S. + b. + g. to the f. I = *hihauna ami ni razana ahu.*

13

108.   *Secondly:* the future made by means of enclitic words
of form.   These are all prepositions indicating the direction
" whither ".   How they come to denote the future has been
discussed in Section III.

I.   The Western languages, those of Sumatra, the Malay
Peninsula, and Madagascar, employ the preposition *ka*, which
in extended form becomes *kan* and *akan*, and in variant form
ku.   Thus *ka* is used as a preposition, *e.g.*, in Mal.; *akan* in
Day.; *ku* in Karo.   As a sign of the future *ka* is used, *e.g.*, in
Mkb.; *akan* in Day.; *hu* < *ku* in Hova.

II.   The Eastern languages, including those of Southern
and Central Celebes, employ the preposition *la*, which in certain languages has the form *da* in conformity with the RLD-
law.   As a preposition *la* occurs, *e.g.*, in Kupangese; the sign
of the future is *la* in Mak., *da* in Bareqe, and, far away from
the Eastern group, in Nias.

III.   Bont. uses *ad* as a preposition and as a sign of the
future.   It is conceivable that this *ad* is identical with the *da*
= *la* in II. above.   For, in the first place, metathesis is a very
common phenomenon in the IN languages; and, secondly,
another preposition in Bont., synonymous with *ad*, appears
both as *is* and as *si*.

109.   Like Hova, Day. also employs the preposition *ku* to
indicate the future, but it has made it into a verb: *maku*.
Precisely analogous cases are the Bug. *matu* < *ma* + *tu* and
the Tettum *atu* < *a* + *tu*; the preposition *tu* exists independently, *e.g.*, in Toba.

110.   Illustrations to the two preceding paragraphs. Mkb.,
from the Story of Manjau Ari: " I shall go " = *den ka pai*.
Mak., from the Jayalangkara: " I shall now go and sleep "
= Shall go I sleep = *la mañey aq tinro*.   Bareqe, from the
Story of the Migrating Mouse: " I shall emigrate " = S. e. I
= *da melinja (mo) yaku*.   Tettum, from Matthijsen's Dialogues: " To-morrow morning (the) horses will come " =
awan sawan kuda atu mai.

111. The *third* way of indicating the future consists in the use of auxiliary words meaning " will " and the like, *e.g.* *hĕndaq* in Mal., *issa* in Bont., etc. — In the use of the second and third methods we meet with the same state of things as we noticed in connexion with the past tense: the particles are often omitted. In the Mal. Epic Bidasari we ought to find the future expressly indicated more especially in Canto 5, which deals largely with the making of plans for future action; but we find hardly any cases of it.

112. Some languages employ several of the modes of forming the future, for instance Mak., which has both *la* and *sallañ*, and Bont. All the methods possible in Bont. are represented in the Story of the Battle of Kaloqokan:

I. The future is not indicated by any linguistic means: " When will they come?" = When c. t. = *kad* (*nan*) *alian ca ?*

II. Future with formative *-um-*: " We shall run away " = S. + r. + a. we = *lumayao kami.*

III. Future with *ad*: " It will be much " = *ad añsan.*

IV. Future with *issa*: " You will come, the three of you " = W. y. c. the three = *issa kayu* (*'d*) *sumaa ay tolo.*

113. Among the languages which form their tenses with genuine formatives, there are some that have only elaborated two tenses: thus Magindanao only has the present and the past, and has to use a periphrasis for the future. Other languages form all the three tenses, and also bring the imperative into the ambit of this system of tenses. Such elaborated systems are found in Formosa, the Philippines, the intermediate islands, *e.g.* Sangir, and Madagascar. Example:

	Hova	Tagalog
WB	*tadi,* " to bind "	*tawag,* " to call "
Present	*manadi*	*tuñmatawag*
Past	*nanadi*	*tuñmawag*
Future	*hanadi*	*tatawag*
Imperative	*manadia*	*tumawag*

114. Illustrations of the tense-system in Madagascar, from the Old Malagasy Sermons:

I.   Present: " Abu Bekr, who fears the Lord " = The A. B., f. t. L. = *r' Abubakiri matahutru an Dzañahari*.

II.   Past: " My heart has stored it up " = Heart my h. + st. + up = *fu ku nitarimi*.

III.   Future: " They will not see me " = N. w. s. m. = *tsi hahita ahi*.

115. *Tenses of the Causative.* These follow the active closely.   Example from Hova:

	" to speak "	" to cause to speak "
Present	*miteni*	*mampiteni*
Past	*niteni*	*nampiteni*
Future	*hiteni*	*hampiteni*

Illustration from Bont., which, as we already know, uses *pa-* as the sign of the causative and *in-* as the sign of the past tense; from the Story of the Stars: " Mother has made our brother fly " = Has + caused + to + fly m. b. o. = *in-patayaw ina kawwaan mi*.

116. The *tenses of the passive* sometimes follow those of the active pretty closely, as in Hova; in other cases, as in **Tag.**, they diverge further from them.   Examples:

I. Hova—

WB	*ume*, " to give "
Present	*umena*, " to be given "
Past	*numena*
Future	*humena*
Imperative	*umeu*

II. Tagalog—

WB	*tawag*, " to call "
Present	*tinatawag*, " to be called "
Past	*tinawag*
Future	*tatawagin*
Imperative	*tawagin*

117. A peculiar way of forming the past passive is found in Bug. and the closely related Mak.   Bug. *pura* and Mak. *leqbaq*, which mean " finished, completed ", are put before the simple underived WB; it is to be remembered that the WB, as already mentioned above, often has in itself a passive signification. Bug. example:

WB *siyoq,* " to bind "
Past Active *pura maqsiyoq*
Past Passive *pura siyoq.*

It is true that this formation is not found very frequently; in the Injilai the first instance occurs in the first executioner's story. — Illustration of this mode of forming the past tense, from the third executioner's story in the Injilai: " A man who had also been bitten " = *worowane pura oqkoq to.*

SECTION VII : THE PERSONS.

118. The IN languages often possess two parallel series of personal pronouns: full forms and short forms. Thus in very many languages the full form of " I " is *aku*, while its short form in Bont. is *ak*, in Mal. *ku*, in Old Jav. *k*. Full forms are found in all the languages, so that this linguistic fact must be called Common IN; the distribution of the short forms is less extensive, though we find them in nearly all the great areas of distribution: in Celebes, Bug. possesses them, but Tontb. does not. In certain languages the series of the short forms is incomplete; others, on the contrary, have two series of them.

Note.—With the etymological relation between the full and short forms of the pronouns we need not deal here, as this is a monograph on the verb. Nor need we speak of the relation between the short forms of the personal pronouns and the possessive pronouns, which also appear as a species of short forms; *e.g.* Bont.: " I ": full form = *saken*; short form = *ak*; possessive, " my " = *ko*. — Besides, I have said something about this subject in a former monograph.*

119. The full forms of the personal pronouns accompany the verb, either as subject or as object, in precisely the same way as substantives do. Thus in the Day. Story of the Inner Bark of the Tree we find:

The Inner Bark went = I. + B. the w. = *keañ-ñamo tä hagoet.*

He went = *iä hagoet.*

Hence in what follows we shall have but little more to do with the full forms ; we simply refer the reader to Section IX. On the other hand the short forms are eminently deserving of the attention of linguistic students, more particularly of those

---

* [" Sprachvergleichendes   Charakterbild   eines   indonesischen Idiomes ", §§ 65. 157 *seqq.*]

who are concerned with the Indo-European languages and
those who devote themselves to the study of languages in
general, for the combination of these forms with the verb
represents the commencement of a conjugation.

120. We have already learnt that of the languages which
possess short forms of the personal pronouns some exhibit
incomplete, others complete, series.

I. In Mal. only the pronouns " I " and " thou " have short
forms:

	Full form	Short form
I	*aku*	*ku*
Thou	*ĕṅkaw*	*kaw*

II. Mentaway has the two series complete, save that for the
second person plural the full form and the short are identical:

	Full form	Short form
I	*aku*	*ku*
Thou	*äkäw*	*nu*
He	*iña*	*i*
We	*sita*	*ta*
You	*kam*	*kam*
They	*sia*	*ra*

Note.—The Mentaway grammar does not mention the short
form *i*, but there are passages in the texts which admit of no
other interpretation than the existence of such a short form.
A passage of that sort occurs at the beginning of the first
Story of the Great Bear: " Father, he twines yarn at home "
= *ukui i puputärä bakä ka uma.*

III. Bug. in addition to a series of full forms possesses two
complete series of short forms:

	Full form	Short forms	
I	*iyaq*	*u* or *ku*	*aq*
Thou	*iko*	*mu*	*o* or *ko*
He	*iya*	*na*	*i*
We	*idiq*	*kiq*	*kiq*
You	*iko*	*mu*	*o* or *ko*
They	*iya*	*na*	*i*

121. Use of the short forms. In this paragraph we always mean the use of the short form as subject; its function as object will be discussed later.

I. The full forms are employed when the emphasis is on the subject; when that is not the case, the short forms are used. In the Bug. letter from the Princess Weyanu (*i.e.*, Princess X) to Matthes, which is about Bug. manuscripts, occurs the passage: " I myself will give orders to convey them there " = I self order, convey them = *iyaq pa maqsuro panoq i.* Here the word *pa*, " self ", shows that the emphasis is on the subject. In the same letter there is mention of some fragrant oils, but there we find: " I have not handed them over to him " = Not I have + handed + over him = *deq u pati-wiriw i.* Here the important point is the predicate, and hence the short form *u* is used for the subject.

II. When the emphasis is on the subject it very often happens that both forms, the full and the short, are used together. So in the Mak. Jayalangkara we find the sentence: " (Jayalangkara was without fear, but his brothers cried:) ' We are exceedingly afraid ! ' " = Fear exceedingly we we = *mallaq duduw aq inakke.* Here the emphasis is on the subject " we ", because of its antithesis to Jayalangkara, and it is expressed twice, by the short form *aq* and the full form *inakke.*

III. In the case of the third person, when that is expressed by a substantive, the short form of the pronoun is often added as well. But this does not involve any emphasis or any other special effect. If we find in the above-mentioned letter about manuscripts: *na ala i karaeñ riy anu* = " He has taken them, the Prince of X ", this means no more than: " The Prince of X has taken them ".

IV. There are also certain limitations in the use of the short forms, which vary from one language to another. Usually they only accompany the active and causative forms of the verb. Mal. employs the short forms only with transitive verbs. In Mak. this limitation does not hold good; illustration, from the dialogue of the cats in the Jayalangkara: " Come on, let us go " = *umbamo kiq lampa.*

122. We now come to the question: In what manner do the short forms of the personal pronouns combine with the verb?

I. Where the language in question has only *one* series of short forms: in some languages they *precede*, while in others they *follow*, the verb. This does not depend on the usual order of the subject, be it a substantive or a full form of pronoun. In Mal. the subject as a rule *follows* the predicate, but the short forms of the personal pronouns have to precede it. — They *precede* the verb in Toba, Mal., Bareqe, Tettum, etc., but *follow* it in Bont.

II. Where the language in question has *two* series of short forms: in that case the one series always *precedes*, the other *follows*, the verb; that holds good, *e.g.*, of the two Bug. series given above, the *u*-series precedes, the *aq*-series follows.

123. Illustrations to the foregoing paragraph.

I. Position of the forms *before* the verb. Bareqe, from the Song about the Beloved Relatives: " I value (them) like gold " = *ku timba ewa wuyawa*. Mak., from the Sixth Elegy: " God, I pray " = *Batara, ku kanro*. Old Jav., from the fifth canto of the Rāmāyaṇa: " He bent this bow " = *r ayat ikanaṅ laras*. Mentaway, from the Love Dialogues: " I will not " = Not I w. = *ta k' oba* < *ta ku oba*.

It chances that the short forms of all the personal pronouns occur in the Nias Story of Buruti and Futi:

I — " I know my mother well " = I k. w. mother my = *u ila sa nina gu*.

Thou — " Why dost thou steal my child ?" = W. t. s. c. my = *hanawa o tago nono gu*.

He — " The ghost Buruti spake " = He s. B. g. = *i mane Buruti-beχu*.

We — " We will speak " = We s. w. = *ta waqo dania*.

You—" Give me the child !" = You g. me c. = *mi beqe χogu nono*.

They — " They have stolen my child " = *la tago nono gu*.

II. Position of the short forms *after* the verb. Bont., from the Battle of Kaloqokan: " They run into the wood " = R. they i. w. = *umäy ca id pagpag*.

124. In languages that possess two series of short personal pronouns the speaker is free to choose between those that precede and those that follow the verb. In the Jayalangkara we find: " When you arrive at Masereq, you will ascend the mountain " = W. a. y. there at M., y. w. mount up m. = *punna battu ko mañe ri Masereq, nuw eroq naiq ri moncoñ*, but it could equally have been: *nu battu* and *eroq ko*. That appears most plainly from an analysis of the dialogue of the two cats in the Jayalangkara, when they want to go to Masereq, for nowhere else in the whole of the Jayalangkara are the pronouns as frequent as in that passage: we see there that the two series are used indiscriminately.

125. When the short forms of the personal pronouns *precede* the verb, some languages omit the active formatives, others do not. In Mal. the word for " to see " is *mělihat*, but " I see " is *ku lihat*, the *mě-* being dropped. In Rottinese " to seek " is *akaneni* < *aka* + WB *neni*, " he seeks " is *n akaneni*, the *aka-* being retained. — Illustrations. Mal., from the Hang Tuah: " I have taken it away from you again " = I have + t.-a. again from you = *ku ambil pula daripada mu*. Rottinese, from the Animal Play: " He seeks the man " = H. s. m. the = *nakaneni touk a*.

126. The most interesting question is as to the degree of intimacy that exists in the combination of short personal pronoun and verb. In some languages the connexion is a close one, in others it is looser.

127. The *looser* combination. This is found, *e.g.*, in Bug. and Mak.:

I. In these languages it is not absolutely essential that the pronoun should come immediately next to the verb. In the Jayalangkara we find: " Go you !" = *mañe ma ko*, where the verb and pronoun are separated by the emphatic particle *ma*.

II. Genuine suffixes effect a shifting of the accent, but pronouns put after the verb do not.

III. Pronouns can be used with other parts of speech besides verbs. — Illustration, Bug., from the Injilai: "You are a man, I am a bird " = *tau ko, ku manuqmanuq.*

IV. The short form need not necessarily be the subject, it may be the object.

128. The *closer* combination. This is found, *e.g.*, in Mal. Here the short form of the pronoun only goes with verbs; between the pronoun and the verb nothing can be interposed; *ku lihat* can only mean " I see ", not " see me". — The accent does not come into question here, for words that precede do not influence the accent of what follows.

129. But the most intimate combination of the short pronoun and the verb is to be found in Rottinese. The verbal formatives in Rottinese begin with a vowel; and the short forms of the pronouns, which precede the verb, have lost their vowels. *e.g.* " he " = $n < na$. Hence it has become possible for the short pronoun and the verb to coalesce into a real unit. For instance, the WB for " to flee " is *lai*, the verb *alai*, " he flees " is *nalai.* Specimen paradigm:

WB	*hani*
Verb	*ahani*
I wait	*ahani*
Thou waitest	*mahani*
He waits	*nahani*
We wait	*tahani*
You wait	*mahani*
They wait	*lahani*

Note I.—Rottinese usually also puts the full form of the pronoun before this conjugated verb. *e.g.* " I wait " = *au ahani.*

Note II.—The transition from the short form of the pronoun with a vowel to a form without a vowel is neatly illustrated in Mentaway. Whereas in Mak. " I " is only *ku* and " thou " only *nu*, in Mentaway one can say either *ku* or *k*, *nu* or *n*, when a vowel immediately follows. Thus in the same Love

Dialogue we find: " Why don't you care to ?" = Why not you
care = *apa ta nu oba*, and " Don't you care for me ?" = *ta n
oba aku*.

130. Illustrations of the Rottinese conjugation. It so
happens that the whole conjugation is represented in the
Animal Play:

I — " I say " = *au ae*.

Thou — " Don't you know, then ?" = Then thou not
know = *te o ta malelak*.

He — " He seeks the man " = *nakaneni touk a*.

We — " We flee " = *ata talai*.

You — " Eat !" = *mua leonma*.

They — " That they may not see me " = That they n. s.
me = *fo ala boso lita au*.

131. In the languages in which the short pronouns are
closely connected with the verb, the pronoun only does duty
as the subject: Mal. *ku lihat* can never mean " see me ". In
languages where the connexion is a less intimate one the pronoun can also serve as the object. — Illustration from the
Mak. Jayalangkara: " (It were better that we roam around
than that) the snake should eat us " = Us it eat, snake = *kiq
na kanre naga*.

132. In the languages which possess two series of
short pronouns, such as Bug., Mak., and Nias, when *at the
same time* one pronoun is used before the verb and another
after it, then the first one is the subject and the second the
object. — Illustrations. Bug., from the Injilai: " I kill you "
= *u sampělle o*. Nias, from the Story of Buruti: " I love you "
= *u omasiqo o*.

---

133. We have learnt that the IN verb can express genus,
mood, tense and person. That, however, does not conclude
the cycle of its vital manifestations.

I. We have already heard that certain languages are able
to express the *beginning* of an action, by means of the aorist
formative *um*. — Now some languages can also indicate

duration: thus Old Jav. has given the active formative *man-* and the passive formative *-in-* a durative tinge which did not originally belong to them. Illustration, from the Āśramawa-sanaparwa: "As long as Draupadi was being ill-treated" = D. as + long + as she was + being + ill-treated = *Dropadī kāla nira winudan.* — Other languages, again, are able to express the fact that something just intervenes during the *continuance* of an action. But here we do not meet with genuine formatives, but merely auxiliary words of form such as *těnah, sědan,* or *sadan,* and the like. Illustration, Mkb., from the Manjau Ari: "A woman was engaged in weaving" = A person woman "*sadan*" wove = *sa oran padusi sadan batanun.* — Bont. has a formative *naka-* to indicate the *conclusion* of the action. Illustration, from the Story of the Rat and the Two Brothers: "Now they have finished eating" = Now h. + f. + e. they = *kecen nakakanan ca.*

II. Here and there we also find *participial* formatives. Nias has a present participle in *s-,* the formation of which has been discussed in Section III. — Illustration, from the Story of the Fish and the Rat: "A woman drawing water" = Woman d. w. = *alawe sanaqu idano.*

III. In several IN languages *number* can be expressed. Masaretese has a verbal formative which is *da-* in the singular, and *du-* in the plural. Illustration, from the History of the Tagalasi Tribe: "He saw the inhabitants of Tagalasi-Miten sitting there" = Saw i. the T.-M. sit = *daanak geba ro Tagalasi-Miten duptea.* — Nias uses an infixed *g* as a sign of the plural. Illustration, from the Story of Buruti:

Thou weepest   *mee o*
They weep always   *mege-ege ira.*

In Gayo the formative *i* indicates the plural either of the subject or of the object, the latter in the following sentence from the Story of the Blue Princess: "She had all her clothes on" = All had + on clothes = *mbeh sěloki pěkayan.*

Note.—All the phenomena mentioned in this appendix to Section VII occur only sporadically; we cannot draw from them any conclusions as regards Common IN.

SECTION VIII : VERBAL PHRASES AND OTHER MODES OF EXPRESSION.

134. IN often uses the verb in cases where the Indo-European languages with which we are more generally familiar employ a substantive, adverb, etc.; but the opposite also holds good.

135. IN forms abstract substantives just as Indo-European does. Thus from the WB *ro*, " to come ", which is also used without any formative as a verb. Toba derives the substantive *haroro*, " arrival " $<$ *ha* $+$ *ro* reduplicated. — Illustration from the Sangmaima: " In order that they may know the time of my arrival " $=$ In $+$ order $+$ that be $+$ known time of arrival my $=$ *asa diboto bakta ni haroro ñku.*

136. Now the IN languages often use a substantival construction in cases where as a general rule the better known Indo-European languages adopt the verbal construction; and that applies, in particular, to the verbs " to do ", " to intend ", " to think ", " to say ", " to be named ". This phenomenon can be styled Common IN. The IN substantives in question are either substantival WB's like Old Jav. *don*, Tag. *ibig*, " intention ", or else derivative substantives like Old Jav. *pagaway*, " the making ", which exists alongside of the WB *gaway* and the verb *magaway.*

I. Substantival construction with the ideas of " doing ", " making ". Old Jav., from the Prosody of Mpu Tanakung: " Well, what had you to do ?" $=$ What then making your $=$ *mapa kari pagaway ta.*

II. With the idea of intention. Tag.. from Tell: " Why do you crowd upon me (in the open road) ?" $=$ What the intention your with me $=$ *ano añ ibig niniyo sa akin.* Old Jav.

from the Āśramawasanaparwa: " That is what they desire to
attain " = (That that) may + be + attained, (is) aim that =
kapaṅgíha don ika.

III. With the idea of saying. Tontb., from the Story of
the Demon that haunts women in confinement: " Then they
exclaimed " = Then speech their = *siituoka kua era (o).*
Nias, from the Story of Buruti: " Then she spake thus " =
Then thus speech her again = *ba simane li nia zui.* Day.,
from the Story of the Inner Bark: " Then said he to himself "
= Then (was) word of the heart = *tä koa n huañ.*

IV. With the idea of thinking. Karo, from the Story of
the Glutton: " But I think the Glutton is dead " = Heart
mine yet, that dead the Glutton = *ate ku min, ěñgo mate si*
Lagaman.

V. With the idea of being called. Old Jav., from the
Śakuntalā: " There was once a king, who was called Duśwanta
= Was a k., D. name his = *hana sira mahārāja Duśwanta*
ñaran ira. Tontb., from the Description of the Sacrificial
Feast: " This sacrificial feast is called the offering for the
plants " = Name of s. + f. this (is) plant-offering = *ñaran i*
papěligin itu mañusěw.

137. On the other hand, a verb is often used in IN in cases
where the Indo-European languages with which we are more
generally acquainted would employ some other part of speech.
All the instances here enumerated are Common IN.

I. The verb replaces an indefinite *pronoun.* The verb
that serves this purpose is the verb " to be, to be in existence ",
Old Jav. *hana,* Mal. *ada,* Nias *so.* — Illustrations. Old Jav.,
from the Kuñjarakarṇa: " Some had their heads chopped off "
= Were, (whose) chopped + off + were heads their = *hana*
winaduñ kapala ña. Mal., from Abdullah's Journey: " There
were several islands, some big and some small " = Were
several piece islands, were small, were big = *ada běběraṇa*
buwah pulaw, ada kěcil, ada běsar.

II. The verb replaces a *preposition,* namely, the prepositions " at " or " about " etc., with verbs denoting an emo-

tion. The verbs doing duty in these cases are " to see " and
" to hear ".—Illustrations. Day., from the second Sangumang Story: " His mother wondered at what Sangumang said "
= M. his wondered hearing words S. = *indu e heñan mahinin
auh Sañumañ*. Old Jav., from the Āśramawasanaparwa:
" The king wept, being touched by his condition " = Wept
k. t. seeing c. his = *manañis mahārāja kasrĕpan tumon gati
nira*.

III. The verb replaces *adverbs* such as " up ", " down "'
" out ", " back ", and the like. — Illustrations. Kupangese,
from the Story of the Fool: " Then he stepped in into the
midst " = Then he s. entering into the m. = *ti un laok tama
se llala*. Day., from the second Sangumang Story: " I walked
along by the side of the gigantic chopper " = I w. going +
along (by) g. + c. = *aku manañjoñ mahoroy pahera*.

IV. The verb replaces the *affirmative particle*.—Illustration, Nias, from the Story of Futi: " Have you heard the words
of the chief ? She said: ' Yes !' " = You h. w. c. ? She s.:
' I heard ' = *o roño li razo ? i mane: u roño*.

138. With respect to several of the passive forms of the
verb there is a controversy as to whether they should not rather
be regarded as substantival forms. My view is the following:

I. The name " passive forms " is given by the grammars
to certain linguistic phenomena which were undoubtedly
originally substantives. In the Mkb. work Manjau Ari there
is a sentence: " It grows in the field, surrounded by trees ".
" Surrounded by trees " is: *diliñkuañ kayu*. The form
diliñkuañ is explained by the traditional grammar as a passive, and it is further added that the agent *kayu* is annexed
without the preposition " by ". But the WB *liñkuañ* is also
a substantive in Mkb., meaning " something that surrounds ";
and *di* is also a preposition; so I could also take *di liñkuañ
kayu* as meaning " in a ring-fence of trees ", for the genitive
relation is expressed in many IN languages, and in Mkb. in
particular, by the mere order of the words without the intervention of any preposition. Thus in my view *diliñkuañ kayu*
was originally a substantival construction.

II.   In the Old Jav. Kuñjarakarṇa we find the sentence:
" He came upon a door " = A d. was met by him = *babahan
kapaṅgih de nira.*   Here, no doubt, one might also regard
kapaṅgih as a substantive, for *ka-* serves in many IN languages
to form substantives as well as verbs.   But here the agent
is attached by means of the preposition *de*, which never introduces a genitive relation.   I cannot, therefore, without putting
a strain upon it, construe the sentence as: " the door was a
find of his ".   On the contrary, *de* corresponds rather with the
kind of prepositions that are used in our languages to introduce
the agent in passive sentences; that is shown by active con-
structions like the following from the Āśramawasanaparwa:
" To undergo pain through you " = *manĕmu lara de ñu.*

III.   In not a few IN languages the agent can be introduced in both ways, either genitively or by a preposition
meaning " by, through ", as in Mal., where the preposition
is *oleh.*   An analysis of the whole of the Mal. work Hang
Tuah has resulted in showing that though the construction
with the preposition preponderates, the genitive construction is freely represented there too, and no difference in meaning is perceptible as between the two modes of expression.
For example: " It was heard by the chief " = *didĕñar batin*;
but: " It was heard by the mother " = *didĕñar oleh ibu.*
This interchangeability of the two forms indicates, to my
mind, the occurrence of a transformation in the mental attitude with which they are regarded: what was originally substantival has gradually come to be felt as verbal.

IV.   In Bug. the agent is never introduced genitively, but
always by the preposition *ri*, which never indicates the
genitive.   I have analysed the whole of the Paupau Rikadong
— 29 pages of print — from that point of view, and have not
found a single exception.   That, to my mind, shows that
what the Bug. grammar calls " passive " is really felt to be
passive, even though one or other of the forms of the passive
may have been originally substantival.

V.   In individual cases it will often be difficult to put oneself into the mental attitude of the IN native so as to be able

14

to determine whether, for him, a given linguistic phenomenon which the ordinary grammar calls a passive is really substantival or verbal. — Speaking with some reserve, I incline to the view that the construction under I.: *diliṅkuan kayu* is really felt as a passive by the Mkb. people of to-day, and is, therefore, a verbal phenomenon, as the ordinary grammar says it is.

SECTION IX : THE VERB IN THE SENTENCE.

139. Among the linguistic means employed by IN for linking the several parts of a sentence together the following are of particular importance: prepositions, the copula, the status constructus, and the syntactical order of the words.

140. Prepositions.

I. In Common IN the genitive relation has the preposition *n* or *ni*. This preposition links substantive with substantive. There are no active or causative verbs that " govern " the genitive. But, as we have heard, the agent is often linked with the passive predicate like a genitive. — We have also learnt that the genitive can be expressed by the mere order of the words, without any preposition at all.

II. In some languages the dative relation has a special preposition, *e.g.* in Karo: *man*; in other languages the dative is expressed by the same prepositions as the adverbial.

III. The accusative relation is very rarely indicated by a preposition; as a general rule, the syntactical order suffices.

IV. In Common IN the adverbial is introduced by prepositions. Of these the two prepositions *i* and *ri* have a particularly wide distribution.

141. The copula.

I. The Indo-European copula, the verb " to be ", has nothing exactly corresponding to it in IN. Hence the sentence, " What is the reason that it is so ?" is expressed in the Kuñjarakarṇa by: " What reason of it, so ?" = *apa dumeh ña maṅkana*. In Achinese, in the Story of the Pelican, we find the sentence, " Then exclaimed all the fish: ' It is good so ' " rendered by: " Then exclaimed all fish: ' Thus good ' "

211

= *těmar sěut bandum ěnkut : ño měnan.* In Bug., in a letter
of the Princess Aru Panchana we find the expression: " What
is the price of this gold thread ?" = What price of it gold
thread this = *siaga ělli na wěnampulawěn ede.*

II. IN possesses a feature which the grammars rightly call
a copula. Only it is not a verb, but a particle, viz., *i* or *ay*
or *ya*, etc., which links different parts of the sentence, particularly subject and predicate, together. The copula is found
in the Philippines, in Northern Celebes and in Madagascar;
it cannot, therefore, be called Common IN.

142. The status constructus, in Nias.

It is formed principally in two ways: words that begin with
a vowel take *n* or *g* before that vowel; words that begin with
a surd turn it into a sonant. Many words do not form the
status constructus at all. Examples:

	Mother	Rat
Status absolutus	*ina*	*tequ*
Status constructus	*nina*	*dequ*

The status constructus serves the same purpose as the
copula, it links the several parts of the sentence together,
especially the subject with the predicate. " Rat " is *tequ* and
" to go " is *moi*, and in the Story of the Rat and the Fish the
phrase " the rat goes " is: *moi dequ.*

Note.—The first method of forming the status constructus
may be thus explained: the sounds *n* and *g* are the prepositions *n* and *ka*, respectively. The preposition *n* has been
mentioned at the beginning of this section; *ka*, which, in
accordance with the Nias phonetic laws stated in Section III
had to become *ga*, has been repeatedly referred to. But we
have also learnt that *n* is a Common IN preposition for the
genitive relation and *ka* for the place " whither ". We must,
therefore, assume that the two prepositions have considerably
enlarged their sphere of action, or have made it more general.
This assumption is rendered credible by the fact that there
are parallel processes in Mentaway, which is a near neighbour
to Nias geographically and shares a number of special features

with it.   Now in Mentaway the preposition *ka* has also considerably extended its functions, so that it is now able to
introduce almost any syntactical relation; and moreover
before vowels it often appears in the abbreviated form *k*.*

143.   The emphasizing of the predicate.

I.   Nearly all IN languages possess particles which serve
to emphasize some particular part of the sentence, so that
this phenomenon must be styled Common IN.   The most
widely distributed is the particle *ma*, which also appears as
mo, *mĕ*, *mama*, and *man*; it occurs in the Philippines, in
Celebes, in the islands lying near New Guinea, and in Sumatra.
Mal. has an emphatic particle *lah*, Mkb. *ma* + *lah*, etc.

Note.—Though some languages have *ma*, others *mo*, others
again *mĕ*, this change of vowel does *not* as a rule correspond
with the phonetic laws of the languages in question; we must,
therefore, provisionally call it variation.

II.   Now though it is true that these particles can be used
to emphasize any part of the sentence, yet they are most frequently put after the predicate.   In the Sumbawarese text
about Dog's Dung — 27 lines of print — *mo* occurs eleven
times, of which nine are cases where it follows the verb.

III.   A minority of the languages makes but sparing use
of the particles of emphasis; thus Kupangese, for example,
where in the Story of the Fool — 10 pages of print — *ma*
occurs only once, viz., in the phrase *baku ma*, " it is enough ".
The majority use them very plentifully, *e.g.* Toba.   In the
Toba Story of Sangmaima the particle *ma* occurs in the ordinary course of the narrative after nearly every predicate.
Illustration: " Sangmaima ate, and then took his provisions
and went into the depths of the forest " = Then ate the S.,

* [The second mode of formation of the status constructus is explained by the author in his monograph " Indonesisch und Indogermanisch im Satzbau ", § 180, as resulting from the carrying on of the
" voice " of the final vowel (with which all Nias words end) onto the
initial consonant of the following word, when it is closely connected
with what immediately precedes, thus changing the unvoiced consonant
into a voiced one.   See also Essay IV, § 302, II.]

then were + taken p. his, then went into forest deep = *asa
mañan ma si Sañmaima, asa diboan ma bohal na, asa laho ma
tu tombak loño-loño.*

144. Sentences that have a predicate but no subject.

I. The indefinite pronouns " it " or " one ", used as subjects, are not as a rule represented at all in IN. — Illustrations. Mentaway, from the Contest between Sun and Moon:
" I am well, it is raining " = *aku maäru. urat.* Bareqe, from
the Song to the Moon: " It gets dark, before one wends one's
way homewards " = Gets dark, before go + home = *maweñi
(mo) nepa jela.*

It is true that the subject is sometimes indicated in cases of
that kind. In the Bont. Story of the Stars the expression
" it is growing dark " (*i.e.*, night is coming on) is sometimes
rendered by *malafi* and at other times by *malafi nan talon*,
" the daytime is becoming night ".

II. When the verb is in the imperative the pronominal
subject may be added or omitted. Languages that possess
short forms of pronouns are fond of adding the subject in such
cases. Thus in the Bug. Paupau Rikadong the king says to
his servants: " Go, then ! " = Go then you = *lao sa o.* In
Mak.. in the expressions " don't " = *teya ko* and " don't let
us " = *teya kiq*, by means of which the prohibitive is formed,
the pronoun always appears; an analysis of the whole of the
extensive work Jayalangkara has hardly revealed a single
exception to this rule.

145. Having in the preceding paragraph dealt with sentences that have no subject, we have now to speak of sentences
that have no verbal predicate.

I. It has already been mentioned that IN possesses no
verb corresponding to the Indo-European copula.

II. When in an IN sentence there is an adverb or a preposition indicating a direction in space, the verb of going,
coming, or remaining, which would be the predicate, is often
omitted. — Illustrations. Old Malagasy, from the Sermon
Tonih Zañahary: " Where art thou, Moses ? " = Where thou,

the M. = *aiza hanaw, ra Musa*. Day., from the Story of the
Inner Bark of the Tree: " For what purpose do you come ?"
= For what you = *akan kwe kaw*.

III. In IN sentences we very often find the predicate
accompanied by an interjection, mostly an onomatopœic one.
— Illustrations. Old Jav., from the Kuñjarakarṇa: " Hey
presto ! (she) was at the door " = *rĕp datĕn ri n lawan*. Rot-
inese, from the Animal Play: " There is a flash; bang ! the
musket rings out " = *nandela; dan ! sisilo nali*.

Now in such sentences as these the verb may also be omitted,
so that the interjection by itself plays the part of a predicate.
Illustration, Toba, from the Sangmaima: " Then cried the kite
' hulishulis ' " = Then " hulishulis " k. = *asa hulishulis (ma)
lali*.

The phenomena mentioned in this paragraph are to be
regarded as Common IN.

146. Linking the subject with the predicate. *First method:*
the syntactical order.

I. The predicate precedes the subject; this rule is Common
IN. — Illustrations. Old Form., from Vlis's Collection of
Dialogues: " You have evidently been sleeping " = Have +
slept y. e. = *nimesip kaw lawa*. Old Jav., from the Tantri
Fables: " Thus spake the goose, then answered the tortoise "
= Thus word of the g., a. the t. = *mankana lin n ikan hansa,
sumahur ikan pās*. Toba, Sangmaima, from the Burning of
the Book of Magic: " Then his book of magic was burnt, but
a leaf of it fell behind his house " = Then burned magic +
book his, fell at back of house his one leaf magic + book =
*asa gor (ma) pustaha na, timpal (ma) tu pudi ni ruma na sa
lompit pustaha*.

II. But this order is not absolutely obligatory. If special
emphasis is to be laid on the subject, it may precede. —
Enumeration: the Mentaway Story of the Spirit of the Palm
Toddy contains 25 lines and three instances of the order subject + predicate; and in each case this occurs because the
subject is to be emphasized, on account of an antithesis.

III. Certain isolated languages, which have no close connexion with one another, follow the opposite order as a general rule. To this category belong Day. and Masaretese. — Illustrations. Masaretese, from the Story of the Forest Spirit: " Meanwhile men ate pouched rats "* = Meanwhile m. the a. p. + r. = *gamdi geba ro ka tonal*. Day., from the first Story of Sangumang: " The buffaloes were penned by me " = B. the w. + p. by + me = *hadañan tä kuroñ ku*. — Enumeration. In the Masaretese Legend of the People of Tagalasi the order subject + predicate is strictly maintained.

IV. The order of the short forms of the pronouns has been dealt with above.

147. Linking the subject with the predicate.

Second method : The copula. This copula, the particle *i* or *ya* or *dia*, etc., is interposed between subject and predicate, thus linking them together. Illustrations. Tag., from Tell: " That cries to Heaven " = *iya i sumisigaw sa lañit*. Tontb., from the Story of the Water Snail and the Antelope: " I have been requested by the antelope " = I " *ya* " h. + b. + r. by a. = *aku ya tinaqaran i tuqa*. Hova, from the Testament of Umbiasa: " The body requires nourishment " = *ni nufu dia mila hanina*.

148. Linking the subject with the predicate. *Third method:* the status constructus in Nias. The subject, which follows, is put into the status constructus. — Illustration. from the Kawofo: " Then appeared Kawofo " = *ba so Gawofo*.

149. The agent relation in the passive sentence. This has been discussed in Section VIII.

150. Predicate and predicative. The predicative is simply added, without more, to the verb of the predicate. This phenomenon is to be regarded as Common IN. — Illustrations. Modern Jav., from the History of the State of Kĕḍiri: " He was made commander-in-chief " = *kadadosakĕn senapati*. Sund., from Van der Ent's Descriptions of Animals

---

* Cuscus moluccana.

and Plants: " Their leafribs are manufactured into brooms "
= L. t. a. + m. b. = *ñere na diȷiyön sapu.*

151. Predicate and infinitive. In this case also there is,
as a rule, merely juxtaposition. — Illustration, Bug., from the
letter of Princess X, wherein she asks Matthes for a copy of
the Jayalangkara: " That is what I wish to say to you " =
That I wish say to you = *iya uw aqkatta powadada r' idiq.*

Bont., in this case, employs the copula. Illustration, from
the Battle of Kaloqokan: " We are going to take " = Going
we " *ay* " take = *umüy kami ay umala.*

152. Predicate and direct object.

I. The Common IN rule is that the direct object is added,
without more, to the predicate. — Illustrations. Simalurese,
from Westenenk's small Collection of Dialogues: " May I
take these coconuts ?" = M. I t. c. these = *dai u abe bonol
ereh.* Sangirese, from Adriani's Songs: " He longs for the
absent ones " = Desires men absent the = *mĕkati tau tadi e.*
Banggayan, from Riedel's text: " We looked for bulbous
roots " = *ikami moñombolii baku.*

This order is not absolutely obligatory. If the object is
to be emphasized it may precede. In the Masaretese Story of
the Forest Spirit there is *one* case of the order object + predicate, occasioned by the object being emphasized on account
of antithesis: " (Hereafter I shall only come with my voice),
but you shall not be able to behold my body again " = But
body the you get see no more = *bu fatan di kimi beta añak
mela beka.*

II. In a very small number of languages the direct object
is linked to the predicate by means of a preposition. This is
done in Bont. by means of *is* and in Hova, in certain cases,
by means of *ani.* — Illustrations. Bont., from the Battle of
Kaloqokan: " Then we buy the cake " = T. b. we the c. =
keceñ lumago kami is nan kankanen. Hova, from the Testament of Umbiasa: " Men have begotten thee " = *ulumbeluna
(nu) niteraka ani ialahi.*

III. In Nias the direct object is in the status constructus.
Illustration, from the Story of the Woman who wanted to

eat the Lightning: " Wrap up the dog !" = You w. + u. d.
= *mi fanombo nasu.* — The status absolutus is *asu.*

153. It very often happens that verbs which are transitive
in the Indo-European languages most familiar to us also take a
direct object in IN. I have analysed from this point of view
the Old Jav. tale which is embodied in Mpu Tanakung's
Prosody, and the result is as follows. Many verbs take the
accusative that also take it in German; but contrary to the
German idiom are: " Helfen gegen Liebespein " (To be of help
against the pangs of love) = *atuluṅ rimaṅ;* and " Den Ver-
gnügen nachjagen " (To race after pleasures) = *aṅrarah rūm.*

154. All IN languages have verbs of motion which are construed with the accusative, particularly the verb " to go into ".
— Illustrations. Karo, from the Story of the Glutton: " They
went into their house " = T. w. h. their = *si dahi rumah na.*
Mal., from the Hang Tuah: " He went into the house " =
masuq rumah.

Amongst all the IN languages of which I have analysed
texts of some length, Day. is the one that displays this phenomenon most frequently, and I have found it occurring
oftenest in the two Sangumang Stories:

palus huma	to enter into the house
tamä huma	to go into the house
lumpat huma	to mount into the house
blua huma	to come out of the house
buli lewu	to go back to the village
sampay kaleka	to arrive at the place
mahoroy pahera	to walk along the gigantic chopper.

155. In many IN languages we find the phenomenon of
a preposition, particularly the preposition *i,* coalescing with
the verb. Such verbs in that case require no further linguistic
means to link up the object, though *per se* it be an indirect
one, or even the adverbial; in other words, they are construed
transitively. Example, Bug.:

To go on a path:	*joppa ri lalĕṅ.*
To tread a path:	*joppai lalĕṅ.*

I have dealt with this matter in considerable detail in a former monograph.*

156. The object used with reflexive verbs demands special consideration. The IN methods differ to this extent from those of the Indo-European languages best known to us in that they do not say, for example, " I betake myself " but " I betake my body " or " my person ". This phenomenon is Common IN. " Body " or " person " is *awak* in many languages, *ale* in Bug., *droi* in Achinese, and so on. — Illustrations. Basa Sangiang, from the First Dirge for the Dead: " Remove yourselves upstream !" = Remove person your upstream = *tasat arep m ñaju-ñaju*. Bug., from the first executioner's story in the Injilai: " It is to be feared that the king will repent him of it " = To + fear that repent person his king the = *ajajke na sĕssĕi ale na aruñ e*. Achinese, from the Story of the Wise Judge: " He made himself in shape like a man " = He shaped person like mankind = *ji pĕrupa droi sĕpĕrti manusiya*. — Enumeration. In Section I mention was made of an enumeration which showed that reflexive verbs are rarer in Mal. than in German, for instance. An analysis of the whole of the Jayalangkara has had a similar result; yet in the highly coloured description of the fight waged by the hero with the inhabitants of Masereq, for example, there are three consecutive cases: " to guard oneself from ", " to hurl oneself against ", " to throw oneself upon ".

157. It is a neat coincidence that not a few IN reflexive verbs find their pendants in French. Bug., as the above example shows, has a parallel to " se repentir ", Mal. to " se taire ", Mak. to " s'évanouir ", and Mkb. to " s'agenouiller ".

158. The indirect object. It is the Common IN rule that a preposition is used to link the indirect object with the predicate. — Illustrations. Mak., Jayalangkara, from the king's speech:† " This I lay in charge upon you " = *iya (mi) ku*

---

* [" Sprachvergleichendes Charakterbild eines indonesischen Idiomes ", §§ 116-123.]

† Matthes ed., pp. 143 *seqq.*

palaq ri kaw. Old Jav., from the Āśramawasanaparwa: " To reflect on death " = *atutura ri pati.* Bont., from the Kolling: " Tell it to our mother !" = T. you to m. our = *kana m ken ina ta.* Hova, from the Testament of Umbiasa: " He who follows after the low fellows becomes a low fellow (himself) " = *izay miaraka ami ni ambualambu, dia ambualambu.*

159. I have analysed the three books of the Old Jav. Mahābhārata entitled Āśramawasanaparwa, Mausalaparwa, and Prasthānikaparwa from the point of view of studying the dative object, which in Old Jav. is construed with the two synonymous prepositions *i* and *ri*, and the result is as follows. The dative object occurs especially:

I.   With verbs of saying, asking, answering, commanding, and greeting; *e.g., manĕmbah ri*, " to ask someone respectfully".

II.   With verbs of thinking, knowing, remembering, and forgetting; *e.g., atutur ri*, " to think of ".

III.   With verbs of desiring, rejoicing, being content, and being sorrowful; *e.g., alara ri*, " to mourn over ".

160. Since, as has been shown above, many IN languages possess formatives which make verbs, that would otherwise take an indirect object or an adverbial, into transitive verbs, it follows that in such languages the indirect object seldom appears. In the Karo Story of the Glutton the first dative object, introduced by the preposition *man*, does not occur till l. 100: " This stone is suitable for a seat " = Suits stone this for seat = *mĕhuli batu ndai man pĕrkundulkundulĕn.* On the other hand, by way of contrast, the quite short Tontb. Story of the Python contains half a dozen cases of the dative object.

161. Nearer and remoter object together in a sentence. From what has been said above it follows that the former comes next to the predicate without the intervention of any-preposition—and the latter then follows, accompanied by a preposition. I have analysed the whole of Jonker's Book of Laws on this point and find a great many cases of agreement with the corresponding German idiom, *e.g.,* to give refuge to

an offender; to give wages to the man; to lend a weapon to
an offender; to deliver, to pledge, etc., a thing to someone.
But contrary to the German idiom, "to accuse something
to a person", meaning "to accuse a person of something".

162. The adverbial is worked into the sentence by means
of prepositions. Among the widely distributed prepositions
are *di*, *ri*, " in, on, at ", etc., and *ka*, " to, towards "; Tag.
has *sa*, " in, at "; Timorese *bi*, " in "; etc., etc. — Illustrations. Lampong, from Ophuijsen's Collection of Mousedeer
Stories: " If you come down to the water I shall catch you "
= If y. descend to w., you I c. = *asal niku turun di way,
niku ku tĕkĕp*. Bĕsĕmah, from Helfrich's Collection of Proverbs: " Where is there any ivory that has no flaw ? " = In
what i., not flawed = *di manĕ gadiñ diq bĕrĕtaq*. Kangeanese,
from the Story of Kandhulok: " On his way Kandhulok
arrived at a ricefield " = O.-h.-w. the K. a. at r. = *sa-jhalan-
jhalan-na se Kandhulok tĕppaq ka saba*. Timorese, from
Jonker's text: " What is smelling in the room in there ? " =
saan nafo bi keen nanan. Togianese, from Adriani's small
Collection of Texts: " I will not live in my village here any
longer " = Not + more I will live h. in v. my = *tamo ku poru
maroro iriqi ri lipu ñku*. Nabaloi, from Scheerer's Collection
of Dialogues: " We eat on the march " = Eat we during m.
= *mañan tayo chi chalan*.* Tag., from Tell: " You are my
guest at Schwyz, I am yours at Lucerne " = You g. mine at
S., I the yours at L. = *kayo i panaohin ko sa Schwyz, ako añ
iniyo sa Luserna*.

---

* Scheerer gives no description of his *ch*, but as he has based his
spelling on the Spanish usage it seems likely that his *ch* is identical
with the sound rendered in these Essays by *c*.

ESSAY IV

PHONETIC PHENOMENA
IN THE INDONESIAN LANGUAGES

(The original was published in 1915.)

SUMMARY

of Substance + Word of Weak Stress. 326. Accentuation of Loan-words. 327-8. Quality of the Accent. 329. The Unaccentuated Syllables. 330. Original Indonesian Accentuation. 331-2. Comparison with the Accent of the Indo-European Word. 333-7. Sentence Stress.

338-41. Section XV: Lagu.

342-51. Section XVI: As to the Invariability of Phonetic Laws.

———————

SECTION I : FUNDAMENTAL CONSIDERATIONS.

1. The present monograph is a delineation of the *phonetic phenomena* of the IN languages.

Note.—As to the method of transcription, see § 39, as to the abbreviations, § 38.

2. Up to the present no comprehensive work on this subject has appeared, but a sufficient quantity of material for such a work has been published in the shape of IN grammars and vocabularies and a number of treatises. I shall not enumerate these *sources and preliminary works* here, because I intend to refer to them in detail in my " Geschichte der IN Sprachforschung " which is to appear shortly. — The works of my predecessors have furnished me with a relatively small part of the materials, either rough hewn or more or less worked up; the greater part has been collected by myself. In its whole plan, as well as in the execution of the individual sections dealing with the subject from various points of view, my monograph takes its own independent line.

3. I have to delineate the IN *phonetic phenomena* of the *past* as well as those of the present time. The past history of IN sounds can be gathered from the written documents handed down to us, or it can be deduced by the usual methods of linguistic science, above all by the method of comparison. On account of its heritage of written documents dating from former periods, Javanese is of special importance for the study of IN phonetics; Bugis, Sundanese, Malagasy, and some other tongues, are of much less moment.

4. For our deductions we often require a *basis to start from*; and that basis is Original IN. In this matter I follow the same procedure as Brugmann in his " Kurze vergleichende Grammatik der indogermanischen Sprachen ". Just as IE comparative research has inferred from the Sanskrit *dhūmás*, Latin *fumus*, etc., an Original IE *dhūmós*, " smoke ", and as Brugmann (KvG, § 85), in dealing with the vowel *ū*, proceeds from this *dhūmós* and other such Original IE words as by the same method have been shown to contain the vowel *ū*; so from Hova *telu*, Toba *tolu*, etc., there follows an Original IN *tĕlu*, " three ". This *tĕlu*, together with the other words in which an Original IN *ĕ* has been inferred, serves us as a point of departure for the discussion of the sound *ĕ* and its derivatives.

Note.—By far the greater part of the IN words occurring in this monograph have the *accent* on the penultimate syllable. In that case I do not mark it, and accordingly write *telu, tolu*; on the other hand, in § 5 I write *taló*, because this Pangasinan word is accentuated on the final syllable. For the reasons given in § 330 I cannot indicate the accent in the reconstructed Original IN words. — As regards *quantity*, see §§ 67 *seqq.*

5. I will now demonstrate by an individual example the nature of the *method* by which I *reconstruct* the Original IN forms.

Thesis.

" Original IN possessed a neutral, colourless vowel, styled in Javanese, and accordingly also in IN comparative linguistics, the pĕpĕt, which is represented (not very aptly) by the symbol *ĕ*, and occurs for example in the Original IN word *tĕlu*, ' three ' ".

Evidence.

I. As " three " in Pangasinan is *taló*, in Hova *telu*, in Sundanese *tilu*, in Toba *tolu*, in Tinggian *tulu*, the variegated character of the vowel of the first syllable can be most satis-factorily explained as a case of differentiation from a neutral original, just such as the pĕpĕt.

II. The pĕpĕt still actually exists, even though in a minority of the IN languages, yet in the most *diverse* local areas of the family.   Thus in Karo in Sumatra, in Balinese next to Java, in Tontemboan in Celebes, etc., the word for " three " is *tĕlú.*

III.   Old Javanese likewise has *tĕlú;* and how important Old Javanese is will be shown in § 6.

IV.   Nias has no pĕpĕt; where other tongues have *ĕ,* Nias has an *o.*   But this *o* has a peculiar pronunciation, it is articulated further back in the mouth than the *o* of a different origin.   If I represent the front *o* by o_1 and the back one by o_2, I get (for example) the equations: Nias *bo₂li,* " price " = Original IN, and likewise Gayo, Malay, etc., *bĕli,* but Nias o_1no_1, " child " = Original IN, and likewise Old Javanese, Tagalog, etc., *anak.*   The peculiarity in the articulation of the o_2 accordingly points to an originally peculiar sound, in fact to the pĕpĕt.

V.   Iloko knows no pĕpĕt; where other languages have a pĕpĕt, Iloko puts an *e.*   But the consonant, which immediately follows this *e,* is doubled; thus the equivalent of Original IN, and likewise Old Javanese, Malay, etc., *lĕpas,* " free ", is Iloko *leppás.*   This doubling of the consonant does not occur after an *e* of any other origin.   Now Madurese says *lĕppas;* it also doubles the consonant, but leaves the *ĕ* unchanged.   If we compare the Mad. procedure with the Iloko, it follows that the Iloko *e,* after which the consonant is doubled, points back to an original pĕpĕt.

VI.   Talautese lacks the pĕpĕt; an *a* occurs where other languages have *ĕ.*   But after this *a* the liquid *l* is articulated differently than it is after an *a* which descends from an Original IN *a.*   So in Tal., too, we have an indication of the existence of the pĕpĕt in Original IN.

VII.   Hova possesses no pĕpĕt; for an *ĕ* of other languages it puts in an accentuated syllable an *e,* in an unaccentuated one an *i.*   Original IN, and likewise Karo, etc., *tĕlĕn,* " to swallow ", has therefore in Hova the equivalent *télina.*   Now before this *i* < *ĕ* Hova preserves Original IN *l* unchanged, whereas before a Hova *i* < Original IN *i* it becomes *d;* thus *télina* < Original IN *tĕlĕn,* but *dimi,* " five " < Original IN *lima.* Here again, then, we find in a language which itself has no pĕpĕt an argument for the existence of the pĕpĕt in Original IN.

Conclusion.

The evidence of I.-VII. *supra*, to which many other testimonies could be added, shows conclusively that the phonetic system of Original IN must be credited with the vowel called pĕpĕt.

6. The *phonetic conditions of Old Javanese* coincide in most cases with the phonetic system of Original IN as inferred by the comparative method. Hence we get, from objective documents, a confirmation of what has been attained merely by inference. — To this harmonious agreement there are two exceptions:

I. Original IN r_2 (= uvular r) disappears in Old Jav.; hence Old Jav. *atus*, " hundred ", from Original IN r_2atus.

II. Original IN successive vowels are often contracted in Old Jav. Original IN, and also Malay, etc., disyllabic *lain*, " other ", becomes *len* in Old Jav.

7. It is not possible in IN linguistic research, any more than in IE, to discover the corresponding original values of *all* the phonetic phenomena of the living languages. Some IN languages possess the sound called hamzah; but, as stated in § 40, I am not at present in a position to decide with absolute certainty whether it should be ascribed to Original IN.

8. Between any of the phonetic types that exist to-day and its corresponding archetype in the original mother-tongue, there may have been *intermediate stages*. *IE* linguistic research possesses the means of determining such intermediate stages in many cases. Thus Kluge, in his " Etymologisches Wörterbuch der deutschen Sprache ", s.v. *Met*, shows that between Original IE *mĕdhus* and the Modern German *Met* (= *mēt*), " mead ", we have to intercalate Original Germanic *mĕdus*, Old High German *mĕto*, and Middle High German *mĕt* as intermediate forms. *IN* research possesses such means to a much more limited extent, seeing that it has only got one single language with really important written records of some antiquity, namely, Javanese; besides which, Old Jav. mostly exhibits the same phonetic state as Original IN. Nevertheless, IN research is in some instances able to detect such intermediate forms, and the cases where it is possible may be taken to fall pretty much under the following heads:

I.   The intermediate form is found in *Old Jav.*:

Original form	Intermediate stage	Final result
Original IN	Old Jav.	Modern Jav.
dir₂us	*dyus*	*adus*, " to bathe "

dir_2us — $dyus$ — $adus$

II.   The intermediate form is represented by the *native spelling*:

Original form	Intermediate stage	Final result
Original IN	Written Minangkabau	Spoken Minangkabau
sĕlsĕl	*sasal*	*sasa*, " to regret "

III.   The intermediate form exists in a *cognate dialect*:

Original form	Intermediate stage	Final result
Original IN	Tunong-Achinese	Achinese Proper
batu	*batéw*	*batéĕ*

IV.   The intermediate form can be ascertained by *inference*. If Original IN *bar₂a*, " glowing embers ", results in Bungku *wea*, we must assume a form *waya* as an intermediate stage: see § 136.

9.   We often have reports that the *older living generation* adheres to an older phonetic stage, while a newer phonetic type has developed in the speech of the younger people.   In Kamberese Original IN *s* becomes *h*, *e.g.* Kamb. *ahu*, " dog ", < Original IN *asu*, but " one often hears old people pronouncing the *s* " (Wielenga).

10.   Phonetic changes either take place unconditionally or are dependent on definite *conditions*.   Original IN pĕpĕt unconditionally, in all cases where it occurs, becomes *e* in Dayak; thus Original IN *tĕkĕn*, " staff ", results in Day.

teken. In Hova, which betrays a somewhat near relationship
with Day., the pĕpĕt only becomes *e* when it bears the accent;
hence Original IN *tĕkĕn* produces Hova *téhina.* Accentuation,
therefore, is the condition for the change of *ĕ* into *e* in Hova.

11. The condition under which a phonetic change takes
place is one thing, and the *cause* which calls it into existence
is another. The conditions are very often recognizable in
IN, but as regards the causes the same observation applies to
IN as Hirt, in his "Handbuch der griechischen Laut- und
Formenlehre", § 71, made about Greek: "We are often
unable to detect the causes of phonetic change". Nevertheless IN linguistic students have set up many a theory on this
subject, and I here repeat some of them, without commenting
thereon: "A peculiarity of certain of the Toraja languages is
the change of *s* into *h*. It appears to us that the custom of
filing the teeth quite short or partially knocking them out,
may be the cause of this phonetic change" (Adriani). — In
Karo, Original IN *a* remains *a*, but alongside of *jah*, "yonder",
a form *joh* has appeared, "in consequence of a movement of
the lips, with which one indicates the direction 'yonder'"
(Joustra). — "The custom of chewing betel explains why the
Javanese often pronounce a velar instead of a labial, *e.g.,*
kĕstul for *pĕstul,* 'pistol'" (Roorda).

12. In the evolution of IN sounds a number of other
forces bear sway, which operate in the way of influencing,
furthering, hindering, crossing, etc., though they cannot be
called "causes" or "conditions" in the strict sense. These
are analogy, popular etymology,* the tendency towards
differentiation, phonetic symbolism, onomatopœia, euphemism, and the tendency towards disyllabism.

13. *Analogy* plays as great a part in the phonetic evolution of the IN languages as it does in the IE family. Thus
among the IN, as among the IE languages, there is hardly one
in which the numerals have not been affected by its influence;

* [The tendency which produces forms like "Hobson-Jobson",
"sparrow-grass", etc.]

cf. Paul, " Prinzipien der Sprachgeschichte ", under the heading " Kontamination ".

In Original IN, " hundred " is r_2atus and " thousand ", r_1ibu, but for " thousand " Bajo says *ribus*, having transferred to it the *s* of r_2atus.

14. *Popular etymology* also has the same importance in IN as in IE. Persian *lāzuwerdi*, " sky blue ", becomes in Javanese *rojowĕrdi*, in imitation of *rojo*, " king ", as if it meant the royal colour. — Particularly frequent is the occurrence in IN of a species of popular etymology which I will style *grammatical popular etymology*. From Sanskrit *yoga* comes Karo *iyoga*, " yoke ". But as *i-* in Karo is a prefix, it appears to the people who speak Karo as if *iyoga* were made up of the prefix *i* + the intermediary sound *y* + *oga*, and hence they have abstracted out of *iyoga* a WB *oga*, which is now employed alongside of *iyoga*. Or, since *ka-* is a very common prefix in Old Javanese, the Sanskrit *kawi*, " poet ", makes the impression of being a derived word, and from it is extracted a WB *awi*, " to compose (poetry) ", from which in its turn various derivatives are formed, *e.g.,* *awiawian*, " poetry ".

15. *Tendency towards differentiation.* Where the originally single meaning of a word is differentiated, a phonetic differentiation may also be induced, in IN as in IE. Just as in the dialect of Lucerne the Middle High German *mĕsse* has evolved into *Mäss*, " the religious ceremony styled the mass ", and *Määs*, " an annual feast and fair ", so too the Original IN *ulu*, " head ", appears in Bimanese as *ulu*, " formerly ", and *uru*, " beginning ".

16. *Phonetic symbolism.* In many IN languages we find phonetic symbolism at work in the duplication of words, as in the Sundanese *uncal-ancul*, " to hop hither and thither ", alongside of *ancul*, " to hop ". So too the substitution of a sonant for a surd in the Nias $aizo_2\text{-}aizo_2$, " somewhat sour ", beside $aiso_2$, " sour ", and other cases, may be due to phonetic symbolism. On the other hand, I do not share the view that in durative formations such as the Old Javanese *mamanah* from the WB *panah*, " to shoot ", the *m* replacing the *p*, that is a continuous sound instead of a momentary one, indicates duration; in a former monograph I have given a purely mechanical phonetic explanation of this phenomenon, and I am convinced that all *IE* scholars will approve of *my* view.

Madurese exhibits a peculiar phenomenon in connexion with words where the WB is partially reduplicated, after the fashion of *los-alos*, " very fine ", *te-pote*, " quite white "; *alos*, " fine ", is evolved phonetically from the Original IN, and likewise Malay, etc., *halus*, and similarly *pote* from *putih*. But alongside of *los-alos*, *te-pote*, we also find forms which have preserved the Original IN vowels, viz., *lus-alus*, *ti-puti*, and these denote a still higher or more superlative degree than *los-alos*, *te-pote*. In these cases, then, it is the more archaic phonetic type that denotes the higher degree of quality.

17. *Onomatopœia* exercises its influence on the evolution of the IN sounds mainly in the way of impeding the consistent operation of phonetic laws. It manifests itself in the first place in interjections that mimic a sound. In Minangkabau an Original IN liquid at the end of a WB disappears; Original IN *lapar*, " hunger ", is also written *lapar* in Mkb., but pronounced *lapa*. Further, Original IN final explosives turn into hamzah in spoken Mkb.: thus Original IN *atĕp*, " roof ", > spoken Mkb. *atoq*. So no *r* and no *p* can occur as finals in spoken Mkb. But interjections like *gar*, " crack !", *dapap*, " plop !", etc., are exceptions to this rule. — Besides these, the operation of onomatopœia is seen in words of substance, mostly in names of animals, which have been formed in imitation of natural sounds. In Tontemboan, in the case of WB's consisting of a doubled root, the final consonant of the first half must as a rule become *q*: thus Original IN *korkor*, " to scratch ", becomes Tontb. *koqkor*. But the onomato- pœically formed *kerker*, the name of a species of bird, retains the *r* in the first half.

18. *Euphemism.* For reasons of euphemism certain words, especially such as are connected with sexual matters, have been deliberately deformed in the IN languages. A number of these are given in Van der Tuuk's Toba vocabulary, *e.g.*,

ilat, disfigured from *pilat*, " membrum virile ". Such deformations usually occur on the analogy of some other, more or
less connected, word : thus *ilat*, on the analogy of *ila*, " shame ".

19. *Tendency towards disyllabism.* Whereas the forces
thus far mentioned, analogy, popular etymology, etc., operate
in IE as well as in IN, the tendency towards disyllabism is
exclusively peculiar to IN. Its significance was already
recognized by Humboldt in his " Kawisprache ", pp. ccccii
seqq. The WB's of the IN languages are as a rule disyllabic,
and the genius of the IN languages is often impelled to
squeeze into this mould such words as are not really disyllables at all or have lost that form in the course of linguistic
evolution. Thus the Dutch word *lijst*, " list ", appears in
several IN languages under the form *ĕles*, with a prothetic
formative *ĕ* which has no meaning or significance; and
" Rome ", *i.e.*, Constantinople, is called *Ruhum* in Minangkabau, not *Rum*.

20. Between the *written language* and the *colloquial* in IN
there are often phonetic differences. The one of most frequent occurrence is that the colloquial allows abbreviations
which are avoided in the written language. Thus spoken
Javanese says *dulur*, " brother or sister ", for the written
sĕdulur.

21. The phonetic phenomena hitherto described occur in
ordinary, normal speech. Besides this we find in IN certain
special modes of speech. These are the language of children,
the language of animals in the beast fables, poetic language,
and various artificial languages.

22. The *language of children* in IN has the four following
characteristics :

I. *Substitution of one sound for another.* " As long as a
Bareqe child is unable to pronounce the velars, it regularly
replaces them by the dentals; thus it says *atu* for Original IN,
and also Bareqe, *aku*, ' I '. Small children often pronounce
c for *s*, and accordingly say *cucu* for Original IN, and likewise
Bareqe, *susu*, ' breast ' " (Adriani).

II. *Infantile repetition.* By the change of a consonant, words are adapted to this type. Thus Bareqe children say *jeje* for *keje*, " membrum virile "; Tontemboan children, *kiqkiq* for *kiqciq*, " to bite ". In Tontb. *titiq* for *kiliq*, " to sleep", both changes have occurred, viz., substitution of the dental for the velar and also adaptation to the infantile habit of repetition.

III. *Transformation* of combinations of sounds which are *difficult* for children *to pronounce.* Thus Karo children say *a-pe* for *lañ-pe*, " not at all ".

IV. Besides the above, the language of children exhibits other *isolated phenomena*, which cannot be classed under any general category. Thus Tontemboan children say *lileq* instead of *lĕlcq*, " to bathe ".

23. When parents speak with children, they use either the normal form of speech or the children's language; but they also sometimes make a compromise between the two. In the preceding paragraph, under subsection I, we saw that the Bareqe children use *cucu* for *susu*, " breast ". But in normal Bareqe the palatal tenuis only occurs after the nasal, so that forms like *cucu* do not exist in the speech of adults. On the other hand, the palatal media is not subject to the same restrictions as the tenuis, and so it comes about that parents, when they speak to children, say neither *susu* nor *cucu*, but *juju*.

24. It is not uncommon for childish words to make their way into the language of adults, particularly the forms involving infantile repetition. In Original IN and in most of the living IN languages, " father " is *ama*, " mother ", *ina*; but several languages employ the infantile forms *mama* and *nina*. In Tontemboan, " grandfather " is *apoq*, and " uncle ", *itoq*; but the *vocatives* of these words are *papoq* and *titoq*. — In Bugis the word for " little girl " is *bĕsseq* or *bĕcceq*, the first form being used only of princesses. According to subsection I of § 22, the form with *s* is the normal one, while the one with *c* was originally the infantile form.

25.   The phenomena of childish speech recur to a great
extent in IE.   In certain of the Swiss dialects the word for
" father " is *Ätti*, but other dialects replace it by *Tätti*, using
therefore the form that involves infantile repetition: see
" Schweizerisches Idiotikon ", I, 585.

26.   The *language of animals* employs (*inter alia*) the method
of infantile repetition, like the language of children.   In the
sixteenth tale in Adriani's " Leesboek in de Bareqe taal ",
p. 17, l. 10, the old mouse says *kuko*, for *duñko* " crust of the
rice-pap in the pan ".

27.   *Poetic language.*   The requirements of rhythm and
rhyme produce all sorts of phonetic changes.   Certain literatures, it is true, *e.g.* the Bareqe, do not tolerate such disfigure-
ments, but others put up with a great deal in this respect.
Such poetical deformations may be divided into two classes,
viz., those which exhibit changes that are still within the
limits of linguistic possibility, and on the other hand such
as exemplify deliberately artificial modification.

I.   To the first category belongs the poetic licence in
Bisaya, whereby *i* before a vowel may be treated as a consonant, *e.g.*, *motya*, for the trisyllabic *motia*, " pearl ".   The
change of *i* in this position into a consonant is found in the
normal form of many IN languages: the Old Javanese WB
ipi, " to dream ", has a conditional *añipya*.

II.   To the second category belong the most varied forms
of licence, which for the most part are based on no principle.
Sometimes they result from *metric* difficulties.   Thus in the
Balinese Epic Megantaka, strophe 318, verse 7, we find *tos*,
for *totos*, " descendant ", because if *totos* had been used the
verse would have had one syllable too many.   In the second
place, they may be due to difficulties connected with the
rhyme.   In the Minangkabau Epic " Kaba Sabay nan
Aluyh ", verses 446, 447, read: " That we say yes, yes, that
we say no, no " = *maq kami bario-io, maq kami batido-tido*.
Here the form *tido* is a deformation of the normal *tidaq*, " no ",
made to suit the rhyme, which consists in a similarity of both

vowels of the WB's. Thirdly, these changes may be produced by the requirements of the *lagu*, *i.e.*, the current mode
and fashion of reciting. Achinese has (*inter alia*) a special
lagu for the recitation of solemn or tragic poems. In this
lagu the several syllables are pronounced very long, and here
and there extended into two syllables by pronouncing the
vowel twice over with the intercalation of an *ñ* between the
two: for instance, *puñucoq* instead of the normal *pucoq*, " tip ".

28. In IE we also find both kinds of poetic licence, as de-
picted in the preceding paragraph. If in the Aeneid we have
to scan *conubjo*, that corresponds to *motya* in subsection I,
while the mutilated form *navyasā vacas*, cited in Wackernagel,
" Altindische Grammatik ", I, p. xvii, is parallel to the deliberately artificial deformations of subsection II.

29. In *reading aloud*, certain phonetic peculiarities also
occur. " It is customary at the Javanese Court, in reading
out official documents, but only in that case, to aspirate
initial vowels, *e.g.* to say *hadalĕm* for *adalĕm*, ' to dwell ' "
(Poensen).

30. *Artificial languages.* In IN there are quite a considerable number of artificial languages: *e.g.*, priestly languages,
languages of ceremonious politeness, languages specially used
when hunting, thieves' languages, etc. The peculiarities of
these artificial forms of speech are lexicographical and
morphological, but also phonetic. . From the phonetic point
of view two principles in particular are operative:

I. *Metathesis.* The Toba thieves' language, for example,
interchanges the two syllables of the WB, saying therefore
tema for *mate*, " dead ".

II. *Analogical transformation.* The Dayak priestly language says *rohoñ*, " sword ", for the *dohoñ* of normal speech,
by analogy with *rohes*, " to slay ". The Javanese language
of ceremonious politeness changes *kurañ*, " too few ", into
kirañ, by analogy with *lirañ*, " half ".

31. One of the methods of formation of the Javanese
language of ceremonious politeness consists in replacing

various word-endings by *-jiṅ* or *-jĕṅ*: thus from *esuq*, " morrow ", it makes *enjiṅ* and from *buru*, " to hunt ", *bujĕṅ*. I shall style this mode of formation the *jĕṅ*-type. Now we find isolated representatives of this *jĕṅ*-type in other languages also. Malay has a word *anjiṅ*, " dog ", Makassar a word *tojeṅ*, " true ", with *e* instead of *ĕ*. These words do not belong to an artificial stratum of these two languages, but to their normal form of speech. But inasmuch as *anjiṅ* coexists with the Original IN, and likewise Old Javanese, etc., *asu*, and *tojeṅ* with the Dayak, etc., *toto*, one must assume that *anjiṅ* and *tojeṅ* were originally artificial forms, transformations of *asu* and *toto* in accordance with the *jĕṅ*-type, and that they subsequently found their way into normal speech and displaced *asu* and *toto*. This is an interesting case of the influence of the artificial type of language upon the normal type.

32. The word *anjiṅ* is genuine Malay, the word *tojeṅ* is genuine Makassar, they are not borrowed from Javanese, for the simple reason that Javanese does not possess these words. Thus we find the *jĕṅ*-type of word formation as an established institution in several widely separated languages. Hence we may perhaps be entitled to ascribe this particular mode of artificial word formation even to Original IN.

33. *Influence of foreign languages.* This influence, it must be admitted, shows itself most strongly in the vocabulary, and only slightly in phonetic evolution.

I. Phonetic influence of *other IN languages*. Kulawi changes *s* into *h*, and accordingly says *tahi*, " lake ", for Original IN *tasik*. " But many of the men, who nearly all know Palu, which has preserved the *s*, often pronounce the *s* even now, whereas the women, who for the most part only know Kulawi, regularly use *h* " (Adriani). In Ruso-Talautese the normal Talautese *k* of a final syllable is pronounced *s*, e.g., *ápuka*, " lime ", becomes *ápusa*; " but this peculiarity has been steadily disappearing since the settlement in Ruso of a number of people from Niampak, who mock at this idiosyncrasy of the Ruso population " (Steller). The Tojo-Bareqe has par-

tially adopted the accentuation of its neighbour, the Bugis.
"His dwelling-place" in Bareqe is *banúa-ña*, in Bugis *wanuwá-
na*; but Tojo-Bareqe under Bugis influence says *banuá-ña*.

II.   Influence of *non-IN languages*.   Madurese had originally no *f*, but the Madurese have no difficulty in pronouncing
the sound and therefore mostly preserve it unchanged in
loan-words from Arabic or from European languages, so that
we must now include the sound *f* in the Mad. phonetic system.
Bimanese rejects all original final consonants, and treats loan-
words in the same way, thus saying *asa* for the Arabic *aṣal*,
"origin".   "But *educated* Bimanese often pronounce the
final consonant" (Jonker).

34.   *Influence of school teaching.*   Tontemboan has changed
the Original IN, and likewise Old Javanese, Malay, etc.,
media *g* into the spirant *γ*.*   "Under the influence of school
education, which is given in Malay, the younger generation
now uses the media instead of the spirant" (Adriani).

35.   The *native systems of writing and spelling* are of importance for linguistic research in two sets of cases:

I.   The spelling of certain languages, particularly in Sumatra, exhibits *a more archaic phonetic stage* than the pronunciation.   IN research establishes that the word for "free" in
its original form was *lĕpas*.   Minangkabau says *lapeh*, but
writes *lapas*; the written language, therefore, has preserved
the original final of the word.   Such spellings accordingly
confirm the conclusions of linguistic comparison.

II.   Words that lean proclitically or enclitically on a principal word are in several languages *written continuously* with
it.   Thus in the Makassar tale I Kukang, p. 5, l. 15: "He
was always presented (with) money" = *nanitanrotanrówimo
doweq*.   Here *na*, "he", and *mo*, an emphatic particle, are
written together continuously with the principal word *nitan-
rotanrówi*, "to be always presented (with)".   From the
point of view of linguistic science this habit must be regarded
as correct.

* [See § 41, IV, footnote.]

36. For the understanding of IN phonetic phenomena it is absolutely necessary *to study texts*. Naturally those texts are most satisfactory which mark accent, quantity, sandhi, and the like. One can often get more light from the texts than from the explanations of the manuals. For instance, Seidenadel, in his grammar of the Bontok language, gives no theory of quantity, but out of his most conscientiously edited texts we can construct the theory for ourselves. Not infrequently the texts even correct the data of the grammars. Matthes, in his Bugis grammar, § 193, says that the pronoun of the first person *ku* is abbreviated proclitically, but never enclitically, to *u*, but in the Budi Isětiharatě, edited by himself, p. 294, l. 8, we find: " My husband loves me " $=$ He loves me, husband my $=$ *na-clóriy-aq worowané-u*. Moreover for several languages we possess carefully edited texts, indicating accent, quantity, sandhi, etc., but as yet no grammars or vocabularies.

37. *Comparison of IN with IE.* In this monograph l compare, where it seems to me feasible, the phonetic conditions of IN with those of IE. The idea of comparing IE linguistic phenomena with IN is nothing new. Humboldt and Bopp did it, though with an inadequate comprehension of the IN material. Kern does it with a true insight into both the IN and the IE material, and the critical student is grateful to Kern for his work. But recently certain voices have made themselves heard, denying the desirability of such comparisons. Therefore I must adduce some considerations in support of my point of view.

I. IE research has advanced further than IN, its subtle and highly developed methods can, indeed *must*, serve as a guide to IN research. For example, many IN scholars classify the IN languages according to the sounds they admit as finals; others have classified them on the basis of their genitive construction, particularly as regards the position of the genitive before or after the principal word. Both systems depend upon *a single* linguistic phenomenon. In the IE sphere we find (*inter alia*) a classification of the Germanic languages into East Germanic and West Germanic. But Kluge, " Urgermanisch ", § 146, bases this division not upon *a single* criterion, but upon a whole series of them, and yet the classification is not accepted by all scholars. That sort of thing ought to make IN scholars wake up; either they must discover additional criteria or abandon their classification of the IN languages.

Note.—The classification of the IN languages on the basis of one single linguistic phenomenon would only be reasonable if it were proved that it was the most important, significant, and characteristic, of all linguistic phenomena. But no such proof has been given, either in support of the phenomena of final sounds or of the position of the genitive. For my own part, I do not see why the phenomena of final sounds should be deemed more important than those that affect sounds in the interior of words (see §§ 193 *seqq.*), or the position of the genitive in relation to the principal word more important than (*e.g.*) that of the predicate in relation to the subject. In the last few years IN research has devoted an undue amount of attention to the genitive.

II. Conversely, the results of IN linguistic research may also be applied with profit to IE study. For example, in Meyer-Lübke's " Historische Grammatik der französichen Sprache ", I, § 43, the word *tante*, " aunt ", is explained as having been formed under the influence of the principles of infantile repetition from an older form *ante* < Latin *amita*. This explanation finds its parallel and confirmation in the IN phenomena of our § 22.

III. Students of linguistic psychology make use of IN material, often in fact they seem to prefer it, as a basis for their inferences. But as their own training has been IE, they will be enabled to feel their way with greater certainty into the sphere of IN linguistic phenomena, if these are presented to them accompanied by IE parallels. For I have shown clearly enough in a former monograph* how even the most

* [See " Prodromus ", § 28.]

eminent students of linguistic psychology may err, when they venture into IN without definite guidance.

IV. Many scholars who compare the vital phenomena of different families of speech, *inter alia* IE and IN, have it as their aim, either principal or subsidiary, to ascertain what linguistic phenomena should be esteemed as expressions of the higher intellectuality. Without exception, they arrive at the conclusion that the IN languages, as compared with the IE, bear the mark of inferiority. Now if the deductions which led them to that conclusion were unassailable, one would have to submit to them; but so far as the IN languages are concerned, I will undertake to show that these arguments, also without exception, betray inadequate knowledge, partiality, etc. As regards two scholars, Durand and Taffanel, I demonstrated that in a former monograph.* Let us now take a more recent case. Finck, in his work " Die Haupttypen des Sprachbaues ", p. 94, deals with the structure of the sentence in Samoan, and in connexion therewith, rightly enough, discusses the part which is played by the numerous particles — *i.e.*, prepositions, conjunctions, words of emphasis, etc. — in knitting together the several portions of the sentence. He then arrives at the conclusion that these particles have not the power to weld the Samoan sentence into a unity, and his final verdict is that Samoan does not possess the complete, definite sentence-structure that IE has. This implies a judgment that convicts a language of the IN-Polynesian family of inferiority in an important manifestation of its linguistic vitality. But Finck overlooks the fact that Samoan, like all the languages of the IN-Pol. family, has other means of attaining the completeness, and in particular the definite rounding off, of the sentence, means which can be employed in addition to, or in lieu of, the particles. One such means, for example, is the tonal accentuation of the sentence (see § 335), whereof Finck says not a syllable. And how inadequately Finck—and his authorities — grasped the real nature of these very particles, is drastically illustrated by the way in which he translates the title of the Samoan text selected by him as an

* [See " Tagalen und Madagassen ", §§ 12, 56.]

example. This reads: '*o le tala i le fuñafuña*, and Finck (p. 86, l. 12 from the bottom) translates it: " O ! (or " indeed ") the tale in the sea-cucumber ". In reality '*o* (in my spelling *qo.* § 39), which is derived from an older form *ko*, is a *preposition* accompanying the nominative (see Kern FI, p. 30, l. 1); and *i* is a preposition *with an extensive* (*i.e.*, vague and general) *sphere of meaning* which in several IN-Pol. languages happens also to serve for the genitive relation. So Finck has rendered a preposition by an interjection, and has arbitrarily and wrongly translated a preposition of vague and general import by a locative one. — Now if as against this sort of faulty comparison of IN and IE another method of comparison is propounded, which avoids the mistakes of the former and may therefore be termed the objective method, it would follow that the former method could no longer maintain itself. And if our objective method had no other aim or purpose than to cut away the ground from under the feet of that unscientific, unjust mental attitude, which is so offensive to our common sentiment of humanity as well, would not that be a sufficient justification for its existence?

38. In this monograph the following *abbreviations* (besides such as are obvious) have been used:

IN = Indonesian.

IE = Indo-European.

WB = Word-base.

Brugmann KvG = K. Brugmann, " Kurze vergleichende Grammatik der indogermanischen Sprachen."

Meillet GvP = A. Meillet, " Grammaire du vieux Perse."

Kern FI = Kern, " De Fidjitaal."

Bijdr. = Bijdragen tot de Taal-, Land- en Volkenkunde van Nederlandsch-Indië.

Schwarz-Texts = Tontemboan texts, edited by J. Alb. T. Schwarz.

Steller-Texts = The texts in K. G. F. Steller, "Nadere Bijdrage tot de kennis van het Tala-oetsch."

Seidenadel-Texts = The texts in C. W. Seidenadel, " The first Grammar of the language spoken by the Bontoc Igorot."

Tuuk Lb = H. N. van der Tuuk, " Bataksch Lees-boek."

Hain-Teny = Jean Paulhan, " Les Hain-Teny Méri-nas."*

* [See also Essay II, § 15.]

SECTION II: ENUMERATION AND DESCRIPTION OF THE INDONESIAN SOUNDS.

The Original Indonesian Phonetic System.

39. Original Indonesian must be credited with the following phonetic system:

Vowels	a	i	u	e	o	$ĕ$
Semi-vowels	y	w				
Liquids	r_1	r_2	l			
Laryngal	q^*					
Velars	k	g	$ṅ^*$			
Palatals	c^*	j	$ñ^*$			
Dentals	t	d	n			
Labials	p	b	m			
Sibilant	s					
Aspirate	h					

40. *Observations* on this table of sounds:

I. The two vowels *e* and *o* in the living IN languages are mostly of secondary origin. In a former monograph† I was able to prove their existence as Original IN sounds only in two words, viz., *bela*, " companion, avenger, to share the same fate ", and *sor*, " below ".

II. The liquid r_1 is a lingual *r*, while r_2 is a uvular *r*.

III. The laryngal *q*, also called hamzah, is almost always secondary in the living IN languages. Only in a single case (see § 181) can it with some probability be ascribed to Original IN.

IV. The palatals are regarded by some scholars as not being original; in their opinion they have been evolved from

---

* [See also Essay I, § 11, I, footnotes.]

† [See Essay II, § 26.]

dentals. But no valid arguments have been advanced against my view, which I supported in a former monograph.*

V. Precisely the same applies to the labial media, which some scholars likewise refuse to attribute to Original IN.

VI. We must not overlook the fact that the picture which we are at present able to draw of the Original IN sounds is very much in the rough. For example, it is certain that Original IN possessed the dental series, but we are not in a position to form any precise view as to whether they were postdental, or supradental, etc.

VII. The symbolization of the pĕpĕt by ĕ is clumsy and misleading, but in general use. It is quite a mistake to represent the hamzah by an apostrophe, since the latter has also to serve entirely different purposes, e.g. to indicate the omission of a sound. The objectionable ambiguity caused by using the apostrophe for the hamzah is plainly shown by such a book-title as "De Bare'e-sprekende Toradja's": here the first apostrophe stands for the hamzah, while the second one serves to separate the sign of the plural from a noun. — For my part, I denote the hamzah by q.

The Phonetic Systems of the Living Languages, compared with that of Original Indonesian.

41. The modern IN languages exhibit the following peculiarities in phonetics as compared with Original IN:

I. Some languages have lost certain of the original sounds; some more, some less. In Old Javanese, r_2 has disappeared. Rottinese has lost the pĕpĕt, the palatals, and r, and has got y and w only in interjections.

II. Some languages have created new sounds; thus Hova has created the spirants f and z.

III. Some languages have lost certain of the Original IN sounds, but have formed them again out of other sounds. Original IN h has disappeared in Hova, hence Hova *fulu* <

* [See Essay II, §§ 37-40.]

Original IN *puluh*, " ten ", but *h* has again been evolved from *k*, hence Hova *hazu* < Original IN *kayu*, " tree ".

IV. The sounds found in living IN languages, which cannot however be ascribed to Original IN, are:

The modified (" Umlaut ") vowels *ä ö ü*.*

The nasalized vowels.†

The cerebrals.‡

The spirants *γ, χ; š, z; f.* §

42. Some of the IN languages possess some sound or other in two distinct shades; thus Nias has two *o*'s (see § 5), Talautese two *l*'s (see § 5); Original IN had two *r*'s (see § 129).

43. Sounds with unusual articulation, *i.e.*, such as rarely occurs in human speech in general, are scarce in IN. Busang has a labio-dental *b*, formed by the contact of the lower lip with the upper teeth. Buli has an *h* formed by expelling the breath through the nose.

Fixed and Varying Pronunciation.

44. Some of the IN languages have a constant pronunciation of their sounds, others exhibit variations in some sound or other. In the Philippine languages " *i* is often not to be distinguished from *e* " (Scheerer). In Dayak " the sound of *o* varies between *o* and *u*, indeed the same person in uttering the same word will pronounce the sound sometimes more like an *o*, and at other times more like a *u* " (Hardeland). Probably Bontok exhibits the extreme of arbitrariness in this respect; thus (*inter alia*) in the short story entitled Kolling in Seidenadel-Texts, pp. 555 *seqq.*, one and the same narrator pronounces the word for " then " sometimes *isaed* and sometimes *išaed* (see Kolling 1 and Kolling 10).

45. Such varying pronunciation may be a *preparatory step* towards certain phonetic changes. Dayak is somewhat

* [Pronounced as in German, or nearly so.]
† [As in French.]
‡ [As in Sanskrit, and some other Indian languages.]
§ [See § 65; *γ* is the voiced sound corresponding to the unvoiced *χ*.]

closely related to Hova, and it is to be observed that in Hova
the sound *o* no longer varies between *o* and *u*, but has become
completely identified with the latter, so that Hova no longer
possesses any *o* at all.

46. The varying pronunciation of sounds also occurs in
certain IE languages. Thus Finck in his " Lehrbuch des
Dialekts der deutschen Zigeuner ", § 1, note 4, notices a case
of variation between *w* and *b*.

Full and Reduced Pronunciation.

47. In some IN languages certain sounds are pronounced
not in their normal, full form, but in a weak, reduced form.
In Bontok, final *g*, *d*, *b* " are often scarcely audible " (Seidenadel). In Gayo " in the combinations *ṅg*, *ñj*, *nd*, *mb* the media
is so very much weakened in pronunciation that in many
cases it is impossible to make out whether it is present at all "
(Hazeu). In Hova " final vowels are on the point of disappearing altogether " (Rousselot).

48. This weak pronunciation is displayed particularly by
such furtive vowels as the Minangkabau *ă* in such a word as
púluăh (disyllabic) < Original IN *puluh*, " ten "; by vowels
that owe their existence to the principle of the repetition of
sounds mentioned in § 232, like the *y* in the Hova phrase *ari
gyaga*, " and is surprised ", for *ari* + *gaga*; by such sounds as
merely serve to separate or link together two vowels, like the
w in Bugis *wanuwa*, " land ", for which some other languages
say *wanua*. The weak pronunciation of the last-named class
of sounds is reflected in the varying spelling of the manuscripts,
which sometimes write and sometimes omit the corresponding
letter. In the Bugis tale Paupau Rikadong the phrase " to
the child " = *ri* + *anaq* is written *riyanaq* (p. 4, l. 4) and
rianaq (p. 10, l. 18).

49. Weak pronunciation is the *preparatory step* towards
complete disappearance. Thus the media after the nasal,
which as mentioned in the preceding paragraph is weakly

pronounced in Gayo, has disappeared altogether in certain other languages, *e.g.* in Rottinese; hence Rot. *tana*, " mark " < Original IN *tanda*.

50. Reduced pronunciation of certain sounds is also found in IE. In Latin *n* was weakly pronounced before *s*, *e.g.* in *mensa* (see Sommer, " Handbuch der lateinischen Laut- und Formenlehre ", § 136). Here too reduced pronunciation is a preparatory step towards complete disappearance, hence the Romansch form *mesa*.

Preciser Description of the Several Indonesian Sounds.

51. In the following I give a somewhat more precise description of the several IN sounds, so far as seems to me necessary and sufficient for the purposes and aims of the present monograph.

52. *Vowels.* These will be described in greater detail in the following Section, with reference both to their quantity and quality. Only the pĕpĕt will be discussed here.

53. I. The *pure* pĕpĕt. " The Javanese pĕpĕt is the indeterminate vowel, the sound of the voice when the mouth is not put into any particular position so as to form a definite vowel like *a*, *i*, etc." (Roorda). The shape of the mouth-cavity in pronouncing the Madurese pĕpĕt is " the same as in ordinary breathing " (Kiliaan).

II. The *modified* pĕpĕt. In this the articulation inclines somewhat towards the position of *a*, or *i*, or *u*. " The pronunciation of the Bugis ĕ partakes somewhat of the sound of *a* " (Matthes). In Old Javanese the articulation of the pĕpĕt must have approximated somewhat towards the position of *u*, for it changes into *w* when, after the loss of a consonant, it happens to stand before a vowel; hence Old Jav. *bwat* for *bĕat* < Original IN *bĕr₂at*.

This shade of *a*, *i*, or *u* is the *transitional stage* to the perfect *a*, *i*, or *u*. In Bugis the pĕpĕt has the shade of *a*, while in Makassar, which is very closely related to Bugis, it appears as a perfect *a*.

III. The *fleeting* pĕpĕt. In some languages the pĕpĕt shares the characteristics of the other vowels: it can occur in long and short form, accentuated and unaccentuated. In other languages, *e.g.* in Tontemboan, it only appears as a short vowel. Or else, as in Gayo, it cannot carry the accent: hence Gayo *túluk*, " to verify ", but *tĕlúk*, " bay ".

This *fleeting* character of the pĕpĕt is causally connected with various IN phonetic phenomena. So far as I am aware, the pĕpĕt does not become a diphthong in any of the IN languages. In Old Jav., *u* before a vowel turns into a consonant, hence the conjunctive of *tĕmu*, " to meet with ", is *atĕmwa*; but before the pĕpĕt the *u* persists, and the pĕpĕt is simply absorbed, without any lengthening of the *u*; hence the gerund *tĕmun* $<$ *tĕmu* + *ĕn*.

54. The *modified (Umlaut) vowels* are described and discussed in another connexion (§§ 251 *seqq.*).

55. The *nasalized vowels* are not largely represented in IN. The nasalization is caused either by a preceding or a following nasal consonant.

I. The nasal consonant *precedes*. " In Achinese the nasals impart their strongly nasal sound to the following vowel " (Snouck Hurgronje).

II. The nasal consonant *follows*. " In Hova, as in French, the nasalization is coincident with the commencement of the vowel " (Rousselot). " In Sakalava, in the case of nasal vowels, one also hears the nasal, *e.g.* in the first *a* of the word *mandea*, " to go ", the *n* sound " (Fahrner).

56. The *semi-vowels y* and *w*. " Javanese *y* is a semi-vowel like the French *y* in *il y a* " (Roorda). " Dayak *y* is to be pronounced as in the English *you* " (Hardeland). " Bontok *w* is as in (the English) *winter*; a consonantal *u* " (Seidenadel). " Makassar *w* is to be pronounced like the *ou* in the French *ouate* " (Matthes).

With this articulation of the two semi-vowels all sorts of IN phonetic phenomena are connected. " When speaking slowly the Dayak pronounces *y* as a short *i*, thus *yaku*, " I ", as a trisyllable, *iaku* " (Hardeland). In several languages initial *w* receives a prothetic *u*; thus Original IN *walu*, "eight ", is pronounced *walu* and *uwalu* in Tontemboan.

There are however also other ways of pronouncing the semi-vowels in IN. " Bungku *w* is dentilabial " (Adriani). As *w* is represented in Rottinese by *f*, *e.g.* in *falu* < Original IN *walu*," eight ", and *y* in Hova by *z*, *e.g.* in *hazu*, " tree " < Original IN *kayu*, we must assume as transitional stages semi-vowels accompanied by fricative sounds.

57. The *liquids r* and *l.*

I. The *liquid r.* " In certain regions the Malay *r* is formed by the tongue and teeth, in others by the tongue and palate, in others again it is uvular " (Ophuijsen). " In the north (of the Peninsula, the Malay *r*) is guttural " (= uvular) (Winstedt). " Madurese *r* is coronal-cacuminal " (Kiliaan). " The northern dialects of Sangirese have a labial *r* " (Talens).

A few IN languages have two differently articulated *r*'s; thus Běsěmah possesses a lingual one and a uvular one. That was also the case in Original IN (see § 40).

II. The *liquid l.* " The Gayo *l* is formed by the articulation of the tip of the tongue against the roots of the upper teeth " (Hazeu). " Madurese *l* is pronounced by the articulation of the edges of the tip of the tongue against the foremost part of the hard palate, the tip of the tongue being bent upwards and backwards " (Kiliaan). " Bada has a prepalatal *l* as well as a supradental one " (Adriani).

58. The *laryngal q.* " The hamzah is the explosive formed by the glottis " (Adriani). " The hamzah is formed by the sudden opening of the closed vocal chords " (Snouck Hurgronje). " In Ampana the hamzah is as a rule weakly pronounced " (Adriani).

59. *Velars.* As regards these there is nothing further to be said.

60. *Palatals.* " In the Madurese palatals the back of the tongue, more precisely the middle part of it, articulates against the back part of the hard palate " (Kiliaan). " The Javanese *c* is supradental (alveolar), the Malay one palatal, but not purely explosive like the Tontemboan one, but to some extent fricative " (Adriani). " Bontok *j* and *c* " (which Seidenadel writes *dj* and *tj*) " are dentals, not palatals; frequently they are near *ds* and *ts* (*d* and *t* ' mouillé ') " (Seidenadel).

61.   From these and other descriptions of the palatals, it appears that their articulation varies very considerably in the several languages, so that the name " palatal " is often inappropriate, but more particularly that in several languages they are not purely explosive but accompanied by a fricative sound; in that case they do not represent a single consonant but rather two.   From this circumstance many IN linguistic phenomena can be explained:

I.   Just as no IN word may have more than one consonant at the end, so too a palatal is not permissible in that position.

II.   In Dayak two consonants coming together make the preceding vowel short, as in *sănda*, " pawn, pledge ", a simple media makes it long, as in *lādiñ*, " knife ", but before the palatal media the vowel is always short, as in *măja*, " to visit ".   Thus *j* operates like two consonants together.

III.   In Sundanese the accent falls on the last syllable when the penultimate contains a pĕpĕt; thus for example in *tĕlúk*, " bay "; save that if two consonants follow immediately after the pĕpĕt, as in *dĕñki*, " envious ", the accent can remain upon the *ĕ*, and similarly if a palatal follows, as in *sĕja*, " plan ".

Note.—After the descriptions in § 60 we can understand why the native alphabets sometimes write the palatal nasal and sometimes the dental one before the palatals, thus *tuñjuñ* or *tunjuñ*, " water-lily ".

62.   *Cerebrals* or *cacuminals.*   " In Madurese the cacuminals are produced by the articulation of the tip of the tongue against the front part of the hard palate, the tip of the tongue being bent upwards and backwards " (Kiliaan).

63.   *Dentals.*   " The Achinese *d* is formed by the articulation of the tip of the tongue against the gums close to the roots of the upper teeth " (Snouck Hurgronje). " Malay *d* and *t* are supradental " (Fokker). " In Lebonese *d* and *t* are supra-dental " (Adriani).

64. *Labials.* Here there is nothing more to be said.

65. *Spirants.* " The Dayak *s* is hard, like the hard *s* in German "* (Hardeland). " The Tontemboan *s* is supra-dental " (Adriani). " The Gayo *s* is pronounced a little be-tween the teeth, somewhat lisping " (Hazeu).

" The Nias χ sounds like the German *ch* in the word *wachen* " (Sundermann). " Tontemboan has no velar media; in place of it there is a spirant which is pronounced at the back part of the hard palate " (Adriani). Bontok *š* is like " *sh* as in (the English) *shield* " (Seidenadel). Bontok *f* is " as in (the English) *fine* " (Seidenadel). " Buli *f* is bilabial " (Adriani).

66. The *aspirate h*. " Gayo *h*, as in Dutch, distinctly audible even at the end of a syllable " (Hazeu). " Javanese *h* is mute when it is the initial of a word, and very weak as the final of a word, likewise between two different vowels. while between two similar vowels it is like the Dutch *h* " (De Hollander).

* [Or in English.]

SECTION III: QUANTITY AND QUALITY OF THE VOWELS, DOUBLING OF THE CONSONANTS.

Quantity in General.

67. In most of the IN languages there are two gradations of quantity: long and short. In Bontok "lengthened syllables are but little longer than short syllables" (Seidenadel). "In figures the quantity of the German long *ā* might be estimated to be 2, the Malay long *ā* 1½" (Fokker). Sangirese has three gradations, the long vowels resulting from contraction being longer than the rest. Madurese has no gradations of quantity.

Quantity of the Accentuated Syllable in Words of More than One Syllable.

68. In a considerable number of IN languages there prevails a law of quantity which we may call "the IN law of quantity" and which in its two branches is as follows:

I. The *law of length*: The vowel is long when followed by *only one* consonant, *e.g.* in *wālu*, "eight".

II. The *law of brevity*: The vowel is short when followed by *more than one* consonant, *e.g.* in *găntuṅ*, "to hang".

69. In several languages the IN law of quantity is modified by the interference of special laws, *e.g.*:

I. In Dayak the IN law of length is restricted by the fact that before unvoiced sounds the vowels are mostly short, *e.g.* the *a* in *ăso*, "dog"; and even before the voiced palatal the vowels are short, always (see § 61).

II. In Modern Javanese the IN law of brevity is restricted by the fact that before a nasal + a cognate explosive the vowels are mostly long, *e.g.* in *dīntĕn*, " day ".

III. Seidenadel, in his Bontok grammar, gives no theory of quantity, but an examination of his texts leads to the following results: The law of brevity exhibits hardly any exceptions; in Lumawig 69 we find the word *ākyu*, " sun ", which is contrary to that law. The law of length exhibits more exceptions, especially the one whereby a short vowel is frequently found before a nasal, as in Lumawig 1 *ănak*, " child ", 13 *tănub*, " reed, hollow stalk ", Kolling 10 *wănis*, " trousers ". Before *f* all the texts exhibit no exceptions; thus we find only forms like *tukfīfi*, " star ", etc.

70. There are however also IN languages that display a law differing entirely from the IN law of quantity, *e.g.* Daïri. In Daïri the vowel of *every* accentuated syllable is long; thus for example in *pōstĕp*, " to begin ".

71. When the accent is shifted from the penultimate syllable to the final one, as happens in the case of contractions and in many languages in the vocative, two separate tendencies assert themselves:

I. The vowel is *long*. So in Old Javanese in contractions, where the fact is indicated by the symbol of length in the manuscripts; *e.g.*, Rāmāyaṇa, VII, 40, 2: " In order to enter into the interior " = *tumamā riṅ abhyantara*. Here *tumamā* = the aorist *tumama* + the sign of the conjunctive *a*, the WB being *tama*. — Or in Gorontalese in the vocative, of which Breukink says: " *Suku akhir itu boleh mĕnjadi panjaṅ, jikalaw kata itu ditilik sapĕrti kata sĕruhan ataw suruhan* " = " The vowel of the final syllable becomes long when the word is used as a vocative or a command ".

II. The vowel is *short*. So in Hova in contractions, according to Ferrand. Thus it appears that the Hova imperative *milazá*, " tell !" < indicative *miláza* + imperative sign *a*, has a short final vowel.

72. Many parallels can be drawn between the IN and IE phenomena of quantity. The IN law of quantity coincides with the German one; *cf.* Siebs, "Deutsche Bühnenaussprache", in the section entitled " Vokale ". Madurese knows no differences in quantity, precisely like Rumanian; *cf.* Tiktin, " Rumänisches Elementarbuch ", § 15.

Quantity of Vowels in Monosyllabic Words.

73. In some languages the monosyllabic *words of substance* are long, *e.g.* in Karo. Thus even the Karo word *pĕt*, " to seek ", wherein *ĕ* is — inaptly — used for the *pĕpĕt*, is pronounced long. In other languages such words are short; so in Hova, *e.g.* in *lă*, " negation ".

74. The monosyllabic *affirmative a* or *o* is long in most languages, as is shown especially by the spelling of the texts; thus in the Kamberese Story of the Top, Bijdr. 1913, p. 83, l. 28, we find: " Yes, yes, said they " = *ā ā hiwada.*

75. Monosyllabic *words of form* are mostly short, because (for one thing) they have but a weak stress in the sentence. But they may be long; thus according to Meerwaldt the Toba *bē*, " every ", and *pē*, " even ", are long. When a shortly pronounced word of form is formed by composition into a word of substance, length of vowel may ensue. In the Bareqe Tale "The Monkey and the Pig", Bareqe Leesboek, p. 15, l. 4, we find: " To dig up roots " = *mankae toraa.* Adriani's spelling with *aa* indicates the length of the final vowel. " Root " = *torā*, with the accent on the *ā*, really stands for " that (which is) in (the earth) ", the word for " in " being *ră.*

Quantity of Unaccentuated Syllables.

76. The syllables which *precede* the accentuated one are almost always short. Bugis has some long ones, but a search through the dictionary only reveals about half a dozen cases, and these are mostly unexplained etymologically, as *mĕñcána,* " shallow ".

77. Syllables which *come after* the accentuated one are not infrequently long, especially when they end in a vowel. In Dayak all vowels at the end of words are long; thus *hūmā*, " house ", has both vowels long, the penultimate one being accentuated. Bugis in certain cases has vowel length in the unaccentuated final syllable, even when it ends in a consonant, *e.g.* in *dīmēṅ*, " longing ".

78. The phenomenon that syllables which precede the accent are hardly ever long, while those that follow it are often long, is parallelled by the fact that the former hardly ever contain diphthongs, whereas the latter often do (see § 171).

79. In Bugis, when a word accentuated on the final syllable becomes the first member of a compound, the accent may be thrown back; in that case, if the final syllable was long, *e.g.* on account of contraction, it loses its length. From WB *táppa* is derived *tappáṅ*, " creation, model " < *tappa* + *aṅ*, with the accent on the final syllable; in the compound *táppaṅ-matuwa*, " model for a father-in-law " = " future father-in-law ", the accent has been thrown back and the vowel has become short.

Quantity in Old Javanese.

80. The Old Javanese manuscripts indicate the length of the vowels. But it is noticeable how seldom the marks of length occur in them. Judging from the quantity of Modern Javanese they ought to be much more frequent. In the Rāmāyaṇa the long vowels are found, apart from Sanskrit loan-words, only in interjections, in certain monosyllabic words of substance, as in *kūṅ*, " longing ", but not in *sih*, " pity ", in contractions like *matī*, " to let die " < *mati* + *i*, and in compensatory lengthenings, as in *ikū*, " tail " < Original IN *ikur₂*. Hence we meet with whole verses without a single long vowel, *e.g.* Rāmāyaṇa, V, 68, 2: " She then, quite alone, entered unafraid " = *sira juga tuṅga-tuṅgal anusup tamatar matakut*. Were there perhaps in Old Javanese *three* gradations of quantity, as in Sangirese (§ 67), and is only extreme length marked in the manuscripts ?

Quantity in Original Indonesian.

81. As we have got an " IN law of quantity ", but it is counteracted by all sorts of special laws, as further there are difficulties about quantity in Old Javanese, and lastly as in not a few IN languages the available data about quantity are insufficient, we are not at present in a position to form a definite and trustworthy picture of quantity in Original IN.

Quality of the Vowels.

82. As regards the quality of vowels in IN we chiefly meet with two tendencies:

I. The quality depends upon the *quantity*. Long vowels are close, short ones are open. This law holds good for several languages.

II. The quality depends upon the *sounds that follow*. Thus in Minangkabau accentuated *e* before *s*, as in *leseq*, "zealous", is close, while before *r*, as in *lereṅ*, "slope, descent ", it is open.

Doubling of the Consonants.

83. What is called gemination, doubling of consonants, and the like, may represent several different phonetic values: see Sievers, " Phonetik ", in his chapter entitled " Silbentrennung ". As regards the nature of the IN double consonants, the following definitions (*inter alia*) give us some information. " In all these (*i.e.*, certain Philippine) languages the gemination is real, that is, the two consonants are distinctly pronounced " (Conant). " In Bugis the consonants that are written double are pronounced so that the consonant both closes the preceding syllable and begins the following one " (Matthes). " The dividing line of syllabic stress* lies in the

* [The author gives the following illustration of what is meant by " the dividing line of syllabic stress " (Druckgrenze) : " In the Italian word *anno*, " year ", the *an-* is spoken *decrescendo*, and the *-no crescendo*. After the *n* of *an-* the voice is feeblest, weakest, and this is the ' Druckgrenze '."]

geminate consonant itself " (Kiliaan).—In Bontok the two
consonants may also be separated by a hamzah as well; thus
in Seidenadel-Texts, Headhunters' Ceremonies, 4, we find:
" The old people " = *nan amamqma*.

84. The rarest cases of doubling are those of *h* and *q*.
Madurese has a few instances, *e.g.,* *ĕhham,* " ham ", and
leqqer, " neck ".

85. As a rule doubling only occurs between vowels; before
a consonant it is rarer, *e.g.,* as in the Madurese *lommra,* "accustomed ", in accordance with the law given in § 86, III.

86. Consonantal doubling in the living IN languages owes
its origin to several distinct factors; these are:

I. *Doubling of the root,* which is one of the methods of WB-
formation, when the root begins and ends with a similar consonant, as in the Kangeanese *tottot,* " tame ". This case also
occurs especially in the language of children, *e.g.* in the
Achinese childish word *mammam,* " cakes ".

II. *Derivation from the WB.* Here it may be simply a case
of mere addition, as when in Toba from the prefix *mar* + WB
rara there results the adjective *marrara,* " red ". Or it may
involve phonetic processes, as when in Madurese from *ñator*
+ the suffix *aghi* we get *ñatorraghi,* " to offer ".

III. *Various phonetic laws.* Before *r* or *l* Madurese doubles
every consonant except *ñ,* *n,* and *w;* hence the above-cited
lommra, as compared with *lumrah* in other languages. In
Talautese *r* is pronounced double when it follows immediately
after the accentuated vowel.

As for consonantal doubling after the pĕpĕt, see § 5.

IV. *Assimilation.* In spoken Toba, in the combination
nasal + cognate tenuis, the nasal is assimilated to the tenuis:
thus Original IN and written Toba *gantuñ* > spoken Toba
gattuñ. Certain cases of assimilation also especially occur in
sentence-sandhi; thus in Tuuk Lb, I, p. 1, l. 11, we find
written: " Red because of their ripeness " = Red now because
r. their = *marrara do dibahen lamun-na;* but the spoken language says *dibahel lamun-na.*

V. *Haplology*, as for example when in Iloko *apó-apó* becomes *appó*, " grandfathers ", from the singular *apó*.

VI. *Sandhi phenomena* not dependent upon assimilation. These occur for example in Timorese, as instanced in the text " Atonjes Nok ", Bijdr. 1904, pp. 271 *seqq*. There we find, *e.g.*, p. 271, l. 7: " To marry a woman " = M. w. a = *sao bifel-l-es*, from *sao* + *bifel* + *es*.

VII. *Analogical transference*. In Makassar, final *ṅ* is assimilated to the immediately following possessive *na*, hence " His king " = *karaeṅ-na* > *karaénna*; through transference this *nna* is also added to words ending in a vowel, hence *matánna*, " his eye ", from *mata*, " eye ".

VIII. Some *interjections*, *e.g.* Madurese *awwa*.

87. Of all these cases of consonantal doubling only the one mentioned under I. *supra* can be positively ascribed to Original IN.

88. The phenomena connected with the doubling of consonants have many parallels in IE. Thus, for example, the Madurese doubling mentioned in III. *supra* may be compared with the West Germanic consonantal lengthening (Kluge, " Urgermanisch ", §§ 157 *seqq*.). The IE doubling of consonants in personal names (Brugmann, KvG, § 366, 6) has nothing corresponding to it in IN.

SECTION IV: PHONETIC LAWS OF THE SIMPLE SOUNDS, SUMMARILY STATED.

Preliminary Observations.

89. I have prepared for my own use a list of all the phonetic laws of all the hitherto known IN languages. From that list I here give a selection of the more important phenomena, being guided in my choice by the interests of IN research on the one hand and those of IE study on the other.

90. Phonetic changes are either unconditional or conditional (see § 10); in the latter case I add the condition. But it may happen that the condition is composed of several different factors, which it would take too long to go into; or alongside of the cases that follow the law there may be a serious number of exceptions; or the material at my disposal may be incomplete: in such cases I employ the neutral formula: "the phonetic change occurs *in certain cases*".

Laws of the Vowels.

91. Original IN *a*. I. It persists for the most part unchanged in the living languages. Original IN *anak*, "child", appears as *anak* in Old Javanese, Dayak, etc., as *anaq* in Bugis, etc.

II. Original IN *a* becomes *o* in several languages; thus in Tontemboan before *w*, hence Original IN *awak* > Tontb. *owak*, "body". — It becomes *e* in several languages; thus in Sumbanese by Umlaut,* hence Original IN *tasik* > Sumb. *tesi*, "lake". — It becomes *i* in several languages; thus in Taimuruna by complete assimilation, hence Original IN *lima* > Taim. *limi*, "five". — It becomes *ö* in certain cases in Gayo,

* ["Umlaut" is a particular case of partial assimilation: see § 251.]

264

hence Original IN *ina* > Gayo *inö*, " mother ". — It becomes
ĕ in Bĕsĕmah when final, hence Original IN *mata* > Bĕs.
matĕ, " eye ". — It becomes *aw* in Sĕraway when final, hence
Original IN *mata* > Sĕr. *mataw*.

III.   Original IN *a* rarely disappears altogether; it does so
in certain cases in Hova after Original IN *y*, hence Original
IN *laya.₂* > Hova *lay*, " to sail ".

92.   Original IN *i*.   I.   It persists for the most part unchanged in the living languages.   Original IN *lintah*, " leech ",
appears as *lintah* in Old and Modern Javanese, Malay, etc.,
as *dinta* in Hova, etc.

II.   Original IN *i* becomes *e* in a few languages, thus in
certain cases in Madurese, hence Original IN *lintah* > Mad.
lenta. — It becomes *ey* in several languages when final; thus
in Tiruray, hence Original IN *tali* > Tir. *taley*, " rope ". —
It becomes *oy* in certain cases in Achinese when final; hence
Original IN *bĕli* > Ach. *bloy*, " to buy ".

III.   Original IN *i* rarely disappears altogether; it does so
in Tontemboan under the exigencies of metre.   In Schwarz-
Texts, p. 317, Songs of Martina Rompas, 13, we find: " Do
you mean ?" = *cua-mu*.   That *cua* < *icua* = prefix *i* + WB
kua has really lost an *i*, is proved by the presence of the *c*,
which can only occur after an *i* (see § 103).

93.   Original IN *u*.   I. It persists for the most part unchanged in the living languages.   Original IN *tunu*, " to
burn ", appears as *tunu* in Old Javanese, Hova, etc.

II.   Original IN *u* becomes *o* in a few languages; thus in
certain cases in Madurese, hence Original IN *putih* > Mad.
pote, " white ". — It becomes *ü* in Bontok by Umlaut, hence
Original IN *babuy* > Bont. *fafüy*, " boar ". — It becomes *i*
in Loindang by complete assimilation, hence Original IN
kulit > Loi. *kilit*, " skin ". — It becomes *ew* in several languages when final; thus in Tiruray, hence Original IN *pitu* >
Tir. *fitéw*, " seven ". — It becomes *ee* in Achinese in certain
cases when final, hence Original IN *palu* > Ach. *palée*, " to
strike ".

III. Original IN *u* rarely disappears altogether; it does so in Kupangese owing to sentence-sandhi. In Kup. the word for " to draw (liquor) ", when pronounced by itself or in a pause, is *sulu*. But in the Story of the Fool, Bijdr. 1904, p. 259, l. 13, we find : " And drew in order to pour (into another vessel) " = *ti sul le doan*.

94. The vowel *e*. I observed in § 40 that *bela*, " companion, avenger, to share the same fate ", is the only word I have hitherto positively ascertained as possessing an original *e*. This *bela* remains unchanged in the several languages where it occurs, such as Gayo, Bimanese, etc., only the Achinese has *bila*.

95. The vowel *o*. I mentioned in § 40 that *sor*, " below ", is the only word I have positively ascertained as possessing an Original IN *o*. This *o* persists unchanged everywhere, thus in the Old Javanese *sor*, Tontemboan *sosor*, etc.

96. The vowel *ĕ*: see §§ 121 *seqq*.

Laws of the Semi-Vowels.

97. Original IN *y*. I. It persists unchanged in many living languages. Original IN *layar₂*, " to sail ", appears as *layar* in Malay, Sundanese, etc., as *layag* in Tagalog, etc.

II. Original IN *y* becomes *j* in several languages, thus in Bugis between *a*, *o*, or *u*, and an immediately following vowel, hence Original IN *layar₂* > Old Bugis *lajaq*, " to sail ". — It becomes *z* in certain cases in Hova, hence Original IN *kayu* > Hova *hazu*, " tree". — It becomes *l* in Sangirese between vowels, hence Original IN *kayu* > Sang. *kalu*.

III. Original IN *y* disappears altogether in several languages; thus in Toba, hence Original IN *kayu* > Toba *hau*.

98. Original IN *w*. I. It persists unchanged in many living languages. Original IN *walu*, " eight ", appears as *walu* in Tettum, as *waluh* in Gayo, etc.

II. Original IN *w* becomes *u* in Toba when initial, hence Original IN *walu* > Toba *ualu*, " eight ", a word of three syllables, also pronounced *uwalu*. — It becomes *b* in Mentaway, as in *balu*, " eight ". — It becomes *f* in Rottinese, as in *falu*, " eight ". — It becomes *ww* in Old Javanese, hence Original IN *wara* > Old Jav. *wwara*, " to be " (the substantive verb). — It becomes *gu* in Inibaloi, as in *qualo*, " eight ". — It becomes *h* in Mamuju, hence Original IN *tawa* > Mam. *taha*, " to laugh ".

III.   Original IN *w* disappears altogether in a few languages, thus in Modern Javanese between a consonant and a vowel, hence Modern Jav. *lir*, " manner ", for Old Jav. *lwir*.

Laws of the Liquids.

99.   Original IN r_1, the lingual *r*.   I. It is preserved in many living languages, but pronounced in various ways. Original IN *pira*, " how much ", is also *pira* in Old Javanese, Kamberese, etc., *firi* in Hova, etc.

II.   Original IN r_1 becomes *l* in several languages; thus in certain cases in Bisaya, as in *pila*, " how much ". — It becomes *d* in several languages; thus in certain cases in Balinese, as in *pidan*, " how much ". — It rarely becomes *g*; thus in certain cases in Toba, hence Original IN $ir_1uñ$ > Toba *iguñ*, " nose ". — It becomes χ in Nias in the cases where Toba has *g*, as in *iχu*, " nose ".

III.   Original IN r_1 disappears altogether in several languages when final; thus in Hova, hence Original IN $butir_1$ > Hova *wutsi*, " bud ".

100.   As for Original IN r_2, see §§ 129 *seqq*.

101.   Original IN *l*.   I. It mostly persists unchanged in the living languages.   Original IN *lañit*, " sky ", is also *lañit* in Old Javanese, *lanitra* in Hova, etc.

II.   Original IN *l* becomes *r* in several languages; thus in Toba by a regular assimilation whenever the word contains an *r*, hence Original IN *lapar* > Toba *rapar*, " hunger ". — It becomes *y* in several languages; thus in Bareqe between vowels, hence Original IN *jalan* > Bar. *jaya*, " path ". —

It becomes *w* in several languages; thus in certain cases in Tagalog, hence Original IN *puluh*, " ten " > Tag. *powo*. — It becomes *n* in certain cases in Timorese, hence Original IN *kali* > Tim. *hani*, " to dig ". — It becomes *d* in several languages; thus in Hova before an original *i*, not an *i* derived from *ĕ*, hence Original IN *lima* > Hova *dimi*.—It becomes *g* in several languages; thus in certain cases in Batanese, hence Original IN *ulu* > Bat. *ogo*. — It becomes *h* in some Formosan dialects in certain cases, hence Original IN *ulu* > Form. *uho*, " head ".

III. Original IN *l* disappears altogether in several languages; thus in Boano, hence Original IN *balay*, " house " > Boa. *bae*.

Laws of the Laryngal *q*.

102. For the laws of the laryngal *q*, see §§ 140 *seqq*.

Laws of the Velars.

103. Original IN *k*. I. It persists for the most part unchanged in the living languages. Original IN *kuraṅ*, " deficiency ", appears also as *kuraṅ* in Old Javanese, Makassar, etc., as *koraṅ* in Tarakan, etc.

II. Original IN *k* becomes *g* in several languages; thus in Tiruray between vowels, hence Original IN *laki* > Tir. *lagey*, " man " (as opposed to " woman "). — It becomes *h* in several languages; thus in Hova when initial or between vowels, hence Original IN *kuku* > Hova *huhu*, " claw ". — It becomes *q* in several languages; thus in Bugis when final, hence Original IN *anak* > Bug. *anaq*, " child ". — It becomes *c* in Tontemboan when an *i* precedes, hence Original IN *tasik* > Tontb. *taqasic*, " lake ". — It becomes *t* in Hova in sentence-sandhi before *s*, e.g., Hain-Teny, p. 264, l. 4: " Young lark " = *zanat surúhitra* < *zanak* < *zánaka*, " young " + *surúhitra*, " lark ". — It becomes *s* in Kawangkowan Tontemboan in the cases where the standard Tontemboan has *c* < *k*, thus Kaw. *taqasis* for the above *taqasic*.

III. Original IN *k* disappears altogether in several languages; thus in certain cases in Bugis, hence Original IN *kulit* > Bug. *uliq*, " skin ".

104. Original IN *g*. I. It mostly persists unchanged in the living languages. Original IN *gantuṅ*, " to hang ", appears in Old Javanese, Sundanese, etc., as *gantuṅ*, in Bugis as *gattuṅ*, etc.

II. Original IN *g* becomes *k* in Bugis after *ṅ*, hence Original IN *tuṅgal* > Bug. *tuṅkĕ*, " alone ". — It becomes *gh* in Madurese, hence *ghantoṅ*, " to hang ". — It becomes a velar spirant in Tontemboan (see § 65). — It becomes *h* in Hova when initial, hence Hova *hantuna*, " to hang ".

III. Original IN *g* rarely disappears altogether; it does so in Rottinese after *ṅ*, hence Makassar, etc., *geṅgo* appears in Rot. as *ṅgeṅo*, " to rock to and fro ".

105. Original IN *ṅ*. I. It mostly persists unchanged in the living languages. Original IN *aṅin*, " wind ", is also *aṅin* in Old Javanese, Malay, etc., *haṅin* in Tagalog, etc.

II. Original IN *ṅ* becomes *n* in several languages; thus in Hova, save before a velar, hence in *ánina*, " wind ". — It becomes *ñ* in several languages; thus in certain dialects of Tontemboan after *i*, hence Original IN and Tontb. *liṅa* > dialectic Tontb. *liña*, " to hear ". — It becomes *k* in several languages by assimilation; thus in spoken Toba, hence Original IN *baṅkay* > written Toba *baṅke* > spoken Toba *bakke*, " corpse ".

III. Original IN *ṅ* disappears altogether in several languages when final; thus in Nias, hence Original IN $ar_1 \breve{e}ṅ$ > Nias *aχo*, " charcoal ".

Laws of the Palatals.

106. Original IN *c*. I. It is preserved in some of the languages. Original IN r_1acun, " poison ", appears in Old Javanese and Malay as *racun*, in Bimanese as *racu*, etc.

II. Original IN *c* becomes *s* in many languages; thus in Tagalog, hence *lason*, " poison ".

107. Original IN *j*. I. It persists unchanged in some of the languages. Original IN *jalan*, " path ", appears also in Bontok, Běsěmah, etc., as *jalan*, in Bareqe as *jaya*, etc.

II. Original IN *j* becomes *c* in Bugis after *ñ*, hence Original IN *jañji* > Bug. *jañci*, " promise ". — It becomes *jh* in Madurese, as in *jhalan*, " path ". — It becomes *d* in several languages; thus in certain cases in Old Javanese, as in *dalan*, " path ". — It becomes *z* in certain cases in Hova, hence Original IN *tuju* > Hova *tuzu*, " direction ". — It becomes *s* in Lalaki, as in *sala*, " path ".

108. Original IN *ñ*. I. It persists unchanged in some of the languages. Original IN *pěñu*, " turtle ", appears also in Old Javanese as *pěñu*, in Madurese as *pěñño*, with doubling of the *ñ* in accordance with the law in § 5, V, etc.

II. Original IN *ñ* becomes *n* in some languages; thus in Toba, as in *ponu*, " turtle ".

Laws of the Dentals.

109. Original IN *t*. I. It mostly persists unchanged in the living languages. Original IN *tali*, " rope ", appears also in Old and Modern Javanese, etc., as *tali*, in Tettum as *talin*, etc.

II. Original IN *t* becomes *d* in several languages; thus in certain cases in Sawunese, hence Original IN *mata* > Saw. *mada*, " eye ". — It becomes *ts* in Hova before *i*, hence Original IN *tilik*, " to peep at " > Hova *tsidika*. — It becomes *k* in several languages ; thus, according to Aymonier and Cabaton, in Cham before *l*, hence Original IN *tělu* > *tlu* > Cham *klaw*, " three ". — It becomes χ in certain cases in some of the Formosan dialects, hence Original IN *tai*, " dung " > Form. χ*e*. — It becomes *h* in several languages; thus in certain cases in Kamberese, hence Original IN *pitu* > Kamb.- *pihu*, " seven ". — It is cerebralized in several languages; thus in certain cases in Madurese. — It becomes *s* in Bolaang- Mongondou when in contact with *i*, hence Original IN *kulit* > Bol.-Mong. *kulis*, " skin ".

III. Original IN *t* disappears altogether in several languages; thus in Nias when final, hence Original IN *kulit*, " skin " > Nias *uli*.

110. Original IN *d*. I. It persists unchanged in many languages. Original IN *dagañ*, " stranger ", appears also in Old Javanese, Toba, etc., as *dagañ*, in Bimanese as *daga*, etc.

II. Original IN *d* becomes *t* in several languages when final; thus in Malay, hence Original IN *añud*, " drift " > Mal. *hañut*. — It becomes *dh* in certain cases in Madurese, hence Original IN *damar* > Mad. *dhamar*, " resin ". — It is cerebralized in several languages. — It becomes *r* in several languages; thus in Bugis after *n*, hence Original IN *linduñ* > Bug. *linruñ*, " shade ".

III. Original IN *d* disappears altogether in some languages; thus in Kulawi after *n*, hence Original IN *tanduk* > Kulawi *tonu*, " horn ".

111. Original IN *n*. I. It is preserved in the living languages in a great majority of the cases. Original IN *anak*, " child ", appears also in Old Javanese, etc., as *anak*, in Nias as o_1no_1, etc.

II. Original IN *n* becomes *ñ* in several languages when final; thus in Bugis, hence Original IN *añin* > Bug. *añiñ*, " wind ". — It becomes *l* in several languages; thus in certain cases in some of the Formosan dialects, as in *alak*, " child ". — It becomes *t* by assimilation; thus in spoken Toba, hence Original IN *gantuñ* > spoken Toba *gattuñ*, " to hang ".

III. Original IN *n* is lost in several languages; thus in Nias before *t*, hence Original IN *lintah* > Nias *lita*, " leech ".

Laws of the Labials.

112. Original IN *p*. I. It mostly persists unchanged in the living languages. Original IN *pitu*, " seven ", is also *pitu* in Old Javanese, Masaretese, etc., *opitu* in Gorontalese, etc.

II. Original IN *p* becomes *b* in Achinese when final, hence Original IN *idup* > Ach. *udeb*, with metathesis of the vowels

and change of *i* into *e*. — It becomes *f* in many languages;
thus in Hova when initial or between vowels, as in *fitu*,
" seven ". — It becomes *w* in Nias in sentence-sandhi in
accordance with the law changing surds into sonants (§ 302).
Original IN *par₁ay*, " rice ", appears in Nias as *faχe*; but in
the Dancing Hymn in Bijdr. 1905, p. 12, l. 4 from the bottom,
we find: " I winnow rice " = *u siχ waχe*. — It becomes *k*.
" Some of the tribes of the Eastern Toba cannot pronounce
p and make a *k* of it, thus *kiso* for the standard Toba *piso*,
' knife ' " (Van der Tuuk). — It becomes *h* in Rottinese, as
in *hitu*, " seven ".

III.   Original IN *p* disappears entirely in several languages;
thus in certain cases in Kissarese, hence Original IN *pira* >
Kis. *ira*, " how much ".

113.   Original IN *b*.   I. It persists unchanged in many of
the living languages.   Original IN *bañaw*, " heron ", appears
also in Malay, Dayak, etc., as *bañaw*, in Old Javanese as *baño*.

II.   Original IN *b* becomes *bh* in certain cases in Madurese,
hence Original IN *buru* > Mad. *bhuru*, " to hunt ". — It
becomes *p* in Buli in certain cases, hence Original IN *bulu* >
Buli *plu*, " hair ". — It becomes *w* in several languages; thus
in Hova when initial or between vowels, as in *wanu*, " heron ".
—It becomes *f* in Rottinese, hence Original IN *r₁ibu* > Rot.
lifu, " thousand ". — It becomes *h* in the Silayarese dialect
of Makassar in certain cases, hence Original IN *beli*, " price "
> Mak. *balli* > Sil. *halli*.

III.   Original IN *b* disappears altogether in several languages; thus in Gayo in certain cases when initial, hence
Original IN *batu* > Gayo *atu*, " stone ".

114.   Original IN *m*.   I. It persists for the most part unchanged in the living languages.   Original IN *mata*, " eye ",
is also *mata* in Old Javanese, Bagobo, etc., *matan* in Tettum,
etc.

II.   Original IN *m* becomes *n* in several languages: thus in
Hova when final, hence Original IN *inum*, " to drink " >
Hova *inuna*, " to drink poison ". — It becomes *ñ* in a few

languages when final; thus in Bugis, as in *inuñ*, " to drink ".
— It becomes *p* by assimilation; thus in Toba, hence Original
IN *lumpat* > spoken Toba *luppat*, " to jump ".

III.   Original IN *m* disappears altogether in several languages when final; thus in Bareqe, as in *inu*, " to drink ".

Laws of the Spirant *s*.

115.   Original IN *s*.   I. It mostly persists in the living
languages.   Original IN *susu*, " breast ", is also *susu* in Old
Javanese, Malay, etc.

II.   Original IN *s* becomes *š* in several languages; thus in
Mentaway when initial, hence Original IN *siwa* > Ment.
šiba, " nine ". — It becomes *h* in several languages; thus in
Kamberese, as in *hiwa*, " nine ". — It becomes *t* in several
languages; thus in Buol, hence Original IN *si*, the article >
Buol *ti*.

III.   Original IN *s* disappears altogether in several languages; thus in Hova in certain cases, hence Original IN *běsi*
> Hova *wi*, " iron ".

Laws of the Aspirate *h*.

116.   Original IN *h*.   I. It persists unchanged in a minority of the IN languages.   Original IN *pěnuh*, " full ".
appears also as *pěnuh* in Old Javanese, as *panuh* in Tarakan,
etc.

II.   Original IN *h* becomes *q* in a few languages; thus in
certain cases in Tontemboan, hence Original IN *lintah* >
Tontb. *lintaq*.

III.   Original IN disappears altogether in the majority of
the living languages; thus in Bugis, hence Original IN *pěnuh*
> Bug. *pěnno*, " full ", and Original IN *ilih* > Bug. *ile*, " to
choose ". — In such cases a *u* or *i* preceding the *h* becomes
o or *e* in Bug., whereas final Original IN *u* and *i* remain unchanged, hence Original IN and likewise Bug. *tunu*, " to
burn ", *kali*, " to dig ".

18

Laws of the Simple Sounds in Indo-European and in Indonesian.

117. A large majority of the IN phonetic changes also occur in IE, partly under similar conditions, and partly under different ones. I give here a selection of parallels between IE and IN:

Sanskrit and Toba: $s + s > ts$. — Sansk. *vatsyāmi*, " I shall dwell " $< vas + syāmi$; Toba *latsoada* $< las + soada,$ " not yet ".

Old Persian and Kamberese: $s > h$. — Old Pers. *hainā*, as compared with Sanskrit *senā*, " army ", Meillet GvP, § 130; Kamb. *hiwa* $<$ Original IN *siwa*, " nine ".

Armenian and Rottinese: $p > h$. — Arm. *hing*, " five ", as compared with Sanskrit *pañca*, Greek *pente*; Rot. *hitu*, " seven" $<$ Original IN *pitu*.

Greek and Modern Javanese: $w > $ nil. — Gr. *oikos*, as compared with Sanskrit *veśa*; Modern Jav. *lir*, " manner " $<$ Old Jav. *lwir*.

Latin and Toba: y between vowels $>$ nil. — Lat. *tres* $<$ *treyes*; Toba *hau*, " tree " $<$ Original IN *kayu*.

Old Bulgarian and Makassar: All original diphthongs become simple vowels, *cf.* Leskien, " Grammatik der altbulgarischen Sprache ", §§ 43 *seqq*.

Old Prussian and Cham: $tl > kl$. — Old Prus. *stacle*, " support " $<$ *statle* (Trautmann, " Die altpreussischen Sprachdenkmäler ", § 67); Cham *klaw* $<$ *tlu* $<$ Original IN *tĕlu,* " three ".

Germanic and Hova: $k > h$. — Gothic *hilan*, " to conceal ", as compared with Latin *celare*; Hova *hazu*, " tree " $<$ Original IN *kayu*.

Old Irish and Rottinese: $w > f$. — Old Ir. *fer*, " man ", as compared with Latin *vir*; Rot. *falu*, " eight " $<$ Original IN *walu*.

Sicilian dialect and Bugis: media after nasal $>$ tenuis. — Sic. *ancilu*, " angel " $<$ Latin *angelus*; Bug. *jañci*, " promise " $<$ Original IN *jañji*.

German dialect of Lucerne and Mori: *nt* > *nd*. — Luc. dialect *Määndig*, " Monday " (High German *Montag*); Mori *mondasu*, " sharp ", as compared with Petasia *montaso*, from the Original IN WB *tajĕm*.

118.   There are two IN phonetic laws for which I know of no parallels in IE; both are peculiar to Achinese and both appear in the word *lhee*, " three " < Original IN *tĕlu*: Initial Original IN *tĕl* > Ach. *lh*, and final Original IN *u* > Ach. *ee*. See also Section V, *ad fin.*

SECTION V: THE MOST IMPORTANT INDONESIAN PHONETIC LAWS, SET FORTH IN DETAIL.

Preliminary Observations.

119. The most important IN phonetic laws are four in number: the pĕpĕt-law, the RGH-law, the hamzah-law, and the law of the mediæ.

120. Now the course of our enquiry is as follows:

I. In the case of the pĕpĕt-law we have to ascertain what are the representatives of the Original IN pĕpĕt in the living IN languages.

II. In the case of the RGH-law our enquiry has to pursue the same course as with the pĕpĕt-law, we have to find out by what sounds the Original IN uvular r (r_2) is represented in the living IN tongues. This law is also called, after its discoverer, by the name of "Van der Tuuk's first law". I have preferred to designate it by the more convenient and significative name of "RGH-law", a name based on the fact that Original IN r_2 is represented in many of the living languages by g, in some by h; and I observe that this designation is gradually gaining ground.

III. In the case of the hamzah-law our business is to set forth from what Original IN sounds or by what linguistic processes the sound hamzah has originated in the living IN languages. Here, therefore, the procedure differs from that which is to be followed in the case of the pĕpĕt-law and RGH-law; we start from an Original IN multiplicity and arrive at one uniform result in the living languages, viz., the hamzah. For the hamzah is a secondary sound in IN; we cannot therefore proceed from an Original IN hamzah. The hamzah-law is peculiarly interesting for the following reason: in IN the hamzah is very widely distributed, in IE on the other hand it is very little known; the phenomena connected with the hamzah therefore mark an important difference between IE and IN.

IV. The law of the mediæ. In a number of IN languages media and continuant interchange in one and the same word. Thus in Bugis the WB for " to cut off " appears sometimes as *bĕtta* and sometimes as *wĕtta*, thus at times with the momentary media *b*, and at other times with the continuant *w*. Probably there was nothing corresponding to this in Original IN; so in this case (in contrast to the other three laws) we cannot have recourse to Original IN at all.

The Pĕpĕt-Law.

121. Original IN possessed the vowel *ĕ*, described in § 53, produced with the mouth-cavity in a position of indifference, and often called pĕpĕt.

122. This pĕpĕt has been preserved in a minority of the IN languages, *e.g.* in Old Javanese, Karo, Bugis, etc. Thus Old Jav. has preserved the original phonetic condition in the case of the pĕpĕt, while abandoning it in the case of the RGH-law.

123. The pĕpĕt can change into all the other vowels: *a*, *i*, *u*, *e*, *o*. Original IN *tĕkĕn*, " staff ", results in Makassar *takkaṅ*, Dayak *teken*, Tagalog *tikín*; Original IN *ĕnĕm*, " six ", becomes in Toba *onoṁ*, in certain Formosan dialects *unum*.

124. In several languages Original IN *ĕ* has a multifarious resultant.

I. The *accent* is the determining factor. In Hova *ĕ* in an accentuated syllable becomes *e*, in an unaccentuated one *i*, hence Original IN *ĕnĕm* > Hova *énina*. In Kolo in the same way the resultants are *o* and *u*, hence Original IN *ĕnĕm* > Kolo *onu*. Notice the parallel between the more sonorous *e* and *o* and the less sonorous *i* and *u* of Hova and Kolo respectively.

II.   The *consonant* following the pĕpĕt is the determining factor.   In Pabian-Lampong, *ĕ* before *r* becomes *a*, while before *m* it becomes *u*, etc.   Hence Original IN *sĕmbah,* " respectful salutation " > Pab.-Lamp. *sumbah.*

III.   The determining factors *cannot be ascertained*; thus in Bimanese, where the pĕpĕt can be replaced by all the other vowels.

125.   In Old Javanese, in consequence of the loss of an r_2, the pĕpĕt may be left standing before a vowel, in which case it changes into *w* and forms with the vowel a rising diphthong, as in *bwat* < Original IN *bĕr₂at*, " heavy ".   In its further evolution the diphthong becomes a simple vowel, hence Modern Jav. *abot* < Old Jav. *bwat.*

126.   In a few languages the pĕpĕt disappears altogether.

I.   Disappearance *before* the accentuated syllable, in several languages, when the pĕpĕt stands between a mute and a liquid, *e.g.,* Original IN *bĕli*, " to buy " > Gayo *bli*, also however pronounced *bĕli*. — In Tagalog this phenomenon only occurs when the word is also extended by a prefix, so that even after the loss of the *ĕ* the word remains disyllabic, as in *itlóg*, " egg " < Original IN *tĕlur₂.*

II.   Disappearance *after* the accentuated syllable, in several languages, when the pĕpĕt stands between a semi-vowel and a consonant.   Thus Original IN *dawĕn*, " leaf ", results in Dayak in *dawen*, which is quite in conformity with the rule (§ 123), but in Malay it is not represented, as one might have expected, by *dawan*, but by *daun* (a disyllable).

III.   In Old Javanese inscriptions the pĕpĕt is often omitted.   Thus we find in Kawi Oorkonden, II, 10, b: " Shall be seized by tigers " = *dmakĕn iñ macan*.   As Modern Javanese pronounces the pĕpĕt in these cases, thus saying *dĕmaq*, " to seize ", I do not quite know what to think of this omission of the pĕpĕt.

127. Languages that are closely related to one another often display a similar treatment of the pĕpĕt. But that also happens in the case of tongues that are widely apart; thus both in Toba and in Bisaya, *ĕ* changes into *o*, hence *tĕlu*, "three" > Toba *tolu*, Bis. *toló*. Finally, it also happens that languages which are very closely related to one another differ just in their treatment of the pĕpĕt; thus in the two principal dialects of Minangkabau it is precisely the difference in the representation of the Original IN *ĕ* that forms the chief differentia between them: the Agam dialect has *a*, hence Original IN *bĕr₂as*, "rice" > Agam *bareh*; the Tanah Datar dialect has *o*, hence *boreh*.

128. The pĕpĕt and prosody. In some languages the pĕpĕt is replaced by another vowel when the verse accent falls upon it. In Tontemboan it is changed into *e*. "God" in Tontb. is *ĕmpun*, "friend", *rĕñan*, "friends", *rĕña-rĕñan*; but in a poem in Schwarz-Texts, p. 139, l. 16, in an iambic verse, we find: "Now, gods, friends, ho!" = *ja empuñ reña-reñan e*. — In Talautese, *ĕ* has become *a*, but under the influence of the verse accent even this *a* is replaced by another vowel, either *e* or *o*; thus in Steller-Texts, p. 66, l. 2, we find *sasobañ* for *sasabbañ*, "to appear", and *elo* for *allo*, "sun".

Note.—For other phenomena occurring in connexion with the pĕpĕt, see §§ 5 and 148.

The RGH-Law.

129. Original IN had two *r* sounds, a lingual *r* (= r_1) and a uvular *r* (= r_2). "Thousand" in Original IN was r_1ibu, but "hundred" was r_2atus.

130. The Original IN condition has only been preserved in very few of the living languages, and even there not quite undisturbed, for example in Bĕsĕmah. Bĕs. r_1ibu, "thousand", r_1aeon, "poison", $sur_1oñ$, "to push", contain r_1, like the corresponding Original IN words r_1ibu, r_1acun, $sur_1uñ$; Bĕs. dar_2at, "mainland", jar_2om, "needle", $nior_2$, "coconut palm", are pronounced with r_2, like Original IN dar_2at, jar_2um, $niur_2$.

131. In several languages r_1 and r_2 have coalesced: thus Madurese pronounces the r in *soroñ* $<$ Original IN *sur₁uñ* just like the one in *jharum* $<$ Original IN *jar₂um*, both being cacuminal.

132. Original IN r_1 becomes l in some languages, as in Tagalog *libo* $<$ Original IN *r₁ibu*, in others it becomes d, in others again some other sound (see § 99). I have included these phenomena of the r_1 sound under the designation of " the RLD-law ", a name which is analogous to that of the RGH-law.

133. Original IN r_2, that is to say, the r of the RGH-law, in some languages remains r, which need not however be uvular; in some others it turns into g, or into h; in a few it also becomes l or y or q. Example: Original IN *ur₂at*, " vein " $=$ Malay *urat* $=$ Tagalog *ugát* $=$ Dayak *uhat* $=$ Pangasinan *ulát* $=$ Lampong *uyak* $=$ Tontemboan *oqat*. See also §§ 135 and 139.

134. A comparison of the two preceding paragraphs shows that the further developments of r_1 and r_2 are in part identical, *e.g.* both r_1 and r_2 can result in l. But they never have an identical evolution *in one and the same language*. Thus, for example, in Tagalog, r_1 does in fact become l, as in *libo* from *r₁ibu*, " thousand ", but r_2 turns into g, as in *ugát* $<$ *ur₂at*, " vein ".

135. In several languages Original IN r_2 is represented by more than one sound.

I. Its *position in the word* is the determining factor. In Talautese, r_2 becomes k when final, otherwise r; hence Original IN *bar₂at*, " west " $>$ Tal. *bárata*, but Original IN *niur₂*, " coconut " $>$ Tal. *niuka*.

II. The *contiguous sounds* are the determining factor. In Sangirese, r_2 results in h, but after $o < ě$ it appears as γ; hence Original IN *r₂atus*, " hundred " $>$ by metathesis *r₂asut* $>$ Sang. *hasuq*, but Original IN *běr₂as*, " rice " $>$ Sang. *bóɣasěq*.

III The determining factors *cannot be ascertained*. In Hova, Original IN r_2 sometimes produces r as in *awáratra* < Original IN *bar₂at*, " west ", sometimes s as in *wésatra* < Original IN *běr₂at*, " heavy ", sometimes z as in *zatu* < Original IN *r₂atus*, " hundred ", and sometimes disappears altogether as in *wau*, " new " < *bar₂u*.

136. When Original IN r_2 becomes y, further developments may occur. The semi-vowel y may unite with the preceding vowel to form a falling diphthong, as in Lampong *ikuy*, " tail " < Original IN *ikur₂*. By a further phonetic process such diphthongs may become simple vowels, as in Pampanga *iki* < *ikuy* < *ikur₂*.

137. In some languages Original IN r_2 disappears altogether, particularly in Old Javanese. as in *dyus* < Original IN *dir₂us*, " to bathe ". When the r_2 was final in Original IN, then in Old Javanese the preceding vowel is lengthened by way of compensation for the disappearance of the r_2, as in Old Jav. *ikū*, " tail " < Original IN *ikur₂*.

138. It is to be supposed that this disappearance was not a single, momentary change. In Old Javanese, r_2 probably first turned into h, as in Dayak; such an h is still preserved in *wahu*, " new " < *bar₂u*. — In other languages where r_2 has likewise disappeared the hamzah may have been the transitional sound. In Tontemboan, Original IN r_2 becomes q, but in several cases this q has disappeared: Original IN *ular₂*, " snake " > Tontb. *ulaq*, but Original IN *timur₂*, " south " > Tontb. *timu*.

139. Languages that are closely related to one another often exhibit a similar treatment of the r_2. But this also occurs in the case of languages that are widely distant from one another; thus both in Lampong and in Pampanga, $r_2 > y$. Finally, it may happen that languages, which differ so little from each other that one can only call them dialects of one another, nevertheless diverge in this matter of the treatment of the r_2; thus in the various dialects of Talautese it is just the divergent representation of the r_2 that forms the differ-

entia between them. The chief dialect turns final Original
IN r_2 into k, hence Original IN $niur_2$, " coconut " $> niuka$,
with the supporting vowel a; for this $niuka$ other dialects
have $niuca$, $niuha$, $niuta$.

The Hamzah-Law.

140. In the living IN languages the hamzah is found as
an initial sound before vowels, as a medial sound between
vowels or between a vowel and a subsequent consonant, and
as a final sound after vowels; in such positions, in fact, as in
the Achinese $qancó$, " to melt ", Madurese $leqer$, " neck ",
Bugis $biriqta$, " report ", Makassar $anaq$, " child ". — Other
positions are rare, such as in the Bontok $allqo$, " pestle ",
Tontemboan $ĕlaqb$, " torch "; and the words in question
nearly always offer etymological difficulties.

141. Hamzah is found occasionally as initial, medial, or
final of the WB, in which case it is not derived from another
sound.

142. In many IN languages words that " begin with a
vowel " are pronounced with an emphatic enunciation, whereby in fact a hamzah is sounded as *initial* before the vowel;
this rule holds good for Achinese, Tontemboan, etc.   It is
true that neither the native script nor the transliteration made
by scholars is in the habit of representing this hamzah; thus
the word for " child " in Tontb. is written $anak$, but in reality
pronounced $qanak$, with an initial hamzah.

143. In several languages we find hamzah as a *medial*
between the two vowels of the WB, when there is no other
consonant there.   In Nias, as the dictionary shows, this is
often the case, though it is of course true that a percentage
of these q's result from k, as in $ataqu$, " to fear " $<$ Original
IN $takut$, and so fall under § 147.   In Madurese such a hamzah
is found in cases where other languages in the respective
words have h or w or no sound at all, as in Mad. $poqon$, " tree "
$=$ Malay $pohon$ $=$ Bugis $pōṅ$, or in $soqon$, " to carry on the
head " $=$ Javanese $suwun$.

144. In many languages hamzah is found as a *final*, abruptly closing the final vowel.

I. In very many *interjections*, thus in Bugis, Tontemboan, etc.; the interjection " fie !" in particular very often has a *q* as final: Makassar *ceq*, Bugis *caq*, Sangirese *siq*, etc. The frequent occurrence of *q* in interjections is connected with the emphatic, abrupt way in which they are uttered.

II. In names of relationship in the *vocative*. Original IN *ama*, " father", results in the Tontemboan *amañ*, with a particle welded on to it; but the vocative is *amaq*. Here the abrupt utterance has created the *q*.

III. In *names of relationship* generally. Thus alongside of Original IN *pu*, " grandfather", we find the Tontemboan *apoq*, beside Old Javanese *bi*, Modern Javanese *bibi*, " woman, aunt", the Madurese *bhibbhiq*, etc. These forms with *q* were originally vocatives.

IV. In *numerals*. In Madurese the numerals which in Original IN ended in a vowel are pronounced with a final *q*, whenever they are used by themselves, thus Original IN *tĕlu* > Mad. *tĕlloq*, " three ", but *tĕllo ratos*, " three hundred ". The occurrence of the *q* is either due to the force of analogy, on the pattern of *ĕmpaq*, " four " < Original IN *pat*, where the *q* is in accordance with rule, or else it is connected with the abrupt enunciation which sometimes occurs in counting.

V. In *negatives*, very frequently. Thus alongside of Original IN, and likewise Old Javanese, *aja*, a vetative negative, we find the Bugis *ajaq*, beside the Malay *tiada* a form *tidaq*, etc.

VI. In *words of any category of meaning*. In Busang an Original IN final vowel usually has a hamzah added to it; in particular, Original IN *i* becomes *eq* and *u* becomes *oq*, hence Original IN *bĕli*, " to buy " > Bus. *bĕléq* and Original IN *batu*, " stone " > Bus. *batóq*.

145. Just as in several languages the interjections often end in *q*, so in other languages they are particularly frequently found with an *h* as final, thus in Madurese.

146. Just as vocatives and negatives may have a final *q* added to them, so in certain languages they may receive a final *a*. Toba has a vocative *aṅgiá* corresponding to *aṅgi*, " younger brother "; alongside of the Tagalog negative *di* there is a Dayak *dia*.

147. Hamzah proceeds from certain Original IN sounds *in conformity with phonetic laws*:

I. From Original IN *k* in several languages, thus in Talautese; Original IN *aku*, " I " > Tal. *iaqu* = article *i* + *aqu*.

II. From *r₂* in several languages, thus in Makelaqi; Original IN *jar₂um*, " needle " > Make. *raqum*. From *h* (see § 116).

148. While some languages double the consonant that follows upon an accentuated *pĕpĕt* (see § 86), others develop a hamzah between the *pĕpĕt* and certain consonants that follow it. In Makassar the *pĕpĕt* becomes *a*, but the hamzah persists; thus Original IN *kĕdĕm*, " to close the eyes ", becomes *kaqdaṅ* in Mak.

149. Hamzah arises in several languages from special laws of the *interior sounds* of words, when the interior is of the *taptap* type (see § 198), thus in Tontemboan; hence Original IN *pukpuk*, " to break in pieces " > Tontb. *puqpuk*.

150. Hamzah results in many languages from special laws of the *final sounds*:

I. In some languages Original IN final *k* > *q*, thus in Malay, hence Original IN *anak* > Mal. *anaq*.

II. In Minangkabau all Original IN final explosives result in *q*, hence Original IN *atĕp*, " roof " > Mkb. *atoq*.

III. In Bugis, *q* results from all final consonants save the nasals and *h*, hence Original IN *nipis*, " thin " > Bug. *nipiq*.

151. Many IN languages add to the Original IN final consonant a supporting vowel, thus Hova, hence Hova *ánaka* " child " < Original IN *anak*; several languages employ *supporting vowels + hamzah*, thus Makassar, hence Original IN *nipis*, " thin " > Mak. *nipísiq*.

152. Hamzah arises in sentence-sandhi from the abbreviation of words that are weak in stress. Thus the Sangirese preposition *su* can be pronounced *q*. We find in the " Children's Games ", Bijdr. 1894, p. 520, l. 2: " Yonder in the inland country " = *dala q ulune* for *dala su ulune*.

153. Initial and final hamzah may be lost in sentence-sandhi, either regularly or arbitrarily. Tontemboan *añe.* " hither ", is pronounced *qañe* in conformity with § 142, but in the text Weweletĕn (Sacrificial Prayers), Schwarz-Texts. p. 309, l. 7, we find: " Come eat here !" = *mai cuman añe*, the *q* being lost. In Busang the word for " house " is *umaq*. But in the poem Boq Uyah Batang, p. 285, l. 2, we find: " The house (named) Lang Dĕhaq " = *umaq Lañ Dĕhaq*, and on p. 284, l. 2, *uma Lañ Dĕhaq*.

The Law of the Mediæ.

154. We meet with the law of the mediæ especially in Celebes and the neighbouring smaller islands, thus in Sangirese, Talautese, and Tontemboan, three languages that are closely related to one another, in Cenrana, and in Bugis; also apart from Celebes in Ibanag, Nias, Mentaway, and Hova.

155. I. The *Sangirese* law. In Sang. the media comes after a consonant; after vowels, the media *g* turns into the spirant *γ*, the media *d* into the liquid *r*, the media *b* into the semivowel *w*; thus the instantaneous mediæ become continuants; and this holds good both of a single word and of words in a sentence. As initial of a single word pronounced by itself or at the beginning of the sentence, the media persists. Hence *bera*, " to speak ", *mĕqbera*, the future active of the same, but *iwera*, the future passive. In the story in Bijdr. 1893, p. 354, l. 1, we find: " I will tell of the ape " = *iaq mĕqbio n baha*, but l. 4: " Said the ape " = *añkún i waha*.

II. The *Talautese* law agrees with the Sangirese. Thus the word for " house " is *bale*, as in Sang., and the word for "edge" is *biñgi*, but in the Story of Parere, Steller-Texts, p. 89, l. 2, we find: "At the edge of the river" = *su wiñgi n sáluka*.

III. The *Tontemboan* law. The media *g* becomes *γ* in all cases; *d* and *b* interchange with *r* and *w* as in Sangirese. But as initial of a single word pronounced by itself or at the beginning of a sentence, the continuant is used, in contrast with the Sangirese usage. Original IN *balay*, "house", therefore, is Sang. *bale* but Tontb. *wale*; "to remain at home" in Tontb. is *maqmbale*. Within the sentence the law only operates in certain cases. Thus in the Story of the Newly Wed, Schwarz-Texts, p. 82, l. 3 from the bottom, we find: "In the house" = *am bale* < *an wale*; but l. 20: "Yet corals" = *taqan wiwin*, without alteration of the *w*.

IV. The *Cenrana* law. The mediæ *d* and *b* become *r* and *w* respectively after a vowel, *e.g.*, *dami*, "only", but *mesa rami*, "one only".

V. The *Ibanag* law. Initial *d* becomes *r*, when an *a* is put before it: *dakay*, "badness", but *marakay*, "bad".

VI. The *Bugis* law. In Bug., initial *w* and *r* turn into *b* and *d* respectively, when a prefix is put before these sounds, no matter whether the prefix ends in a vowel or a consonant. Thus from *wĕnni*, "night", are formed *maqbĕnni*, "to spend the night (somewhere)", and *pabĕnni*, "to cause (somebody) to spend the night (somewhere)", and from *rĕmme*, "soft", *maqdĕmme*, "to soften", and *padĕmme*, "to cause to soften". But the rule is not consistently carried out: from *wĕtta*, "to cut", comes *maqbĕtta*, "to cut off", but also *pawĕtta-wĕtta*, "headhunter". Evidently compromise has been at work here, and probably the regular rule is the one exemplified in *pawĕtta* in relation to *maqbĕtta*.

VII. The *Nias* law. When a WB begins with *d* or *b* and a prefix is put before these sounds, *b* becomes *w* and *d* becomes *r*; in similar circumstances *χ* becomes *g*, thus conversely the continuant turns into a media. Thus *bua*, "fruit", but *mowua*, "to bear fruit"; *dua*, "two", but *darua*, "to be a pair "; χaru, " dig ", as a WB, but mogaru, the verb " to dig ". In Nias also the rule is not strictly observed.

VIII. The *Mentaway* law. We always find the media *b*, never *w* instead of it. As initial the media *g* always appears, but in the interior of words *g* and *γ* interchange pretty irregularly. An examination of the whole of Morris' texts shows that the word for " banana (plantain) " occurs four times under the form of *bago* and twice under that of *baγo*. " The media *d* is mostly a variant in pronunciation for *r* " (Morris).

IX. The *Hova* law. In Hova, Original IN initial *g* $>$ *h*, hence *hántuna* $<$ Original IN *gantuñ*, " to hang ", and *húruna* $<$ Original IN *guluñ*, " to roll ". But Original IN *k* also becomes *h*, hence Hova *húditra* $<$ Original IN *kulit*. " skin ". When the prefix *ma* $+$ nasal is put before *h* $<$ *k*, the *h* $<$ *k* disappears in conformity with § 16,* hence *manúditra*, "to peel ". But if this same prefix appears before *h* $<$ *g*, the *g* reappears, hence *mañgúruna*, " to roll ". But here too there have been changes based on analogy, for from *hántuna* is formed *manántuna*, instead of the *mañgántuna* which one would have expected. From *húdina* $<$ Original IN *guliñ*, " to turn", is formed the verb *manúdina*, but the substantive *sañgúdina*, " top ".

Comparisons with Indo-European.

156. We do not find many parallels in IE to the four principal IN laws.

I. The IE indeterminate vowel turns into *i* or *a* (Brugmann KvG, § 127), just as in IN *a* and *i* (*inter alia*) result from *ĕ*, but after the description in § 53 we cannot absolutely identify the pĕpĕt with the IE indeterminate vowel.

II. In contrast with the IN *r*, the IE *r* is a very constant sound.

III. The hamzah plays but a very small part in IE. Just

* [See also Essay III, § 30.]

as IN possesses many interjections ending in hamzah, so in the Lucerne dialect the word for " yes " is in certain cases pronounced *yŏq* instead of *yō*.

IV. With the law of the mediæ may be compared certain instances in Italian dialects, such as *donna* and *la ronna* (Gröber).

SECTION VI: THE TWO MOST IMPORTANT PHONETIC COMBINATIONS AND THEIR LAWS.

Preliminary Observations.

157. The two most interesting phonetic combinations in IN are the combination of a vowel with a semi-vowel and the combination of an explosive with the aspirate *h*. The first are called diphthongs, the second aspirates. In the diphthongs the semi-vowel may precede, as in the Dayak *yaku*, " I ", or follow, as in the Tagalog *patáy*, " to kill ". Only the second kind can lay claim to special interest, and we shall therefore deal only with it.

158. In many writings on IN subjects — to some extent, I regret to say, in my own former monographs also — the semi-vocalic components of the diphthongs have not been distinctly indicated. Thus in Malay textbooks one meets with such spellings as, for example, *bau*, " smell ", and *rantau*, " coast ", the end of the word being spelt in each case in the same way, though it is only in the second case that the end is a diphthong, while in the first word the *a* and the *u* belong to two separate syllables; I now write *bau*, and, on the other hand, *rantaw*.

159. Madurese spelling has no means of denoting aspiration, and accordingly spells *ghuluñ*, " to roll ", and *guluñ*, " a delicacy made from glutinous rice ", in the same way.

The Diphthongs and their Laws.

160. The IN diphthongs are mostly combinations of vowels with one or other of the two semi-vowels *y* and *w*. Other possible combinations are rare: Original IN final *i* becomes in certain Achinese dialects the diphthong *oy*, thus Ach.

bloy, " to buy " < Original IN *bĕli,* but the standard dialect says *bloe,* with a semi-vocalic *e.*

161. The IN diphthongs only appear exceptionally in the accentuated syllable of the WB. That is a contrast with IE, if we call to mind such cases as the Greek *kairios,* " fitting ", or the Gothic *skaidan,* " to sever ". Hova has certain cases like *táwlana,* " bone ", where contraction has produced the diphthong, as there is an Old Javanese *tahulan* corresponding to *táwlana.* Mentaway has also a few cases, *e.g., räwru,* " to journey downstream "; they are mostly words of which the etymology is obscure.

162. In by far the greater number of the cases the IN diphthong appears in the final syllable of the WB, and constitutes the end of it. Though that is usually the syllable that does not bear the principal accent, its sonority is, nevertheless, not very much weaker than that of the accentuated syllable (see §§ 329 *seqq.*).

163. The diphthongs most commonly met with in the IN languages are *aw, ay,* and *uy,* and these we must ascribe to Original IN. The words *paraw,* " hoarse ", *bañaw,* " heron ", *patay,* " to kill ", *balay,* " house ", *apuy,* " fire ", *babuy,* " pig ", which are found in many IN languages, must also be regarded as Original IN, the first of them in the form *par₂aw.*

164. The Original IN diphthongs *aw, ay,* and *uy,* have undergone various vicissitudes in the living IN languages:

165. In many languages the diphthongs, as mentioned in § 163, have been *preserved.* Iloko has, for example, the words *patáy, apuy,* etc.

166. The *a* of *ay* and the *u* of *uy* may, under the influence of the *y,* be *modified* in the manner technically termed " Umlaut ", hence Dayak *atäy,* " heart " < Original IN *atay.* Bontok *fafüy,* " pig " < Original IN *babuy.*

167. The first component of the diphthong may *change into another vowel,* thus in certain dialects of Borneo both *ay* and *uy* appear as *oy,* hence *patoy* as well as *baboy.* — As Original IN *patay* results in Bontok in *padöy*, we must there assume *patoy* as an intermediate stage.

168. The diphthongs become *simple sounds*:

I. The first component of the diphthong disappears, as in Malay *api* < Original IN *apuy*.

II. The second component disappears, as in Hova *afu* < Original IN *apuy*.

III. The two components unite into a simple vowel, the sound of which lies intermediately between the two components, as in Toba *pate* < *patay* and *poro* < *paraw*.

169. The Original IN vowel sequences *au* and *ai*, where the vowels belong to two distinct syllables, as in *tau*, " man ", *lain*, " other ", are in several languages contracted to *o* and *e* respectively, hence *e.g.*, Old Javanese *len* < *lain*. Here we must assume their pronunciation as diphthongs as an intermediate stage, thus: *taw* and *layn*.

170. This contraction to simple vowels takes place:

I. Without limitations, in several languages.

II. Only when the word is burdened with an enclitic, in Karo. Thus, " water " = Karo *lau*, " his water " = *lo-na*, " distance " = *dauh*, " his distance " = *doh-na*.

171. In several IN languages *new diphthongs* have arisen, which do not therefore represent Original IN diphthongs:

I. Several languages turn the *i* and *u* of the final syllable of the Original IN WB into *ey* and *ew* respectively, for example, Tiruray; hence Tir. *taley*, " rope " < Original IN *tali*, Tir. *fitéw*, " seven " < Original IN *pitu*.

II. Other languages turn *i* into *ay* or *oy*, *u* into *iw* or *aw*. Thus Original IN *běli*, " to buy ", becomes in Daya-Achinese *blay*, in Tunong-Achinese *bloy*; Original IN *batu*, " stone ", appears as *batiw* in Lamnga-Achinese, and as *bataw* in Miri, a Borneo dialect.

III. Sĕraway turns Original IN final *a* into *aw*; thus Sĕr. *mataw*, " eye " < Original IN *mata*.

172. All the cases of diphthongization mentioned in the preceding paragraph occur as a rule only when the original vowel, from which the diphthong has proceeded, was a *final*. This phenomenon runs parallel with the fact that the Original IN diphthongs *aw, ay,* and *uy* also appear only as finals. Only in certain languages of Borneo are vowels closed by consonants also sometimes turned into diphthongs, thus in Dali and in Long Kiput, hence Dali *lañayt,* " sky " < Original IN *lañit* and Long Kiput *pulawt,* " gum " < Original IN *pulut.*

173. Diphthongization may also be the result of various other phonetic processes. Such processes are:

I. Vocalization of consonants, in Lampong, *e.g., ikuy,* " tail " < Original IN *ikur$_2$.*

II. Reduction of vowels that originally belonged to two distinct words, as in Bangkalan *saybu,* " a thousand " < *sa + ebu.*

III. Reduction of vowels after the dropping out of a consonant, as in Hova *fay,* " ray (fish) " < Original IN *par$_2$i.*

174. When originally simple vowels are turned into diphthongs, as in Tiruray *taley,* " rope " < *tali,* the process of diphthongization must have been preceded by length of the vowel; from § 77 we know that final vowels are often long.

175. As stated in § 76, syllables coming before the accentuated syllable are very seldom long, and similarly diphthongs very rarely occur before the accentuated syllable. In a few Sanskrit loan-words beginning with *s,* Lampong has the diphthong *ay* in that position, as in *saygara,* " sea " < Sansk. *sāgara.*

176. I know of no case of the pĕpĕt turning into a diphthong. After what has been said in § 40, I, there can be no question of the diphthongization of Original IN *e* or *o.*

The Aspirates and their Laws.

177. As the majority of the IN languages only tolerate combinations of consonants to a limited extent, some of them merely the combination of a nasal with a cognate explosive, the aspirated consonants are not widely distributed in IN.

178. Aspirated consonants have arisen in the living IN languages in the following ways:

I. They are found in WB's formed by the *doubling of roots* having *h* as their initial and an explosive as their final, as in Old Javanese *hathat*, " to take care ", Bisaya *haghag*, " texture ". These cases are not numerous.

II. A few languages, like Tagalog, allow the *combination of most of the consonants* with a subsequent *h*, and consequently also that kind of combination which we call the aspirates. Hence in Tagalog a word like *bugháw*, " blue ", is just as permissible as a word like *panhík*, " to ascend ".

III. In Madurese, aspirates arise *in conformity with phonetic law* by the change of Original IN mediæ into aspirated mediæ; hence Original IN *gantuñ*, " to hang " > Mad. *ghantoñ*; Original IN *jalan*, " path " > Mad. *jhalan*; Original IN *dayañ*, " stranger, trader " > Mad. *dhaghañ*; Original IN *këmbañ*, " bud " > Mad. *këmbhañ*, " flower ".

IV. In a few languages, as in Cham and Achinese, aspirates arise through the *elision of vowels*. Hence Original IN *pohon*, " tree " > Cham *phun*; Original IN *tahu*, " to know " > Ach. *thee*.

V. Aspirates are found in *loan-words* from the Sanskrit, as in Tagalog *katha*, " speech ".

VI. Achinese renders the *Arabic f* by *ph*, as in *kaphé*, " the infidel ".

179. Only the few isolated cases of aspiration mentioned under § 178, I, can be ascribed to Original IN. There is therefore a great difference in the relative importance of the aspirates as between Original IN and Original IE.

SECTION VII: SPECIAL PHENOMENA OF INITIAL, INTERIOR, AND FINAL SOUNDS.

Preliminary Observations.

180. We have often been able to notice in Section IV that the condition under which a phonetic change takes place consists in the fact that the sound in question is an initial, interior, or final sound. Thus Original IN *a* changes in Běsěmah into *ě* when it ends a word, but otherwise remains unchanged. We will not discuss these phenomena again in this place, but will deal with a series of phonetic facts which are particularly characteristic of the nature of the initial, interior, and final sounds and which we have, on that account, reserved for this Section. Hereto belong also the phenomena connected with the enunciation of vowels, whether as initial, medial, or final, in *words*.

Initial, Medial, and Final Enunciation.

181. The *enunciation* of IN words, that begin with a vowel, may be soft, hard, or aspirated. Hard enunciation, that is to say the sounding of a hamzah before the vowel, is evidenced for a considerable number of IN languages (see § 142), and we may therefore with very fair certainty ascribe this phenomenon to Original IN. Moreover, hard and aspirated enunciation may interchange. " At the beginning of Achinese words *h* and *q* occasionally interchange, either because one dialect uses *q* and another uses *h*, or because the choice between them is left to the fancy of the individual speaker " (Snouck Hurgronje). The Minangkabau vocabulary contains a great number of words beginning either with or without *h*, such as *hindu* and *indu*, " mother ".

182. Initial hamzah is replaced in certain languages by other sounds: γ, y, w.

I. In Muna we find γ, as in *γate*, " heart " $<$ Original IN *atay*, or more precisely: *qatay*.

II. In Buli we get y, as in *yataf*, " roof " $<$ Original IN *atĕp*, or more precisely: *qatĕp*.

III. In Bulanga-Uki we meet with w, as in *wina*, " mother " $<$ Original IN *ina*, or more precisely: *qina*.

183. The occurrence of these sounds, γ, y, and w, instead of q, is explained by the phenomena of sandhi. In Malay the word *ĕmpat*, " four ", when it stands alone or at the beginning of a sentence, is pronounced *qĕmpat*. In the phrase " four pieces of sugar-cane " $=$ s. f. p. $=$ " *tĕbu wĕmpat buku*, the initial q is replaced by w ", under the influence of the preceding u (Fokker). Now in Bulanga forms such as *wina* this w has simply become permanently affixed, and the y of Buli and γ of Muna are the result of similar processes.

184. *Medial enunciation.* In some IN languages the most various vowels may succeed one another. The sequence of vowel $+$ pĕpĕt or pĕpĕt $+$ vowel is rare; it is found in a few instances in Madurese, as in *taĕn*, " rope ". In some languages intermediary or separating sounds arise between two vowels. And here two cases in particular are to be observed:

I. Between $u +$ vowel or $i +$ vowel the appropriate semi-vowel steps in. Some of the IN languages say *buah*, " fruit ", others *buwah*; some say *ia*, " he ", others *iya*.

II. In some languages q or h appears between vowels, especially when they are similar, as in Malay *leher*, Madurese *leqer*, " neck ".

185. *Final enunciation* of a word ending in a vowel may, like initial, be soft, aspirated, or hard (with a hamzah). In Madurese every word ending originally with a vowel receives a final h, Mad. *matah*, " eye " $<$ Original IN *mata*. — In

Busang in the like case a hamzah is used, and *i* turns into *e*, *u* into *o*. Table of examples:

Original IN		Busang	
lima		*limáq*,	" five "
dĕpa		*dĕpáq*,	" span "
buta		*butáq*,	" blind "
bĕli		*bĕléq*,	" to buy "
laki		*lakéq*,	" man "
tali		*taléq*,	" rope "
asu		*asóq*,	" dog "
batu		*batóq*,	" stone "
kayu		*kayóq*,	" tree ".

186. In Madurese all three grades of enunciation may occur in the same word. If a word in Original IN ends in a vowel or diphthong, as *mata*, " eye ", *laju*, " to proceed ", *patay*, " death ", the word is pronounced in Mad. with aspirated enunciation, hence *matah*, *pateh*, *lajhuh*, " thereupon ". In the interior of a sentence the aspiration is lost, and thus in the texts appended to Kiliaan's Grammar, I, p. 124, l. 12, we find: " Thereupon (he) died " = *lajhu mateh*. Before a pause, due to the speaker being at a loss how to proceed, the word is pronounced with a hamzah, thus *lajhuq . . . mateh*.

The Initial.

187. IN words can, as a rule, begin with a vowel, a semi-vowel, or a simple consonant; and this state of affairs is to be regarded as Original IN. In connexion therewith the following points are also to be noted:

I. Before the initial *vowel* some languages sound a hamzah (see § 181).

II. Few words in the IN languages begin with the *semi-vowel y*, and none of them can be shown to be Original IN. Initial *w* is more frequent, but it mostly originates from *b*. Of Original IN *w* there are only three cases: *walu*, " eight ", *wara*, " to be, to exist ", and *way*, " water ".

III. In contrast with the IE languages, *ṅ* is not a rare phenomenon among the initial *consonants*.

188. Some IN languages also admit an initial formed of *two consonants*. The commonest cases are mute + liquid and nasal + cognate explosive. In connexion with initial double consonants the following points are also to be noted:

I. Initial consonantal sequences are the same as those that occur in the interior of words; thus in Nias, where we have, for example, *mb* both initially and medially, as in *mbawa-mbawa*, "spotted", alongside of *mambu*, "to forge (as a smith)".

II. The initial allows fewer consonantal sequences than the interior of words, as in Hova. The sequence $n + t + s$ does in fact occur medially, *e.g.* in *untsi*, "banana (plantain)", but not initially.

III. The initial admits of more consonantal sequences than the interior of words, as in Rottinese. The sequence $n + d$ does in fact occur initially, as in *ndala*, "horse", but not medially.

189. *Three consonants*, mostly nasal + cognate explosive + liquid or semi-vowel, rarely occur initially. Nias, for example, has $n + d + r$, as in *ndrundru*, "hut". Old Javanese has $n + d + y$, as in *ndya*, "where, what".

190. When words begin with two or three consonants, they usually remain unchanged in all positions in the sentence. In the Gayo text, "The Blue Princess", p. 46, l. 4, *a sentence begins* with a word having the initial *nt :* "That I may not marry" = N. I m. = *nti aku kěrjön*. In Rāmāyaṇa, VIII, 171, the above-mentioned *ndya* occurs after the word *toh*, "well", *which ends with a consonant.*

191. Initials of more than one consonant are not Original IN; they have arisen through various phonetic processes:

I. *In conformity with phonetic law, e.g.* in Hova. Original IN *d* changes in certain cases in Hova into *tr*, as in *trúzuna* < Original IN *duyuñ*, "sea-cow".

II. Through *loss of a vowel*, as in Gayo *bli* < Original IN *běli*, "to buy", or in Makianese *mto*, "eye" < Original IN *mata*.

III. Through *word-formation*. Alongside of the Old Javanese *ndya* we find an Old Jav. *ndi* and a Toba *dia*, with the same meaning; accordingly *ndya* is analysable into the three elements $n + di + a$. I have dealt with such combinations of words of form in previous monographs.

192. Through the process of *word-abbreviation* (§§ 274 *seqq.*) initials arise which would not otherwise be possible in the languages in question. Examples:

I. In Tontemboan *k* is pronounced *c* when an *i* comes before it, either in a word or in a sentence, but in no other case. Thus from the two elements *raqi + ka* comes the negative *raqica*. This is often abbreviated into *ca*, and then the initial *c* is allowed to remain unchanged even if there is no *i* before it, as several passages prove. Thus in Schwarz-Texts, p. 61, l. 17, we find: "He said: He does not catch " = *kuanao : ca maindo.*

II. In conformity with the law of the mediæ (§ 155, III) an initial media must become a continuant in Tontemboan. But in proper names abbreviated as explained in § 276 the media persists, as in *Biraq*, abbreviated from *Imbiran*, a personal name.

The Medial.

193. In the interior of the IN WB, which is mostly disyllabic, thus between the two vowels of it, we meet either with no consonant, or one, or two, but rarely three.

194. Of the cases where there is *no consonant*, or *only one*, between the two vowels, there is nothing more to be said.

195. Among the cases where *two consonants* occur between the two vowels, two types in particular are frequent, the *Lintah-type* and the *Taptap-type*. Both are to be ascribed to Original IN.

I. The *Lintah-type*. In almost all the IN languages the combination of nasal + cognate explosive is permitted medially. Thus, for example, the word *lintah*, "leech", recurs, with $n + t$, in nearly all the IN languages.

II. The *Taptap-type* has originated from the doubling of the root, as in Old Javanese, etc., *taptap*, " to strike ".

196. Now some of the living IN languages have preserved both the Original IN types, others have modified them.

197. The *Lintah-type* has remained unchanged in by far the greater number of IN languages; only a small percentage of the languages has altered it, entirely or partially, and in the following ways:

I. Some languages, such as Toba, assimilate the nasal in the combination of nasal + tenuis to the tenuis; thus spoken Toba *gattuṅ*, " to hang " < written Toba, and likewise Original IN, *gantuṅ*.

II. Some few languages allow the nasal to disappear entirely; thus Nias, as in *lita* < Original IN *lintah*. But *mb* and *ndr* < *nd* persist, as in *tandru*, " horn " < Original IN *tanduk*, *tandra*, " mark " < Original IN *tanda*.

III. Conversely, other languages allow the explosive to disappear; thus Rottinese, as in *tana*, " mark " < Original IN *tanda*.

198. The *Taptap-type* has remained unchanged in Old Javanese, Karo, Tagalog, etc., but yet in fewer languages than the Lintah-type. The modifications it has undergone are of the following kind:

I. Assimilation has taken place, as in Makassar; Original IN, and likewise Old Javanese, *paspas*, " to cut off ", appears in Makassar as *páppasaq* = *pappas* + the supporting syllable *aq*

II. The first of the two medial consonants becomes a hamzah, as in Tontemboan, which accordingly says *taqtap* instead of *taptap*.

III. The first of the two consonants disappears entirely, as in Bĕsĕmah, hence Bĕs. *tatap*.

Note.—The rules mentioned in this paragraph do not hold good of *all* possible cases of the Taptap-type, but they always apply to certain classes of cases, determined by regular laws.

199. Sequences of *three consonants* in the interior of words are rare and cannot be ascribed to Original IN. They arise chiefly in two ways:

I. *By mere operation of phonetic law.* The sequence *nd* in Nias becomes *ndr*, hence Nias *tandra* < Original IN *tanda*, " mark ".

II. By the springing up of *intermediary sounds.* From the Old Javanese WB *prih* is derived the verb *amrih*, " to strive ". for which Madurese has *ambri*, the *b* having arisen as an intermediary sound forming the transition from the *m* to the *r*. Of like origin is Modern Javanese *ambral* < *amral* < *admiral*.

The Final.

200. In Original IN a word could end in a vowel, a diphthong, or a *single* consonant, other than a palatal (see § 61, I). A final palatal is quite rare in the living languages, though found in Tontemboan as the resultant of *k* (see § 103).

201. The developments in the living languages of the Original IN final *vowels* have been dealt with in §§ 91 *seqq.*, those of the *diphthongs* in §§ 160 *seqq.*; those of the *consonants*, which can lay claim to very special interest, will now be discussed.

202. The Original IN condition as regards final consonants persists unchanged in Old Javanese, and also, with very few exceptions. the loss of *h* for example, in several of the Philippine languages.

203. In the remaining IN languages we can discern three tendencies in the treatment of consonantal finals: unification, loss, and addition of a supporting vowel.

204. *Unification.* This is applied in various degrees in the several languages, as will be shown here by reference to the explosives:

I. Malay unifies the mediæ with the tenues. Original IN *bukid*, " hill " > Mal. *bukit*. Thus among the explosives only the three tenues *k*, *t*, and *p*, are in this case capable of serving as finals.

II.   Masaretese behaves like Malay and further unifies *p* with *t*, hence Original IN *atĕp* = Malay *atap* = Masaretese *atet*, " roof." Here, therefore, among the explosives only two tenues, *k* and *t*, are capable of serving as finals.

III.   Primitive Bugis, as I showed in a former monograph, unified all the explosives into *k*, hence Primitive Bug. *lañik*, " sky " < Original IN *lañit*, and *atĕk*, " roof " < Original IN *atĕp*. Here, therefore, out of all the explosives only the one tenuis *k* is capable of serving as a final.

205. *Loss.* The disappearance of the final consonants takes place in the several IN languages in various degrees:

I.   Makassar allows only one consonant, namely *h*, to disappear, as in *panno* < Original IN *pĕnuh*, " full ".

II.   In Hova, *s*, *h*, and the liquids disappear, hence Hova *manifi* < Original IN *nipis*, " thin ", *fenu*, " full " < Original IN *pĕnuh*.

III.   In Bimanese, Nias, and some other languages, all final consonants disappear.

206. *Addition of a supporting vowel.* In this connexion two tendencies may be discerned among the several IN languages:

I.   The same supporting vowel is added in all cases: in Talautese and Hova *a*, in Ampana *i*, in Kaidipan *o*, or exceptionally *u*, etc. Hence Original IN *inum*, " to drink " > Tal. *inuma* = Hova *inuna* = Kaid. *inumu*; Original IN *putih*, " white " > Kaid. *pitiho*.

II.   The supporting vowel imitates the vowel that immediately precedes the final consonant, as in Mentaway, hence Ment. *tukulu*, " to push ", alongside of Karo *tukul*, but *rápiri*, " wall ", *bóbolo*, " a species of lily ", etc.

III.   A few languages, such as Makassar, further add a hamzah after the supporting vowel, hence Original IN *nipis* " thin " > Mak. *nipisiq*, *lĕpas*, " free " > Mak. *láppassaq*, *atur*, " to put in order " > Mak. *átoroq*.

IV. The consonant saved by the supporting vowel may nevertheless disappear owing to further phonetic processes, while the supporting vowel may be preserved, as in Ambon; hence Original IN *tuwak*, " palm-wine " > Amb. *túwao*, Original IN *atĕp*, " roof " > *áteo*.

207. Some of the IN languages only recognize one of the tendencies delineated in §§ 204 *seqq.*, others two, others again all three of them.

I. Nias only has loss of the final: all Original IN final consonants disappear.

II. Minangkabau has both unification and loss. The explosives are unified to *q*, the liquids disappear. The nasals and *h* persist, *s* becomes *h*.

III. Makassar employs all the methods. The aspirate disappears, the nasals are unified into *ṅ*, the explosives into *q*, the liquids and *s* receive a supporting vowel + hamzah.

208. In all the IN languages we meet with the pheno-menon that final consonants are *interchanged*. In Malay alongside of *butir*, " grain ", which is in conformity with phonetic law, there is also a form *butil*. Hova has as a pendant to the Malay *burut*, a phonetically regular word *wúrutra*, but alongside of it it also has a form *wúruka*, " broken, torn, rags ", etc. This phenomenon occurs everywhere in isolated cases, mostly only in a few cases. Probably these are due to prehistoric formative processes, or to the working of the principle of analogy, and the like.

209. We very often meet with the phenomenon that in some language a word ends in a consonant, while the Original IN and some of the other living languages have a vowel as final. Here we are dealing with words of form that have become annexed to the original word. " How much " in Original IN is *pira*, but in Makassar *piraṅ*; " this " in Old Javanese is *ika*, but in Modern Jav. *kaṅ*. The *ṅ* is an article welded on, originating from such formulas as the Old Jav. for " this child " = Greek *tuto to teknon* = Old Jav. *ika ṅ anak*. Such annexed articles are also not uncommon in the IE sphere; we find one for example in the French *lierre*, " ivy ", etc.

210. Now, when *a suffix is added* to a final that has been modified through the influence of the laws affecting finals, we observe the following phenomena:

I.   The *original state* of the final, as it was in *Original IN*, again appears. When from the Bugis *nipiq*, " thin " < Original IN *nipis* a verb " to thin " is formed by means of the suffix -*i*, it does not take the form *nipiqi* but *nipisi*. More correctly expressed, the formation *nipisi* has been handed down from a period when people still said *nipis*.

II.   The derivative exhibits the *modern state* of the final. Original IN *bañun*, " to stand up," appears in Makassar as *bañuñ*, and from it is derived the verb *bañuñañ*. " to raise ". This formation dates from a period when *n* had already turned into *ñ*.

III.   The derivative displays an *intermediate state* of the final, a stage of development lying *between* the Original IN and the modern form. As shown in a previous monograph, Original IN *sĕlsĕl*, " to regret ", turned in Primitive Bugis into *sĕssĕr*, whereof the Modern Bug. has made *sĕssĕq*. The derivative " reproof" in Modern Bug. is *pasĕssĕrrĕñ*; it dates from a period when people no longer said *sĕlsĕl*, and had not yet begun to say *sĕssĕq*.

IV.   The derivative has *both* the original and the modified state of the final, *side by side*. Original IN *lĕpas*, " free ". appears in Minangkabau as *lapĕh*. The derivative " to free " is both *malapasi* and *malapĕhi*. To this there is an exact parallel in Hova. Original IN *lĕpas* appears in Hova as *lefa*. But the passive imperative is both *alefasu* and *alefau*.

V.   The derivative shows *none* of the forms we should be disposed to expect; for just in this sphere there have been many cases of analogical transference. Original IN *ĕpat*, " four ", appears in Primitive Bugis as *ĕppak*, in Modern Bug. as *ĕppaq*, but the derivative " to divide into four " is *ĕppári*. This formation is based on the analogy of words like *appaq* :

appári, " to display ", where the *r* is in conformity with phonetic law, for Malay and other languages have the form *hampar*.

211. Behaviour of the *supporting vowel in derivatives* and *with enclitics* :

I. On the addition of a *suffix* the supporting vowel is dispensed with. From Makassar *sássalaq* < *sĕlsĕl* comes the derived verb *sassáli*, " to refuse ".

II. Before *enclitics* we find both persistence and dis-appearance of the supporting vowel. In the Makassar romance Jayalangkara, p. 72, l. 9, is the expression : " The people of Egypt " = P. E. the = *tu-Máserek-a*. *Másereq* < *Meṣir* has the supporting syllable *-eq*, and this *persists* before the enclitic article, the hamzah turning into a *k*. In the Hova Fables of Rahidy, V, l. 3, we find : " Killed by him " = *nuwunúini*, for *nuwunúina + ni*. Here the supporting vowel has *disappeared*, and the two *n*'s coming together have coalesced into one.

The Final in Rottinese.

212. Rottinese displays peculiar phenomena in the final, which require special consideration.

213. In Rot. three of the consonants are capable of serving as finals, viz. *k*, *n*, and *s*, Original IN *awak*, " body " > Rot. *aok ;* Original IN *ur₁an*, " rain " > Rot. *udan ;* Original IN *nipis*, " thin " > Rot. *niis*. But Original IN *bĕr₂at*, " heavy " > Rot. *belak ;* Malay, etc., *ruañ* > Rot. *loak*, " room ".

214. One might endeavour to explain these facts by the principle of unification (§ 204).

215. But we are faced by a circumstance which excludes any explanation based on the principle of unification ; the circumstance is this, that in an extraordinary number of cases the final is different from what one would expect on general linguistic principles or from IN usage. Examples : Original

IN *jalan*, " path " > Rot. *dalak* ; r_2atus, " hundred " > *natun*; *matay*, " to die " > *mates*, " dead "; *lidi*, " nerve of a leaf " > *lidek*. And alongside of the above-mentioned *niis* > *nipis* there is a form *niik*.

216. To explain this state of affairs, one might then have recourse to the principle of the interchange of finals, as in § 208. But this is countered by the fact already mentioned, that the phenomena illustrated in the preceding paragraph are exceedingly common in Rot., whereas interchange of finals in other languages only occurs in isolated cases.

217. Accordingly we must look around for another explanation, namely the following one:

I. *Negative part* of the explanation. The cases in question are not really instances of a law affecting finals. The three final consonants, *k*, *n*, and *s*, are not the representatives of Original IN finals; even the *n* in *udan* is not a survival of the *n* of Original IN ur_1an.

II. *Positive part.* In a former period of its existence Rot. cast off all its final consonants; there was, therefore, a time when it said *dala*, " path ", *uda*, " rain ", *nii*, " thin ". This condition is the same as the closely related Bimanese has preserved to this day, *e.g.* in *ura*, " rain ", *nipi*, " thin ", etc. The finals which occur nowadays in Rot. are *articles, which have become annexed and have lost their force.* like the ones mentioned in § 209.

218. Articles and demonstratives beginning with *k*, *s*, or *n*, are found very frequently in the IN languages. It is also no uncommon phenomenon for such words of form to occur without a vowel. The Old Javanese article for things is *añ* and *ñ*. The Bontok article for persons *si* is often abbreviated into *s*, and so is the Inibaloi *si*. Thus in the text " Kalinas ", in Scheerer, " The Nabaloi Dialect ", p. 149, l. 5, we find: " I have met the captain " = H. + m. I the c. = *inaspol ko s kapitan.*

219. The article is put after the principal word in many IN languages, and particularly in those that are near neighbours.

and relatively close connexions of Rot., for example in Sawunese. Thus in the Sawunese Story of Pepeka, Bijdr. 1904, p. 283, l. 10 from the bottom, we find: " In the cave " = In c. the = *la roa ne*. The Modern Rottinese article *a* also follows the principal word.

220. The fact that we therefore have to credit Rottinese with four articles, *k*, *n*, *s*, and *a*, makes no difficulty, for the number of articles in Bugis is even larger, as I showed in a previous monograph.

221. We therefore assume that in a former period of its evolution the final in Rottinese had become exclusively vocalic, and that in the modern period it has again to a large extent resumed the consonantal form owing to the welding on of articles containing no vowel. The assumption of such a divergency in development involves no impossibility. As was remarked above, the Bimanese is a language with purely vocalic finals, yet it employs certain enclitic pronouns even in forms devoid of vowels. " Child " in Bim. is *ána* < Original IN *anak*, " my child " is *aná-ku* or *aná-k*. And such forms even occur at the end of a sentence; thus in Mpama Sañaji Ali in Jonker's " Bimaneesche Texten ", p. 55, l. 15 from the bottom, a sentence ends with the words: " At the house of our prince " = At p. o. = *labo rumá-t*. In Bim. such pronouns are still mobile, they have not been welded together with the principal word to form a new WB as in Rot.

222. The *crucial test* of the correctness of these conclusions consists in the following: If the finals *k*, *s*, and *n*, are articles that have been annexed and have lost their original force, they must not occur in verbal words, vocatives, or the like. And that is really the case.   The word *taek*, " young man ", is *tae* in the vocative.   " To rain " is *uda*, " (the) rain " *udan*. Accordingly the Original IN *ur₁an* has undergone the following development in Rot.:

Original IN	*ur₁an*.
Rot., older period	*uda*.
Modern Rot., verb	*uda*, " to rain ".
Modern Rot., substantive	*udan*, " rain ".

It is true that there have also been compromises and cases
of transference. In *niik* or *niis* (§ 215) we should not have
expected to find an annexed article but a vocalic final.

223. Phenomena similar to those of Rot. are also exhibited
by some other languages spoken on islands in the same part
of the sea, for example by Timorese.

Comparison with Indo-European.

224. The IN phenomena of initials, medials, and finals
have a very large number of parallels in IE. Only a few of
them will be selected for mention here:

I. Old Slavonic and Buli. Before an originally *initial*
vowel an *i*-sound appears. Buli *yatof* < Original IN *atĕp*;
for the Old Slavonic see Leskien, " Grammatik der altbulgarischen Sprache ", § 57.

II. Greek and Madurese. Between *medial m* and *r* the
intermediary sound *b* appears. Mad. *ambri* < *amrih* (§ 199);
Gr. *mesēmbria*, " noon ", alongside of *hēmera*, " day ".

III. Portuguese dialect of Alta Beira and Talautese.
Final consonants receive a supporting vowel. Alta Beira
deuze, " God "; Tal. *inuma* < *inum*, " to drink ".

SECTION VIII : CERTAIN SPECIAL CLASSES OF PHONETIC PHENOMENA.

225. In this Section will be discussed certain phonetic phenomena which occupy a somewhat special position and are also usually dealt with separately in the IE textbooks. These phenomena are: prothesis, anaptyxis, repetition of sounds, metathesis, haplology, assimilation, " Umlaut ", dissimilation, and fracture.

226. The most frequently occurring kind of *prothesis* is the affixing of a pĕpĕt before words that were originally monosyllabic or had become monosyllabic through some process of phonetic change. The cause of this phenomenon is the tendency towards disyllabism (§ 19). Old Javanese *goṅ*, " gong ", appears in Modern Jav. as *ĕgoṅ* as well as *goṅ*. Original IN *dur₂i*, " thorn ", passes through *rur₂i* into Old Jav. *rwi*, in accordance with the principle mentioned in § 137, and then in Modern Jav. undergoes a further evolution into *ri*, by the side of which now appears a form *ĕri*. Dutch *lijst*, " list ", appears in IN languages as *les* and *ĕles*.

227. This prothetic *ĕ* is also subject to the phonetic laws of change; hence " gong " in Toba is *oguṅ*, as Toba alters the pĕpĕt into *o*.

228. Instead of the pĕpĕt, *i* may also appear before *y* and *u* before *w*. The Old Javanese conjunction *ya*, " that ", is likewise *ya* in Tontemboan, but people also use both the forms *ĕya* and *iya*, in accordance with what has been said above. Original IN *buwah*, " fruit ", becomes Old Jav. *wwah*; from this is regularly derived the Modern Jav. *woh*, but alongside of the latter there is also a form *uwoh*.

229. Besides this prothetic $\breve{e}$, i, or u, we meet in various languages with yet other vowels affixed before words that originally had a consonantal initial. Original IN, and likewise Old Javanese, Malay, etc., *lintah*, "leech", appears in several languages as *alintah*; Original IN *tĕlur₂*, "egg", is represented in Tagalog by *itlóg*, etc. I am not in a position to decide whether these are cases of a purely phonetic process or whether we are here dealing with creations of a formative import. Parallel phenomena offering similar difficulties of explanation are also found in IE: see (*inter alia*) Hirt, "Handbuch der griechischen Laut- und Formenlehre", §§ 193 *seqq.*

230. *Anaptyxis* is found in Pabian-Lampong, where an $\breve{e}$ appears between r and the immediately following consonant. To Malay, Karo, etc., *sĕrdan*, corresponds a Lamp. form *surĕdan*, "a species of palm". This sort of anaptyxis may be compared in the IE sphere with phenomena like the Oscan *aragetud* = Latin *argento*. Of another kind is the appearance of vowels between consonants in loan-words, where facilitation of pronunciation is the cause of the phenomenon (see § 284).

231. *Repetition of sounds* may affect vowels or consonants, may be progressive or regressive. and may occur merely in isolated cases or in series of cases.

232. When in Hova an i is put before a velar, it is without exception repeated after the velar, in consonantal form and at the same time very softly pronounced. "Surprised" in Hova is *gaga*, and "to be surprised" is not *migaga* but *migyaga*.

233. Bajo "fractures"* an a of the second syllable of a WB into *ea*, when the word ends in $\dot{n}$; Original IN *bĕnan*, "thread", therefore appears in Bajo as *bĕnéan*. In the one case of *geantéan* < Original IN *gantan*, "a particular measure of capacity", the e has been repeated in the first syllable.

234. In very many cases in IN languages there appears before a consonant a nasal, which is wanting in other IN

* [See § 260.]

languages, and which we cannot ascribe to Original IN either. The word for " brain " in some of the languages is *utĕk*, in others *untĕk*; " to pursue " is *usir* and *uṅsir* in Old Javanese. Now there are in the IN languages a great number of very commonly used prefixes and suffixes containing nasals, and it is from these that the nasal has forced its way into the interior of the WB by means of the principle of the repetition of sounds. From the Old Jav. WB *usir*, for example, comes the active *aṅusir* or *maṅusir*, and from this *aṅ-* or *maṅ-* the *ṅ* has been projected into the variant form *uṅsir* of the WB.

235. Repetition of sounds is also found in IE, and IE research avails itself of the same explanations that have been applied above to IN: see (*inter alia*) Zauner, " Altspanisches Elementarbuch ", § 78.

236. *Metathesis* is a phenomenon of very frequent occurrence in IN; it turns up in all sorts of forms, either sporadically or in regular series.

237. The following are the sorts that occur most frequently:

I. The vowels of the two syllables of the WB change places. Original IN, and likewise Malay, etc., *ikur*, " tail ", is pronounced *ukir* in some other languages; thus in some dialects of Madagascar: *uhi* < *ukir*.

II. The consonants of the first half of the word change places. Original IN, and likewise Old Jav., etc., *waluh*, " pumpkin ", appears in Bugis as *lawo*.

III. The consonants of the second half of the word change places. Original IN *r₂atus*, " hundred ", appears in several languages as *rasut*.

IV. Two interior consonants change places. Toba *purti* < Sanskrit *putrī*, " daughter ".

238. Tontemboan possesses a peculiar, optional kind of metathesis, which will be illustrated by the following example. In the Story of the Poor Woman and her Grandchild, Schwarz-Texts, pp. 107 *seqq.*, we find on p. 110, 1. 5: " Why should we respect ? " = What the cause-for-respect = *sapa ĕn ipĕsiriq*.

On p. 109, l. 1, we find as an equivalent for the same phrase *sapa im pĕsiriq*. From *ĕn ipĕsiriq* there has been metathesis to *in ĕpĕsiriq*, then the initial *ĕ* has disappeared, making *in pĕsiriq*, and finally by assimilation *im pĕsiriq* has resulted.

239. Metathesis may either be definitive or optional, permitting both forms, the original and the modified one, to exist side by side. Original IN *par₂i*, " ray (fish) ", appears in Tontemboan as *pair*, and in no other form; but in Sundanese *ayud* and *aduy*, " soft ", exist side by side.

240. We notice in various languages a certain preference for particular kinds of metathesis.

I. The preference is connected with the *position* of the sounds in the word. The Mantangay dialect of Dayak favours metathesis in the case of the first syllable of trisyllabic words; it has *dahañan* for the *hadañan*, " buffalo ", of the standard Dayak dialect.

II. The preference is related to a particular *result*. In Sawunese metathesis mostly operates so that an *a* of the second syllable comes into the first one, the *a* also changing into *ĕ* ; hence Original IN *pira*, "how much " $>$ Saw. *pĕri*, *r₂umah*, " house " $>$ *ĕmú*, etc.

241. In certain languages we meet with metatheses occurring in regular series. When in Original IN an *l* immediately precedes the second vowel of a word and an *r* immediately follows it, then these consonants invariably change places in Gayo; hence Gayo *tĕrul*, " egg " $<$ Original IN *tĕlur₂*, *arul*, " brook " $<$ *alur₂*, etc.

242. *Haplology.* This occurs in IN in the first place *sporadically* in various languages, thus in Tsimihety. In " Chansons Tsimihety ", Bulletin de l'Académie Malgache, 1913, p. 100, v. 10, we find *mañi-reboño*, " growing densely ", for *mañiri-reboño*, from the WB *tsiri*, " to grow ".

243. Haplology also occurs in most *regular* series in connexion with the doubling of words. Here either the first or the second term of the duplication may be abbreviated by the method of haplology. The first kind, the abbreviation of the *first term*, appears in every imaginable form, whereof we now give a selection:

I.   The last sound is omitted: Dayak *luyu-luyut*, " somewhat soft ", from *luyut*, " soft "; similarly *aki-akir*, " to push slightly ", etc.

II.   The last two sounds are omitted : Buli *lis-lisan*, " broom ", from *lisan*, " to sweep ".

III.   All sounds except the last are omitted: Tontemboan *u-anu*, " such and such a person ", " Mr. What's his name ", from *anu*, " some one ".

IV.   All sounds except the first are omitted : Mentaway *o-ogdog*, " a tool for opening coconuts ", from the WB *ogdog*.

244.   The *second term* is abbreviated by the method of haplology.   This case is rare.   Padoe *laqika-ika*, " hut ", from *laqika*, " house ".   Javanese *Roso-so*, familiar mode of addressing a person whose name is *Roso*.

245.   As all the species of haplology instanced in §§ 243 *seqq.* are cases of the elimination of sounds that were not in direct contact with the corresponding similar ones, they are analogous to the haplological phenomena of IE described in Brugmann KvG, § 338, A, 2, like the Latin *latrocinium* < *latronicinium*.

246.   *Assimilation* displays in IN all the possibilities that also occur in IE: compare the cases in Brugmann KvG, §§ 319 *seqq.*, with the following scheme.   In the IN languages assimilation may be:

Ia.	Vocalic:	Original IN *tau* > Tontemboan *tow*, " man ".
Ib.	Consonantal:	Original IN *gantuṅ* > Toba *gattuṅ*, " to hang ".
IIa.	Progressive:	Original IN *garuk* > Bimanese *garo*, " to scratch ".
IIb.	Regressive:	Original IN *tau* > Tontemboan *tow*.
IIIa.	Unilateral:	Original IN *tau* > Tontemboan *tow*.

IIIb.	Mutual:	Original IN *aur*	> Bimanese *oo*, " bamboo ".
IVa.	With contact:	Original IN *gantuṅ*	> Toba *gattuṅ*.
IVb.	Without contact:	Original IN *kulit*	> Loinan *kilit*, " skin ".
Va.	Partial:	Original IN *babuy*	> Bontok *fafüy*, " pig ".
Vb.	Complete:	Original IN *kulit*	> Loinan *kilit*.

247. Assimilation occurs in IN not only within the WB, but also, though not often, between the WB and the formative:

I.   The formative affects the WB: Dayak *tuli*, " to moor ", *talian*, " mooring place ".

II.   The WB affects the formative: Tontemboan *sĕraq*, " to eat ", *sĕraqan*, gerundive of the same $<$ *sĕraq* + formative *ĕn* ; *siriq*, " to honour ", *siriqin*, gerundive of the same $<$ *siriq* + formative *ĕn*; and so with all the vowels, when the WB ends in a vowel + hamzah.

248. Assimilation of one part of a compound word by the other is rare. In Busang *do*, " day " + *halĕm*, " past ", becomes *dahalĕm*, " yesterday ".

249. Certain assimilations occur in IN in regular series. If in an Original IN word there is an *l* together with an *r*, then in Toba the *l* is in all cases assimilated to the *r*; hence Original IN *lapar₂*, " to hunger " $>$ Toba *rapar*. The assimilations between WB and formative mentioned in § 247 also occur invariably.

250. We find in several IN languages the change from Original IN final *aya* and *ayu* to *ay*. We may believe that in these cases there was first assimilation into *ayi* and then simplification of the *y* + *i*. Examples: Original IN *kayu* $>$ Sigi *kay*; Original IN *layar₂*, " to sail " $>$ Hova *lay*.

251. The term *Umlaut* is really a superfluity in linguistic terminology, for it only denotes a species of partial assimilation. But the term is used in IN as well as in IE, and usually denotes the partial assimilation of the three vowels *a*, *o*, and *u*, under the influence of *i*.

252. Umlaut is fairly widely distributed in IN. Examples:

Umlaut of *a* $>$ *ä* : Original IN *lima* $>$ Dayak *limä*, "five".

Umlaut of *a* $>$ *e* : Original IN *hatay* $>$ Sumbanese *eti*, "heart".

Umlaut of *a* $>$ *ö* : Original IN *patay* $>$ Bontok *padöy*, "to kill".

Umlaut of *o* $>$ *e* : Toba subdialect *oyo* $>$ Toba *eo*, "urine".

Umlaut of *u* $>$ *ü* : Original IN *babuy* $>$ Bontok *fafüy*, "pig".

Note.—The symbol *ä* is used by Hardeland for an *a* modified by Umlaut in Dayak, and I have retained it.

253. Gayo has a sound similar to the German *ö*, but not originating through the modifying influence of an *i*, as in *dödö*, "breast" $<$ Original IN *dada*.

254. Umlaut may be a preliminary step towards more complete assimilation. Original IN *lima* appears in Dayak as *limä*; and Hova, which is very closely related to Dayak, has *dimi*.

255. *Dissimilation* is rarer in IN than assimilation.

256. Dissimilation occurs:

I. If *two* similar sounds would otherwise follow one another. The duplication of Modern Javanese *ro*, "two", takes the form of *loro*. Original IN *babuy*, "pig", and *babah*, "to carry", appear in Mandarese as *bagi* and *baga* respectively.

II. If *three* similar sounds would otherwise follow one another. Original IN *añin*, "wind", appears in Bugis as *añiñ*, but *mañinañ*, "to dry in the air", has preserved the *n* through the operation of dissimilation. As in *wañuñěñ*, "to raise", from *wañuñ*, "to stand up" $<$ Original IN *bañun*, the same principle has not been at work, we may assume that in *mañinañ* the vowel *i* has been a contributing factor. — Or is this case simply an application of the rule in § 210, I?

257. Dissimilation operates either with or without contact:

I. Dissimilation with contact: *e.g.* in Toba in the case of *s + s*, when these two sounds would otherwise come together, *e.g.* in *'lat-soada*, "not yet" $<$ *las*, "yet" $+$ *soada*, "not".

II.   Dissimilation without contact: thus in Dayak in the case of *s : s,* *e.g.* in *tuso,* "breast" $<$ Original IN *susu,* *tisa,* "remainder" $<$ Sanskrit *seša.*

258.   Dissimilation operates between WB and formative. In Sangirese the suffix *-an* is replaced by *-en* when the last syllable of the WB contains an *a.*

259.   A special case of dissimilation is the one that goes so far as to cause one of the two sounds to disappear entirely. Whereas Dayak says *tisa* for *sisa* $<$ *seša* (§ 257), in Minangkabau the word takes the form *iso,* alongside of *siso.* This is a proceeding similar to the elision of the *r* in the dialectic Greek *phatria,* "brotherhood" $<$ *phratria* (see Brugmann KvG, § 336).

260.   *Fracture** is a term used in IE research to denote various processes; I use the term for the change of *a* into *ea.* Bajo changes the *a* in final *an* into *ea,* at the same time transferring the accent on to the *e;* hence Bajo *padéan,* "grass" $<$ Original IN *pádan.* The cases are numerous.

* [In the original, " Brechung ".]

SECTION IX : PHENOMENA CONNECTED WITH THE AGGREGATION OF SOUNDS INTO SYLLABLES.

261. Each individual syllable has a *summit*. In IN this is almost always a vowel, and only quite exceptionally a voiced sound of some other kind. It is true that IN possesses words of form having no vowel, such as *n*, " of ", *m*, " thy ", but these appear almost invariably only after a vowel, with which they then combine to form a syllable. " Thy gain ", in Toba, is *labám* $<$ *laba* $+$ *m*, but " thy house " is *bagasmu*. — An exception is formed by Gayo, where *n*, " of ", can stand between two consonants, as in *bĕt n se*, " (after the) fashion of this ". Here the nasal *n* is placed between two sounds that are deficient in sonority; it must therefore be a *nasalis sonans*, and is accordingly the summit of a syllable. The same is the case in Dayak phenomena like *blióñ-m*, " thy chopper ", where *m* for *mu* also comes after a consonant and is a nasalis sonans. An illustration in support of this is to be found in the Story of Sangumang, Bijdr. 1906, p. 201, l. 10: " How many choppers hast thou ?" $=$ How $+$ many are choppers thine $=$ *pirä aton blióñ-m*. — Seidenadel says in § 17 of his Bontok grammar: " Final *l* often becomes a sonant liquid, similar to *l* in our (English) word *bottle* "; but he gives no instance, and in all the texts I have found nothing to correspond with this assertion.

262. Certain phonetic processes may cause a *shifting of the summit of a syllable*. Most of the IN languages (as stated in § 4) accentuate the penultimate, thus *áwak*, " body ", *báyar*, " to pay ", and the like. The summit of the first syllable of each of these words is the *a* before the semi-vowel. Toba changes *awak* into *aoak*, Tawaelia turns *bayar* into

baeari. It must not, however, be imagined that the *o* and *e*
here merely fulfil the consonantal function of the *w* and *y* : they
become full vowels, and hence take on the accent and become
the summits of syllables; accordingly the results are the
trisyllabic *aóak* and the quadrisyllabic *baéari.*

263. When a word consists of several syllables, there
arises the question where the *limits* of the syllables lie. In
Bontok " two intervocalic consonants are divided and distributed among two syllables ", but " *ds* (and) *ts* are considered as one sound " (Seidenadel). According to § 60, *ds*
and *ts* represent Original IN palatals. " In Achinese, when
there is a combination of nasal with explosive or even of
nasal + explosive + liquid, as in *cintra*, ' wheel ', the first
syllable ends with the vowel and the second begins with the
combination " (Snouck Hurgronje). This rule must also hold
good for some other IN languages; various phenomena point
in that direction. In several languages, as in Nias (§ 188), a
WB can begin with nasal + explosive; in others, as in Modern
Javanese (§ 69), such a combination does not make the preceding vowel short. And is perhaps also the *bĕt n se* of § 261
to be regarded as *bĕt + nse* ?

264. *Variability in the division into syllables* also occurs.
" In Madurese a hamzah between vowels may be pronounced
as the end of the first syllable or the beginning of the second "
(Kiliaan): accordingly *poqon*, " tree", is either *poq-on* or *poqon*, or even *poq-qon.*

265. In Bontok we find a few cases where the limit between syllables is further marked by the shutting of the vocal
chords, *i.e.* by hamzah; thus in the Headhunters' Ceremonies,
Seidenadel-Texts, p. 512, l. 3: *totokqkoñan*, " to watch ".

SECTION X: PHONETIC PHENOMENA CONNECTED WITH THE COMBINATION OF WORD-BASES WITH FORMATIVES.

266. In the IN languages the WB's occur either unchanged or else *combined with formatives, i.e.* prefixes, infixes, or suffixes. In Ophuijsen's "Bataksche Texten, Mandailingsch Dialect ", p. 16, l. 14: "The story of the old ox " = S. of ox which old = *hobaran ni lombu na tobaṅ*, the words *lombu* and *tobaṅ* are unchanged WB's, but *hobaran* consists of the verbal WB *hobar*, " to tell a story " and the suffix *-an*, which is used to form substantives.

267. The addition of formatives may, or may not, involve phonetic changes. In the "Pantun Mĕlayu", edited by Wilkinson and Winstedt, Pantun 4, l. 1, we find: " Whence flies the dove?" = W. d. f. = *dari-mana punay mĕlayaṅ*, and 5, l. 1: " How can one catch a porcupine ?" = How catch p. = *bagay-mana mĕnaṅkap landaq*. The WB's are *layaṅ* and *taṅkap*; in the derived form *mĕlayaṅ* we observe no phonetic change, but in *mĕnaṅkap* the *t* has turned into *n*.

268. The phonetic phenomena occurring in connexion with the extension of the WB by means of formatives are either the same as those which we also observe in the interior of the WB itself, or they are different. Old Javanese contracts the Original IN sequence $a + i$ in a WB into e; but it similarly contracts if this sequence should happen to occur in a derivative word. Original IN *lain*, " other " > Old Jav. *len*, but likewise *ma + iṅĕt* > *meṅĕt*, " to take care ". — Toba assimilates the *r* of a prefix to an immediately following *l*, and accordingly pronounces *par + lanja* as *pallanja*, " carrier of burdens ". But in a WB, such as *torluk*, " bay ", the *r* persists unchanged.

269. The phonetic phenomena which we observe in the various IN languages in connexion with the addition of *suffixes*, are chiefly and more particularly the following; and it is to be noted incidentally that the suffixes nearly all begin with a vowel:

I. *Intermediary sounds* appear; after *i*-sounds naturally *y*, after *u*-sounds *w*. Hence Bugis *tunuwaṅ*, " to set on fire " < *tunu* + *aṅ* from WB *tunu*, " to burn ". Or the intermediary sounds are *h* or *q*; thus in Southern Mandaïling *parkalahan*, " prophetic tables " < *par* + WB *kala* + *an*; or in Madurese *mateqe*, " to kill " < *pate*, " death " + *e*.

Such intermediary sounds may interchange. After *e* in Makassar the intermediary sound is *y*, after *o* it is *w*; but in the " Journal of the Princes of Gowa and Tello " we always meet with *Bontoya*, " the (country of) Bonto " < *Bonto* + the article *a*, instead of the modern form *Bontowa*, *e.g.* on p. 8, l. 15.

II. The final vowel of the WB becomes *consonantal* before the suffix: thus in Old Javanese *i* > *y*, *u* > *w*, as in *katunwan*, " to be burnt " < *ka* + WB *tunu* + *an*.

III. The vowel of the WB and that of the formative are in many languages *contracted together*. Old Javanese WB *kĕla* or *kla* + the gerundial termination -*ĕn* results in *klān*, as in Kawi Oorkonden, I, 3, 20: " Shall be cooked in (the) cauldron of Yama " = *klān i kawah saṅ Yama*.

IV. The consonantal final of the WB is *doubled* in Madurese and a few other languages. From the WB *ator* Mad. forms the verb *ṅatorraghi*, " to offer " < *ṅ* + *ator* + *aghi*.

V. In Gayo a final *nasal* of the WB *changes into cognate media* + *nasal*, *e.g.* in *kuödnön*, " more to the right " < WB *kuön*, " right " + *ön*. Mentaway inserts the tenuis instead of the media, as in *mämäräpman*, " to want to sleep ", from WB *märäm*. Illustration: Ghost Stories, in Morris' texts, p. 82, l. 8: " I want to sleep there " = Sleep + want + to there I = *mämäräpman lä aku*.

VI. In Bontok *a media becomes a tenuis*. From WB *kaeb* is formed the verb *kapen*, " to make ", from *facy*, " to whip ", *ʃayeken*.

VII. In Madurese *a tenuis becomes a media*. The WB for " to suck " in Old Javanese and Mad. is *sĕpsĕp*, and " to suckle a child " in Mad. is *ñĕpsĕbbhi*.

VIII. In the combination nasal + cognate media between the two vowels of the WB *the media is lost* in Maañanese. From WB *endäy*, " to take ", there is a derivative form *enäyan*.

270. *Quantity* in *contraction*.

I. In most cases vowel-length results; thus in Makassar, *e.g.* in *kasalán*, " compensation (for a wrong done) ", which has a long *a* in the final syllable $<$ *ka* + *sala*, " to err " + *añ*.

II. In other languages length of vowel does not result; thus in Toba, as in *parhután*, " locality of a settlement ", with short *a* in the final syllable $<$ *par* + *huta*, " settlement " + *an*; see also § 71.

271. The phonetic phenomena to be observed upon the addition of *prefixes* to the WB are less multifarious than in connexion with the addition of suffixes. They are the following:

I. *Elision*. In Bugis from WB *onro*, " to dwell ", are formed both *paonro* and *ponro*, " to cause to dwell ".

II. *Contraction*. In Old Javanese, from *ma* + WB *iñĕt* is formed *meñĕt*, " to take care ".

III. Appearance of *intermediary sounds*. Thus in Daïri *pĕhuwap* $<$ *pĕ* + *uwap*, " steam ".

IV. *Change of the explosive*, with which the WB begins, *into the cognate nasal*, as in Malay *mĕnañkap*, " to catch ", from WB *tañkap*, see § 16.

272. Upon the addition of formatives vowel-harmony may also supervene (see § 247).

273. We noticed in § 168 that the Original IN final diphthongs, as in *punay*, " dove ", *patay*, " to kill ", become reduced to simple vowels in several languages, as for instance in Bugis, which says *pune*. — But in connexion with this

appearance of simple vowels instead of diphthongs we meet
in several languages with phenomena that cannot be simply
explained as contraction, weakening, and the like. For the
consideration of these cases we will use the following table
as a basis:

Original IN:	*gaway*, " to make "	*patay*, "to kill"	*punay*, " dove ".
Tagalog:	*gaway*, " to bewitch "	*patáy*	*punay*.
Old Javanese:	*gaway*	*pati*	
Later Old Jav.:	*gawe*		
Malay:		*mati*	*punay*.
Dayak:	*gawi*	*patäy*	*punäy*.

Here we are struck by two sets of facts. Why do Malay
and Dayak in some of these cases have the diphthong, as in
punay and *punäy*, respectively, while in others they have a
simple vowel, as in *mati* and *gawi*? Why does Original IN
ay appear in the Old Jav. *pati* as *i*, while in *gawe* we observe
that it is regularly contracted into *e*?

The answer to these questions is given by certain phenomena of the Philippine languages. In these a word ending
in a diphthong appears in different forms according to whether
it stands alone or has a suffix or enclitic attached to it. Original IN *balay* is also in Ibanag *baláy*, " house ", but " their
house " is *balé-ra*. In Tagalog the word for " to give " is
bigáy, but its passive is *bigyán*. Now I assume that a similar
change used to take place in Original IN, so that one and the
same word was *e.g.* sometimes pronounced *gaway* and sometimes *gawi*; Old Javanese, Malay, Dayak, etc., then com-
promised the matter, so that in some cases the form with the
diphthong and in others the form with the vowel came to be
used exclusively, and hence *e.g.* Malay *mati* side by side with
punay.

SECTION XI : ABBREVIATION OF WORDS.

274. Abbreviation of words occurs in very various kinds of cases; certain languages use it in words of every category, others in certain sorts of words, *e.g.* proper names. Most commonly a word is abbreviated at the beginning, less often at the end, and least frequently in its interior, as for example in the case of Napu *au* < Original IN *anu*, " such and such a one, that which ". Very rare indeed are such cases of irregular compression as the Karo *ĕrbubai*, " to announce a marriage formally " < *ĕrdĕmu bayu*. Abbreviation always occurs in isolated cases, here and there pretty commonly, but never in definite series determined by phonetic laws, apart from the haplological abbreviations in the doubling of words (§ 234), which are, however, a special phenomenon. The full form may give rise to *several* short forms: thus of the above mentioned *anu* there are in Napu the two short forms *au* and *u*. All three forms figure side by side in the Napu text, " The Creation of the World "; p. 393, l. 6: " that which we see " = *anu ta-ita*; p. 394, l. 11: " that which is wild " = *au maila*; p. 394, l. 11: " that which lives " = *u tuwo.*

275. Abbreviation in WB's, *irrespective of the category to which they belong.*

I. In Achinese, in consequence of the accentuation of the last syllable, the first syllable of many WB's is dropped. In the Story of the Clever Blind Man, appended to Van Langen's grammar, p. 109, l. 12, we find in the second sentence two abbreviated WB's next to one another: " To climb a coconut-palm " = *ik ur*. Here *ik* < Original IN *naik* and *ur* < *niur₂*.

II. In Cham we meet with similar abbreviations, *e.g.* in *lan*, " month ", " aphæresis from Original IN *bulan* " (Cabaton).

Cham has a very large number of loan-words from neighbouring
languages having monosyllabic WB's, and these loan-words
have had their influence on a part of the disyllabic WB's of
IN stock.

276. Abbreviation *in certain categories or functions* of
words.

I. In *exclamations.* In various languages a disyllabic WB
will lose a·syllable when it is used as an exclamation, thus
imitating the interjections, which are very often monosyllabic.
— In Tontemboan they say *deq*, "oh, horror!", from *indeq*,
"horror". Thus we find in "The Burning of Kinilow",
Schwarz-Texts, p. 156, l. 2 from the bottom: "Horror, oh
horror for me!" = *deq e deq aku.*

II. In *vocatives.* In many languages abbreviations are
used in the vocative. Vocatives, like exclamations, imitate
interjections, and besides that, many languages accentuate
the last syllable of a word when used in the vocative.* Such
vocative abbreviations are found, in the first place, in words
of relationship and friendship, as in the Madurese *coñ*, "lad!"
< *kacoñ*, "the lad". Thus in the Story of Kandhulok in
Kiliaan's Texts, II, p. 153, l. 9 from the bottom, we find:
"Well, lad!" = *kĕmma coñ!* Longer formations are reduced
to disyllables or trisyllables, as in the Toba vocative *maén*
from *parumaen*, "daughter-in-law". — In the second place,
they occur in personal names, as in the Modern Rĕmbang-
Javanese vocative "*Wir!*" < *Wiryadimejo.* — In some languages such abbreviations are also used when the word is not
employed vocatively, *e.g.* Tontemboan *itow*, "the little boy"
< *mañalitow.* — The Rottinese *feo* < *feto*, "sister", is pri-
marily a vocative but is also used in other ways.

III. In the *imperative*, which is very similar in its nature to
the vocative. *e.g.* Toba *botson*, "give (it) here!" < *boan tuson.*

IV. In *proper names*, especially those of persons. In some
languages, as for example in Dayak, personal names are formed
from descriptive words by omitting the initial consonant.

* [See Essay II, § 79.]

Such Dayak names are, *e.g.*, *Agap* $<$ *tagap*, " strong ", *Adus*
$<$ *radus*, " stout ", *Ilak* $<$ *kilak*, " love ", *Inaw* $<$ *ginaw*,
" to shine ". These abbreviations imitate the words of
relationship " father ", " mother ", and " child ", which in
most of the IN languages begin with a vowel, the Original IN
types being, of course, *ama*, *ina*, and *anak*.

V. In *technical terms*. Here we often meet with very
drastic abbreviations, just as in similar cases in IE: *cf.* English
pops $<$ *popular concerts* (Brugmann KvG, § 366, 5). Thus
the Bugis *ida-ida*, which denotes a certain poison, is an abbreviation of " quickly-working poison " $=$ p. q.-w. $=$ *racun*
maqpacidacida.

VI. In *compounds*. Here, in the first place, the abbreviation may occur at the point of junction of the two words.
The first member of the compound loses its final vowel, more
rarely a consonant and in that case mostly the aspirate *h*.
Examples: Ampana *torarue*, " water-spirit " $<$ spirit $+$ water
$=$ *torara* $+$ *ue*; Minangkabau *tigari*, " a festival " $<$ *tiga*,
" three " $+$ *hari*, " day ". Or else the first member of the
compound, which usually has the weaker stress, may be abbreviated; as in Busang *bĕtaóq*, " right side " $<$ *beh*, " side "
$+$ *taóq*, " right ".

Particular notice is due to certain Bugis abbreviations
wherein the first member of the compound loses a final *ñ*, as
in *po-lila*, " back part of the tongue " $<$ *poñ*, " stem " $+$
lila; similarly *po-lima*, " back part of the hand ". The abbreviation is explicable by the fact that a sequence like *ñ* $+$ *l* is
not permissible in the interior of a WB; but why should there
be abbreviations like *po-kanuku*, " back part of the nail ",
seeing that the sequence *ñ* $+$ *k* occurs very often in WB's?
The reason is that these are analogical formations; *po-kanuku*
has imitated *po-lima*.

VII. In *groups of words* that denote a single idea and
therefore approximate to compounds. In the first place,
such groups as have for their first element a *title*. In the story
Ja Bayur, in Ophuijsen, " Bataksche Texten, Mandailingsch
Dialect ", p. 74, l. 4 from the bottom, we find: " His name

became Ja Bayur " = N. h. the b. J. B. = *gorar nia i man-jadi Ja Bayur*, where *Ja* is an abbreviation for *raja*, " prince ". — Other abbreviations falling under the present category are, *e.g.*, Sawunese *dupamu*, " wife " < " person in (the) house " = *dou pa ĕmu*; Napu *anaṅkoi*, " little child " < *ana*, " child " + *anu*, " which " + *koi*, " little ". — We particularly often meet with such cases of compression in words of form, as in Dayak *ranen*, " and so on " < *ara*, " name " + *enen*, " whatever ".

VIII. In *numerals*. In Javanese, in counting (according to Poensen), or in counting *rapidly* (according to J. N. Smith), the disyllabic digits 1-10 are usually docked of the first syllable, *e.g.* people say *tu* for *pitu*, " seven ". Here the abbreviated forms imitate the forms which are really monosyllabic, like *pat*, " four ".

IX. In *auxiliary verbs*. In verbs which are usually followed by another, dependent, verb that contains the leading idea, abbreviation may occur in several languages, the medial sounds of the word being reduced. Thus, for example, in Karo, *dapĕt*, " to be able ", is abbreviated to *dat*. In Minangkabau the full form of the word which would correspond to the Malay, etc., *pĕrgi*, " to go ", no longer occurs, but only the short form *pai* or *pi*. But an analysis of the Manjau Ari shows that *pai* or *pi* mostly occurs only in the above-mentioned kind of context; thus p. 8, l. 1: " We go to fetch (him) " = written: *kita pi japut* = spoken: *kito pi japuyq*.

X. In *enclities* and *proclities*: see § 302.

XI. In *euphemisms*: see § 18.

XII. In *loan-words*: *e.g.* Modern Javanese *dĕler* < Dutch *edele heer*. Here the tendency towards disyllabism very often asserts itself.

XIII. In *colloquial language*: see § 20.

XIV. In *poetry*: see § 27.

277. Abbreviation, particularly in the case of compounds, may go so far that the significative nucleus is *lost altogether*. This is especially the case with compound negatives in several

languages. The Tontemboan negative *raqi* is often strength-
ened by the particle *ka*, thus forming *raqica* (in accordance
with the rule in § 103, II), which again by abbreviation becomes *ca*. As appears from an examination of all the texts,
this *ca* is especially found in dialogues.

278. The full form and the short form may serve *side by
side* in the language. In Cham " a certain " is *haley*, or, abbreviated, *ley*. Now, in the story Mu Gajaung, p. 22, l. 29, we
find: " On a certain day " = *harey haley*; but in l. 11: *harey
ley*.

279. In abbreviations, phonetic phenomena may occur
which are not otherwise possible in the language in question.
Rottinese has a word *bindae*, " a sort of vessel " < *bina*,
" shell " + *dae*, " earth "; but in the interior of Rot. WB's
the sequence *n* + *d* does not occur.

280. A considerable proportion of the IN abbreviations of
words have *parallels in IE*. In IE, as in IN, the species of
abbreviation whereby sounds in the interior of words are
eliminated, is the rarest: see Brugmann KvG, § 366, 5. —
Elimination of the final vowel of the first part of a compound
is found in Gothic, *e.g.* in *hauhhairts*, " proud ", as compared
with *armahairts*, " merciful ": see Wilmann, " Deutsche Grammatik ", the section entitled " Der Vokal in der Kompositions-
fuge ". Abbreviations of titles are found, *e.g.* Middle High
German *ver* < *vrouwe*, Italian *na* < *donna*. An instance of
abbreviation in exclamations is the Swiss-German *mänt* <
Sakrament. A case of the abbreviation of the negative going
so far as to deprive it of its significative nucleus is the Swiss-
German *üt*, " nothing ".

SECTION XII: PHONETIC PHENOMENA IN LOAN-WORDS.

281. When a loan-word is taken up into an IN language, its sounds must accommodate themselves to the phonetic capacities of the language that accepts it. Exceptions are rare and are found mainly among educated persons; but here and there a foreign sound has persisted even in popular pronunciation. Madurese has no *f*, but loan-words containing that sound preserve it even in popular pronunciation " pretty generally " (Kiliaan).

282. The change of sounds takes place in certain cases because the recipient language absolutely does not possess the *sound* that occurs in the loan-word.

I. Loan-words from *IN languages*. The commonest case is that of the palatals, which are wanting in certain IN languages; they are replaced by a velar, a dental $+ i$, or by the semi-vowel *y*. Table:

Malay *jambatan* > Napu   *gambata*, " bridge ".
Malay *janji*   > Sangirese   *diandi*, " to promise ".
Malay *jaga*   > Tontemboan *yaga*, " watch, guard ".

II. Loan-words from *non-IN languages*. The commonest case is that of the various sibilants, as most of the IN languages possess only one, viz. *s*. Thus the Dutch *sjaal*, pronounced *šāl*, " shawl ", appears in Madurese as *sal* or *cal*.

283. The sound may occur in the loan-word in a *position* which it is not allowed to occupy in the recipient language. In Busang no word ends in *s*, Original IN r_2atus, " hundred ", becomes *atu*, and hence *Bugis* > *Bugit* and *English* > *Iṅĕlit*. The *s* has only persisted in *kĕrtas*, " paper ". — A particularly common case is that an IN language having only vocalic finals adds a vowel to loan-words that end in a consonant. In the Tsimihety Poem on the Telegraph, p. 116, we find *telegrafi*, *Parisi*, and *Madagasikara*.

284. The *phonetic combination* may be alien to the recipient language. Here it is mostly a case of combination of consonants. The linguistic methods then applied by the IN languages are the following:

I. *Elimination.* In Jonker's Rottinese Texts, p. 44, l. 1, we find: "Service letter" = L. s. = *susula dis*; *dis* being from the Dutch *dienst*.

II. *Metathesis*, as in the Old Malagasy *Serafelo*, the name of a certain angel < Arabic *Asrafil*. This form is found in Ferrand's text Niontsy, p. 24, l. 1 from the bottom: "Where art thou, O Asrafil?" = *aiza hanaw ra Serafelo?*

III. *Insertion* of a sound, as in the Bugis *porogolo* < Dutch *verguld*, " gilt ".

285. The selection of the inserted vowel is determined:

I. By the nature of the neighbouring *vowel*, as in Makassar *parasero* < Portuguese *parceiro*, " partner ".

II. By the nature of the neighbouring *consonant*. Between the *s* and the χ of a Dutch initial *sch* Makassar inserts an *i*, as in *sikau* < *schout*, " mayor ".

286. Special consideration is due to the developments of the phonetic combinations of explosives + *h*, *i.e.* the *aspirates* of loan-words in languages which themselves have no aspirates.

I. The aspiration disappears altogether, as in Malay *bumi* < Sanskrit *bhūmi*, " earth ".

II. A vowel appears between the explosive and the aspiration: Makassar *pahala*, " utility " < Sanskrit *phala*. Madurese, in accordance with the principle in § 184, II, has *paqalah*. Daïri *dĕhupa* < Sanskrit *dhūpa*, " incense ".

III. Owing to some secondary process the aspiration disappears, but the inserted vowel persists; hence Toba *daupa* and *budá* < *budaha* < *buddha*.

287. The phonetic phenomena hitherto delineated are either sporadic or else form regular series. Of the latter kind is the Bugis rendering of the Dutch initial *sch-*; the dictionary contains half a dozen ca̍ses, and in all of them *sch-* is rendered by *sik-*, *e.g.*, *sikemboro* < Dutch *schenkbord*, "tray". The Hova dictionary has eight loan-words which in their original languages began with *br*. In five cases *br-* becomes *bur-*, as in *burákitra* < English *bracket*. In the three other cases the inserted vowel is determined by the neighbouring one, as in *biriki* < English *brick*.

288. Loan-words may either submit to the laws of phonetic change governing the several IN languages or they may struggle against them. In Saqdanese *w* is omitted in loan-words as it is in native words. That appears from the text "Tunaq Pano Bulaan", where (*inter alia*) on p. 225, l. 6 from the bottom, we find *saa*, "snake" < Original IN *sawa*, and on p. 228, l. 8, *deata*, "God" < Sanskrit *dewatā*. — In Minangkabau an Original IN final *at* becomes *eq*, but loan-words preserve the pronunciation *at* unchanged even in colloquial, hence Mkb. *adat*, "customary law".

289. In connexion with the reception of loan-words the forces of analogy and popular etymology are particularly operative. The word for "veil" in Bugis is *bowoñ*, or in its contracted form *bōñ*, and in imitation of it the Dutch *bom*, "bomb", appears not only as *bōñ* but also as *bowoñ*. In Hova it chances that no words begin with *l + a + b*, but several with *l + a + m + b*, hence the French *la bride* appears in Hova as *lamburidi*. In the Old Sundanese legend Purnawijaya, verse 154, the hound of hell is called *Sirabala*; that is a deformation of the Sanskrit *śabala* made under the influence of the article *si*, which in Sund. is used with names of animals.

290. In the reception of loan-words IE displays much the same sort of phenomena as IN. To mention only a single case, we observe in Italian as in Makassar the insertion of vowels into awkward consonantal combinations, hence Ital. *lanzichenecco* < German *Lanzenknecht*, "spearman", like Mak. *parasero* < *parceiro* (§ 285).

SECTION XIII : PHONETIC PHENOMENA IN THE SENTENCE.

291. In the interior of the sentence we may either meet with the same phonetic phenomena as in the interior of words, or with different ones.

I. In the standard dialect of Tontemboan a *k* after an *i* changes into a *c*, both in the sentence and in the individual word. Hence in the story told by S. Pandey, Schwarz-Texts, pp. 12 *seqq.*, we not only get on p. 13, l. 25, *lalic* < *lalik*, " to go to law (about something or other) ", but also in l. 23 *si cayu* < *si kayu*, " the tree ".

II. In the Kawangkoqan dialect the change of *k* into *c* takes place only within the word, not in the sentence. Hence in the story told by A. W. Rompas in the Kawangkoqan dialect, p. 156, l. 5, we read *pasicolaan*, " school-house ", from WB *sicola* < *sikola*, but on p. 155, l. 11, we find *si kayu*, " the tree ".

292. A sentence may either be a perfect unit, or may contain within it certain parts which combine into a more closely connected group. Such groups may either be knit together more intimately by the *sense*, thus to the linguistic consciousness of the people of Nias the combination of " principal word + subjective genitive " is more intimate than that of " principal word + objective genitive ". Or the closer relation between certain parts of a sentence may be constituted by the fact that they are *subordinated to a single accent* (or *stress*). This is the case with the group of " proclitic or enclitic + word of substance ". — Now in these groups of more intimate relation phonetic phenomena may occur which otherwise do not appear in the body of the sentence (see § 302).

293. The *phonetic phenomena* that appear in the *sentence*, as such, are especially the following: assimilation, metathesis, appearance of intermediary sounds, doubling of final consonants, turning of vowels into consonants, contraction, loss of vowels, and loss of consonants. These phenomena are to a great extent similar to those that have been noticed in connexion with the combination of the WB with formatives (§§ 266 *seqq.*).

294. *Assimilation*, in many languages, *e.g.* in Toba. In the story Nan-Jomba-Ilik, Tuuk Lb, p. 1, l. 4 from the bottom, we find written: " Why comest thou ?" = *di-bahen ro hamú*, but it is pronounced *di-baher ro hamú*.

295. *Metathesis*, in Kupangese. According to the text Bihata Mesa, Bijdr. 1904, metathesis occurs in certain cases in the second syllable of a WB when used in a sentence. Original IN *aku*, " I ", appears also in Kup. as *aku*, and *laku*, " to go ", as *lako*; hence on p. 253, l. 1, we find: " Then (he) went and reported (it) " = Then w., then r. = *ti lako, ti tek*. But on p. 253, l. 2, we find: " I went to hang him up " = I w. hang + up = *auk laok tai*.

296. Appearance of vowels or consonants as *intermediary sounds*. In the Tontemboan story " Kariso and his Children ", Schwarz-Texts, p. 129, l. 8 from the bottom, we find: " A relation of his " = *ĕsa taranak-ĕ-na*. The intercalated pĕpĕt is the intermediary sound ; *na* = " of him ". Hain-Teny, p. 186, verse 5, has: " To be able to keep back the stream " = *nahatan-d-riaka*. Here Hova employs the consonant *d* as an intermediary sound between *nahatan(a)* and *riaka*.

297. *Doubling of final consonants*, in Ibanag. " I am big " = B. I = *dakall ak* < *dakal* and *ak*.

298. *Change of vowels into consonants*, in several languages, as in Old Javanese, Timorese, etc. Old Javanese, from Mpu Tanakung's Prosody, str. 41, v. 1: " A bird likewise " = *paksy adulur* < *paksi* and *adulur*.

299. *Contraction*, in Old Javanese and other languages. Rāmāyaṇa, II, str. 43, v. 1 : " His big bow " = Bow his big = *laras nirāgöñ* < *nira* and *agöñ*.

300. *Loss of vowels.*

I. When the vowel ends the word and the next one begins with a vowel, *e.g.* in Hova. Hain-Teny, p. 136, v. 6: " To be disquieted " = Have disquiet = *manan eritreritra* < *manana eritreritra.*

II. When the vowel ends the word and the next one begins with a consonant, in Kupangese. From the story Bihata Mesa, Bijdr. 1904, p. 257, l. 3: " (They) sit together " = *dad buan* < *dada* and *buan.*

III. When the vowel is closed by a consonant, in Timorese. From the story Atonjes, Bijdr. 1904, p. 271, l. 17: " This mother " = M. t. = *ainf i* < *ainaf* and *i.*

301. *Loss of consonants,* in Kamberese. From the Story of the Top, Bijdr. 1913, p. 82, l. 7: " Pasture (for) horses " = *pada njara* < *padaṅ* and *njara.*

302. Special phenomena of the *groups of intimate relation* mentioned in § 292.

I. In Old Javanese certain pronouns when in a proclitic position may lose a final vowel, even before a word that begins with a consonant. Thus Rāmāyaṇa, XXII, str. 17, v. 1: " Then shall I recognize thy love " = *ṅke k tona asih ta.* The *k* is an abbreviation of *ku,* the proclitic pronoun of the first person, which appears in that form and with that function in many IN languages; *tona* is the future of *ton,* " to see ". Apart from these cases Old Javanese does not employ elision but only contraction or the change of a vowel into a consonant.

II. In Nias after a final vowel in certain groups of intimate relation the *voiceless* initial consonant of the next word is *changed into* a *voiced* (or sonant) one; thus in the combination " principal word + subjective genitive ", or the combination " preposition + principal word ". The word for " heart " in Nias is $to_2do_2,$ but in the story Siwa Ndrofa, Bijdr. 1905, p. 34, l. 7, we find: " In (the) heart " = *ba* $do_2do_2.$

303. The phonetic phenomena of the sentence sometimes take place with strict *regularity,* sometimes less regularly.

1. Voicing in Nias takes place with strict regularity.

II.   Elision in Hova in the group " predicate + object " is left to the discretion of the speaker, at least so it appears from Hain-Teny.   On p. 188, v. 2, we find: " To want to swallow stones " = W. to sw. st. = *hitelim batu* < *hitelin (a) watu*, but p. 80, v. 2: " To smell (of) lemons " = *manitra wuasari*.   Elision of the vowel would produce *mani buasari*.

304.   *Interjections* often decline to conform to the laws affecting the sentence.   In Toba the final *a* of a word invariably disappears before an initial *a* of the next one, as in the Riddle Stories, III, Tuuk Lb, I, p. 50, l. 1 from the bottom: " If it is not permitted " = *molo soada adoñ*, which is pronounced *molo soad adoñ*.   But if the word with final *a* is an interjection, the *a* persists, as in Riddle Stories, I, Tuuk Lb. I, p. 49, l. 11: " No, O father " = *indadoñ ba amáñ*.

305.   Within a group of intimate relation the *operation of the phonetic laws of change is* often *suspended*.

I.   In *words of substance*.   In Makassar, final *k* changes into *q*, as in Mak. *anaq* < Original IN *anak*, " child ", but before the article added enclitically this change does not take place, *e.g.* in *anak-a*, " the child ".

II.   In *proclitics and enclitics*.   In Minangkabau, final *a* changes into *o*, as in *mato*, " eye ", < Original IN *mata*; but proclitic words like the preposition *ka* keep their *a* unchanged.

306.   Finally, here are some *parallels between IN and IE* :

I.   *Assimilation* in Greek and in Toba.   Greek dialect in Thumb, " Handbuch der griechischen Dialekte ", § 203: *tõl Labyadãn* < *tõn Labyadãn*.   Toba *sal lappis*, " one layer " < *san lampis*.

II.   *Voicing* in Sardinian and in Nias.   Sardinian *tempus*, " time ", but *su dempus*, " the time ".   Nias *to₂do₂*, " heart ", but *ba do₂do₂*, " in (the) heart ".

III.   *Loss of vowel*.   The word of substance loses a vowel before an enclitic: Rumanian and Balinese.   Rumanian: *casa*, " the house " < *casă* and the article *a*.   Balinese, from the texts appended to Eck's grammar, p. 62, l. 2: " To be contained in the letter " = *muñgw iñ surat* < *muñguh iñ surat*.

— The enclitic loses a vowel: Latin and Karo. Latin *viden,* " seest thou ?" < *vides* + *ne.* Karo, from the story Dunda Katekutan, p. 34, l. 17: " (It is) done " = *ĕṅgom* < *ĕṅgo* + the emphatic particle *mĕ.*

IV. *Resistance of interjections* to the phonetic laws affecting the sentence: Sanskrit and Toba. Sanskrit, in Wackernagel, " Altindische Grammatik ", I, § 270. Toba: *ba amáṅ* (see § 304).

SECTION XIV: ACCENT.

In General.

307. Accent in the IN languages is either *determinate* or *free*. It is determinate, when its place in the word is determined by definite rules; it is free, when such rules are wanting.

308. The *position* of the accent in the WB is either on the penultimate or the final syllable. Other modes of accentuation are rarer phenomena.

Accentuation of the Word-Base.

309. There are four systems of accentuation applicable to the IN *word-base*:

I. All WB's accentuate the penultimate. This is the *penultimate type*.

II. All WB's accentuate the final. This is the *final type*.

III. The WB's accentuate either the penultimate or the final, according to definite rules. This is the *Toba type*.

IV. The WB's accentuate either the penultimate or the final, but without definite rules. This is the *Philippine type*.

310. The *penultimate type* is the most widely distributed one. — Moreover in the Toba type also, and in many representatives of the Philippine type, accentuation of the penultimate syllable preponderates. This appears clearly from an examination of accentuated texts, *e.g.* the Mandaïling texts in Van der Tuuk's Toba grammar, p. 31 (which exemplify the Toba type) or the text Lumawig in Seidenadel-Texts, pp. 485 *seqq.* (Philippine type). Hence by far the greater number of the IN WB's have the accent on the penultimate

311. The languages which accentuate the penultimate, however, admit exceptions to the general rule.

I. In several languages of the penultimate type the *pĕpĕt* cannot take the accent. Therefore if the penultimate contains a pĕpĕt, the accent falls on the final syllable, as in Gayo *sĕlúk*, "tortuous". If both syllables have a pĕpĕt, some of the languages accentuate the penultimate, others the final.

II. Some languages of the penultimate type have a small number of *words of substance* that are accentuated on the final; thus Mentaway, *e.g.*, *arát*, "to go in". These are mostly words for which no cognates are to be found in the other IN languages.

III. Several languages of the penultimate type possess a few *words of form*, especially demonstratives, that are accentuated on the final. Examples: Mentaway, *otó*, "so", Bugis *manrá*, "yonder", Hova *iti*, "this". Nias accentuates most of its demonstratives on the final syllable.

In various languages of the penultimate type we find words of form that are accentuated either on the penultimate or the final, but with variations in meaning; *e.g.* Sangirese *táïu*, "on that account", *taïú*, "thereupon".

IV. In *interjections* too we not infrequently meet with accentuation of the final, as in Bugis *awi*, "indeed!" (implying surprise).

312. The *final type* comprises but few languages. It includes, for instance, Busang, which accordingly pronounces *anák*, for "child".

313. The *Toba type* comprises Toba and cognate languages, such as Mandaïling. Here too the accent mostly falls on the penultimate. But in certain definite cases, determined by rules which are given in the grammars, accentuation of the final occurs. One such rule is: Verbal WB's denoting a condition that has been *caused* (by some external agency), accentuate the final; hence the accentuation of *tanóm*, "to be buried", as against *húndul*, "to sit".

314. In the languages of the *Philippine type* some WB's accentuate the penultimate and others the final, without there being any rules on the subject. We can form no idea why Bontok says *pitó*, " seven ", but *wálo*, " eight ", the more so as there is no certain etymological explanation of these words.

315. *Unusual* modes of *accentuation*: accentuation of the *antepenultimate* results from the addition of a supporting vowel in all languages that add it. Hence Hova *ánaka*, " child " $<$ Original IN *anak*, Makassar *nípisiq*, " thin " $<$ Original IN *nipis*.

Equal accentuation of both syllables of the WB is found in some languages in onomatopœic formations, as in Toba *búmbám*, " to beat ".

Accentuation of Derivatives from the Word-Base.

316. When a *disyllabic* — or *polysyllabic* — WB is extended by means of *prefixes*, the accentuation is not affected thereby; Bugis *pésĕq*, " to feel ", and *papésĕq*, " feeling ", are accentuated alike.

317. When *suffixes* are added, we observe the following phenomena:

I. In languages of the penultimate type the accent is *shifted*, so that it always falls again upon the penultimate. From the Bugis *tíwiq*, " to bring " $<$ Primitive Bug. *tiwir*, are derived: *tiwíri*, " to bring to somebody ", and *patiwiríyaŋ*, " to give something to somebody to take with him and bring it ". Only a few languages of the penultimate type fail to shift the accent, *e.g.* Gayo, which accordingly accentuates *kĕbáyakan*, " riches " $<$ *báyak*, " rich ".

II. The other types also shift the accent, hence Toba *isían*, " vessel " $<$ *isi*, " contents ". But alongside of this they also possess suffixes which attract the accent to themselves. In Toba the suffix -*an* of the comparative takes the accent, thus: *biroŋán*, " blacker ", from *biroŋ*, " black ", as against the above-cited *isían*.

III. When contraction results upon the addition of suffixes, accentuation of the final syllable is also produced, as in
Toba *haduwán*, " the day after to-morrow " < formative
ha + duwa, " two " + formative *an*. — If the feeling, that
the word is a derivative, becomes lost, the accent may be
shifted back again; hence Mandaïling *hadúwan*, " the day after
to-morrow ".

318. When suffixes are added to *monosyllabic* WB's —
which in all the IN languages amount to only a very small
percentage of the vocabulary — there is nothing new to be
remarked as to the accent. From the Bugis *noq*, " downwards " < *nor* < *sor* (§§ 40, I, 150, III), is derived: *nóri*, " to
bring down ", which gives rise to no observations.

319. When prefixes are added to monosyllabic WB's, the
general rule is that the accent does not shift away from the
WB, *e.g.* Bugis *panóq*, " to let down " < *noq*, " downwards ".
Here, therefore, even the languages of the penultimate type
have the accent on the final. — But if the feeling of derivation
becomes obscured, the accent may shift back. Bungku has
opá, " four ", from *ĕpat* = prothetic *ĕ* (§ 226) + Original IN
pat, but Nias has *o₂fa*, with *o* < *ĕ* in conformity with § 227.

Accentuation of Doubled Words and Compounds.

320. When a word is *doubled*, the first element preserves
its accent in some of the languages, but loses it in others. In
Dayak both alternatives occur side by side, with differentiation in meaning: *gila-gíla*, " all stupid ", *gila-gíla*, " somewhat
stupid ".

321. Here too the Toba type has all sorts of peculiarities,
e.g., *jalák-jalák*, " to seek everywhere ", alongside of *manjálak*,
" to seek ", from the WB *jálak*.

322. In Bugis a certain number of words that have a long
and accentuated final syllable, such as *apĕllán*, " cooking
utensils ", *atinrón*, " sleeping apartment ", *arún*, " king ",
shift back the accent, and thereby also lose the length of the

final syllable, whenever they serve as the first element of a compound; *e.g.*, *árum-póne*, " king of Bone " $<$ *aruṅ* and *Bone*. In a Bug. sentence it hardly ever happens that two accentuated syllables follow one another, for almost every word is accompanied by enclitics; hence in a compound an accentuation like *arúm-póne* makes a disagreeable impression, and is therefore altered. As to *mp* $<$ *mb* $<$ *ṅ* + *b*, see § 117.

Accentuation of the " Complex ": *i.e.* Word of Substance + Word of Weak Stress.

323. The complex (or conglomerate) may consist of a word of substance + a *monosyllabic* enclitic. In that case we sometimes find the accent shifted, and sometimes not, in accordance with definite rules:

I. In Makassar, for example, when the article *a* is affixed, the accent shifts if the principal word ends in a vowel, but not if it ends in a consonant: hence *úlu*, " head ", *ulúw-a*, " the head ", *járaṅ*, " horse ", *járaṅ-a*, " the horse ".

II. If the enclitic loses its vowel, that does not prevent the shifting: Bimanese *aná-t*, " our child " $<$ *ána* + *ta*.

III. The Toba particle *tu*, " too ", attracts the accent to itself: *madae-tú*, " too bad " $<$ *madáe* + *tu*. This is in imitation of the accentuation of the comparative (§ 317, II).

324. Again, when *disyllabic* or *several monosyllabic* enclitics are added, shifting of the accent may result, or it may not, or the complex may even have two accents. An instance with two accents is found in Paupau Rikadong, p. 19, l. 4 from the bottom, in Matthes' Bugis grammar: " They also reported it " $=$ T. r. a. it $=$ *na-léttúri-tó-n-i*. Here *n* $<$ *na* is an emphatic particle, homonymous with *na*, " they ".

325. There is little to remark in connexion with the addition of *proclitics*. When a monosyllabic proclitic combines with a monosyllabic WB, some of the languages accentuate the WB, others the proclitic. Toba says *si-gák*, " the crow " $<$ the article *si* + *gak*; Sundanese, on the other hand, *si-pus*, " the cat ".

Accentuation of Loan-words.

326. Loan-words mostly accommodate themselves to the native laws of accentuation; thus the Dutch *gezaghebber*, " ruler ", becomes *sahébar* in Dayak. Exceptions are rare, *e.g.* the Bugis *sikelewá* < Dutch *schilderacht*. This cannot have been a case of imitation, for Bug. native words never end in an accentuated *a*.

Quality of the Accent.

327. All our previous researches have been concerned with the *position* of the accent. Let us now enquire as to its *quality*. In IN the accentuated syllable may differ from the unaccentuated ones thus: by greater loudness, by a higher pitch, or by increased length.

328. Select descriptions of the quality of the IN accent: " Accent in the IN languages is of a different kind from what it is in the IE. In Dutch, and particularly also in English, the principally accentuated syllable is pronounced loudly, the other syllables softly. That is not the case in the IN languages. There the unaccentuated syllables receive fairer treatment, but in consequence the accent is of course less distinct. In some languages the accent is nothing more than a lengthening or extension of the accentuated syllable. But Sangirese has not gone to such lengths as that; its accent is distinctly audible " (Adriani). — " In the IE languages accent is stress, but in many IN languages it is a rise in pitch of the voice. It is true that this rise in pitch is accompanied by an increase in loudness, but that does not cause the unaccentuated syllables to be pronounced in a more cursory manner. As in Toutemboan the accent is produced by a rise in pitch and the unaccentuated syllables are all distinctly and perfectly pronounced, the Tontb. accent gives one the impression of being weak. It is, however, distinctly audible that it falls upon the penultimate " (Adriani). — " In Rottinese the accent is distinctly audible and falls upon the penultimate " (Jonker). — " In Minangkabau all the syllables have the same loudness but the penultimate one sounds somewhat longer or more extended and thus has the accent " (Van der Toorn). — " When pronounced alone, in fact simply mentioned, all Achinese words are sounded so that both syllables have an equal stress, but the second syllable is pronounced in the higher tone " (Snouck Hurgronje).

The Unaccentuated Syllables.

329. It appears from § 328, that so far as the loudness of the tone is concerned the unaccentuated syllables do not differ very considerably from the accentuated. At the same time the syllable *preceding* the accentuated one is somewhat weaker than the one *following* the accentuated syllable. On this fact are based all sorts of phenomena that we have noticed in the preceding parts of this monograph, *e.g.* that the syllable after the accentuated one is pronounced long in several lan guages, and that it is capable of becoming a diphthong. On the other hand, length is of very rare occurrence in syllables preceding the accentuated one, and diphthongization is still rarer. Ampana sounds the syllables before the accentuated one so softly, " that it is only when a person speaks slowly, that one can hear what vowel they have " (Adriani). In several languages a syllable preceding the accentuated one may lose its vowel: in Dayak they say *blaku* as well as *balaku*, " to ask ". Loss of a vowel following after the accentuated syllable is very rare; it is found in Makianese, which has *lim*, " five " < Original IN *lima*.

Original Indonesian Accentuation.

330. In former monographs I assumed that the deter minate system of accentuation, and in particular the penul timate type, was the modern representative of the Original IN law of accentuation. Since then, doubts have arisen in my mind. In *IE* there are languages with determinate, and others with free, accentuation, and Original IE is credited with the free system, the IE languages with the determinate accent being taken to represent a secondary development. Might not something of the kind be possible in IN also? In that case the free Philippine type would be the primitive original, and not the determinate penultimate type. This supposition arose in my mind when I observed that in the languages of the penultimate type, there occur, though very sporadically, cases of accentuation which are at variance with the law of penultimate accentuation and coincide with corresponding Philippine cases. The Philippine languages often accentuate personal pronouns on the final syllable, and Nias (which in other respects follows the penultimate type) also has *ami*, " you ".

Comparison with the Accent of the Indo-European Word.

331. In this sphere also a large number of parallels between the two families of language may be found. For instance, Latin and Makassar have quite similar systems of accentuation:

I. *Principal rule.* The accent falls either on the penultimate or on the antepenultimate, as in Lat. *cadáver*, " corpse ", Mak. *kandáwo,* " hollow ", Lat. *cádere*, " to fall ", Mak. *káttereq*, " to cut ".

II. *Subsidiary rule.* In a minority of cases the accent is on the final syllable, viz. as a result of contraction, as in the Lat. perfect *audīt < audivit* (Sommer, " Handbuch der lateinischen Laut- und Formenlehre ", § 71, I, c), Mak. *kodí*, with a long *i*, " to make bad " $<$ WB *kodi* + the suffix *i*.

332. It is true that the principal rule in Latin has a different linguistic basis from the one in Makassar. In Latin the quantity of the penultimate is the determining factor, while in Makassar the question turns upon the origin of the final, viz. whether it is an original syllable or merely a syllable added as a support.

Sentence Stress.

333. Under this head we must consider the relative accentuation of the several parts of the sentence, and especially the phenomena connected with the accentuation of the end of the sentence, for these are of great importance as characteristics of the IN languages.

334. Relative accentuation of the several parts of the sentence. " Toba only has accentuation of a syllable of a word. It does not employ word-stress, which we use in order to throw emphasis upon a particular word in the sentence " (Van der Tuuk). — " Busang accentuates the final syllable of the last word of the sentence; but one can also accentuate any word in the sentence, if it contains a leading idea " (Barth). — " Accent in Javanese consists merely in this, that the last two syllables of each subdivision of a sentence are pronounced somewhat long and slowly, but both in an equally high tone. All the other syllables of a subdivision of a sentence are pronounced in a similar tone. If it is desired to throw special emphasis upon a word, it is given a position just before a break in the sentence, so that its last two syllables are as a matter of course pronounced more slowly, with the accent as defined above " (Roorda). — " In the Achinese sentence it is not the several words that are the units for the purpose of accentuation, but rather groups of two or three words, linked together as one whole. In the phrase, ' a new-born child ' = c. n. b. = *anöq baro na*, the *na* deprives the other two words altogether of any distinctive accent; they become, if one likes to put it that way, unaccentuated " (Snouck Hurgronje).

335. Relative accentuation of the *end of the sentence*. " The end of a Sundanese sentence is always pronounced long and in a singing (*zangerig*) tone, and the penultimate syllable of the sentence mostly receives a special emphasis " (Coolsma). — " The pronunciation of the Mantangay dialect of Dayak is much like that of the Pulopetak dialect, only the last word of each sentence is pronounced longer and louder " (Hardeland).

— " In Minangkabau the last word of a sentence, or its final syllable, bears the principal accent; thus they say, with a stronger intonation : ' He sleeps ' = *inyo lalóq* " (Van der Toorn). " In Bada the last syllable of a sentence is spoken with a rising (*opgang*) of the voice, *i.e.* with a rising accent " (Adriani). — " As regards rise and fall of tone, or the musical accent, Malay pronounces the phrase: ' Is that a stone ?' = That stone = *ini batu*, in a rising tone, but: ' That is a stone ' = *ini batu*, in a falling tone " (Van Ophuijsen).

336.   The *interrogative sentence.*   In the Bontok interrogative sentence the intonation rises and reaches " its highest tone at the final vowel of the sentence " (Seidenadel). — " The assertive and the interrogative sentence in Dayak may be illustrated by the following examples.   Assertive: ' He is sick ' = *iä hábăn*.   Interrogative: ' Is he sick ?' = *iä hábán*, in an interrogative tone which somewhat accentuates, and makes half long, even the last syllable of *haban* " (Hardeland).

337.   In many IN languages the *vocative*, whether standing by itself or forming part of a sentence, throws the accent on to the last syllable of the word or group of words.   Hence in many languages: *iná*, " O mother ", the vocative of *ina*, " mother ".   Karo, from the story Raja Kĕtĕñahĕn, in Joustra, " Karo-Bataksche Vertellingen ", p. 92, l. 19: " Weep not, father !" = Not thou w., f. = *ola kam tañis bapá.   Ibid.*, p. 91, l. 18: " Let us go home to eat, my prince " = Eat we to house, prince mine = *man kita ku rumah, raja-ñkú.* — This fashion of accentuating the vocative must be regarded as Original IN.

SECTION XV : LAGU.

338. The word *lagu* in IN signifies " modulation of the voice, melody, tempo, and style, in speaking or reciting ".

339. We may distinguish between three kinds of lagu, viz. those characteristic of particular languages, particular individuals, and particular circumstances, or the emotions arising therefrom, respectively. Of the second sort there is nothing to be said here.

I. The lagu of particular *languages.* " The Sundanese are in the habit of speaking slowly and quietly, in a peculiar tone, lagu, which sounds singing and prolonged " (Coolsma). — " The Achinese speak rapidly " (Snouck Hurgronje). — " The Puqu-m-Boto dialect is spoken in a tone that sounds more cheerful and is more prolonged, than the average Bareqe. The tone of the To-Lage dialect sounds somewhat proud and mocking, even in the mouths of slaves and children " (Adriani).

II. The lagu of particular *circumstances.* Here the excessive lengthening of vowels and even of consonants is a phenomenon of particularly frequent occurrence. " In Minangkabau, if one wants to express pity for the person addressed, one says: *tuaaan,* ' lord !' ; if a man sees a runaway horse, he shouts out: *kudooo !* " (Van der Toorn). — " In Madurese, they say *kab . . . bhi,* ' all !', instead of *kabbhi,* if they want to express astonishment ".

340. From the *tempo* there result certain phonetic phenomena, viz. the lento an d allegro forms. In Dayak the article *i* coalesces with the pronoun *aku* to form *yaku,* " I ". When speaking slowly the Dayak says *iaku.* This *iaku* is the lento form, and at the same time the exceptional one, the normal form being *yaku.* According to Ophuijsen the Malay *duwa-*

345

bĕlas, "twelve", when spoken rapidly, is sounded *dobĕlas*. This *dobĕlas* is the allegro form, and likewise the exceptional one. In Achinese *bah + le*, "let be !", has become *bale*, but when people are speaking *quite* slowly the *h* reappears, *bahle* being therefore the lentissimo form.

341. On the differentiation into lento and allegro forms depend such double forms in Latin as *nihil* and *nil* (Sommer, "Handbuch der lateinischen Laut- und Formenlehre", § 80); the case of the Karo negative *lahaṅ*, beside *laṅ*, is exactly similar.

SECTION XVI: AS TO THE INVARIABILITY OF PHONETIC LAWS.

342. When one studies certain descriptions of IN phonetic conditions, it appears not infrequently as if the IN languages were less consistent in their phonetic phenomena than the IE ones. But the trouble is not always in the language, it may be due to the writer:

I. Something may be given as a striking instance of a phonetic phenomenon, though in fact it is *not a phonetic phenomenon at all*. On the assumption that the phrase " come here !" is *mari* in Malay and some other languages, but *mai* in Bugis, it has been asserted that in Bugis the *r* has disappeared. This would be the only case of the loss of *r* in Bugis. However, *mari < ma + ri* is a verbal derivative from the locative preposition *ri*, while *mai* is a derivative from the locative preposition *i*, and does not mean " come here !" but " to go yonder ". So the Bug. *mai* is not a case of phonetic change at all.

II. *False etymologies* are propounded. Thus in the Old Javanese dictionary (Kawi-Balineesch-Nederlandsch Woordenboek), vol. IV, p. 226, the Old Jav. *pula*, " to plant ", is connected with the Dayak *pambulan*, " garden ". But Dayak *pambulan <* prefix *p(a) + imbul*, " to plant " + suffix *ɩ a*. In conformity with a strict law of Dayak phonetics (§ 247), the *i* of *imbul* has had to assimilate itself to the *a* of the suffix.

III. The phonetic phenomena are *wrongly explained*. Original IN *tunu*, " to burn ", appears in Pampanga as *tɪ:ɪ*. Now according to Conant, in his article entitled " Mono-syllabic Roots in Pampanga ", *Journal of the American Oriental Society*, 1911, p. 392, *tun < tunu* has lost the final *u*

by apocope. That would, however, be the only case of apocope in a WB in Pampanga; and accordingly every representative of *IE* scholarship will regard this explanation as unaccept-
able, because it leaves the case standing as an isolated phenomenon. — In reality, Original IN *tunu* was changed by metathesis (an extremely common phenomenon in IN, as we saw
in § 236) into *tuun*, which was then contracted to *tun*.

IV. Too little consideration is given to the *meaning* of
words. Conant (*ibid.*, p. 392) adduces yet another instance
of apocope: *sut* as compared with the Bisaya *suta*. But
according to Bergaño *sut* means " humillarse, rendirse yendo
à la presencia de aquel à quien se humilla "; while *suta*,
according to Encarnacion, signifies: " descubrirse, hacerse
patente, publico ". The meanings of *sut* and *suta* are therefore very divergent, so that it is impossible to connect these
two words together.

V. But there is, above all, yet another thing which makes
it *appear* as if the phonetic evolution of the IN languages were
less subject to the rule of law than is the case with the IE
ones. And that is a certain *practice*, widely spread in IN
research, and not exactly wrong *per se*, but defective and apt
to give rise to confusion. It is this: many lexicographers are
in the habit of adding etymologies to their key-words; but in
doing so they omit to indicate whether the words adduced
for comparison from other languages are to be considered
identical with the particular key-word in conformity with
some phonetic law, or are merely in some way or other related
to it. Example: in the " Kawi-Balineesch-Nederlandsch
Glossarium ", p. 313, we find: " *Panas*; Malay, Sundanese,
Madurese *idem*, Bimanese *pana*, Malagasy *fana*, ' warmth ' ".
Here the words *panas*, *pana*, and *fana* coincide *with one
another, in perfect conformity with phonetic law*. — But on
p. 302 we find: " *Pakan*; Sundanese *hakan*, Madurese
kakan, Malay *makan*, ' to eat ' ". Here the words *do not
coincide according to phonetic law*, for in no case does, *e.g.*, an
Old Jav. *p* correspond with a Sund. *h*; we have here several
variant formations from the WB *kan*, which in its monosyllabic

shape exists in many IN languages. In Old Jav. the WB *kan* has been combined with the formative syllable *pa-*, in Sund. with *ha-*. — The IN lexicography of the future must perform this part of its work more precisely than has been the case hitherto.

343. In reality the occurrence of phonetic phenomena in IN is certainly not attended by any greater irregularity than it is in IE. We observe in IN the *strictest regularity* in a very great number of cases. Brugmann KvG, § 19, 7, remarks: " That certain phonetic changes take place in regular conformity with some law, is often enough an obvious fact, *e.g.* the change of Original IE *-m* at the end of a sentence into *-n* in Greek ". We can say precisely the same of the treatment of Original IN *-m* in Hova, for it appears there invariably as *-na* = *n* + the supporting vowel, *e.g.* in *inuna* < Original IN *inum*, " to drink ".

344. Though on the one hand we observe in many cases the strictest consistency in IN, yet on the other we also sometimes observe the contrary, but such instances are not more frequent than in IE nor do they differ in kind from IE cases.

345. There is a series of phonetic phenomena, in IN as in IE, in which science neither can, nor does, expect absolute invariability. Such are metathesis, assimilation, dissimilation, and the like. But even here IN not infrequently displays a thorough-going consistency (see § 241).

346. A strikingly large percentage of the IN vocabulary is of onomatopœic origin; and it has already been observed in § 17 that onomatopœic formations may evade the operation of phonetic laws. For the actions of beating, tapping, and pounding, there are in the various IN languages the interjections *tuk* or *duk* or *puk* or *bug*. Now from these interjections are derived a large number of WB's, whose meaning preserves the fundamental idea of beating or the like, or has diverged from it by transference. Examples: Karo *tuktuk*, " to knock "; Gayo *tumbuk*, " to beat "; Malay *tumbuq*, " to pound "; Old Javanese *gĕbug*, " to beat "; Karo *batuk*, " cough "; Malagasy dialects *túluka*, " beak "; Old Javanese *tutuk*, " mouth "; in several languages *tuktuk*, " woodpecker "; Karo *pukpuk*, " to labour hard "; Tontemboan *sinduk*, " pounded rice "; Javanese *pupugan*, " fragment ".

Here, for example, there is no question of any phonetic connexion between *duk* in Tontb. *sinduk* and *buq* in Mal. *tumbuq*, for a Tontb. *d* never corresponds with a Mal. *b*.

347. In IN and IE the operation of phonetic laws is very often countered by the powerful influence of analogy and popular etymology. The power of popular etymology is very aptly and generally noticeable in names of animals, especially trisyllabic ones, as exemplified by the " Schweizerisches Idiotikon " on the one hand and the Old Javanese vocabulary on the other: see *e.g.* in the former s.v. *Ameise*, " ant ", and in the latter s.v. *alipan*, " centipede ".

348. In IE research difficulties arise in connexion with certain phenomena that have been termed root-variation, root-determination, and the like: see Brugmann KvG, § 367. I refer to such cases as the existence alongside of one another of forms like the IE *trep: trem: tres*, in the Latin *trepidus*, " timid ", *tremere*, " to tremble ", and the Sanskrit *trasati* < *treseti*, " to tremble ". We find precisely similar phenomena in IN also: thus in Tontemboan there are the forms *rĕp*, *rĕm*. and *rĕs*, in *urĕp*, " to cover ", *rĕrĕp*, " to overlap "; *urĕm*, " to clasp round ", *tirĕm*, " to enclose "; *kĕrĕs*, " to clasp round ", *kurĕs*, " to cross one's arms ". And in IN such phenomena are even less easy to tackle than they are in IE. As a rule we are not even in a position to form any certain idea that they really involve *phonetic* questions.

349. But there still remain in IN as in IE some phonetic phenomena, of which one can only say either: " Here lawless chance holds sway ", or: " Research has failed to discover the principle of the occurrence ". To such alternatives I feel that I have to resign myself after considering the representation of Original IN *t* in Bimanese and Original IN *k* in Nias.

I. Original IN *t* in Bimanese:

Original IN	Bimanese
tanda	*tanda*, " mark ".
tanah	*dana*, " earth ".
r₂atus	*ratu*, " hundred ".
batu	*wadu*, " stone ".

II. Original IN *k* in Nias:

Original IN	Nias
karaṅ	*kara*, " coral ".
kandaṅ	*kandra*, " stable ".
kima	*gima*, " shell ".
kasaw	*gaso*, " rafters ".
kĕn	χo_2, " to ".
kait	χai, " hook ".
kayu	*eu*, " wood ".
kulit	*uli*, " skin ".

350. Regularity in the occurrence of phonetic phenomena is greater in some languages than in others; it is greater, for instance, in Minangkabau than in Bimanese. It is also greater in some sounds than in others: in the nasals very much more than in the liquids, so that Bopp in his " Ueber die Verwandtschaft der malayisch-polynesischen Sprachen mit den indischeuropäischen ", p. 66, l. 15, rightly speaks of a " fluctuation of the liquids ".

351. When we observe the phonetic processes of the IN languages we often get the impression that the movement is still going on and tending towards some end, which it has not yet attained. Such a presumable end, for example, is that " in Bugis initial tenues are endeavouring to disappear ".

I. Initial *k* has *to a great extent* disappeared already, as in *uliq*, " skin " < Original IN *kulit*.

II. Initial *p* has disappeared *in two words*, viz. *uso*, " heart " < Original IN *pusu* and *uro*, " quail " < Original IN *puruh*.

III. Of the disappearance of initial *c* and *t* there are *no certain instances*.

WORKS BY DR. BRANDSTETTER
ON ORIENTAL SUBJECTS

MONOGRAPHS ON INDONESIAN LINGUISTICS.

1. Die Beziehungen des Malagasy zum Malaiischen.*
2. Die Geschichte von König Indjilai. Eine bugische Erzählung ins Deutsche übersetzt.†
3. Tagalen und Madagassen.‡
4. Ein Prodromus zu einem vergleichenden Wörterbuch der malaiopolynesischen Sprachen.
5. Mata-Hari.
6. Wurzel und Wort in den indonesischen Sprachen.§
7. Sprachvergleichendes Charakterbild eines indonesischen Idiomes.
8. Gemeinindonesisch und Urindonesisch.§
9. Das Verbum.§
10. Der Artikel des Indonesischen verglichen mit dem des Indogermanischen.
11. Indonesisch und Indogermanisch im Satzbau.
12. Die Lauterscheinungen in den indonesischen Sprachen.§

MONOGRAPHS ON INDONESIAN LITERATURE.

1. Der Natursinn in den älteren Litteraturwerken der Malaien.
2. Die Geschichte von Hang Tuwah. Translated from Malay.
3. Die Geschichte von König Indjilai. Translated from Bugis. (Already mentioned above on account of its detailed linguistic commentary).
4. Die Gründung von Wadjo. Translated from Bugis.
5. Die Geschichte von Djajalankara. Translated from Makassar.

MINOR WORKS.

1. (a) Das Lehnwort in der bugischen Sprache. (b) Die Lehnwörter, welche der Luzerner Mundart und der bugischen Sprache gemeinsam angehören. In *Drei Abhandlungen über das Lehnwort.*
2. Anlaut und Auslaut im Indogermanischen und Malaio-polynesischen. In *Album Kern.*
3. Die Sprache der Liebe in der makassarischen Lyrik. In *Mélanges de Saussure.*
4. Die Stellung der minahassischen Idiome zu den übrigen Sprachen von Celebes einerseits und zu den Sprachen der Philippinen anderseits. In F. Sarasin, *Versuch einer Anthropologie der Insel Celebes.*

* Translated into English under the title: " The relationship between the Malagasy and the Malayan languages ", by R. Baron, in the *Antananarivo Annual and Madagascar Magazine*, 1894-95, Antananarivo.

† Translated into Dutch under the title: " Geschiedenis van Koning Indjilai ", by M. C. Poensen, in the *Indische Gids*, 1900.

‡ Translated into Spanish under the title: " Tagalog y Malgache ", by P. L. Stangl, the first part in the *Revista Historica de Filipinas*, año I, the second in the *Biblioteca Nacional Filipina*, año I, Manila.

§ Translated in the present volume.

BILLING AND SONS, LIMITED, PRINTERS, GUILDFORD, ENGLAND.

ROYAL ASIATIC SOCIETY'S PUBLICATIONS

ON SALE AT THE ROOMS OF THE SOCIETY
22, ALBEMARLE STREET, LONDON, W.

ORIENTAL TRANSLATION FUND

NEW SERIES

(1–5) REHATSEK (E.). Mīr Khwānd's "Rauzat-us-Safā" or "Garden of Purity." 1891 to 1894. Price 10s. a volume.

(6) TAWNEY (C. H.). The Kathā Koṣa. 1895. Price 10s.

(7) RIDDING (Miss C. M.). Bāṇa's Kādambarī. 1896. Price 10s.

(8) COWELL (E. B.) and THOMAS (F. W.). Bāṇa's Harṣa Carita. 1897. Price 10s.

(9) CHENERY (T.). The first twenty-four Makāmāts of al Harīrī. 1898. Price 15s.

(10) STEINGASS (F.). The last twenty-four Makāmāts of al Harīrī. 1898. Price 15s.

(11) GASTER (M.). The Chronicles of Jerahmeel. 1899. Price 10s.

(12) DAVIDS (Mrs. Rhys). The Dhamma Sangani. 1900. Price 10s.

(13) BEVERIDGE (Mrs. H.). Life and Memoirs of Gulbadan Begum. 1902. Price 10s.

(14, 15) WATTERS (T.). On Yuan Chwang's Travels. Edited by T. W. Rhys Davids and S. W. Bushell. 1904–5. Price 10s. a volume.

(16) WHINFIELD (E. H.) and MIRZA MUHAMMAD KAZWINI. The Lawā'iḥ of Jāmī. Facsimile of an old MS., with a translation and a preface on the influence of Greek philosophy upon Sufism. Second edition, 1914. Price 5s.

(17) BARNETT (L. D.). Antagaḍa-dasāo and Anuttarovavāiya-dasāo. From the Prakrit. 1907. Price 5s.

(18) KEITH (A. Berriedale). The Śāṅkhāyana Āraṇyaka. 1908. Price 5s.

(19. 22) ROGERS (A.). Memoirs of Jahāngīr. Edited by H. Beveridge. Vol. I. 1909. Price 10s. Vol. II, 1914. Price 10s. a volume.

(20) NICHOLSON (R. A.). The Tarjumān al-Ashwaq of Ibn al-ʿArabī. Text and Translation. 1911. Price 7s. 6d.

(21) WARDROP (Miss M.). The Man in the Panther's Skin. By Shot'ha Rust'haveli. 1912. Price 10s.

(23) WARDROP (O.). Visramiani. The Story of the Loves of Vis and Ramin. A romance of Ancient Persia. Translated from the Georgian Version. Price 10s.

MARGOLIOUTH (D. S.). The Hesht Bihisht. (*In preparation*.)

ASIATIC SOCIETY MONOGRAPHS

(1) GERINI (Colonel G. E.). Researches on Ptolemy's Geography (Further India and the Indo-Malay Peninsula) 8vo. 1909. Price 15s.

(2) WINTERNITZ (Dr. M.). Catalogue of Sanskrit MSS. in the R.A.S.. with an Appendix by F. W. Thomas. 8vo. 1902. Price 5s.

(3) HIRSCHFELD (Dr. H.). New Researches into the Composition and Exegesis of the Qoran. 4to. 1902. Price 5s.

(4) DAMES (M. Longworth). The Baloch Race. 8vo. 1904. Price 5s.

(5) LE STRANGE (Guy). Mesopotamia and Persia in the Fourteenth Century A.D., from the Nuzhat-al-Kulūb of Ḥamd-Allah Mustawfī. 8vo. 1903. Price 5s.

(6) BROWNE (Professor E. G.). Chahár Maqála of Nidhámí-i-ʿArúdí-i-Samarqandí. 8vo. 1899. Price 3s.

(7) CODRINGTON (O.), M.D.. F.S.A. A Manual of Musalman Numismatics. 8vo. 1904. Price 7s. 6d.

(8) GRIERSON (G. A.), C.I.E. The Piśāca Languages of North-West India. 8vo. 1906. Price 5s.

(9, 10) DAMES (M. Longworth). Popular Poetry of the Baloches. Text and translation. Two vols. 8vo. 1907. Price 15s.

(11) SAYCE (Professor A. H.) and PINCHES (T. G.). The Tablet from Yuzgat in the Liverpool Institute of Archæology. 8vo. 1907. Price 5s.

(12) BAILEY (Rev. T. Grahame). The Languages of the Northern Himalayas, being studies in the Grammar of Twenty-six Himalayan Dialects. 8vo. 1908. Price 5s.

(13) BAILEY (Rev. T. Grahame). Kanauri Vocabulary. 8vo. 1911. Price 3s.

(14) LE STRANGE (Guy). Description of the Province of Fārs, in Persia, from the MS. of Ibn-al-Balk̲h̲ī. 8vo. 1912. Price 5s.

(15) BRANDSTETTER (R.). An Introduction to Indonesian Linguistics, translated by C. O. Blagden. 8vo. 1916. Price 7s. 6d.

(16) PINCHES (T. G.). Tablets from Lagaš and other Babylonian Sites in the possession of Randolph Berens, Esq. 8vo. 1915. Price 5s.

(17) BAILEY (Rev. T. Grahame). Himalayan Dialects. (*In the press.*)

GASTER (M.). El-Asatir, or the Samaritan Apocalypse of Moses. (*In preparation.*)

ROYAL ASIATIC SOCIETY PRIZE PUBLICATIONS FUND

(1) HULTZSCH (Professor E.). Prākṛitarūpāvatāra of Simharāja. The Text in Nāgarī characters, with Notes, Introduction, and Index. 8vo. 1909. Price 7s. 6d.

(2) BODE (Mabel Haynes), Ph.D. The Pali Literature of Burma. 8vo. 1909. Price 5s.

(3) HULTZSCH (Professor E.). The Mēghadūta with Vallabha's Commentary. 8vo. 1911. Price 7s. 6d.

(4) BRAY (Denys de S.). The Life-History of a Brāhūī. 8vo. 1913. Price 5s.

A special discount is allowed to members of the Society.